REPORT

ON THE

GEOLOGICAL SURVEY

OF THE

STATE OF IOWA:

EMBRACING THE RESULTS OF INVESTIGATIONS MADE
DURING PORTIONS OF THE YEARS 1855, 56 & 57.

BY

JAMES HALL, *State Geologist;*
J. D. WHITNEY, *Chemist and Mineralogist.*

VOLUME I.

PART I : GEOLOGY.

PUBLISHED BY
AUTHORITY OF THE LEGISLATURE OF IOWA.
1858.

PRINTED BY CHARLES VAN BENTHUYSEN.

TABLE OF CONTENTS.

CHAPTER V.

GEOLOGY OF CERTAIN COUNTIES : BY A. H. WORTHEN.

CHAPTER VI.

COUNTY GEOLOGY (CONTINUED) : BY J. D. WHITNEY.

CHAPTER VII.

CHEMISTRY AND ECONOMICAL GEOLOGY : BY J. D. WHITNEY.

PART II.

CHAPTER VIII.

PALÆONTOLOGY OF IOWA : BY JAMES HALL.

TO HIS EXCELLENCY

THE HON. RALPH PHILLIPS LOWE,

GOVERNOR OF THE STATE OF IOWA.

SIR :

THE Report addressed to your predecessor in November last has been delayed in its publication much longer than could have been anticipated, and from circumstances beyond our control. One of these has been the time required for engraving so large a number of plates in a style worthy of the subjects illustrated ; and, furthermore, an unexpected delay in the work of the engraving from causes not discovered till it had been some time in progress. It is hoped, however, that the later publication of the work will be in some measure compensated by the increased interest which this part of the Report will have for the scientific public, and which will render the volumes more acceptable in the public libraries of this and other countries.

It may be proper to mention, in this place, that during the interval which has elapsed since the commencement of the printing in December 1857, several discoveries in Western Geology have been made. The most interesting of these, so far as regards the geology of Iowa, is the determination of the existence of the Permian system; the discovery of which was announced almost simultaneously by Prof. SWALLOW and Mr. HAWN, and by Messrs. MEEK and HAYDEN, while the pages of this volume were passing through the press. I have cited these publications in a note on page 143, and I have likewise incidentally noticed some fossils of the same character from Illinois, though their geological relations have not been determined. The paper of Messrs. SWALLOW and HAWN*, showing the relations of

* Mr. HAWN, who has been engaged in the linear surveys of Kansas Territory, has likewise devoted himself to the study of its geological structure, bringing out the sections which for the first time have clearly shown the relations of the Gypsum formation with the Cretaceous above and the Carboniferous rocks below.

the Gypsum formation of the west with the Permian rocks, had not then been published, or I should have availed myself of the information there given to cite from its pages some facts regarding this interesting geological formation. My remarks on the supposed relations of these beds were chiefly drawn from the observations of Mr. WORTHEN in 1856, which are more fully detailed in his Report; and from information obtained at a later period, regarding the occurrence of peculiar fossils in the Desmoines valley, in connection with, or in the locality of the Gypsum beds.

The inference (page 143) that these beds are unconformable with the Coal measures, is probably incorrect; the appearance indicating this condition in the Desmoines valley being of local extent, and due to the absence of some members of the series. It would moreover appear that the same may be true of the overlying formations ; and the hitherto supposed want of conformability may be due to the local absence of a portion of the series, as is so well shown in the relative position of the Coal measures to the underlying rocks along the valley of the Mississippi river.

Among other discoveries has been the announcement of Jurassic rocks in the region of the Black hills, from the explorations of Dr. HAYDEN, whose previous discoveries in that region, connected with what was before known of the geology of the country still further to the north, and also in the south, had rendered the existence of Jurassic rocks in that latitude more than probable. The hiatus heretofore existing in the sequence of formations in the West is thus being rapidly filled up. Dr. HAYDEN has also discovered in the same region the Potsdam sandstone, containing its characteristic fossils*. There is thus evidence of this lower member of the Palæozoic series as far west as the Black hills; a fact which had been inferred from its increasing thickness in that direction, as shown by Prof. SWALLOW in Missouri. We have long possessed metamorphic slates and other rocks indicative of Lower Silurian age from points still farther west, along the line of the Rocky mountains; and Lower Silurian fossils were brought by Col. EMORY from the same range, on the United

* I have elsewhere had occasion to notice more fully the discoveries of this zealous and indefatigable explorer, who has done more than all others of the present time towards giving us a true knowedge of the geology and palæontology, particularly of the Cretaceous and Tertiary formstions of the interesting country bordering the Upper Missouri and its tributaries.

States and Mexico Boundary Survey : showing that these formations, however attenuated in that direction, still preserve their characteristic features, reappearing from beneath the broad area of newer formations which occupy the great eastern slope of the Rocky mountains.

The third volume of the Geological Report of Kentucky, and several interesting palæontological papers, have appeared during the same period; and, as far as possible, these have been cited, and the names of the species there published have been adopted for several of those described in this volume, where no doubt of identity existed. If others have been overlooked, it has been from no intention or want of desire to identify and give credit for all such as have been previously described. The expansion of the volume so far beyond what was originally anticipated has precluded citations from and comparisons with the new facts and forms brought out in many of these papers; and, for the same reason, one or two subjects proposed for the second part of this volume have been postponed to the next.

The drawings of the Plates of this volume have been made by Mr. F. B. MEEK; and the diagrams of the Crinoideæ, illustrating the text, have been drawn with great care and accuracy by Mr. R. P. WHITFIELD, and will afford valuable aid in the comparison of species. The steel engravings are by Mr. JAMES DUTHIE, and those of the Crinoideæ especially may be regarded as very superior illustrations.

JAMES HALL, *State Geologist.*

SEPTEMBER, 1858.

RESOLUTIONS OF THE LEGISLATURE OF IOWA.

Joint Resolution to provide for the printing of an additional number of the Report of the State Geologist, and for the disposal of the same.

Resolved by the General Assembly of the State of Iowa, That the Governor be and is hereby authorized to procure the printing of one thousand copies of the Report of the State Geologist, in addition to the two thousand copies directed to be printed by the Sixth General Assembly.

Resolved, That the copies of said Report ordered to be printed by the foregoing resolution shall be disposed of as follows : Two hundred and fifty copies of the same shall be distributed under the direction of the Governor, to such of the Governments and Scientific Societies of Europe, and to such of the State Governments and Scientific Societies of this Union, as the Governor in his discretion shall determine. Fifty copies shall be given to the present State Geologist, twenty-five copies to Ex-governor Grimes, and ten copies each to Ex-governors Briggs and Hempstead ; and the remaining copies shall be disposed of by the Secretary of State, by sale for the benefit of the State, at the rate of five dollars per copy.

Resolved, That the Governor be further authorized to draw his warrant or warrants on the Auditor of State for the expenses incurred in accordance with the foregoing resolutions, who shall audit and allow the same.

APPROVED : February 12, 1858. RALPH P. LOWE, *Governor.*

Joint Resolution to provide for the distribution of the State Geological Reports.

Resolved by the General Assembly of the State of Iowa, That the Secretary of State be and is hereby authorized to distribute the two thousand copies of the State Geological Reports that were ordered to be printed by the last General Assembly, according to the following manner : One copy to each member of the last General Assembly, agreeable to a resolution passed by that body; and eighty copies to the State Historical Society, and ten copies to the State Library, and five copies to the Deaf and Dumb Asylum, and twenty-five copies to the State University, and one copy to each county in the State (to be held in the care of the county treasurer), and twelve copies to each State officer for distribution, and twelve copies to each member of this General Assembly for distribution within the State; and one copy to each State, one copy to the person or persons who edit each weekly newspaper or periodical in the State, one copy to each organized college or academy in the State, one copy to each of the chaplains of the General Assembly, and one copy to each of the secretaries and clerks of the General Assembly; and the remainder are to be disposed of by the Governor in the way of exchange for other valuable works, to be placed in the State Library.

Resolved, That for the distribution of said Reports, that the Secretary be authorized to draw his order on the State Auditor for the necessary expenses, to be paid out of any funds in the State treasury.

APPROVED : February 24, 1858. RALPH P. LOWE, *Governor.*

TO HIS EXCELLENCY

THE HON. JAMES WILSON GRIMES,

GOVERNOR OF THE STATE OF IOWA.

SIR :

THE accompanying Report on the Geology of Iowa comprises the results of the Survey to the close of the season of 1857. Under the law of 1855, the field work of the Geological Survey was commenced in September of that year, and has been carried on as rapidly, and extended over as much ground as the means at our disposal would permit ; one or two parties being employed in the field during the months of May and June, and of September, October and November of each year.

Mr. A. H. WORTHEN* was engaged as Assistant at the commencement of the Survey, and was employed, during the seasons for exploration, until the close of 1857 : by his services in the field, and the loan of his magnificent collection of carboniferous crinoids, he has added greatly to the value and interest of this Report. Messrs. B. J. HALL of Burlington (Iowa), and E. HUNGERFORD, offered their services and were employed as volunteer assistants ; the former in the autumn of 1855, and the latter in the corresponding season of 1856. Subsequently Mr. HUNGERFORD† was engaged as Assistant during the spring campaign of 1857 ; and the results of his observations will be found incorporated in Chapter VI. Mr. EDWIN A. COOLEY of Marion, Linn County, Iowa, joined the Survey in the summer of 1857, and continued to the close of the season.

The geological explorations have hitherto been confined to the eastern counties of the State, as shown in the Report. It is proposed to complete the publication of the results of the Survey in another volume, which shall contain the geological description of the western portion of Iowa, with a discussion of such subjects of theoretical and practical interest, including agriculture and the capacity of the soils, as can only be properly treated after having gone over the whole State.

* Since appointed State Geologist of Illinois.

† Since appointed Professor of Geology in the University of Vermont.

Among geological facts of interest brought out in this Report is the determination of the existence of the Hudson-river group at numerous points in Iowa and Illinois ; and although the occurrence of the blue shales had been previously noticed in Illinois, their true relations had not been recognized. The same strata have also been shown by the Missouri Report to exist in that State, and their identity with the " Blue limestone" of Cincinnati is now generally admitted.

The investigations in the Iowa Survey have shown the existence of an important limestone formation, above the Niagara limestone, not heretofore recognized in the Mississippi valley : this limestone occurs at Leclaire, forming by its undulations the Upper rapids of the Mississippi. Being a magnesian limestone, and holding the same relative position as the limestone of Galt, Canada West, it is not improbable that the two will be proved, by their fossil contents, to be identical. At the present time we know too little of the fossils of the Leclaire limestone to speak with certainty of its palæozoic relations.

Although the Hamilton and Chemung groups are recognized, both in their lithological aspect and in some of their more important fossils, it is yet an interesting and significant fact that the larger number of the species are distinct from those of more eastern localities, and, in some forms, more nearly allied to European species.

The subdivisions proposed in the Carboniferous limestones, below the Coal measures, are founded both upon physical and zoological differences, which seem to warrant the separation of the several members of the series. In Part II of this Report, these subdivisions have been illustrated by some of their more characteristic fossils ; from which it is believed the successive formations may be everywhere recognized.

In concluding these remarks, we acknowledge with much pleasure and satisfaction our obligations to the citizens of the State generally for their kind treatment, and the readiness with which they have furnished information in aid of the objects of the Survey ; and would more particularly mention the names of ALEXANDER M'GREGOR, of M'Gregor; Prof. J. ALLEN, Dr. J. SPRAGUE, H. DE WERTHERN, Esq., RICHARD BONSON, Esq., R. OSEE ANDERSON, Esq., and Dr. SCOTT, of Dubuque ; Dr. C. C. PARRY, of Davenport ; T. S. PARVIN, Esq., and Mr. REED, Engineer, of Muscatine ; and E. R. BLACKWELL, Esq., of Keokuk.

JAMES HALL, *State Geologist.*
NOVEMBER, 1857. J. D. WHITNEY, *Chemist and Mineralogist.*

ORGANIZATION OF THE SURVEY.

In the month of January, 1855, the Legislature of the State of Iowa passed the following Act to provide for a Geological Survey of the State.

AN ACT PROVIDING FOR THE GEOLOGICAL SURVEY OF THE STATE.

Section 1. ***Be it enacted by the General Assembly of the State of Iowa,*** That the Governor may appoint, by and with the advice and consent of the Senate, a State Geologist, who shall be a person of competent scientific and practical knowledge of the sciences of geology and mineralogy, who shall hold his office for the term of two years, unless sooner removed by the Governor.

§ 2. The said State Geologist shall, by and with the consent of the Governor, appoint one suitable person to assist him in the discharge of his duties, who shall be a skilful analytical and experimental chemist.

§ 3. It shall be the duty of said Geologist and his assistant, as soon as may be practicable after the appointment, to commence and carry on, with as much expedition as possible, a thorough geological and mineralogical survey of the State, as also of the character and quality of the soil for agricultural purposes.

§ 4. It shall be the duty of the Assistant to make full and complete examinations and assays of all rocks, ores, soils, or other substances which may be submitted to him by the State Geologist for that purpose, and to furnish him with a detailed and complete account of results so obtained.

§ 5. It shall be the duty of the State Geologist, on or before the first Monday of December in each year, during the time not necessarily occupied by said survey, to make report of said survey and the progress thereof, accompanied with such maps, drawings, and specifications as may be necessary and proper to exemplify the same to the Governor, who shall lay a copy of the reports before the General Assembly.

§ 6. It shall also be the duty of such Geologist to forward to the Governor, from time to time during the progress of said survey, such specimens of rocks, ores, coals, soils, fossils, and other mineral substances discovered and examined, properly labeled, as may be proper and necessary to form a complete cabinet of collections of specimens of geology and mineralogy of the State; and the Governor shall cause the same to be preserved for the benefit of the State, for public inspection. Said Geologist shall cause to be represented on the map of the State, by colors and other appropriate means, the various areas occupied by the different geological formations in the State, and mark thereon the localities of the respective beds of deposits of the various mineral substances discovered, and the character of the soil; and, on the completion of the survey, to compile a memoir of the geology and mineralogy of the State, comprising complete accounts of the leading subjects and discoveries which have been embraced in the survey.

§ 7. For the purpose of carrying into effect the provisions of this Act, the sum of two thousand five hundred dollars is hereby annually appropriated for the said term of two years, to be expended under the direction of the Governor. The salaries of the Geologist and Assistant shall be fixed by the Census Board of the State : the salaries of the Geologist and Assistant, however, shall not commence until they have respectively entered upon the discharge of their duties; and upon the completion of said survey and the duties connected therewith, the same shall cease and determine.

§ 8. This Act shall take effect, and be in force from and after its publication in the Iowa Republican and Iowa Capital Reporter.

REUBEN NOBLE,
Speaker of the House of Representatives.

MATURIN L. FISHER,
President of the Senate.

Approved — January 23, 1855.
JAMES W. GRIMES, *Governor.*

Under the authority given by this Act, James Hall of Albany (New-York) was appointed the State Geologist, and J. D. Whitney of Northampton (Massachusetts) was appointed to the department of chemistry, mineralogy, etc.

In accordance with the provisions of the Act, a report of progress was communicated to Governor Grimes at the end of the year 1856, accompanied by the following letter.

TO HIS EXCELLENCY JAMES W. GRIMES, GOVERNOR OF IOWA.

I HAVE the honor to submit herewith a report of a geological reconnoissance of the State of Iowa, made in 1855, together with a general statement of the results of the examinations made during the year 1856.

In order to conduct the work intelligibly, and to accomplish the object desired, it became necessary to obtain, in the first place, a general knowledge of the geological structure of the territory to be examined. For this purpose, geological sections were to be carefully made in different directions across the State. The northern and central parts, being to a great extent deeply covered by drift and modern accumulations, offered few facilities for such an object. The course of the Mississippi river presented the best exposures of the rocks; and likewise flowing generally in the direction of the dip of the strata, I was enabled to determine the successive formations and beds of rock from the Lower sandstone on the north, to the Coal measures, which approach the river at Davenport and Muscatine, and again in the vicinity of Keokuk; the intermediate space being occupied by limestones of Carboniferous age.

The reconnoissance of 1855, which was commenced only in the latter part of the season, was made chiefly along the course of the Mississippi river, and the observations extended into the interior at various points. These examinations have enabled me to present a brief general sketch of the geological formations of the State, which include some interesting and important groups not before noticed on the Upper Mississippi river. I have also given a sketch of the successive members of the series of Carboniferous limestones; showing, as I believe, for the first time, the true order and succession of the several masses or groups constituting this important and interesting geological series which underlies the greater part of the Coal measures of the Mississippi valley.

In the present state of the work, it would be impracticable to give, with any satisfaction, the details of the geological examination of counties or particular portions of the country: these, in order to be made available, require to be accompanied by maps and sections, the material for which has been obtained as far as the examinations have progressed.

While this reconnoissance of the geology occupied my attention, Professor WHITNEY was engaged in the Lead region, with a view to a complete investigation of that portion of the State occupied by the Lead-bearing rock, and the phenomena connected therewith. I understand from him that his investigations are not yet finished, and that much of the material collected is not yet in a state to be reported.

During the past season, Mr. WORTHEN has been chiefly occupied in making a detailed section along the valley of the Des Moines, and in local examinations in the southern part of the State. Much of this work is not yet in a condition to be reported upon. The collection of rocks and fossils are to be examined, and the coals require to be analyzed before the full results can be given.

The preliminary work is now so far accomplished, that the detailed examination of counties and particular districts may be at once begun, with a view to the preparation of a geological map of the State, which shall indicate the localities and limits of the several geological formations.

Extensive collections of the rocks, minerals and fossils, have been made from all parts of the State examined : these, with the exception of specimens taken for subsequent investigation, have been forwarded to Iowa city in accordance with the directions of your Excellency.

It is very important, both for the advantage and progress of the survey, as well as for the future value of this collection, that some proper place be assigned for its reception, in order that the specimens now lying in boxes may be arranged and labelled with their proper names and localities.

I have the honor to remain
Your Excellency's very obedient servant,

December, 1856. JAMES HALL, *State Geologist.*

On the receipt of this Report by Governor Grimes, the subject was brought before the Legislature of the State, and the following enactment and resolutions were passed.

AN ACT MAKING PROVISION FOR THE CONTINUATION OF THE GEOLOGICAL SURVEY OF THE STATE.

Section 1. ***Be it enacted by the General Assembly of the State of Iowa***, That there be and is hereby appropriated from the treasury of the State, out of any monies not otherwise appropriated, the sum of ten thousand dollars, to aid in the further prosecution of the geological survey of the State, and to be expended under the direction of the Governor.

§ 2. All geological specimens and fossils collected during said survey are hereby granted to the State University, and shall be deposited and carefully kept in a cabinet to be by that institution devoted to this purpose.

§ 3. This Act shall take effect, and be in force from and after its publication in the Iowa City Republican and the Iowa Capital Reporter.

SAMUEL M'FARLAND,
Speaker of the House of Representatives.

W. W. HAMILTON,
President of the Senate.

Approved — January 24, 1857.
JAMES W. GRIMES, *Governor.*

JOINT RESOLUTIONS TO PROVIDE FOR THE PRINTING OF THE REPORT OF THE STATE GEOLOGIST.

Resolved by the General Assembly of the State of Iowa, That the Governor be and is hereby authorised to procure the printing of two thousand copies of the Report of the State Geologist; and that he cause one copy thereof to be transmitted to each member of the General Assembly, and the remainder to be deposited in the office of the Secretary of State.

Resolved, That the Governor be further authorized to draw his warrant on the State Auditor for the expense thereof, who shall audit and allow the same.

APPROVED — January 29, 1857.
JAMES W. GRIMES, *Governor.*

After the passage of the foregoing Act and Resolutions, Governor GRIMES returned the Report of progress to the State Geologist, requiring him to prepare a volume which should include the results of the field work of 1857, and to " cause the same to be printed in large good type on excellent paper, with wide margins, with all proper and necessary illustrations, bound in cloth". The volume was directed to be of such a character as to form a part of the complete work on the geology, palæontology, agricultural and other economical resources of the State, as contemplated in the original act.

The accompanying volume has been prepared in accordance with the enactments and directions above given. It is hoped that it may meet the expectation of the enlightened legislators who have enacted the laws, as well as of the Executive who has on all occasions manifested the most lively interest in the progress of the work, and that the results here given may prove of real interest and importance to the People of the State.

ERRATA ET CORRIGENDA.

Page 40, line 3 from top, after 'recognized', add 'as the Hudson-river group'.

Page 48, sixth line, for 'Iowa river', read 'Upper Iowa river'.

Page 73, first line of note, for '*Spirigera*', read '*Nucleospira*'.

Page 174, diagram fig. 23, for 'coal 1 foot', read 'coal 3 foot'.

Page 203, thirteenth line from top, for 'lily stars', read 'lily stones'.

Page 479, under the generic description of *Megistocrinus*, seventh line from bottom, for 'five', read 'four'.

Page 484, under generic formula of *Pertremites*, second line, for '1×9', read '1×5'.

Page 484, under generic description, line 5, for 'pentagonal plates', read 'pentagonal basal plates'.

Page 485, for 'Plate ii, fig. 3', read 'Plate i, fig. 4'.

Page 492, ninth line from top, for '*L. demissa*', read '*S. demissa*'.

Page 499, for 'Plate vii, fig. 1', read 'Plate vii, fig. 2'; and the same in the reference to Plate vii, page 500.

Page 504, for **'Spirifer submucronatus'**, read **'Spirifer subattenuatus'**; and same on page 505, fifteenth line from top.

Page 507, twelfth line from bottom, for '*S. submucronatus*', read '*S. subattenuatus*'.

Page 512, line 17, for '*Spirifer parryanus*', read '*Spirifer biplicatus*'.

Page 529, in references to figures on Plate viii, erase letter *c*.

Page 540, in description of *Platycrinus nucleiformis*, read 'anal plate large, hexagonal'.

Page 560, note at bottom of page, last line, for '*Agaricocrinus*', read '*Agaricocrinites*'.

Page 562, under generic formula of *Agaricocrinus*, after 'interradial plates', add '1–3'.

Page 568, *Actinocrinus unicornis*, fifth line of description, read 'first radial plates, two heptagonal and three hexagonal'.

Page 569, explanation of diagram, third line, for 'second radials', read 'second interradials'.

Page 570, twelfth line from bottom, for 'first radials heptagonal', read 'first radials, two heptagonal'.

Page 574, under *Actinocrinus symmetricus*, second line of description, for 'heptagonal', read 'pentagonal'.

Page 576, under *Actinocrinus cornigerus*, fourth line of description, for 'first radial plates hexagonal', read 'two heptagonal'.

Page 577, under *Actinocrinus pentagonus*, third line of description, for 'two equal hexagonal', read 'two equal and irregularly hexagonal'.

Page 578, first line: 'Second radials, one hexagonal, the others octagonal'.

Page 580, second line from top, for 'pentagonal', read 'hexagonal'.

Page 581, sixth line from top, after 'hexagonal', add 'and heptagonal'.

Page 581, second line from bottom, for 'Fig. 19', read 'Fig. 10'.

Page 583, *Actinocrinus ornatus*, fourth line of description, for 'Radial', read 'First radial'.

Page 585, seventh line from bottom, read 'Third radials supporting', etc.

Page 589, under *Actinocrinus longirostris*, eighth line of description, read 'Third radials hexagonal or heptagonal'.

Page 596, under references to plate, add 'Fig. 6 *c*, base of specimen'.

Page 603, under references to plate, add 'Fig. 4 *e*, interior of ventral valve, showing the dental lamellæ'.

Page 607, under reference to figure 1, for 'half as great', read 'twice as many'.

Page 638, under *Productus setigerus*, for 'Plate xviii', read 'Plate xix'.

CHAPTER I.

PHYSICAL GEOGRAPHY.

Boundaries of the State of Iowa—Area—Configuration of its Surface—Sections across the State from east to west—Amount of Descent of the Mississippi River—Obstructions to navigation—Fall of the Missouri—Character of its navigation—Tributaries of the Mississippi—The Des Moines—The Cedar—The Iowa—The Wapsepinicon—The Turkey and Upper Iowa Rivers—Rivers tributary to the Missouri—Mounds—Prairies—River or Bottom Prairies—River Bluffs—Rolling Prairie—Elevation and Distribution of the Prairie Region—Character of its Surface—Peculiarities of Soil—Vegetation—Theories of the formation of the prairies—Climate of Iowa—Meteorological Tables—Inferences from the Tables.

Before entering upon a description of the geological structure of the State of Iowa, which is the especial object of this Report, it will be proper to give a sketch of the physical geography of the region whose geology we have been investigating. In every part of the world we see a most intimate connection between the configuration of the surface and the geological structure of any particular district ; and it will be shown in the course of this Report, that every peculiarity of the topography of the Northwest is the faithful reflection of the nature of the underlying rocky strata, or the final result of those agencies whose workings it is the province of the geologist to investigate.

The State of Iowa has nearly the figure of a rectangular parallelogram; its extreme length from east to west is about 300 miles, and its breadth a little over 200. Its northern boundary is the parallel of 43° 30′, which separates the

State from Minnesota; its southern limit is nearly in the latitude of 40° 31′. The two great rivers of the North American continent form its eastern and western boundaries. The Mississippi, on the east, has a general north and south course; but forms an irregular arc, of which the convexity is turned towards the east. Between the mouth of Turkey river on the north, and the city of Muscatine on the south, this bending of the river is quite regular, and gives a chord of about 90 miles in length between the extremities of the arc, and a distance of nearly 50 miles from this chord to the point where the river reaches farthest to the east. The States of Wisconsin and Illinois border Iowa on this side, their mutual boundary being the parallel of 42° 30′. The western limit of the State is the river Missouri, as far north as the mouth of the Big Sioux, which river the boundary line on this side follows, until it cuts the parallel of 43° 30′.

The State, as thus bounded, includes an area of nearly 60,000 square miles*.

The surface of Iowa is remarkably uniform in its altitude. It nowhere rises into an elevation which can be called a mountain, nor are the water-shed lines marked by distinct and easily recognizable ridges. In general, the western border of the State is more elevated than the eastern, and the northern higher than the southern. The Missouri has a more rapid descent than the Mississippi in the latitude of Iowa; and, besides, has a much longer course from the northwestern corner of the State to its entrance into the Mississippi, than the latter has from the northeastern corner to their mutual junction. If, therefore, we start from the Mississippi and proceed westward, we shall find ourselves gradually rising, until we reach the water-shed between the two rivers; and on descending into the valley of the Missouri, we shall be at a height above our starting point, which will be greater,

* The exact number of square miles in the State is not known at the Surveyor General's office: by a rough calculation, it was estimated at 57,024.

in proportion as the line we have traversed is nearer to the north boundary of the State. Each successive crossing of the streams emptying into the Mississippi, we shall find to be a little higher than the preceding one, as we advance from the east towards the west. This will be exemplified by the following tables of heights, obtained from the Engineers of the "Dubuque and Pacific" and "Mississippi and Missouri" railroads.

TABLE OF HEIGHTS ABOVE LOW-WATER IN THE MISSISSIPPI RIVER AT DUBUQUE.

Locality.	Distance from Miss. River at Dubuque, in miles.	Elevation, in feet.
Railroad track, ascending the Catfish valley..	4	84
"	5	133
"	6.3	170
"	7.3	188
"	8.3	230
"	9.2	271
"	10.3	302
"	13.6	444
"	21.2	492
"	22.2	520
North fork of Makoqueta, high water.......	28.8	352
Railroad track	30.9	350
"	40.2	489
South fork Makoqueta river	45.9	325
Railroad track	50.3	456
Prairie creek	53.1	404
Railroad track	57.2	485
Buffalo creek........................	59.5	405
Railroad track	60.3	451
Independence	68.5	330
Wapsepinicon river (300 feet wide).........	69	310
Railroad track	74.2	402
Cedar river (high-water mark)	92.4	
Railroad track	106.7	307
"	115.3	350
South fork Beaver creek..................	116.9	345
Summit between Iowa and Cedar rivers......	135	575

Locality.	Distance from Miss. River at Dubuque, in miles.	Elevation, in feet.
Iowa river (bed of stream)................	141.7	463
Summit between Iowa and Boone rivers......	162	750
Boone river (bed of stream).............	169	410
Summit between Boone and Des Moines rivers,	175	550
Des Moines river (300 feet wide)..........	189.2	377
Summit between Des Moines and Coon......	231	719
Coon river (bed of stream)...............	236	669
Summit between Coon and Little Sioux......	250	849
Little Sioux river.......................	263	504
Summit between Little Sioux and Floyds....	271	819
Floyds river...........................		515
Missouri river..........................		347

The above elevations are on the route of the Dubuque and Pacific railroad, which has its eastern terminus at Dubuque, and its western near the mouth of the Big Sioux at Sioux city. The table which follows gives the elevation of some of the principal points along the line of the Mississippi and Missouri railroad which extends from Davenport to Council Bluffs.

TABLE OF HEIGHTS ABOVE LOW-WATER OF THE MISSISSIPPI RIVER AT DAVENPORT.

Locality.	Distance from Mississippi river, in miles.	Elevation, in feet.
Iowa river, low-water mark................	56	98
Summit between Iowa and Skunk rivers......	122	440
North Skunk river.......................	130	290
South Skunk river......................	155	235
Summit between North and South Skunks....	150	425
Des Moines river.......................	180	227
Summit between Mississippi and Missouri....	245	967
Missouri river..........................	310	425

From the above levellings, it will be seen that the Dubuque and Pacific road ascends the valley of the Catfish by a grade averaging about 30 feet to the mile for a distance of 15 miles from Dubuque, when the general level of the prairie is reached, and the road runs along at a level varying from

450 to 500 feet above the Mississippi, until it reaches the valley of the North Makoqueta, which it crosses at an elevation of 352 feet. Thence, the surface of the country west to the South Makoqueta varies in altitude from 400 to 450 feet; attaining, at the highest point between those two streams, an elevation of 489 feet, at the distance of 40.2 miles from Dubuque. At the point where the south fork of the Makoqueta is crossed by the railroad, its elevation is 325 feet; and from here west to the Wapsepinicon river, a distance of twenty-three miles, the general height of the surface is about 450 feet, with variations of 40 or 50 feet of depression or elevation. From the Wapsepinicon to Cedar river the general level of the country is lower than it was farther east, being about 350 feet; and the Cedar itself is 50 feet lower than the Wapsepinicon. The Iowa is, on the other hand, over 200 feet higher than the Cedar, and the elevation of the surface between that river and the Des Moines is between 550 and 650 feet. The Des Moines is lower than the Iowa river, by a little over 50 feet; the former river being much the larger of the two, and having cut its channel deeper in proportion. From the Des Moines, the road runs in almost a straight line, for a distance of about 60 miles to the head waters of the Little Sioux river, and crosses Coon river at an elevation of 670 feet, while the general level of the region between the two rivers is from 630 to 660 feet. West of the Coon the ground rises gradually, and at its culminating point, 250 miles from Dubuque, attains an elevation of 849 feet. The road strikes Floyd's river about 18 miles from Sioux city, at an elevation of 574 feet above the Mississippi, and descends along its course to the Missouri, which is 347 feet higher than the Mississippi at Dubuque.

Thus it appears that there is a gradual rise of the surface from the east to the west, as far as the water-shed between the streams flowing into the Missouri and the Mississippi, which is much nearer to the former than the latter river, more than three-quarters of the surface of the State being drained by streams flowing to the southeast.

The elevation of the eastern border of the State, above the level of the sea, is at M'Gregor about 624 feet; opposite the mouth of Platte river 613 feet, according to the Wisconsin railroad surveys.

The annexed table exhibits the elevation of the Mississippi river, above the sea level, at some of the more important points between the mouth of the Ohio and Prairie du Chien.

Locality.	Elevation in feet.
Prairie du Chien (by R. R. surveys)...	625
Mouth of Platte river "	613
Dubuque "	610
Head of Upper rapids "	581
Rock island "	555
Flint river (Nicollet)..............	486
Mouth of the Des Moines "	444
St. Louis (Engelmann)	381
Mouth of the Ohio (R. R. surveys)..............	290

From Dunleith, opposite Dubuque, to Cairo, at the mouth of the Ohio, according to the Illinois Central railroad surveys, the descent is about 320 feet; the railroad track at Dunleith being 347.72 feet above low-water mark at Cairo, and 27 feet above low-water at Dunleith. This would give for the descent of the river, the distance being estimated at 586 miles, 0.54 foot or about six and a half inches per mile. From Prairie du Chien to Cairo, by railroad levellings, the fall is 334 feet, the distance being estimated at 652 miles: these data give a descent of 0.51 foot per mile, or just about six inches. This fall, however, is not uniformly distributed, as there are two important rapids within the limits of the State of Iowa, the only ones which interrupt the navigation of the river between its mouth and the Falls of St. Anthony, a distance of about 2200 miles. The obstructions here alluded to are called the Upper and Lower Rapids. The Lower rapids, or Des Moines rapids, extend from about three-fourths of a mile above Keokuk, nearly up to Montrose, a distance of eleven miles. The fall in this distance, according to Captain LEE, is a little over twenty-four feet (24.015 feet), or more than four times the usual descent of the river in the same distance. The Upper rapids extend from the lower extremity of Rock island, at the point where the river is now crossed by the railroad bridge, to the town of Le Claire, about fourteen miles. The fall of the Upper rapids is, on the same authority before cited, 25.74 feet. There is no doubt that it is possible, at a moderate expense, to render the passage of both the Upper and Lower rapids much less difficult than at present, and indeed Congress has more than once taken the matter in hand; but, the appropriations having been too small to effect the object at once, so that the work could not be continuously carried on, but little has been accomplished compared with that which would have been done, had the work gone on uninterruptedly. The obstructions being ledges of rocks, and not shifting sand-bars, whatever is once done will not require to be done over again, and it is much to be desired that this important work should be resumed and finished without delay. At present the Lower rapids amount almost to a total interruption of the navigation of the river, as it is only at the highest stage of water that loaded boats can pass, and a railroad has been constructed from Keokuk to Montrose for facilitating the transfer of freight and passengers. The Upper rapids can be passed by small boats, lightly loaded, during almost the entire season of navigation; but there is always more or less danger, the channel being exceedingly crooked; and, besides the danger of running aground, there is always a delay at low stages of water, if the air is not still, as the channel cannot be kept by the pilot, except when the surface of the water is unruffled.

The navigation of the Missouri is vastly more difficult and dangerous than that of the Mississippi. The current is much more rapid, as the descent of the Missouri is nearly one foot per mile, from the mouth of the Big Sioux to its entrance into the Mississippi. According to NICOLLET, the elevation of the Missouri at Council Bluffs, derived from a series of barometrical observations continued during several months, is 1023 feet. This result agrees pretty nearly with the railroad levellings, which make the river at Council Bluffs 425 feet higher than the Mississippi at Davenport; and if we take 550 feet as the height of the last named point, it will give 975 feet as the elevation of the Missouri. The altitude of the mouth of the latter river is 388 feet, and the distance from Council Bluffs to this point about 673 miles. These data will give a fall of about one foot per mile between these two points, a rate of descent just about the double of that of the Mississippi in the corresponding portion of its course. It may be here noted, for convenient reference, that the fall of the united rivers, from the mouth of the Ohio to the Gulf of Mexico, has been made out by Mr. ELLET to be about 2.8 inches per mile, or four times less than that of the Missouri in the lower part of its course. In consequence of the extreme rapidity of the current and the shifting sand bars with which it is encumbered, and which it is not in the power of the engineer to control, the Missouri river will probably cease to be of much value to the western part of Iowa as a means of transportation, after the system of railroads crossing the State from east to west shall have been completed.

The smaller streams which drain the State of Iowa may be divided into two systems, one of which comprises the rivers emptying into the Mississippi, and the other those which run into the Missouri. Much the larger part of the State is watered by affluents of the former river. This will be seen at once by reference to the annexed diagram, fig. 1, on which is designated the water-shed between the streams flowing into the two great rivers which form the eastern and western boundaries of the State.

FIG. 1.—Diagram of water-shed.

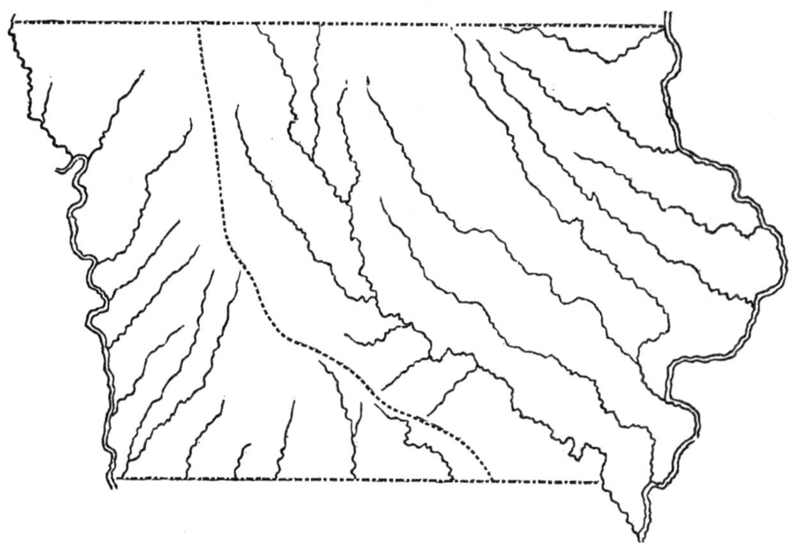

These two systems of rivers run nearly at right angles with each other, those falling into the Mississippi having a course from northwest to southeast nearly, while those which empty into the Missouri run towards the southwest; except along the southern border of the State, where they have a nearly south course. This would indicate the existence of two sets of flexures or fractures, at right angles to each other, as having determined the course of the drainage of the State. There is no evidence of actual fractures having occurred in the rocky strata, as the vallies seem in all cases to be vallies of erosion; but it seems hardly possible not to admit that the surface must have been folded or bent in a series of low swells, having a northwest and southeast direction, with minor flexures at right angles to this. The existence of these two lines of elevations or flexures may be traced over a great extent of surface, in Missouri, Nebraska, and Minnesota.

Of the streams which are tributaries to the Mississippi or Missouri, the most important is the Des Moines*, which rises in a group of lakes just on the border of Iowa and Nebraska, and flows diagonally across the State from northwest to southeast, entering the Mississippi at the extreme southeastern corner of the State, and forming its southern boundary for the last twenty-five miles of its course. A large extent of surface in the interior of the State is drained by this river and its tributaries, of which the Racoon, or Coon as it is usually called, is the most important. A company, called the "Des Moines Navigation and Railroad Company", has been organized to improve the channel of this river by building dams at the various rapids, in order to establish a system of slack-water navigation. There are twenty-eight dams proposed between the mouth of the river and Des Moines, which will afford valuable water-power; but, as the valley of the river is not a lumbering country, it is not to be supposed that river navigation, when interrupted by so many locks, will be able to compete with railroads in the conveyance of either freight or passengers. The importance of our rivers, especially of the smaller ones, as affording facilities for transportation, is rapidly diminishing, as the vast network of railroads is extending over the western country.

* According to NICOLLET, the name Des Moines, which has been attached to the largest river and the capital of the State (Des Moines city), is a corruption of an Indian word signifying "at the road". He remarks, "but, in later times, the inhabitants associated this name (*Rivière Des Moins*) with that of the Trappist Monks (*Moines de la Trappe*) who resided on the Indian mounds of the American bottom. It was then concluded that the true reading of the *Rivière Des Moins* was the '*Rivière Des Moines*', or River of the Monks, by which name it is designated on all the modern maps." NICOLLET's Report, page 22.

The above-mentioned company has a grant of land, to aid in the construction of their improvements, sufficient to enable them to build a railroad up the valley of the river.

The Red Cedar, or Cedar as it is usually called, is the next stream in importance. Its sources are in the lake region of Southern Minnesota, a few miles north of the Iowa line, and its course is nearly parallel with that of the Des Moines, until it arrives within ten miles of the Mississippi, when it bends gradually to the southwest, a course at right-angles with its former one, and after flowing about 25 miles empties into the Iowa, which, although considerably the smaller stream, retains its name after the junction of the two. Water-power is abundant along this stream and its tributaries, especially in the upper part of its course, as on Shellrock and Lime creeks, in Worth, Cerro Gordo and Floyd counties.

The Wapsepinicon, or Wapsi, as it is generally designated by the settlers, drains a narrow belt between the Cedar and Turkey rivers. The stream is probably over 250 miles in length, following its meanderings; while the width of the area drained by it is, for a considerable part of its course, n than from eight to twelve miles, a remarkable illustration of the ridging of the surface of the State in narrow folds as previously mentioned.

The remaining portion of the northeast corner of the State is drained by the Turkey, Yellow and Upper Iowa rivers and their tributaries. This region is more broken and irregular than any other part of the State, and the streams have usually cut deep into the rocks. Their descent is quite rapid, and they furnish ample water-power at numerous points. The Upper Iowa runs through a remarkably picturesque valley, bordered by bluffs which are from 300 to 400 feet high, and display a variety of gracefully curving slopes, interrupted by bold and striking precipices.

The western side of the State is traversed by numerous water-courses, which have a general direction at right-angles to that of the principal streams on the eastern side. None of them are navigable, unless it be the Big Sioux, which forms part of the western boundary of Iowa. In regard to the topography of this portion of the State, we have but little information, and its consideration will be deferred until a future Report.

Although there are no elevations within the borders of the State which can be called mountains, yet there are, in its northern portion, a few isolated rocks, or hills, to which the name of "mounds" is given. These mounds are small patches of rock which have escaped the general denudating influences which have removed the rocky strata over a great extent of country and to a considerable depth. The region in which they occur is nearly coextensive with that in which lead has been found, and they are all geologically identical, as they are capped with the hard beds of the Niagara group, and have, at their bases, the soft shales of the Hudson-river group.

The most easterly of the mounds are within the borders of Wisconsin, and on the extreme eastern edge of the lead region. These are the Blue mounds, two dome-shaped eminences, which rise in the midst of the prairie, and are quite conspicuous objects, owing to their isolated position in a gentle undulating country. Farther west are the Platte mounds, a group of three detached elevations, about six miles northeast of Platteville. Sinsinnewa mound, six miles east of Dubuque, is also in Wisconsin; it is 591 feet above the Mississippi, at Dunleith, and about 225 feet above the general level of the prairie at its base.

In the vicinity of Galena, in Illinois, there are several similar mounds, of about the same height as Sinsinnewa. Pilot Knob, near the mouth of Fever river, is a conspicuous object to those passing up and down the Mississippi, and has long been a well known land-mark to the pilot and raftsman. Waddle's mound just east of the city is a horse-shoe shaped elevation, from the summit of which a most beautiful view of the surrounding country can be obtained, as, indeed, is true of all the other mounds. Other outliers of the Niagara in this region are Hinckley's mound, Jackson's mound, and others to which no name has been given.

In the vicinity of Dubuque, Table mound is a conspicuous object. It is situated about five miles southwest of the city, and is elevated 472 feet above the Mississippi, which is about the height of the outcrop of the Niagara limestone encircling the city of Dubuque, at a distance of from six to ten miles. The summit of Table mound is a flat, narrow ridge extending about 700 feet in an east and west direction, and connected by a low spur running off to the southwest, with the main ridge of the Niagara to the south. Sherald's mound is another elevation of a similar character; it lies in sections 13 and 14, T. 90, R. I. E. Like Table and Sinsinnewa mounds, this also is elongated in an east and west line; as if the current, by which the rocks were scooped out, so as to leave these outlying masses, had acted in one or the other of these directions. The French mounds are eminences between the middle and south forks of the Little Makoqueta, along the outcropping edges of the Niagara in that region. They are about 550 feet above the Mississippi, while Sherald's mound is a little over 600. The limit of the Niagara limestone is distinctly marked by a bold bluff extending to the northwest, after crossing the Little Makoqueta, up the valley of Turkey river on the south side of the stream, and gradually becoming less and less conspicuous in that direction. This outcropping edge is cut by numerous ravines, and worn into long projecting points, in this direction; but there are no isolated masses, or mounds, which are distinct enough to have received a special name. As a geological fact, the formation of the mounds by denudation will be noticed more at length in another part of the Report, and some sections will be given illustrating the facts stated above.

The most striking feature in the topography of the northwest is the predominance of *prairies*, a name first applied by the early French settlers, and now universally adopted, to designate natural grass-land, in contradistinction to the wooded region, or, as it is generally called throughout the west, *timber-land*, or simply *timber*. Probably nine-tenths of the eastern, and a still larger proportion of the western, half of the State of Iowa is prairie. The timber is, in general, found skirting the streams, while the prairie occupies the whole of the higher portion of the country, with the exception of here and there an isolated group of trees, standing like an island in the midst of the ocean.

In ascending from the level of a river to the high land in its vicinity, we first cross the "bottom-land" or "bottom", the portion of the valley which is level, and, being but little elevated above the surface of the stream, is usually liable to overflow, especially at the time of the spring freshets. These bottom-lands are almost always heavily timbered and with a great variety of trees, among which the elm, linden, black walnut, white and burr oak, poplar and ash are the most common; with a great number of others, forming, especially in the valley of the Mississippi, a forest which can hardly be rivalled in the variety of species and vigor of their growth. The breadth of the river bottom is very variable: along the last-named river, it frequently expands to six or eight miles, while, in other places, there is hardly more than room for the stream itself to pass between the bluffs. Generally, the width of the valley is proportioned to the size of the stream; so that, on the smaller tributaries, there is but a narrow belt of low land, within which the stream meanders, with a very crooked course, crossing and recrossing from one side of the valley to the other. On the tributaries of the Mississippi there are but few traces of terraces in the river vallies; while on the great river itself there are, in portions of its course, indications of two distinct stages of elevation. More usually, however, even on the Mississippi, we rise from the river bottom up to the foot of the bluffs by a gradual ascent, without steps or terraces, the face of the country indicating an uninterrupted and gradual drainage, rather than one interrupted by epochs of repose.

The river bottoms are not always timbered. In the Mississippi valley, there are newly-formed islands and patches of land, often of considerable extent, which have not as yet been covered with vegetation, owing to their too recent formation; but which will, in process of time, as we may suppose, support as dense a growth of timber as any other part of the bottom, unless the capricious stream shall again sweep them away, before a sufficient time has elapsed for them to become covered with soil, by the growth and decay of vegetable matter and the deposition of river mud. Besides these temporarily bare patches, there are strips of land along the Mississippi of considerable extent, just above the level of the highest rise of the river, which are called prairies, and are indeed destitute of trees, although quite different in character from the highlands to which that name is usually applied. Prairie la Crosse, Prairie du Chien, Prairie la Porte (the site of the town of Gutenberg), the site of Cassville and other strips of land, especially on the left bank of the river, as far down as Dubuque, belong to this class of prairies. Prairie du Chien for instance, which has given its name to a rapidly-growing town, is a belt of land extending from the junction of the Wisconsin river north for six or eight miles, and having a width of from one to one and a half miles. It slopes gradually upwards from the river, and has an elevation of about thirty feet above the usual stage of water. The soil is a dark reddish-brown sand, with layers of small pebbles as shown in the annexed section (fig. 2), which represents a depth of about six feet, exposed in an excavation in the town near the Mondell House. Back of this strip of unwooded plain, the bluffs rise almost perpendicularly to the

Fig. 2.

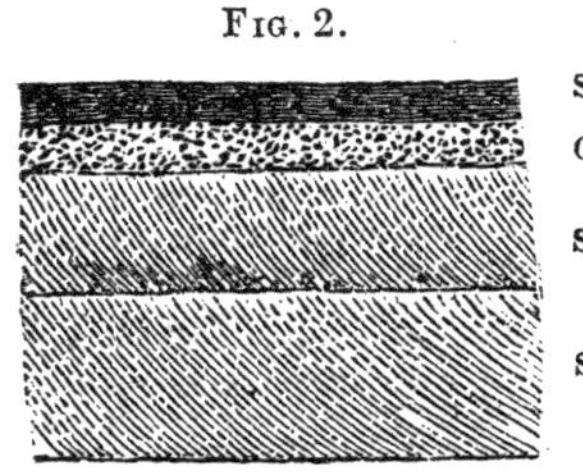

height of nearly 400 feet. sometimes the edge of the prairie adjacent to the river is more elevated than that portion which is nearest to the bluffs, as at Prairie la Porte, for instance, where the river, at its highest stage, almost surrounds the town and converts the plain into an island, as shown in the annexed section, fig. 3, in which *a* represents the level of high water, and *b* that of the ordinary stage of the river.

Fig. 3.—Section at Gutenberg.

The soil of all these low prairies is almost a pure silicious, somewhat ferruginous, sand, very different from that of the high prairies, although in both cases characterized by the absence of trees. The cause of this peculiarity seems to be the combined influence of an extremely sandy soil with the proximity of the river, which, under the peculiar climatological relations of the northwest, exposes it to extremes of moisture and dryness, unsuitable to the growth of arboreal vegetation. Where the soil is more clayey, or not made up so exclusively of sand, there seems to be no obstacle to the most vigorous growth of forest trees.

Farther down the river, within the limits of Missouri, the bottom prairies are largely developed, and are almost as important as the timbered bottom lands. They seem to be different in their origin and nature from the river prairies described above as occurring on the upper part of the Mississippi. The character of their soil, a succession of layers of vegetable mould, clay and sand, assimilates them rather to the high prairies, and the cause of the absence of timber is probably the same in both cases.

After leaving the river bottom, we usually come directly upon the "bluffs", as the steep rise out of the vallies of the streams on to the general level of the country is usually designated at the West. The bluffs form, next to the prairies, the most marked peculiarity of the surface throughout the Northwest. Over a great portion of the region south and west of the great lakes, the rivers flow in vallies, which are sometimes so narrow as to become almost ravines, and which appear to have been eroded by the action of water, their depth and breadth increasing with the magnitude of the stream and its distance from its source. These vallies do not connect with the uplands by a gentle rise, or sloping hill-sides, but by precipitous, sharply defined and, usually, rocky ascents or bluffs. These are often perpendicular, or nearly so, for a considerable portion of their height, when the rock is exposed, as is almost always the case if the valley has any considerable depth. More usually, however, a steep talus of rock and rocky fragments, thinly covered with soil, is crowned on the summit with a crest of precipitous rock, worn in a variety of fantastic forms, and cut by the deep ravines of the streams coming in on one side or the other, giving origin to the peculiar and picturesque scenery of the northwest, which is so well known to travellers and tourists upon the Upper Mississippi.

The height of the river bluffs is variable, depending, as before remarked, partly on the size of the stream and the distance from its source, and varying, also, from other and more general causes, in various districts of the State. The streams usually take their rise in small depressions of the high prairies, hardly to be noticed as being below the general level of the region; as their course continues, their beds gradually sink, and soon become bordered at points with steep banks of detrital material and then with vertical walls of rock, which increase in height, pretty regularly, to the entrance of the tributary into the main valley. In the northeastern corner of the State, however, the vallies are deeper and more precipitous than in any other portion of the State yet examined by us, and there is a gradual diminution in their depth towards the south. Thus, on the Mississippi, in the neighborhood of Prairie du Chien, the general level of the high prairie is over 400 feet above the river, and there is an almost vertical rise in the bluffs of about 300 feet. At Dubuque, the edge of the bluff, which ascends steeply from the river, is from 200 to 210 feet in elevation; and there is a farther immediate elevation of about 50 to 100 feet in addition, making the whole height from 250 to 300 feet. At Burlington, the bluffs are from 120 to 140 feet high, a steep talus of from 100 to 120 feet being crowned by a perpendicular wall of from 15 to 30 feet in height. The tributaries of the Mississippi in the northeastern corner of the State have all cut deeply into the rocks, in the lower part of their course. Thus, the Upper Iowa is bordered by bluffs 300 feet high as far up as New Galena; at Decorah their altitude is from 130 to 140 feet, but they are neither as steep nor as sharply defined. In the southern part of the State the streams rarely exhibit sections of as much as 100 feet, where they have worn their channels the deepest.

The prairie region of the west occupies a vast extent of country, extending over the eastern part of Ohio, Indiana, the southern portion of Michigan, the southern part of Wisconsin, nearly the whole of the States of Illinois and Iowa, and the northern portion of Missouri, and gradually passing, in the Territories of Kansas and Nebraska, into the *plains*, or the arid and desert region which lies at the base of the Rocky Mountains. This passage takes place in the region between the parallels of 97° and 100°, west of which belt the country becomes too barren to be inhabited and worthless for cultivation. The passage from the heavily wooded region of the North and East into the treeless plains of the West is a gradual one, and the disappearance of the underwood and the predominance of "oak openings", or groves of oak and other forest trees, not crowded together, but scattered over the surface at a considerable distance from one another, without any low shrubs or underbrush between them, is the characteristic of the border of the prairie region. To one coming from the dense thickets of low and tangled shrubs which choke the forests of the North, and render travelling through them difficult, even to the pedestrian, the open woods of the Northwest offer a striking contrast to that which has been left behind, and forms a natural introduction to the grassy plains or prairies.

The elevation of the prairie region above the level of the sea gradually increases from the east to the west. The lower part of Illinois varies from 100 to 250 feet above the river at Cairo, or 400 to 550 feet above the sea level. In the central portion of the State the levellings along the line of the Illinois Central railroad indicate an average elevation of from 650 to 750 feet, which increases towards the northern boundary to 800 or 900 feet above the sea. Some of the highest swells of the prairie attain an elevation of nearly 1000 feet. The more elevated portions of Southern Wisconsin are about 1100 feet above tide-water. The region from the Mississippi westward is a gradually ascending plain as far as the very base of the Rocky Mountains. Within the limits of Iowa the table-land, along the water-shed between the streams flowing into the Mississippi and the Missouri, the " lateau du Coteau des Prairies" of NICOLLET, attains the altitude of from 1400 to 1500 feet above the sea; and to the west of the Missouri the ascent still continues, the soil being more and more arid, until at the 105th meridian, an elevation of 5000 feet is attained.

The prairie is designated as "flat" or "rolling", its surface in the one case being nearly level, and in the other, gently undulating. The flat prairie is found chiefly south and west of Lake Michigan, on the head-waters of the Illinois and Wabash rivers. In other districts the rolling prairie greatly predominates over the flat, especially in Iowa, where there are but few tracts of any extent, which are not more or less undulating. Even in the rolling prairie the irregularities of the surface are but trifling in amount, compared with the vast extent which can be taken in at one view; so that it often happens that a region which, seen from a distance, appears to be almost a dead level, is, in reality, furrowed by broad depressions, which give a wave-like character to its surface. Thus, the traveller crossing the prairie in any direction, except along its water-shed, will be surprised to find himself constantly ascending and descending, although only hills of moderate elevation. The depth of these depressions below the mean level of the prairie may frequently be as much as 50 feet; but it does not often greatly exceed that amount, without the drainage becoming sufficient to convert the water, which collects in them, into a running stream. The "swales" or "sloughs" of the prairie, as these depressions are called, are wet and marshy except in the dry season ; and, in the spring and autumn make the roads almost impassable.

The prairies are covered with a dense vegetation of grass and herbaceous plants, to the almost entire exclusion of trees' which occur only, under peculiar circumstances of moisture and soil, in scattered groups, called groves, or along the larger streams, or, occasionally, on low rocky ridges which sometimes are met with. This growth of timber in the river bottoms does not entirely disappear until we reach the border of the "plains", about in the longitude of 98° west of Greenwich. In the swales or depressions, which are comparatively humid, the grass grows very tall and rank ; and the higher and drier the prairie, the finer its growth, and more dense and closely interwoven the sod. Among the grasses of the prairie is interspersed a great variety of flowering plants, which bloom in constant succession from spring to autumn, and lend a peculiar charm to the landscape, giving beauty and variety to what might, otherwise, be called a monotonous scene.*

The upper portion of the material constituting the superficial covering of the prairie is always finely comminuted, and usually has few loose boulders or fragments of rock scattered through it, although they sometimes lie upon the surface in isolated groups, or singly. Upon the great prairies in Central Iowa, one may frequently travel over a large extent of surface, without seeing a single stone, not even so much as the smallest pebble. In the swales and in some of the bottom lands, especially in the southern part of the State, the rich black vegetable mould is very deep, but on the prairies it is usually from one to two feet. The subsoil is almost invariably a quite argillaceous loam, and there is a gradual passage downwards into a material in which, though containing sandy portions and occasional pebbles, the argillaceous element greatly predominates.

The thickness of the superficial deposit which must be penetrated before reaching the solid rock is, of course, very variable in different parts of the State. There are sometimes accumulations of clay, sand and loam to a depth of nearly 200 feet; while in other places the rocks are barely concealed. The deepest accumulations, however, we conceive to be

* "The characteristic herbs of the prairies, etc., would seem to be *Compositæ*, especially Helianthoid Compositæ, such as *Helianthus rigidus, lætiflorus, occidentalis, mollis, hirsutus*, and in the river bottoms *H. doronicoides, Actinomeris helianthoides, Coreopsis aristosa* and *palmata, Echinacea purpurea* and *angustifolia*, and especially *Silphium laciniatum* (the Compass plant), *terebinthenaceum, integrifolium*, etc.; to which may be added *Cacalia tuberosa, Nabalus racemosa, asper* and *crepidineus, Ambrosia bidentata* and *psilostachya, Veronica fasciculata, Liatris pycnostachya, Eupatorium serotinum, Solidaga ohioensis, riddellii* and *missouriensis, Aster oblongifolius, azureus, turbinellus* and *sericeus*". GRAY: Am. Jour. Sci. (2) xxiii, 397.

mainly confined to the vicinity of the great rivers, as we have no evidence that, in the interior of the State and away from the water-courses, the superficial deposits have anything like the depth mentioned above. Indeed the wells which are sunk on the prairie are usually quite shallow, and almost never, so far as we have observed, reach the rock, so that we have not the means of ascertaining accurately what the depth of the whole body of superficial material is. In general, water is struck at from 15 to 30 feet in depth, as soon as a more gravelly stratum is intersected. The gravel which is met with, on sinking in the high prairie region, is rather a mixture of sand and clay with pebbles scattered through it, than a proper gravel. Generally, away from the river courses, where a section of the prairie deposits can be observed, the fine material will be found resting directly on the rock in place, the upper layers of which are usually broken into angular fragments, forming a bed two or three feet in thickness upon the surface of the solid portion beneath. These fragments are sharp and angular, and bear all the marks of never having been removed to any distance from their original position.

The material of the superficial covering of the prairie has evidently not been transported to any great distance. It bears the marks of having had its origin chiefly in the decomposition of the rocks which underlie it. The tendency of many of the limestones and shales of this region to undergo decomposition and crumble to powder is very great. This may be seen well exemplified at many of the shafts in the lead mining district, where the limestone rock thrown out is frequently found to have lost its coherence, and become hardly distinguishable from the soil on which it lies, except by its color. It would be difficult to imagine a prairie soil existing on crystalline rocks; and, in fact, the prairies are exclusively confined to regions underlaid by soft sedimentary strata, especially shales and impure limestones.

The subject of the origin of the prairies, or the cause of the absence of trees over so extensive a region, is one which has often been discussed, and in regard to which diametrically opposite opinions are maintained.

The idea is very extensively entertained, throughout the West, that the prairies were once covered with timber; but that this has been destroyed by the fires which the Indians have been in the habit of starting in the dry grass, and which sweep over a vast extent of surface every autumn. A few considerations will show that this theory is entirely untenable.

In the first place, the prairies have been in existence at least as far back as we have any knowledge of the country; since the first explorers of the West described them just as they now are. There may be limited areas once covered with woods, and now bare; but, in general, the prairie region occupies the same surface which it did when first visited by the white man.

But, again, the prairies are limited to a peculiar region, one marked by certain characteristic topographical and geological features, and they are by no means distributed about wherever the Indians have roamed and used fire. Had the frequent occurrence of fires in the woods been the means of removing the timber and covering the soil with a dense growth of grass, there is no reason why prairies should not exist in the Eastern and Middle States as well as in the Western. The whole northern portion of the United States was once inhabited by tribes differing but little from each other in their manner of living.

Again, were the prairies formerly covered by forest trees, we should probably now find some remains of them buried beneath the soil, or other indications of their having formerly existed. Such is not the case, for the occurrence of fragments of wood beneath the prairie surface is quite rare; and when they are found, it is in such a position as to show that they have been removed to some distance from their place of growth.

It has been maintained by some, that the want of sufficient moisture in the air or soil was the cause of the absence of forests in the Northwest; and it is indeed true that the prairie region does continue westward, and become merged in the arid plains which extend along the base of the Rocky mountains, where the extreme dryness is undoubtedly the principal obstaelc to the growth of anything but a few shrubs, peculiarly adapted to the conditions of climate and soil which prevail in that region. This, however, cannot be the case in the region east of the Mississippi and near Lake Michigan, where the prairies occupy so large a surface; since the result of metereological observations show no lack of moisture in that district, the annual precipitation being fully equal to what it is in the well-wooded country farther east in the same latitude. Besides, the growth of forest trees is rich and abundant all through the prairie region, under certain conditions of soil and position, showing that their range is not limited by any general climatological cause.

Taking into consideration all the circumstances under which the peculiar vegetation of the prairie occurs, we are disposed to consider the nature of the soil as the prime cause of the absence of forests and the predominance of the grasses over this widely-extended region. And although chemical composition may not be without influence in bringing about this result, which is a question for farther investigation, and one worthy of careful examination, yet we conceive that the extreme fineness of the particles of which the prairie soil is composed is probably the principal reason why it is better adapted to the growth of its peculiar vegetation, than to the development of forests. It cannot fail to strike the careful observer that where the prairie occupies the surface, the soil and superficial material have been so finely comminuted as to be almost in the state of an impalpable powder. This is due partly to the peculiar nature of the underlying rocks and the facility with which they undergo complete decomposition, and partly to the mechanical causes which have acted during and since the accumulation of the sedimentary matter forming the prairie soil.

If we go to a thickly-wooded region, like that of the northern peninsula of Michigan, and examine those portions of the surface which have not been invaded by the forest, we shall observe that the beds of ancient lakes, which have been filled up by the slowest possible accumulation of detrital matter, and are now perfectly dry, remain as natural prairies, and are not trespassed on by the surrounding woods. We can conceive of no other reason for this than the extreme fineness of the soil which occupies these basins, and which is the natural result of the slow and quiet mode in which they have been filled up. The sides of these depressions, which were once lakes, slope very gradually upwards; and being covered with a thick growth of vegetation, the material brought into them must have been of the finest possible kind, as is proved to have been the case by examination. Consequently, when the former lake has become entirely filled up and raised above the level of overflow, we find it covered with a most luxuriant crop of grass, forming the natural meadows from which the first settlers are supplied with their winter store of fodder.

Applying these facts to the case of the prairies of larger dimensions farther south, we infer, on what seem to be reasonable grounds, that the whole region now occupied by the prairies of the northwest was once an immense lake, in whose basin sediment of almost impalpable fineness gradually accumulated, under conditions which will be discussed in a subsequent chapter; that this basin was drained by the elevation of the whole region, but, at first, so slowly, that the finer particles of the superficial deposits were not washed away, but allowed to remain where they were originally deposited. After the more elevated portions of the former basin had been laid bare, the drainage becoming concentrated in comparatively narrow channels, the current thus produced, aided perhaps by a more rapid rise of the region, acquired sufficient velocity to wear down through the finer material on the surface, wash away a portion of it altogether, and mix the rest so effectually with the underlying drift materials, or with abraded fragments of the rocks in place, as to give rise to a different character of soil in the vallies from that of the elevated land. This valley soil, being much less homogeneous in its composition and containing a larger proportion of coarse materials than that of the uplands, seems to have been adapted to the growth of forest vegetation; and, in consequence of this, we find such localities covered with an abundant growth of timber.

Wherever there has been a variation from the usual conditions of soil, on the prairie or in the river bottom, there is a corresponding change in the character of the vegetation. Thus, on the prairie, we sometimes meet with ridges of coarse material apparently deposits of drift, on which, from some local cause, there has never been an accumulation of fine sediment : in such localities we invariably find a growth of timber. This is the origin of the groves scattered over the prairies, for whose isolated position and peculiar circumstances of growth we are unable to account in any other way.

The condition of things in the river vallies themselves seems to add to the plausibility of this theory. In the district which we have more particularly examined, we have found that where the rivers have worn deep and comparatively narrow vallies bordered by precipitous bluffs, there is almost always a growth of forest; but where the valley widens out, and the bluffs become less conspicuous, indicating a less rapid erosion and currents of diminished strength, their deposition has taken place under circumstances favorable to the accumnlation of a prairie soil, and the result has been the formation of the "bottom prairie," which becomes so important a feature of the vallies of the Mississippi and Missouri below the limits of Iowa. Where these bottom-prairies have become, by any recent change in the course of the river currents, covered with coarser materials, a growth of forest trees may be observed springing up, and indicating by their rapid development the presence of a congenial soil.

In the course of the survey, should it be continued, a careful chemical examination will be made of a number of specimens of soil, collected in different parts of the State, in the wooded tracts as well as on the prairie. It is to be presumed that the results of such an investigation, combined with the extension of the field observations of the survey over the western half of the State, will throw additional light, on the subject of the origin of the prairies, while at the same time they will form a basis for an opinion on the agricultural capacity of different portions of the State, as compared with each other and with other districts of the Northwest.

Having thus sketched the principal features of the topography of the State, we conclude this chapter by a brief notice of its climate; a subject, the importance of which will be a sufficient apology for its introduction into this Report.

Metereological observations have been kept up by the surgeons of the U. S. Army, at the various military posts, in pursuance of an admirable regulation of the War Department, since the year 1819. It is to these records that we are chiefly indebted for what is accurately known in regard to the climate of the Northwest. Mr. Blodget has recently published a valuable work*, in which abstracts of the observations which have been made by the United States officers,

* Climatology of the United States, &c. Philadelphia, 1857.

and of all those made by private individuals, under the direction of the Smithsonian Institute or otherwise, have been placed before the public in a simple and intelligible form. T. S. Parvin, Esq., of Muscatine, has kept a faithful record of the metereological changes at that place since 1850, and has recently published in the American Journal of Science a "Report on the Climate of Iowa," embracing the result of the records of the year 1856, with a synopsis of the seven years from 1850 to 1856 inclusive. Observations have also been made at a few other points within the State, but for too short periods to be of much value as yet.

A synoptical view of the results at most of the points within the State where observations have been made is here appended. The posts at Prairie du Chien, Fort Armstrong, and Council Bluffs are not in Iowa, but are only separated from its territory by the breadth of the Mississippi in the case of the two first-named places, and of the Missouri in the other. At Fort Snelling near St.Paul, Minnesota, the record is continuous from 1819 to 1855, and these observations are added for comparison.

The table on the next page shows the mean temperature for each month, season, and the year, as deduced from the observations made during the periods specified in the table.

We append to the table of temperatures, one indicating the amount of water precipitated, in the form of rain and snow, at the various points where observations of the kind have been made. The numbers in this table indicate inches and hundredths of vertical depth of water fallen, for each month and season, and for the year.

These tables were compiled from Mr. Blodget's work, and are chiefly made up from the records kept at the United States Military Posts. Observations have been made at several other points by private individuals; but they have, as yet, been kept up for too short a period to be of much value in coming at any general conclusion as to the climate of the State.

TABLE OF MEAN TEMPERATURES FOR EACH MONTH, SEASON, AND THE YEAR, FROM OBSERVATIONS FOR A PERIOD OF YEARS AT VARIOUS STATIONS IN THE STATE OF IOWA.

STATION.	Lat.	Lon.	Elev.	Jan.	Feb.	Mar.	April.	May.	June	July.	Aug.	Sept.	Oct.	Nov.	Dec.	Spr.	Sum.	Aut.	Wint.	Year.	Date of Observation.	Authority.
Fort Madison..	40 37	91 28	550′	24.0	27.0	38.2	56.8	65.3	74.2	82.5	77.5	71.5	54.1	40.2	27.2	53.4	78.1	55.3	26.1	53.2	1854–5	M'Cready.
Muscatine.....	41 25	91 00	586.2	20.2	25.5	34.8	46.4	57.9	66.4	70.5	68.9	62.5	48.8	35.4	22.6	46.4	68.6	48.9	22.8	46.7	1847–'55 (ex.1853)	Parvin.
Fort des Moines	41 32	93 38	850	27.4	30.0	39.5	55.8	59.2	66.4	76.5	71.7	61.2	44.7	35.3	29.2	51.5	71.5	47.1	28.9	49.7	1843–Feb. 1846	Mill. Post.
Fort Armstrong	41 30	90 40	528	22.8	24.7	37.8	51.1	62.7	71.4	76.5	74.5	63.9	52.3	39.0	27.1	50.5	74.1	51.7	24.9	50.3	1824–1835	Mill. Post.
Council Bluffs .	41 30	95 48	1350	19.4	25.2	33.8	51.8	62.2	73.0	75.9	75.4	65.6	52.0	36.4	20.6	49.3	74.7	51.4	21.7	49.3	1820–5; 1843	Mill. Post.
Fort Dodge....	42 28	94 03	980	19.6	23.2	29.3	44.3	59.7	72.2	76.2	73.0	67.2	54.2	31.0	19.5	44.4	73.8	50.8	20.8	47.4	Aug.'51–May '53	Mill. Post.
Dubuque......	43 29	90 50	630	19.8	23.3	35.1	53.8	62.3	69.1	75.2	72.0	66.3	52.5	38.7	24.5	50.4	72.1	52.5	22.5	49.4	1854–55	Horr.
Prairie du Chien	42 05	91 00	650	19.4	21.7	34.5	50.9	60.6	69.5	75.3	72.0	61.5	48.9	34.5	22.6	48.7	72.3	48.3	21.2	47.6	1822–25; 29–45	Mill. Post.
Fort Snelling..	44 53	93 10	820	13.7	17.6	31.4	46.3	59.0	68.4	73.4	70.1	58.9	47.1	31.7	16.9	45.6	70.6	45.9	16.1	44.6	1819–1855	Mill. Post.

TABLE OF PRECIPITATION IN RAIN AND MELTED SNOW, IN THE STATE OF IOWA.

STATION.	Jan.	Feb.	Mar.	April.	May.	June.	July.	Aug.	Sept.	Oct.	Nov.	Dec.	Spr.	Sum.	Aut.	Wint.	Year.	Date.	Authority.
Fort Madison..													15.30	15.90	14.50	4.70	50.50	1849–1853	M'Cready.
Muscatine.....	2.05	1.93	2.96	3.31	4.92	4.95	3.42	6.71	3.75	3.43	3.16	2.74	11.19	15.08	10.34	6.72	44.33	1846–1855	Parvin.
Fort Dodge....	0.65	0.42	1.43	3.04	3.45	5.16	1.57	1.42	2.55	3.26	2.38	1.99	7.92	8.18	8.19	3.06	27.32	Aug. 1851–May 1853	U.S. Mill. Post.
Fort Atkinson .	0.71	0.83	2.54	4.68	5.00	6.68	8.67	5.08	2.81	1.51	0.50	0.73	12.22	20.43	4.82	2.27	39.74	May 1844–May 1846	U.S. Mill. Post.
Prairie du Chien	1.19	1.24	1.92	2.99	2.72	3.74	3.48	4.65	4.06	2.04	1.80	1.57	7.63	11.87	7.90	4.00	31.40	May '36–Aug. '45	U.S. Mill. Post.
Fort Snelling..	0.73	0.52	1.30	2.14	3.17	3.63	4.11	3.18	3.32	1.35	1.31	0.67	6.61	10.92	5.98	1.92	25.43	July '36–June '55	U.S. Mill. Post.

The following table, prepared by Mr. Parvin from his observations at Muscatine (lat. 41° 25′ N.; lon. 92° 2′ W.; altitude 586.21 feet), gives the mean temperature of that place, for each of the months and seasons, for the years 1850–1856; also of each for those seven years, with the difference between the means of the year 1856 and those of the whole period of seven years.

Months & Seasons.	Years : Temperature.							Means of 7 years	Difference 1856 and mean.
	1850.	1851.	1852.	1853.	1854.	1855.	1856.		
Dec. 1849	18.34	19.77	21.37	22.18	26.67	26.76	22.40	22.49	− 6.86
January	24.40	23.97	19.60	27.05	16.16	24.46	7.52	20.45	−12.93
February	26.85	27.73	29.00	23.36	28.50	15.64	15.03	23.73	− 8.70
Winter mean	23.19	28.82	23.32	24.19	23.77	22.28	14.98	22.22	− 7.24
March	32.60	38.22	36.15	33.24	39.86	30.51	25.80	33.77	− 7.97
April	41.22	43.52	42.74	47.81	51.13	53.93	49.37	47.10	+ 2.27
May	53.30	58.19	59.96	55.65	60.03	60.42	61.38	58.42	+ 2.96
Spring mean	42.56	46.64	46.28	45.56	50.00	48.28	45.51	46.40	− 0.81
June	70.17	64.64	66.80	71.22	68.96	67.02	71.79	68.65	+ 3.04
July	74.22	71.62	72.36	68.82	76.16	73.01	73.51	72.81	+ 0.70
August	72.22	69.09	68.98	71.08	73.00	70.35	65.40	70.01	− 5.61
Summer mean	72.20	68.45	69.38	70.37	72.37	70.16	70.23	70.44	− 0.21
September	59.83	68.34	59.76	62.21	68.23	67.92	59.00	63.61	− 4.61
October	44.15	50.35	53.18	45.46	54.36	47.14	52.85	49.67	+ 3.18
November	37.55	34.50	30.00	39.73	36.83	37.83	32.79	35.60	− 2.82
Autumn mean	47.17	47.73	47.64	49.13	53.13	50.96	48.21	49.14	− 0.93
Annual mean	46.28	46.66	46.65	47.31	49.81	47.92	44.73	47.05	− 2.32

To this we may add another table, from the same authority, which exhibits the total quantity (in inches) of rain for each of the months and seasons for the years 1850–6; also the mean of each for seven years, with the difference between the total of the year 1856 and the mean of the septennial period.

MONTHS & SEASONS.	YEARS.							Means of 7 years.	Difference 1856 and mean.
	1850.	1851.	1852.	1853.	1854.	1855.	1856.		
December 1849 ..	4.30	2.40	1.90	5.00		0.41	2.02	1.75	+ 4.30
January	4.40	1.50	2.20	0.30		1.50		1.41	— 1.41
February	0.80	4.50	1.00	0.70	1.25		4.24	1.79	+ 2.55
Winter total.....	5.60	8.50	5.10	6.00	1.25	1.91	6.36	4.96	+ 1.40
Winter mean....	1.87	2.83	1.70	2.00	0.42	0.63	2.12	1.65	+ 0.47
March	2.00	3.00	8.60	0.70	1.12	1.22	0.25	2.41	— 2.16
April	3.30	3.60	5.30	11.80	1.76	2.55	3.44	4.54	— 1.10
May.............	3.70	12.60	6.50	4.60	6.21	1.94	4.39	5.70	— 1.31
Spring total	9.00	19.20	20.40	17.10	9.09	5.71	8.08	12.65	— 4.57
Spring mean	3.00	6.40	6.80	5.37	3.03	1.87	2.69	4.16	— 1.47
June	3.50	14.90	2.20	6.40	0.66	4.75	2.68	4.92	— 2.24
July.............	5.00	8.60	3.70	6.60	2.22	2.35	2.74	4.45	— 1.71
August	13.00	14.00	2.80	1.70	3.33	3.51	1.36	5.66	— 4.30
Summer total ...	21.50	36.90	8.70	14.70	6.21	10.61	6.78	17.05	—10.27
Summer mean...	7.16	12.30	2.90	4.90	2.07	3.33	2.26	5.01	— 2.75
September	3.90	3.50	8.30	6.20	1.13	1.84	2.45	3.90	— 1.45
October.........	2.70	1.40	7.60	0.20	4.29	2.81	5.21	3.45	+ 1.76
November.......	3.50	3.50	5.50	4.10	0.09	2.08	3.83	3.23	+ 0.60
Autumn total....	10.10	8.40	21.40	10.50	5.51	6.73	11.49	10.59	+ 0.90
Autumn mean...	3.36	2.80	7.13	3.50	1.81	2.24	3.83	3.52	+ 0.31
Annual total	46.20	73.00	55.60	48.30	22.06	24.96	32.71	43.26	—10.55
Monthly mean ...	3.93	6.08	4.63	4.02	1.84	2.08	2.72	3.44	— 0.72

The complement of the last table is the one next following, which shows the quantity of snow (in inches) of the months and seasons of snow for the years 1850–1856; also the means of each for seven years, with the difference between the total of 1856 and the mean of the septennial period.

MONTHS & SEASONS.	YEARS.							Means of 7 years.	Difference 1856 and mean.
	1850.	1851.	1852.	1853.	1854.	1855.	1856.		
December 1849 ..	4.70	3.70	1.50	11.40	3.20	1.00	13.00	5.50	+ 7.50
January	2.20	0.50	3.20	1.00	4.00	17.50	12.20	5.80	+ 6.40
February		8.40		2.00	5.50	7.10	12.00	5.00	+ 7.00
Winter total.....	6.90	12.60	4.70	14.40	12.70	25.60	37.20	16.36	+20.84
Winter mean	2.30	4.20	1.56	4.80	4.23	8.86	12.40	5.48	+ 5.82
March	0.80	0.30		2.00	1.10	6.50	3.60	2.04	+ 1.56
April	0.20	6.00							
November.......	0.90	1.30	2.60	8.00	1.00	1.50	5.20	2.93	+ 2.27
Annual total	8.80	20.20	7.30	24.40	14.70	33.60	46.00	22.14	+23.86
Annual mean....	1,46	3,36	1.21	4.06	2.45	5.60	7.66	3.68	+ 3.98

The southern boundary of Iowa is nearly on the same parallél with Central Pennsylvania, while the northern border of the State is in the latitude of Central New-York and Southern Vermont and New-Hampshire. The difference in the mean temperature of the year between the northern and southern districts of Iowa is, therefore, quite a perceptible one. In the region bordering on the Atlantic coast, a difference of latitude equal in amount to that between Keokuk and Lansing implies a difference of mean temperature equal to about 6°.5′. It appears from an examination of the tables given above that observations have not been made at a sufficient number of points, especially in the southern portion of Iowa, or kept up for an adequate length of time, to enable us to draw entirely satisfactory conclusions as to the range of temperature in one part of the State as compared with another. The most extended series are those of Muscatine, Rock island (Fort Armstrong), and Prairie du Chien (Fort Crawford). The difference of latitude of the two latter stations is 1° 35′, and the difference of mean annual temperature 2°.7 ; which variation corresponds quite nearly with that observed in the same parallels on the Atlantic slope*.

Early in the history of this country, it was generally maintained that the climate of the Mississippi valley was considerably warmer than that of the Atlantic States in the same parallel. This theory has not been confirmed by the results of the observations which have been made at numerous stations, both in the Eastern and Western States.

Mr. Blodget remarks on this point as follows:

"The early distinction between the Atlantic States and the Mississippi valley has been quite dropped, as the progress of observation has shown them to be essentially the same, or to differ only in unimportant particulars. It is difficult to designate any important fact

* The mean temperature of Muscatine, as given by Mr. Parvin, seems to be lower than that of other points in about the same latitude ; being 2° less than that of Fort des Moines, 3°.6 lower than the mean of the observations of Rock island, and 2°.6 below that of the Council Bluffs record. This discrepancy we are at a loss to account for.

entitling them to separate classification ; they are both alike subject to great extremes; they both have strongly marked continental features at some seasons, and decided tropical features at others, and these influence the whole district similarly, without showing any line of separation. At a distance from the shore of the Gulf of Mexico sufficient to remove its local effects, the same peculiarities appear which belong to Fort Snelling and to Montreal, as well as to Albany, Baltimore and Richmond."*

On comparison of the records, however, it appears that while there is little difference in the mean temperature for the year between places in the same latitude in the Mississippi valley and on the Atlantic border, yet there is a perceptible tendency to extremes in the mean of the seasons as we go farther west. Thus we may make the following comparisons to illustrate this remark.

Locality.	Latitude.	Temperatures.				
		Year.	Spring.	Summer.	Autumn.	Winter.
West Point, N. Y........	41°23′	50.7	48.7	71.3	53.2	29.7
Fort Armstrong..........	41 30	50.3	50.5	74.1	51.7	24.9
Council Bluffs............	41 30	49.3	49.3	74.7	51.4	21.7
Utica, N. Y	43 06	45.7	44.5	66.5	47.3	24.5
Prairie du Chien	43 05	47.6	48.7	72.3	48.3	21.2
Potsdam, N. Y	44 40	43.6	42.9	66.3	45.4	19.8
Fort Snelling............	44 53	44.6	45.6	70.6	45.9	16.1

These data are sufficient to show that the spring and summer are decidedly warmer, and the winter colder, in the Mississippi valley than on the same parallel in New-York. The open character of the prairie region, the want of shelter from the sun of the summer and the sweeping winds of winter, make these peculiarities of the western climate more perceptible than they would seem to be from an inspection of the thermometrical register. The prairie winds, however

* Climatology of the United States, page 126.

unpleasant to those exposed to them in the severity of winter, are of the greatest benefit to the general sanitary condition of the State; since they prevent the accumulation of the malaria which arises from the decomposition of the rich vegetation of the prairies, as is proved by the marked difference in the health of settlers on the prairie and in the timber.

In regard to the distribution of rain, it will be observed, although the statistics are very imperfect, that while the quantity falling during the year in the Mississippi valley within the limits of Iowa is large, being fully equal to that on the Atlantic coast in the same latitude, there is a rapid, and indeed almost abrupt, falling off as we go towards the north and west. Thus, the total precipitation for the year, at Muscatine, is 44.33 inches, while at Fort Snelling it is only 25.43 inches. The observations at Fort Dodge show a similar decrease in a western direction. The most marked feature of the distribution of the amount of moisture precipitated in the form of rain and snow through the year, is a relative increase of the quantity falling in spring and summer, and a very considerable diminution in winter; which condition becomes more and more marked as we advance westward from the Mississippi. The diminution in the quantity of snow, as compared with the eastern States on the same latitude, is one of the features of the climate which is, practically, most felt by the settler from that region.

CHAPTER II.

GENERAL GEOLOGY.

GENERAL REMARKS ON THE GEOLOGY OF THE NORTHWEST, AND THE RELATIONS OF THE FORMATIONS TO THOSE OF THE EAST.

MODERN GEOLOGY is indebted for its rapid advances, and the certainty with which its determinations are made at different and distant points in the sedimentary fossiliferous strata, mainly to Palæontology. The careful study of the rock formations has shown that certain groups of beds or strata which lie one above another may be identified by the fossil remains which they contain; or, in other words, the beds of limestone, sandstone, shale, etc. have each in their turn, while in the state of sand and mud, formed the bed of an ancient ocean, in which the then living forms have been imbedded, and are still preserved in the solid rocky masses. The refinement to which this study has been carried enables us to distinguish, by a few fossil forms, the relative age of certain beds of rock to other strata which have been elsewhere studied; and as all experience has proved that the order of sequence is everywhere essentially the same, though certain beds may be absent or others intercalated, yet the relative position of known beds is never reversed. We are able by this means to determine at once the relations of all formations which come under examination, to all others in the known geological series. We have thus a means everywhere at hand to determine not only the relations of the rocks under examination to other similar or identical formations, but also their relations to rocks of known economical value, or to those containing materials of similar importance, as coal, iron ore, etc., without consuming the time which would otherwise be necessary in every new locality to determine the order and relations of the entire set of strata and their mineral contents.

This principle, in its application, is carrying out only that which any good observer would do to a limited extent without geological knowledge; for if, after examining a limestone over the area of a township or a county, he should find it everywhere marked by certain characters, and the final result proved it only valuable as a limestone, and containing no other economical product, he would conclude that the same rock, when identified at a distance of ten miles, would possess the same characters. Should this limestone, in the area already examined, have resting upon it a sandstone or shale with coal, he would naturally infer the same order, should he meet the limestone above in any locality not before examined.

Upon the same principle, geological and palæontological knowledge acquired in one or many parts of the country, as well as the results of experience in other countries, are brought to bear upon the investigations of any portion heretofore unexplored. Were it otherwise, the process of geological examination would be slow and tedious, and the results unsatisfactory.

The rocks of the Palæozoic series, or those constituting the different divisions or groups, from the known commencement of animal life to the coal measures inclusive, constitute the fundamental rock formations of much the larger part of the area of the State of Iowa.

The true order and sequence of the strata below the Carboniferous formations have been made known through the Reports of the New-York Geological Survey, more clearly and more in detail than from any other course. These results have been confirmed, with many additional facts of great importance, from the investigations in the Canada Geological Survey; and the order of sequence and nomenclature has been established from Gaspe to Lake Superior, and from New-York to the Mississippi river.

The Reports of Pennsylvania and Virginia have given a clear knowledge of the structure of the coal measures, and the sequence of their different members in the eastern part of the great Appalachian coal field; while the Reports of Ohio, and more recently of Kentucky, have shown a corresponding sequence on the western side of the same region. West of the Cincinnati axis, we know the coal measures of Michigan from the Reports of Dr. HOUGHTON; those farther west, from the Reports of Dr. OWEN on Iowa, Minnesota, etc.; and those of Missouri, more in detail from the Roports of Prof. SWALLOW.

The carboniferous limestones, lying beneath the coal measures, and forming so conspicuous a feature along the Mississippi valley and throughout the west and southwest in the coal-measure regions, are scarcely recognizable on the east of the Appalachian chain, or beneath the coal measures of Pennsylvania, Ohio, Eastern Kentucky, and a large part of Virginia.

The great plateau of the Northwest, stretching from the Appalachian chain westward to the slopes of the Rocky mountains, and limited on the north by Lake Huron and Lake Superior, presents great simplicity of geological structure. The entire sequence of formations, from the Potsdam sandstone to the Coal measures inclusive, occupies the greater portion of this area; and the slight disturbances to which they have been subjected, and the tenuity of the formations, have served only to make the successive beds more accessible to investigation.

Towards the Rocky mountains, the palæozoic rocks are overlaid by the Cretaceous formation, which, in its lower arenaceous members, stretches from the northern limits of the United States territories to the Gulf of Mexico, and throughout a great part of this extent rests unconformably upon the Coal measures. The line of junction of these two formations is secured by the denudation of the highest one, and its finely comminuted materials are widely spread over the lower strata, forming with other materials the broad expanse of prairie deposit of the West.

The lower geological formations, therefore, of this great northwestern plateau are the same as those known in New-York and Pennsylvania, which form not only the undisturbed portions of that part of the country, but also the disturbed regions of mountain ranges, whether known as the Green mountains, the White mountains, the Allegany mountains, or the Appalachian chain.

In tracing westward the geological formations as known in New-York and Pennsylvania, we find them, with one or two exceptions, gradually becoming thinner, until at last several of them are scarcely recognizable, or are so attenuated as to be overlooked in a country deeply covered by modern deposits.

The Potsdam sandstone, which can be traced from Northern New-York and Canada by the St.Lawrence, and thence bordering the north shore of Lake Huron and the south shore of Lake Superior, spreads out in Wisconsin, Minnesota and Northern Iowa, preserving mostly a uniform thickness, and showing an elevation above the Mississippi of more than five hundred feet, which is equal to its usual thickness in more eastern localities. The succeeding Calciferous sandstone is likewise traceable, with some interruptions, over the same area, and is a usual accompaniment of the Potsdam sandstone. Not unfrequently the two are so closely incorporated at their junction, as to show that they are parts of one formation, which has become more and more calcareous, until it is seen as a limestone or dolomite.

The succeeding limestones of the Chazy, Birdseye, Black-river and Trenton, can be traced from New-York and Canada, along the northern side of Lake Ontario and Lake Huron, and thence to the north of Lake Michigan and the western borders of Green Bay, where they trend westerly to the Mississippi river. But they have greatly thinned towards the west; and instead of the marked features presented by the same rocks in Pennsylvania, New-York and Canada East, they form low and often inconspicuous escarpments above the upper or St. Peters sandstone, which represents the Chazy limestone in part, and has a thickness of from sixty to eighty feet.

This diminution of the lower limestones is in a measure compensated by the accession of the Galena or Lead-bearing limestone, which is an upper member of the Trenton limestone series not developed in the East, but forming in Wisconsin, Illinois and Iowa, a more conspicuous feature than the Trenton limestone proper.

In the Hudson-river group and succeeding Oneida conglomerate, a most marked change takes place : the former is estimated to have, in Pennsylvania, a thickness of six thousand feet, and the latter a thickness of one thousand eight hundred feet; while the same rocks along the Green mountain range and in Canada, are in even greater force. This group of strata, consisting of green, blue and red shales, shaly sandstones and some beds of limestone, can be traced westward from Canada and New-York, by Lake Ontario and Lake Huron, by Point aux Baies at the northern extremity of Lake Michigan, and thence from below the head of Green Bay and by the eastern side of Lake Winnebago, and at intervals across the State of Wisconsin. Along this line of almost continuous outcrop there is a constant thinning of the beds, until at last the whole group has diminished to a thickness of less than one hundred feet. Thus we see that the group of strata, forming the most conspicuous feature in the Green mountains, with a thickness greater than the actual height of these mountains, and making up a large part of the whole Appalachian chain, has become so insignificant that it had never been recognized along the Upper Mississippi until during the progress of the present survey in the autumn of 1855.

The Medina sandstone and Clinton group, which thin out to a great extent in the State of New-York, have almost entirely disappeared before reaching Wisconsin. These formations are known only at one or two points within that State, and thus far have not been recognized in Iowa.

The Niagara limestone maintains its character, and essentially its thickness, at the west. Extending from Niagara falls through Canada, it forms the peninsula of Cabot's head, the Manitoulin islands of Lake Huron, and the peninsula between Green Bay and Lake Michigan; and thence stretching southwesterly across Wisconsin, it forms an irregular escarpment which reaches the Mississippi river below Galena in Illinois; and thence takes, with the same features, its course through Iowa, leaving on both sides of the river some outliers further to the north, forming the "Mounds".

Above the Niagara group, and corresponding with it in direction, is a limestone formation of considerable thickness, but which, from its disturbed condition, forms no conspicuous feature in the country. This limestone forms the rapids of Leclaire, and is probably the same rock as that developed in the vicinity of Galt in Canada West.

The Onondaga-salt group, which is next in order of sequence, and in New-York succeeds the Niagara limestone with a thickness of one thousand feet or more, has so thinned out, that in Iowa it is not more than one hundred and fifty feet thick.

The strata which in New-York and the east constitute the limestones of the Upper Helderberg series, the Hamilton, Portage and Chemung groups, are all embraced within less than two hundred feet; while in New-York and Pennsylvania these formations have a thickness of from four to six thousand feet, and form conspicuous topographical features; constituting a great part of the White mountains, and important portions of the Appalachian chain.

The Catskill mountain group, having a thickness of more than three thousand feet, and which forms the conspicuous highlands from which it derives its name, is quite unknown to the west of the Cincinnati axis; and the succeeding conglomerates, sandstones and shales are likewise absent from the series in the west, while their places are in a degree filled by the carboniferous limestones which attain far less thickness.

The same remarks hold true in regard to the Coal formation, which, from having a thickness of more than six thousand feet in Pennsylvania, has become reduced to less than as many hundred feet in Iowa.

This remarkable fact of the thinning out westwardly of all the sedimentary formations, points to a cause in the conditions of the ancient ocean, and the currents which transported the great mass of materials along certain lines which became the lines of greatest accumulation of sediments, and consequently present the greatest thickness of strata at the present time. It is this great thickness of strata, whether disturbed and inclined as in the Green and White mountains and the Appalachians generally, or lying horizontally as in the Catskill mountains, that gives the strong features and the hilly and mountainous country of the east, and which gradually dies out as we go westward, just in proportion as the strata become attenuated.

The subdued features of the West are therefore due, not alone to the absence of great disturbing forces, but to the absence or the great tenuity of the formations, or paucity of materials or strata to be disturbed. The thickness of the entire series of sedimentary rocks, no matter how much disturbed or denuded, is not here great enough to produce mountair features; and the most elevated portions of this region are those where no disturbing force essentially affecting the horizontality of the strata has acted.

The mounds, or highest portions of the country in any part of this western plateau, lie in the undisturbed districts, and exhibit nearly horizontal beds; and are simply due to the original accumulation of sediments forming the rocky strata, which have subsequently been denuded, leaving these isolated portions. These are everywhere capped by the highest rock of that part of the country, the Niagara limestone, and have an elevation of from four to six hundred feet above the Mississippi river; and this elevation gives us very nearly the thickness of the strata from the St.Peters sandstone to the Niagara limestone*. Now if we were to measure the entire thickness of the strata from the Potsdam sandstone to the Niagara limestone, on the borders of New-England, or along the Appalachian chain, we should find it to comprise from six to eight or even ten thousand feet. If, therefore, instead of the disturbances which we find in this eastern extension of the same beds, we had the undisturbed strata, denuded as they have been in Wisconsin, Illinois and Iowa, from the Niagara limestone downwards to the Potsdam sandstone, we should have mounds of as many thousands of feet in height as we there have hundreds of feet.

* The St. Peters sandstone in the region of the mounds lies just below, or at the level of the Mississippi river. The Potsdam sandstone lies about two hundred feet below the St. Peters sandstone.

The following section gives very nearly the relative and aggregate thickness of the several members included in the series; the measurements given being the greatest ascertained at any point.

Niagara limestone	150 feet.
Hudson-river group	100 feet.
Galena limestone . . . . , . .	250 feet.
Trenton limestone	100 feet.
St.Peters sandstone	80 feet.
Calciferous sandstone or Lower Magnesian limestones,	200 feet.
Potsdam sandstone	500 feet.

Thus it would appear that the height of these mountains is not due to upheaval from beneath, or to the folding and plication of the beds; but that the dislocations of the strata and consequent denudation render the elevation always less than it would have been made by the actual thickness of the strata, had they remained undisturbed and piled upon each other in their horizontal condition, and these subjected to the same denudating agencies.

Again, in proof that disturbances of the strata do not necessarily produce elevation, several lines along the country, or lines of anticlinal axes, which show the strata to be inclined from ten to thirty degrees, far from producing mountain features, are along the lowest levels of the country. This occurrence of lines of highly inclined strata, accompanied at the same time by a low country, shows that the cause producing such disturbance is not that producing mouutain elevations*.

The general trend of the older strata on the west side of Lake Michigan is from the northwest to the southeast, or nearly at right-angles to the direction of the Cincinnati axis and the lines of disturbance along the Appalachain chain. This feature presents us with a broad expansion of the Potsdam and Calciferous sandstones, stretching to the southwest from the mountains bordering the south side of Lake Superior. Upon the latter, which is an indestructible magnesian limestone, rests the St.Peters sandstone; and upon this, the resisting strata of the Trenton limestone group. Approaching the outcrop we find a few outliers or mounds of the sandstone, capped by the Trenton limestone, which have withstood the denuding action, and stand out as indications of the former extension of the higher beds over the northern portions of this region of country.

After passing the irregular crop of the Trenton lime-

*For a more full exposition of these views, see introduction to the third volume Paæo ntology of New-York.

stone. It forms interruptedly the plateau for a greater or less distance; when we again find outliers of the succeeding or Hudson-river group, capped by the Niagara limestone, and forming the well-known Blue mounds, Platte mound, Sinsinawa mound, Sherald's mound and Table mound, showing a unity in the geological features from Lake Michigan to the northwestern limits of these formations.

Carrying on our observations still in a southwesterly direction, the succeeding formations of the Onondaga-salt group, the Leclaire limestone, the Hamilton and Chemung groups, form no conspicuous feature in the country; and the Coal measures come on almost imperceptibly, first in small outliers, and then in broader areas, lying unconformably over the slightly inclined edges of the lower strata.

The Coal measures extend much farther north along the Mississippi valley in Iowa and in Illinois, than this Carboniferous limestone; and there is clearly a want of conformity between the two, where they occur in conjunction. From the data already collected, it appears almost certain that the Coal measures reach to the northwestern limits of the State of Iowa, and even beyond it into the adjoining territory. In this direction, however, the formation becomes covered by the succeeding deposits of Cretaceous age, and the productive Coal measures are evidently becoming thinner, so that no safe prediction can be made of their real value.

These formations are limited on the north by the older crystalline rocks, which form mountain barriers on the northeastern side of Lake Huron; and which, crossing the lower extremity of Lake Superior, form a belt of varying width on the south side of that lake, and extend thence more or less continuously to the northwest.

NOTE. In the preceding and subsequent chapters, there may be some facts, views or opinions, not entirely coincident with those of other geologists, and for these the writer alone is responsible. J. H.

CHAPTER III.

GEOLOGY OF IOWA.

GENERAL RECONNOISSANCE.

General Remarks—Potsdam sandstone—Calciferous sandstone—St.Peters sandstone—Trenton limestone, with the subordinate beds of Birdseye and Black-river limestone—Galena limestone—Hudson-river group—Medina sandstone—Clinton group—Niagara limestone—Leclaire limestone—Onondaga-salt group—Upper Helderberg limrstones—Hamilton group—Cheemung group—Burlington limestone—Keokuk limestone— Warsaw limestone— St.Louis limestone— Ferruginous sandstone—Kaskaskia limestone—Coal measures.

With a view of acquiring a general knowledge of the geological structure of the State of Iowa, it became necessary to obtain a section of all the rock formations before commencing the examination of the counties in detail. The course of the Mississippi river being the only line along which a complete exhibition of this geological structure is found in an almost continuous natural section from the lower sandstone to the coal measures, was first examined from the borders of Minnesota to the mouth of the Des Moines.

The successive rocks and groups exhibited in a section along the Mississippi river, from the north to the south line of the State, are given below in the descending order. The lowest rocks occur only in the northern part of the State; while the coal measures, as will be seen, occupy the central and southern portions, and the complete series can be seen only by traversing the entire length of the State.

Coal measures;

Place of { Kaskasia limestone and
Ferruginous sandstone not yet known to be developed in Iowa*;

St. Louis limestone (of Missouri Reports), equivalent to the brecciated limestone at the mouth of the Des Moines (OWEN'S Report);

Warsaw limestone;

Shales and marl beds with geodes, subordinate to the limestone above;

Keokuk limestone;

Cherty beds of the Keokuk rapids, subordinate to the limestone above;

Burlington limestone;

Chemung group, consisting of sandstones and shales;

Hamilton group, consisting of shales and shaly limestones;

Helderberg (Upper) limestones;

Onondaga-salt group;

Leclaire limestone;

Niagara limestone;

Hudson-river-group, consisting of shales and limestones;

Galena limestone;

Trenton limestone;

Black-river and Birdseye limestones;

St.Peters sandstone (of OWEN);

Calciferous sandstone, or Lower Magnesian limestone of OWEN;

Potsdam sandstone.

The Mississippi in its course has cut across all these beds, exposing their outcrop in greater or less perfection from one end of the State to the other. The successive members of the series, dipping to the southward, disappear one after the other beneath the level of the river, allowing the next higher members to come in; while the general level of the country gradually declines in the same direction.

Having determined this order in a satisfactory manner, we are prepared to follow out and examine in detail each one of these formations. The different rocks and groups here named have been traced over wide areas in several of the

* Farther to the south, the "Ferruginous sandstone" of the Missouri Reports comes in above the St.Louis limestone; and above that sandstone lie the limestones of Kaskaskia and Chester, Illinois.

United States : their chief characteristics are therefore known, and also the mineral products which they will probably afford. As these formations, however, are of a sedimentary origin, they may, and do, change more or less when carefully traced over wide areas.

It is an object of great importance to examine these rocks in the direction of their line of bearing, or strike, into the interior of the country. This is not easily accomplished in a region like that of Iowa, where the entire surface has been subjected at different periods to extreme denudation, and is now to a great extent covered by modern drift and a later lacustrine deposit.

The Map published by Dr. OWEN exhibits in a partial degree the direction of the strata below the Coal measures; while the accumulation of drift has rendered it difficult, without long continued examinations, to trace these outlines through the State. The general direction of the strata is from the southeast to the northwest, and the strata or beds of rock seen at any point on the Mississippi may be followed in that direction to the northern limits of the State. The extension is of course not in a direct line, but has been interrupted and the outline rendered irregular both by the ancient denudation and by the action of modern streams.

Having therefore already determined the different members of the entire series occupying the State of Iowa, their dip and direction iu general terms, it yet remains to investigate the details of character, exposure and products, over the area occupied by each individual member.

POTSDAM SANDSTONE.

This lower member of the series attains its greatest exposure in Minnesota and Wisconsin north of the limits of Iowa, and about the region of Lake Pepin. From this point, the rock dips both to the northeast and southwest. Its gradual dip to the southward has diminished its area where it enters the State of Iowa on the north. The excavation of the Upper Iowa river, however, has removed the Calciferous sandstone; so that at the junction of that river with the Mississippi, there is exposed a broad belt of the lower rock.

In following up the Iowa river, the sandstone forms the banks for more than twenty miles along its meandering course, and finally disappears as the ascent of the river bottom rises above the level of the outcrop. Below the mouth of the Upper Iowa, this rock forms the bluffs along the Mississippi, extending for a greater or less distance up the ravines and valleys of the larger streams. The tops of the high bluffs near the river, however, soon become capped by the Calciferous sandstone, and we observe alternating beds of the lower sandstone with cherty beds of the higher rock. The sandstone gradually declines from cliffs several hundred feet in height, to the level of the river, beneath which it finally disappears at the foot of Pike's hill, opposite the mouth of the Wisconsin river, and a short distance below M'Gregor's landing.

Some slightly calcareous bands of this rock contain fragments of trilobites; and in numerous localities shells of *Lingula* are found, though by no means so abundant as in the same rock in Minnesota. These fossiliferous bands appear in the vicinity of Lansing, where the bed containing trilobites lies some sixty feet above the river. At this point I found no fossils in any higher position.

In its general characters this sandstone is a friable mass, usually crumbling on exposure to the frost and sun, though certain beds of no great thickness are sometimes more durable. It is usually a light drab color, sometimes nearly white, and not unfrequently stained brown by the oxide of iron, which in some places appears in great abundance; but there are no evidences of continuous bands of iron ore. In one locality near Lansing, the rock, along what appears to be an oblique fissure, is highly charged with oxide of iron, and some portions are a rich iron ore, but the quantity is not sufficient to be of importance. The origin of this ore appears to be from the decomposition of irou pyrites, near or at the junction of one of the cherty beds above, with the sandstone below.

CALCIFEROUS SANDSTONE.

LOWER MAGNESIAN LIMESTONE OF OWEN.

From the point last mentioned, or a little north of it, the outcrop of the Calciferous sandstone bears northwesterly, with various indentations, to the Iowa river; and there making an abrupt bend in a westerly direction, returns upon the opposite side and stretches in the original direction to the north line of the State, and thence into Minnesota. This rock occupies a broad belt of country, extending from near the Mississippi river to the distance of twenty or thirty miles back, interrupted only by a few outliers of the succeeding rock.

The prevailing character of this formation in the West is that of a magnesian limestone; though in its lower part it is often arenaceous, and contains beds of chert of greater or less thickness. The waters at the close of the Potsdam period evidently contained much silica in solution, which has formed these deposits; and the sedimentary sand is not unfrequently associated with the chert, and both are often more or less mingled with the calcareo-magnesian material. Certain portions of the beds are likewise oolitic, and this character sometimes extends to the higher beds of the rock below. The rock is usually checkered with seams and joints on its exposed surfaces, and presents a very rude exterior. In some of its localities, however, it will produce a durable building material; and since the Potsdam sandstone is usually unfit for such purposes, the supply for the northeastern portion of the State will be derived from the Calciferous ssndstone.

Two miles below Clayton city a working has been carried on for twelve or fifteen feet into the Calciferous sandstone, in search of lead ore. The rock is highly brecciated and very siliceous. Galena in small crystals was found among the rubbish thrown out of the opening. A second opening has been made a few feet north of the deepest one, but does not penetrate as far into the rock. A few rods to the south of the last, a small opening has also been made; but in neither of these does there appear to be any indication of a continuous lode.

In this neighborhood, local undulations were observed along the shore, and numerous large concretionary-like masses were seen lying in the direction of the strata or lines of bedding. This locality is probably the place mentioned by Dr. Owen in his Report, where several thousand pounds of lead ore were taken out of the rock; but I was not able to obtain definite information in regard to the working. The indications of the existence of any considerable quantity of lead ore at this point do not appear to be favorable; since in this immediate neighborhood the rock is too close and free from fissures, and is at the same time extremely brecciated and irregular in character. Although lead ore has been found at several other places in this rock, and particularly at one locality in Minnesota, the general absence of fissures and caverns, which are the indications and accompaniment of the lead ores in the limestones of the West, offers a strong presumption against the occurrence of any productive lodes. Nevertheless some rare and fortunate localities may be found where a few hundred pounds of ore may be obtained in a short time, and within a small space; but such instances are not to be regarded as other than isolated ones, and they furnish no ground for concluding that the country occupied by this rock will ever be a productive mineral region.

The Calciferous sandstone forms a conspicuous feature in the bluffs along the river, from below Lansing, to its final disappearance above Gutenberg. From M'Gregor's landing southward, it often presents a remarkably brecciated character : sometimes throughout a thickness of forty or fifty feet or more, it is a huge mass of breccia. The materials of the rock appear to have been broken up while partially indurated; the interstices are often filled with sand; and fragments of friable sandstone, from the weight of an ounce to several pounds, are found mingled with the broken rock itself. In some instances, these included fragments of sandstone present lines of deposition, and sometimes of discordant lamination, showing that they have been torn from masses of rock previously indurated. In many cases the brecciated character seems due in some degree to internal action among the materials of the rock itself, an action that has at the same time produced a concretionary character; since the rock is not only brecciated, but likewise concretionary. A large mass, apparently made up of fragments, will often be found, on breaking, to leave an interior spheroidal nucleus of hard and tough siliceous limestone, which resists heavy blows of the hammer; while large portions of the surrounding mass so readily break into small fragments, that it is difficult to obtain a cabinet specimen of the proper form and size. The outcrop in some places shows one or more lines of large concretionary or spheroidal masses, the interstices between tbem being filled with fragmentary material of the same rock.

In the region where the rock is most extremely brecciated, it presents an uneven outline upon its surface. Sudden depressions occur where the succeeding rock comes in at a much lower level than it occupies on either side. The appearance is that of sudden small faults or downthrows, as if the rock over a certain area were abruptly depressed before the deposition of the succeeding one, which fills the inequality, and is uninterrupted in the continuity of its own beds above.

St.PETERS SANDSTONE (of Dr. Owen's Report).

This formation succeeds the Calciferous sandstone in all the localities examined in tho Upper Mississippi valley.

The rock occurs as a friable or incoherent mass, having a thickness of from fifty to eighty and even one hundred feet. It consists of grains of white or limpid quartz, loosely aggregated, and sometimes having so little coherence as to be removed from the bank like ordinary sand or gravel : more commonly, however, it has the character of a friable rock, which can be readily wrought by a common pick; and when broken out in large blocks, they will scarcely bear handling or transportation. It is even difficult to procure cabinet specimens, unless by selecting the exterior weathered surface, which is slightly more coherent than the inner portions. Although the grains of which it is composed are of white or limpid quartz, the mass is often, and, particularly near the base, much stained by oxide of iron, while the upper portions are frequently quite free from discoloration.

This sandstone will furnish an excellent material for glass making; and whenever that branch of industry shall be established in the Mississippi valley, an abundant supply of silica may be found for the purpose, from the Falls of St. Anthony southward. A similar sandstone, alternating with the Calciferous sandstone in Missouri, is already used in glass-making.

This rock occurs in several outliers on the south side of the Upper Iowa river; some of them occupying considerable areas, when protected by the more resisting Trenton limestone which sometimes succeeds. These outliers are conspicuous features in the country, appearing like artificial mounds; but where the limestone has been removed, they form gentle eminences, and become gradually lost in the general undulatory features of the surface. It is probable that some remains of this rock will be found in places at long intervals north of its outcrop, lying beneath the drift which has covered the entire country.

As this rock approaches the Mississippi, the summits of the cliffs recede abruptly from the terrace formed by the Calciferous sandstone, owing to its less power of resisting denudation. It is not until the Trenton limestone comes on in sufficient force to protect this sandstone, that the cliffs assume their sharp outline above; and, even then, they present a recession above the Calciferous sandstone. Sloping abruptly from this, they are capped by the succeeding limestone which rises in perpendicular or overhanging cliffs. In consequence of this character, as the sandstone approaches the river, the cliffs have the aspect of a double terrace; the first being formed by the Calciferous sandstone, and the second, some eighty feet higher, by the Trenton limestone; beyond which the country slopes more gently to the interior.

This character is well seen on the Iowa side, opposite the mouth of the Wisconsin river, and both above and below this point; but perhaps nowhere more distinctly and beautifully than above the mouth of the Wisconsin river on the east side of the Mississippi, in the terraces rising up from Prairie du Chien. When seen from the cliffs on the western side, each successive member of the several formations stands out in distinct relief.

On the Iowa side of the river, this rock becomes visible in the cliffs a few miles above Gutenberg; thence rising, as the Calciferous sandstone appears from beneath, it forms successively the lower, middle and upper part of the cliffs from this point northward by Pike's hill, M'Gregor's landing, and for some distance above. Beyond this, it gradually recedes from the river : following the extremely irregular outline of the hills, and leaving here and there outliers, it stretches in its main outcrop to the northwest, reaching the State line at a point a little east of north from Fort Atkinson.

This rock is not so conspicuously developed in Iowa as in Wisconsin and Minnesota. On going northward, after passing the broad elevation of the Potsdam sandstone in the vicinity of Lake Pepin, the strata decline to the northward, and this sandstone reappears upon the banks of the river below the Falls of St.Anthony. It is the rock forming a part of the cliff at the falls, while the terrace over which the waters are precipitated is the Trenton limestone. Being also conspicuously developed at the mouth of the St.Peters river, Dr. OWEN has given it the name of *St.Peters sandstone.*

I should not omit to state, that although this rock disappears beneath the river above Gutenberg, it reappears, where the channel makes an abrupt bend to the eastward, below the mouth of Turkey river. This reappearance is not due, apparently, to any undulation in the strata, but to the easterly direction of the river, which brings us again in the line of strike of these beds. The occurrence of the sandstone at a much lower point on the river, and within a few miles of Dubuque, is important in an economical point of view.

TRENTON LIMESTONE, WITH THE SUBORDINATE BEDS OF BLACK-RIVER AND BIRDSEYE LIMESTONE.

Throughout all that part of Iowa, Wisconsin and Minnesota, occupied by these limestones, the beds are usually so thin, and the characters so variable, that no advantage can be derived frum describing them separately.

At several points above Dubuque upon Turkey river and other places in Iowa, at Platteville and Mineral Point in Wisconsin, at the Falls of St.Anthony and at St. Pauls in Minnesota, the three limestones preserve in a greater or less degree their distinctness of character and position. Near the base there is usually a considerable accession of shaly matter, and the beds representing the Birdseye limestone consist of alternations of thin calcareous and shaly bands or laminæ: these latter being acted upon by the weather, rapidly disintegrate, so that this member of the group rarely presents any prominent feature. A large admixture of shaly matter often marks the Black-river limestone, which in some of its bands contains *Ormoceras tenuifilum* and *Gonioceras anceps*; which, so far as at present known, are restricted to this rock.

Sometimes instead of alternations of shaly and calcareous laminæ at the base of the group, there are beds of shale of considerable thickness without defined limestone bands. In these places there are likewise heavier beds above and below; but the normal lithological aspect of the rock, in such cases, is not preserved.

The Trenton limestone proper is marked in some localities by numerous species of its characteristic fossils, while elsewhere fossils are extremely rare. In some places and through a greater or less portion of its thickness, it maintains the usual lithological characters of the same rock in more eastern localities. Drab-colored magnesian (?) beds occur in some places, presenting characters unlike the rock in its normal condition.

This rock is mostly thinbedded; though the magnesian layers are firmer, thicker, and usually free from seams, furnishing building stones of moderate dimensions, and, rarely, of the thickness of eighteen or twenty inchess. The strata, however, constituting this group of limestones are extremely variable throughout the Mississippi valley. The decrease or augmentation in thickness is not uniformly in one direction, though there is a generally increasing thickness towards the south. From the variations exhibited in numerous measured sections along the Mississippi river, it is probable that the variation in thickness and character of the beds is in a great measure due to the original inequalities of the surface upon which the material was deposited.

The accession of beds and the increase in thickness are

chiefly at the base of the formation; while the higher beds present a nearly uniform character, and are everywhere marked by many of the common fossils of the Trenton limestone, such as *Orthis testudinaria*, *Strophomena alternata*, *S. filitexta*, *Leptæna sericea*, and others.

The first opportunity of obtaining a section of the entire thickness of the beds was at Pike's hill, opposite the mouth of the Wisconsin river. The beds exposed are as follows from the top of the hill :

Galena limestone	30 feet.
Trenton and Birdseye limestones, with numerous fossils,	75 feet.
Mágnesian beds below.	
St.Peters sandstone.	

On Turkey river at Elkader mills, the section exposed gives about twenty feet of highly fosiliferous Trenton limestone below the Galena limestone*.

A section in a ravine below Clayton city gave as follows:

Galena limestone : fifty feet or more	50 feet.
Alternations of Trenton and Galena limestones . . .	10 feet.
Trenton and Birdseye limestones in irregularly laminated beds	20 feet.
St.Peters sandstone . . . . , ... , ...	75 – 80 ft.

At this point we have the first evidence of alternations of the Trenton limestone with the Galena or lead-bearing limestone. This condition, however, is more fully shown in sections farther down the river. The junction of the two, in good exposures of the rock, is very distinct, the bluish gray color and fine texture of the Trenton limestone proper contrasting with the coarser and lighter-colored magnesian galena limestone.

* For details of section, see under head of Galena limestone.

The details given in the following section present some variations from the previous ones :

Upper part of a Section shown in a point of the hill at Clayton city; the measurements in detail.

9.	Heavy-bedded Galena limestone, with cavities and fissures,	50 feet.
8.	Thinbedded fossiliferous limestone : some of the layers buff-colored	20 feet.
7.	Slope over debris	6 feet.
6.	Greenish clay and stripes of buff-colored clay, with concretions of limestone	6 feet.
5.	Heavy-bedded limestone, showing fragments of fossils on fresh fracture, and weathering to an ashen or buff color,	10 feet.
4.	Gray Trenton limestone in thin layers (fossiliferous) . .	15 feet.
3.	Heavy-bedded magnesian [?] limestone	20 feet.
2.	Green shale or clay	2–3 ft.
1.	St.Peters sandstone	70–80 ft.

In this section the subordinate division of Birdseye and Black-river limestones cannot be recognized. The thin-bedded Trenton limestone, characterized by numerous fossils, lies between two heavy beds of magnesian limestone*.

No. 9 has all the characters of true Galena limestone; being heavy-bedded, with a rough and irregularly weathering surface.

No. 8 has a somewhat unusual appearance; having the character of a rock produced by the mingling of the materials of the Trenton and Galena limestones.

No. 6 is a green unctuous clay, with occasional calcareous layers and calcareous concretions : it is fossiliferous, but contains few well-preserved fossils. In its character, it re-

* The heavy-bedded gray subcrystaline limestone below has the general aspect and character of a magnesian limestone, though its composition has not yet been determined by chemical analysis. The beds above, or Galena limestone are known to be magnesian.

sembles the green shales of the Hudson-river group. The upper limit of the clay or shale could not be determined, and it probably occupies a greater thickness than here given.

No. 4 has the usual aspect of the Trenton limestone in the west; partaking of the lithological character both of the Trenton and Birdseye limestones, and marked by Trenton fossils. The layers are thin, irregularly laminated, and often with shaly partings.

No. 3 consists of heavy beds of grayish blue limestone, weathering to ashen or buff color, very tough, with remains of fucoids, and showing some shells on fracture. It has the aspect of the Chazy limestone in some of its phases, but holds no fossils by which its relations could be determined.

No. 2, which is a green shale, is everywhere present in this part of Iowa, forming a distinct band above the sandstone.

Following this exposure of the Trenton limestone to the southwest along the river, the lower beds disappear beneath the river bottom above Gutenberg. The cliff at the back of this village consists mainly of the limestones described in the last section : the lower members lie beneath the level of the bottom land, but are reached in quarrying. The lower heavy beds are extensively wrought at this place for building stone, and a large proportion of the buildings in the place are of this rock. The higher portions only are burned for lime.

The following section illustrates the character of the successive beds forming the high cliff in the rear of the town of Gutenberg:

Galena limestone in massive beds	40 feet.
Thin and unevenly laminated limestone, with some regular beds and cherty layers; all containing Trenton fossils	26 feet.
More evenly and thicker bedded gray limestone. The fossil *Receptaculites* occurs near the top of this division	24 feet.

Thinbedded light gray cherty limestone, containing *Receptaculites*	25 feet.
Green clay	1 foot.
Fossiliferous Trenton limestone in thin unevenly laminated beds	25 – 30 ft.
Heavy-bedded magnesian limestone, resting on the St. Peters sandstone	15 feet.

The total thickness of beds above the sandstone, and between it and the Galena l mestone, is about one hundred feet, a greater thickness than was observed in these beds at any other point on this part of the river.

At Buenavista, the top of the Trenton limestone comes to the level of the river; and owing to the easterly direction of the stream from this point, the rock continues at about the same elevation for some distance, until finally the sandstone below it rises above the river, as seen at Potosi.

As the river resumes its southerly direction, the rock again declines, so that at Dubuque the Trenton limestone is but a few feet above the water-level.

The heavy bedded gray limestone in the Trenton group affords good materials for ordinary buildings, and sometimes some of the fossiliferous beds are of sufficient thickness to be dressed into door and window sills and lintels. The entire distance from Dubuque to Clayton city will afford at intervals good building material, and there are abundant opportunities of opening quarries near the bank of the river.

After dipping beneath the river at Dubuque, the Trenton limestone and its associated beds are not seen again in the State to the southward of this point. These limestones, in their northerly extension from Dubuque, form a conspicuous feature in the cliffs for the entire distance to Pike's hill. Beyond this point these strata appear in the heads of the ravines, approaching within from one to three miles of the river, and, upon some of the high summits beyond, extending quite to the margin of the cliff. From this place their outline gradually recedes from the river, taking a northwesterly direction, and extending to the north line of the State, occupying a broad belt in the western half of Winnesheik county.

GALENA LIMESTONE.

This rock, which succeeds the Trenton limestone proper, or, as shown in the preceding sections, alternates with that rock at the junction of the two, is a most important and interesting formation in the State of Iowa. It is a gray or drab-colored, often yellowish, porous and subcrystalline rock, usually friable but sometimes compact, and possessing a considerable degree of tenacity. It varies in different parts of its extent; the porous and friable character being that prevailing in the central part of its greatest development, while other characters supervene towards its northern and northwestern margin.

This rock has been designated by Dr. OWEN as the "Upper Magnesian limestone;" but this term, as originally applied, included also the Niagara limestone, causing the two to be confounded for a long time; and in order to avoid the difficulty arising therefrom, the name of *Galena limestone* has been proposed.

The great interest of this rock arises from its being the chief depository of the lead ore found in the States of Iowa, Illinois and Wisconsin; for although productive workings have been carried on in the beds lying below this rock, as far down as the St.Peters sandstone, which immediately underlies the Trenton limestone, yet the larger portion of the ore has been obtained from the Galena limestone. As we follow this limestone towards the north and west, we find its thickness gradually diminishing, while the upper portion of it has been removed by denudation; and being less exposed in cliffs where it could easily be explored for ore, mining operations have been carried on to but a small extent, and little lead has been found in that direction beyond the town of Gutenberg.

The extent to which lead ore has been found and wrought will form a part of the special report upon that subject.

The first point at which the Galena limestone appears upon the Mississippi river is at Pike's hill, where it forms about thirty feet of the upper part of the section. In tracing it from that point northwesterly, or in the line of strike, it forms no conspicuous feature by which to draw a line between it and the Trenton limestone below. It will only be after a careful examination of all the exposures along its outcrop, as well as the outcrop of the Trenton limestone, that its limits can be accuratcly determined. In all the sections on the river south of Pike's hill, the Galena limestone forms a conspicuous feature. In the section at Clayton city, it constitutes fifty-six feet of the highest part of the cliff; and at Gutenberg, forty feet of the higher beds are of the same rock.

At Elkader mills on the Turkey river there is an exposure of more than fifty feet of this rock, and below that a talus which may cover as much more of the same.

The details are given below:

Evenly-bedded limestone, layers from six to eleven or twelve inches thick with shaly partings; black on fresh fracture, weathering to light gray or drab color	24 feet.
Heavy-bedded gray limestone with harsh rough exterior, weathering into cavities, and with smaller cavities in the interior: of a harsh and sandy texture . . .	28 feet.
A slope covered by debris of the rock above, soil, etc.	70 or 80 ft.
Magnesian limestone: the thickness not determined.	
Trenton limestone, mostly in thin, unevenly laminated beds: some beds continuous without distinct lamination contain the usual Trenton limestone fossils, with the *Receptaculites* abundant	33 feet.

The upper 13 feet of this part of the section is but partially exposed, and is surmounted by a compact magnesian limestone. The base of the Trenton limestone is not seen.

In this section, the Trenton limestone apparently terminates with the magnesian layer at a point about thirty-three feet above the bed of the stream. The limestone above this point, including the slope covered by debris, is not less than 130 or 140 feet, which altogether belongs to the Galena limestone, as is shown by a section in a dry ravine a little distance from the town. The lower part, however, is cherty with beds of shale; and it is only the central portions, which are nearly thirty feet thick, that have in the highest degree the characteristics of the lead-bearing rock. The higher twenty-four feet of the exposure are very similar to what is called the cap rock in the lead region, and is more argillaceous, less porous, and with fewer joints and seams than the heavy-bedded mass below. From all the sections measured, it is very certain that the Galena limestone gradually thins out to the north and northwest, and at the same time loses very much the characteristic features which distinguish it in the productive lead region. From Gutenberg southward, this limestone gradually increases in thickness.

In the vicinity of Dubuque, the Galena limestone has a thickness altogether of about two hundred and fifty feet; the upper portions are more argillaceous and less porous and friable than the beds below, and the layers are separated by shaly partings. This portion of the rock is also comparatively free from open vertical joints and fissures, and in this respect quite unlike the lower beds. The open fissures and cavities in the rocks below, which contain the lead ore, often terminate abruptly above, being covered by this rock in continuous beds*. The extreme upper portions are often highly argillaceous, and the shaly partings are

* The details of the occurrence of the lead ore will be given under the head of "Economical Geology."

very fossiliferous. The *Lingula quadrata* occurs in great abundance in some of the beds of this rock; the shell usually in a vertical position relatively to the bedding.

This upper rock is not always strictly the cap rock; and although often terminating or capping the lead-bearing fissures, it is not always so; for in some instances the fissures penetrate this rock, and contain lead ore. The occurrence of the ore evidently depends upon the presence or absence of the fissures, and not upon the nature of the rock in which it occurs.

When the limits of this limestone shall be accurately determined, and laid down upon a geological map of the State, it will be found that the area now known as the lead producing portion is less in extent than that which is at present unproductive. In its more northerly extension, the lower beds alternate with more shaly or tenaceous limestone, so that no continuous fissures occur, or, if occurring, are of small extent. The thin central portions, having the true character of the lead-bearing rock, are sometimes fissured and cavernous, and lead ore is frequently found in these fissures.

Thus far it appears that the productive area of this rock is not only where it acquires its greatest thickness, but also where its surface has been denuded of all the overlying formations. It is well known to pass beneath the superincumbent rocks which form the mounds of that part of the country, and beneath the overlying formations on the south; but thus far we are not aware that any productive mining has been carried on in such situations. These circumstances, as well as many others, corroborate the view already advanced, that these ores have been infiltrated into the rock, or deposited into the fissures from above, and that there are no evidences of segregation from the surrounding mass.

HUDSON-RIVER GROUP.

In the sections of rocks heretofore gvien of the lead region of the West, the Galena limestone is represented as succeeded directly by the Niagara limestone, the whole forming parts of the "Upper Magnesian limestone," which has thus been divided by Dr. D. D. Owen:

1. "Coralline and Pentamerus beds of the Upper Magnesian limestone".
2. "Lead-bearing beds of the Upper Magnesian limestone".

Now since the upper portions belong to the Niagara period, or Upper Silurian, and the lower are clearly identified with Lower Silurian rocks, it becomes very desirable to find some stronger line of demarcation than that drawn between two portions of a "Magnesian limestone".

From the sections given on the preceding pages, it will be seen that the Trenton limestoue and the Galena limestone are closely allied one with the other, from the intercalation of beds of the higher, among those of the lower, showing such alternations at the line of junction as to prove them parts of one great formation. The view of the snbject previously entertained, supposed the absence of the Hudson-river group altogether. The position of this group is directly above the Trenton limestone, and in the east it occupies a conspicuous position, having in New-York a thickness of from one to three thousand feet*, and in Canada and Pennsylvania of six or seven thousand feet or more. It is there composed of shales, shaly sandstones, sandstones, and sometimes conglomerates with subordinate beds of limestone which are often of great importance. In tracing this group westward, it had previously been shown to decline in thickness; and between New-York and Lake Huron, in its extension through Canada West, it gradually loses its

* The thickness of this group has not been carefully measured on the eastern borders of the State, where it has a greater thickness, reaching probably to five thousand feet.

arenaceous beds, and becomes more argillaceous and calcareous. In this condition it has been traced from Drummond's Island, by Green Bay, as far as Lake Winnebago, where it has greatly diminished in thickness.

The shales of this group have been removed by denudation, to form the broad depressions of Green Bay, and the valley in the same direction as far as the head of Lake Winnebago. Beyond this point these calcareous shales, recognized as the "Blue limestone"*, had been detected by Mr. LAPHAM in several places in the eastern part of Wisconsin.

The occurrence of the shales of this group, above the Galena limestone, was recognized by Mr. PERCIVAL as the "Blue shale", underlying the limestone of the mounds, and is well described by him on page eleven of his first Report of the Geological Survey of the State of Wisconsin.

The first indication of the existence of this group in Iowa was observed in some mound-like elevations near the Mississippi river, about eight or ten miles below Gutenberg. On examination these proved to be above the Galena limestone, and their summits capped by the Niagara limestone, with *Pentamerus oblongus*, corals, etc. The slope afforded no opportunity of obtaining a section of the beds between the two limestones; but from the character of the soil, the gentle slope of the hill, and other indications, it was presumed that these beds occur here. Farther down the river, this slope from the Galena limestone to the Coralline and Pentamerus beds above, is every where of the same character; being more or less gradual, but never exhibiting any outcrop of limestones. Although springs are of common occurrence on these slopes, there are few ravines or water-courses that offer an opportunity of investigating the beds.

Our attention was subsequently directed by Mr. CHILDS to

* The term Blue limestone was originally applied in the Ohio Geological Reports to the shales and limestones of the Hudson-river group as developed in the neighborhood of Cincinnati, and these were formerly supposed to be the continuation of the Trenton limestone of New-York.

the site of an old mill on the Little Makoqueta, from which some fossils had been obtained, and which, from their previous examination, were inferred to belong to the Hudson-river group. At this locality, though the shales were not seen *in situ* above water, it was evident that they had been thrown out in excavating the foundation of the dam; and a slide of gravel and clay on one side of the stream may have covered up what was formerly an outcrop of the same, since fragments are abundant at the margin of the stream. On another branch of the stream, upon the land of Mr. Pitts, there is an exposure of soft shales with calcareous bands containing abundance of *Orthoceratites*; while the shaly strata, in some parts, are filled with *Tellinomya* (*Nucula*) *levata*. The details of this section are given below:

17.	Top of bank of stream: calcareous bed, compact comminuted shells; a few orthoceratites.	
16.	Shale with graptolite-like markings	1 foot.
15.	Calcareous bed, with comminuted fossils	1 foot.
14.	Fissile shale	10 or 12 in.
13.	More compact calcareous bed, with comminuted and minute fossils; some orthoceratites	18 inches.
12.	Shaly calcareous bed, with comminuted and minute shells,	16 inches.
11.	Orthoceratite bed	8 or 10 in.
10.	Shale	6 inches.
9.	Orthoceratite layer	7 inches.
8.	Shaly calcareous matter	6 inches.
7.	Orthoceratite bed	1 foot.
6.	Shale	7 inches.
5.	Calcareous bed, with orthoceratites and minute shells .	8 inches.
4.	Shale with minute fragments of shells and graptolite-like markings	10 inches.
3.	Concretionary layer	1 foot.

2. Calcareous bed, with minute shells like young orthoceratites . . . . 1 foot.

1. Shale with *Lingula*, twelve feet from bed of stream . 12 feet.

The entire section exhibits scarcely more than twenty-five feet in thickness, but is remarkable for the conditions of the beds of which it is composed. The lowest bed of shale is probably not far above the level of the Galena limestone, which forms the top of the hill near Dubuque. The calcareous beds appear to consist in great proportion of comminuted shells, with minute fossils of several species. The *Orthoceratites* are as abundant as if they had been thrown together alone, and the interstices afterwards filled with calcareous mud. Indeed so abundant are these fossils, and so closely packed that it is difficult to procure an entire specimen. The only large bodies are the *Orthoceratites*, some of which are six inches in length and an inch in diameter, though usually smaller : all the other fossils are extremely small. The materials of the beds are very finely comminuted, as if transported by gentle currents and deposited in deep water.

The black shale, at the base of the section, is not unlike the Utica slate, and the presence of *Lingula* of a large and small species enhances the resemblance.

A similar shale, with broken fossils, was subsequently found thrown out of a shaft or pit some two miles west of Dubuque, and directly above the Upper Galena limestone. In the same vicinity the debris above the limestone contains *Nucula* or *Tellinomya*, and *Orthoceratites*. The slope below the top of Table mound, and all the similar mounds of this neighborhood, as well as the slope to the southward from the Galena limestone to the Niagara limestone, are over the same strata. It has been impossible to obtain a measurement of the entire thickness of the beds, but in these outliers there appears to be no more than fifty feet.

Examinations made upon the east side of the river show the presence of these shaly beds in the base of all the mounds above the lead-bearing rock, and in all places where the country rises much above the level of the Galena limestone. At Scales mound, the Chicago and Galena railroad has been cut through the shales of this group, giving a vertical section of a little more than forty feet. This section, however, does not extend to the base of the limestones above, which come on at some distance from the railroad, and at a higher elevation, so that accurate measurements could not be obtained. The entire thickness is probably less than seventy-five feet, and apparently but little more than sixty feet.

After leaving Dubuque, the shales of this group approach the Mississippi. The Galena limestone, gradually dipping to the south, descends beneath the river at Bellevue; and the green shales rise in an abrupt slope at the back of the town, and are capped by about fifty feet of the Niagara limestone. Along this slope the decomposing shales are found wlthin a few feet of the surface.

The section at Bellevue gives the following measurements:

NIAGARA LIMESTONE.	10 feet limestone; a part of it in thin beds. 31 feet limestone, thicker beds, buff-colored; ten feet of the higher beds thicker than those below. 17 feet limestone in thin layers.
HUDSON-RIVER GROUP.	60 feet, or more, green shales: a slope to the river bottom (base not seen).
	Thinbedded Upper Galena limestone, about ten feet above the lowest stage of water in the Mississippi*.

In consequence of the easterly direction of the river, the shales of the Hudson-river group continue above the water-level, and appear at their full development as low down as Sabula; where the cliff at Savannah, on the opposite side

* The actual contact of the shales with the limestone below was not observed; the base of the hill coming out at the gravelly plateau, and the limestone being visible only in the stream and bank of the river at the lower part of the town.

of the river, gives a section of some eighty or ninety feet. At this place the calcareous bands have increased in thickness and frequency; and the whole mass has much the same appearance as at Cincinnati, Ohio, and Madison, Indiana. Among the fossils occurring here are *Orthis occidentalis*, *O. testudinaria*, *Strophomena alternata*, *S. filitexta*, and others which do not occur in the exposures of these shales farther to the north. In general character the section presents the same beds as at Bellevue.

The shales of this group finally disappear beneath the river before reaching Lyons, at which point the Niagara limestone comes to the level of the river. We shall probably be able hereafter to find some sections of this group farther to the northwest, which may prove its character and thickness. All the facts at present known regarding it show that it becomes gradually thinner in that direction; and we infer, from the exposures observed, that it does not exceed seventy-five feet in thickness (and is probably less than that) on the branches of the Little Makoqueta creek. On the Ohio river at Cincinnati it is more than five hundred feet in thickness, while the Geological Report of Missouri gives to this group one hundred and twenty feet. The great development which it attains in eastern localities, compared with these observations, shows that there is a constant diminution to the westward; and we may expect to find its greatest tenuity or absolute disappearance from thinning out somewhere about the head waters of the western branches of Turkey river.

In a country so largely occupied by limestones, the extent and limits of this shaly group are important points to be determined. Along its entire outcrop may be found springs of water, and fresher vegetation than upon the limestones; while its decomposition produces beds of clay fit for brickmaking. Its occurrence, where denuded of the superincumbent limestone, gives a gentle undulating surface to the prairie country; and where capped by the limestone, we observe usually a flat or gently rounded summit with abrupt walls corresponding with the greater or less thickness of the limestone, and below this the slope over the shales. These rocks form those remarkable mounds, such as Table mound near Dubuque, Sinsinawa mound, Blue mound, Scales mound, Pilot Knob, &c., which are so well known and are such striking features in the scenery of the country bordering upon and within the limits of the lead region of the West.

Fig. 4.—Section at Bellevue.

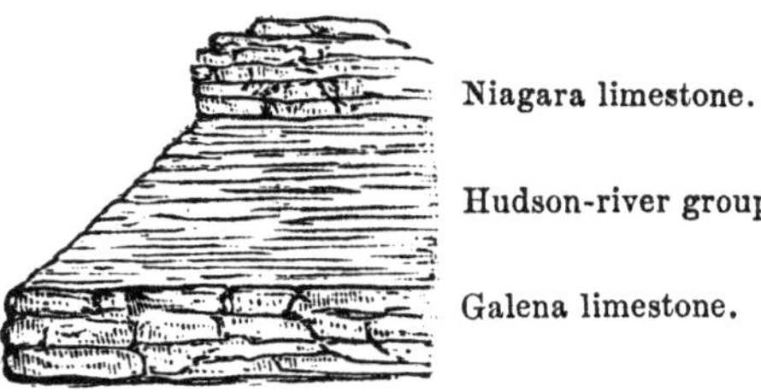

MEDINA SANDSTONE, CLINTON GROUP, &c.

In the States of New-York and Pennsylvania, and in the country to the southward of these, the Hudson-river group is succeeded by sandstones and shales, with limestones, including beds of iron ore, etc. This group of beds is scarcely recognized in the west, and a single locality in Wisconsin is the only authentic one yet known in that region. A thin band of green shale, with a band of ochreous clay, beneath the Niagara limestone near Lyons, indicates perhaps the existence of the Clinton group.

The occurrence of small quantities of iron ore at the base of the Niagara limestone, and disseminated in various parts of that rock, may also indicate the existence of the conditions accompanying the Clinton group, even beyond the point where any considerable accumulation of its sediments occurs.

If existing within this State, the beds marking this group will pr ly be confined to depressions in the strata beneath, which may have been partially or entirely filled by the finer transported materials. Although the iron ore of this age in Wisconsin is of great economical importance in the particular localities where it occurs, it has no wide distribution; and the same will probably be true of Iowa, should similar localities be found.

NIAGARA LIMESTONE.

The Niagara group, where fully developed, consists of shales and limestones sometimes intermingled, and sometimes in separate and successive divisions. In the west the group is represented almost entirely by limestone. This is highly magnesian, often light ash-colored or nearly white on fresh fracture, weathering to a dingy gray or brownish-gray, and porous, or irregularly cellular from the removal of organic bodies. The fossils occur either as silicified casts, or as impressions left by the shell or other body, the original substance of which has been dissolved and carried away. In consequence of this condition, many of the finer fossils which the rock once contained are found only as imperfect casts or impressions.

The rock contains a large proportion of light-colored chert or hornstone, which is sometimes in continuous irregular nodular layers, or in a line of nodules distributed through the rock in parallel layers, and coincident with the lines of bedding. In the decomposition of the rock, the chert is broken into small fragments by the action of frost, and the soil is often filled with this material. To such an extent does it sometimes occur, that the line of its outcrop is marked by a well-formed road made upon the broken chert, which, from affording rapid drainage, and being at the same time very hard, renders it permanent and dry.

The corals in this rock are usually silicified, and are thus well preserved. The *Halysites catenulata* (*Catenipora escharoides*) is a very abundant and characteristic fossil. It occurs everywhere along the exposures of this rock, and we have yet learned of only a single specimen having been found in any rock above or below this in the west*.

The Niagara limestone approaches the river a few miles below Dubuque, and continues to be a more or less conspicuous feature in the cliffs from above Bellevue, to within a few miles of the Upper Rapids; or, more properly, as far as the mouth of the Wapsepinicon river, above the junction of which with the Mississippi it declines beneath the surface. From the point above Bellevue where it recedes from the river, its outcrop continues in a northwesterly direction; and passing to the west of Turkey river, reaches the north line of the State in Howard county. There are several outliers of this rock forming the summits of mounds already noticed to the north of Dubuque, and within a short distance of the Mississippi river. Table mound, and numerous other elevations about the waters of the Little Makoqueta, have their summits of this rock. The southwestery limit of this formation is nearly coincident with the valley of the Wapsepinicon for some distance above its mouth, and the valley of this river will probably be found to mark the line of junction between the Niagara limestones and the limestone of the Rapids at Leclaire.

This rock has been denominated, in the Report of Dr. D. D. Owen, the "Coralline and Pentamerus beds of the upper magnesian limestone". Certain layers are charged with corals of several species, which will be hereafter noticed, while other beds are filled with *Pentamerus oblongus*. This shell is

* A single specimen (a cast) of *Halysites catenulata*, or a species closely corresponding to it, has been found in the Galena limestone. This fact corresponds with discoveries lately made in the Canada Geological Survey, where this coral is found associated with Lower Silurian fossils.

known to mark the formation through Wisconsin and Iowa, and is everywhere a reliable guide for the determination of this rock.

LIMESTONE OF THE RAPIDS OF LECLAIRE.

In descending the Mississippi river, the Niagara limestone is succeeded by a gray or whitish gray limestone, sometimes yellowish gray on fresh fracture. The whole mass is semi-crystalline, very porous, and vesicular from the solution and removal of fossils*. It is sometimes so extremely and uniformly vesicular as to resemble the porous lavas or amygdaloids. The surface is harsh to the touch, and, on fresh fracture, has the sharpness and harshness of a siliceous rock. It would nevertheless appear to be a magnesian limestone, but is reputed to make the best lime in that region of country. The brecciated beds are not restricted to any particular position, but occur near the base of the section measured, in the middle, and near the upper part. These portions are sometimes quite destitute of fossils, and usually they contain but few.

This rock first appears above Leclaire, and dipping gently beneath the river, is lost sight of for some distance; when it reappears on the north side of the town, dipping to the northeast, and soon rises to an elevation of thirty to forty feet or more. It ascends to the southward till near the small stream in the upper part of the village; and here forming an anticlinal axis, dips again to the southward, and, at the present steamboat landing, assumes a nearly horizontal position.

* There is a small species of *Spirigera* scarcely larger than a cherry stone, which occurs in myriads in this rock: the shell is usually entirely removed, leaving innumerable small cavities, in which is sometimes preserved the interior spiral apparatus of the animal. Other portions of the rock contain a great abundance of a small *Littorina*-like shell, which is likewise usually removed, leaving small cavities.

Forming a broad low curve in the synclinal, it again rises to the southward, and forms a continuous low cliff for a quarter of a mile, constantly dipping to the north. With some slight interruptions it extends for a mile farther below, presenting in this distance two low anticlinal and two synclinal axes, and finally disappears with a northerly dip. The lower part of the village of Leclaire lies in a synclinal axis; and towards the north there is another synclinal about two miles distant, above the mouth of Quarry creek.

This limestone in itself, and also in its folded and uplifted condition, is of much interest. From our encampment below the town, this rock was carefully measured in its outcrop along the river bank, noting all changes in character, to the junction of this limestone with the rock above. As it approaches or recedes from the anticlinal and synclinal, the dip varies from five to thirty degrees. The thickness obtained by this measurement was five hundred and forty feet; and between our encampment and the next anticlinal there were not less than one hundred feet*, and probably much more.

In consequence of its disturbed condition, and the enduring character of the beds which have greatly resisted denudation, we have the broad, shallow, rocky bed of the Mississippi at this point, with the rapidly running water, and the consequent interruption of navigation. This place is known as the Upper Rapids of the Mississippi, in contradistinction to the Rapids of Keokuk, known as the Lower Rapids; the latter being over cherty beds of the Keokuk limestone of the Carboniferous period.

So far as we are able to ascertain, this important limestone formation has not heretofore been recognized in western geology; or, if recognized, has been confounded with the Niagara limestone. From this, however, it is quite distinct, both in its lithological character and in its fossil remains.

* Circumstances beyond our control prevented the careful measurement of this part of the section.

The fossils are all in the form of casts, and among them is a small *Spirifer*, a *Spirigera*, a *Pentamerus* undistinguishable from *P. occidentalis*, several gasteropods, and some chambered shells In this reconnoissance no very complete collections were made; but as far as they enable us to form an opinion, the fossils of the limestones of the Leclaire rapids are very similar to those of the limestone of Galt in Upper Canada, although further examination is necessary for this determination. The similarity of position is worthy of notice. The limestone of Galt has been placed in parallelism with the base of the Onondaga-salt group, from a comparison of fossils there found, with some from the lower part of the same group in New-York. At the locality of which we are now speaking, the synclinal axis within the town brings in beds of yellowish magnesian limestone, which are the continuation of the *upper part* of the Onondaga-salt group. Two miles farther up the river, in the valley of a small stream, there is a still more extensive exposure of beds of the same age; which will be shown in the section under that head. The relations of this limestone to the Niagara limestone on the one hand, and to the Onondaga-salt group on the other, correspond precisely with the limestone of Galt.

Should the identity of the limestone of these two distant localities be proved, it will afford sufficient ground for separating these beds from the Onondaga-salt group, and for establishing a distinct group. It seems quite probable that the limestones of this period have their eastern extremity in Central New-York, where, from their small development, as well as from similarity of lithological character, there seemed no sufficient ground for separating them from the non-fossiliferous beds of the Onondaga-salt group. Since, however, in Canada these beds attain considerable importance, and (admitting the conclusions above given) acquire a still greater thickness and more distinctive character on the Mississippi river, it seems necessary to elevate them to the same rank as the other groups of the series.

ONONDAGA-SALT GROUP.

The term *Onondaga-salt group* was adopted by the geologists of New-York as the designation for a set of beds consisting of shale, marl, argillaceous and magnesian limestones, etc., constituting altogether a group well marked by its lithological characters. In the Reports of the third and fourth geological districts, this group was shown to be the source of the principal brine springs of the State, and particularly those of Onondaga county. The same group was shown to embrace the gypsum beds so extensively wrought in the central part of New-York, and to be the source of the remarkable acid springs in the western counties. This group of strata was traced through the length of the State; being very thin at its eastern extremity, having its greatest thickness and importance in the centre of the State, and gradually diminishing to the westward. The same group is also well marked in Canada West, by the presence of gypsum beds and acid springs; and the same series of strata, though much thinner, is recognized in Ohio both by lithological aspect and by the presence of gypsum.

In descending the Mississippi, as already described, the limestones of Leclaire on their first appearance dip gently to the southward, and pass below the river in a shallow synclinal axis, rising again at the northern side of the town. As these beds disappear beneath the river, they are succeeded by thin and evenly bedded drab-colored limestones with shaly partings; the thin beds sometimes shaly throughout, and the more compact ones striped by narrow lines of lighter and darker colors. The lines of lamination are distinctly seen in some of the beds; while others are marked by irregular cavities lined with small crystals. The aspect of the beds is in all respects precisely like the limestones of the upper part of the Onondaga-salt group. Its character, taken in connexion with its position above the Niagara limestone, leaves no doubt in regard to the identity.

These rocks first appear on the river about two miles above Leclaire, where beds of the character described alternate with thin beds containing casts of fossils, as *Atrypa*, etc. One mile above Leclaire, near the mouth of a small stream, the rocks are exposed in the bank of the river, where they have been quarried.

The following beds were measured at this place:

Slaty or thinly laminated beds of limestone	1 foot.
Drab limestone with corals	4 – 12 inches.
Thinly laminated and slaty limestones	2 feet.
Drab limestone in layers 2, 4 and 6 inches thick . .	2 feet.
Porous or vesicular limestone, the lower bed 12 to 14 inches thick; the upper layers from 2 to 4 inches thick	3 feet.
Beds like ordinary hydraulic limestone, the lines of lamination iron-stained	1 foot 8 inches to water level.

All the above have the aspect of the upper part or waterlime beds of the Onondaga-salt group.

In going up the valley of Quarry creek a short distance below the preceding section, a farther exposure of the beds of this group can be seen. The following section commences at a level a few feet higher than the top of the last section; and, with an interval or hiatus of a few feet, is continuous. Every part of this section has been carefully measured, not only on account of its economical importance, but for its extreme interest in a geological point of view, as representing an important group of strata, which in its full development in New-York has a thickness of more than one thousand feet.

Section along the Banks of Quarry creek, three-fourths of a mile above Leclaire.

Thinly laminated beds splitting into slaty layers; the upper 3 feet a little thicker bedded	8 feet.
Layers of half an inch to two inches thick	2½ feet.
Beds similar to those below; the higher beds thinning to 3 or 4 inches . . . . ,	9½ feet.
Yellowish buff-colored limestone, in beds from 4 to 8 and 10 inches, and 2 feet in thickness	35 feet.
A few feet where no rock is seen.	
Drab argillaceous limestone, in layers of 2 to 6 inches thick	10 feet.
Thinly laminated and slaty argillaceous limestone . .	8 - 10 ft.
A few feet where no rocks are seen.	
Thinly laminated beds	4 feet.
Coralline beds	8 inches.
Thinly laminated or slaty layers	3½ feet.
Concretionary layers with deep and large arched cavities,	4 feet.
Drab limestone in 3-inch layers	6 feet.
Thin regular-bedded drab limestone	4 feet.

A space of about ten feet estimated from the base of this setion to the top of the preceding one.

The arched cavities which are seen near the base of the section are so precisely like those containing gypsum in New-York, that there is little doubt the same mineral has existed here. The cavities are from one to three feet in diameter, having the beds below continuous, and those above arching over the cavity and sometimes broken. This condition could only occur from the presence of some solid body over which the strata would be bent. The operation has, in all respects, been the same as that so well known in these beds where gypsum occurs in the State of New-York and in Canada West.

Several of the strata in this section have the character of hydraulic limestone, and can scarcely be distinguished from beds in the same connexion in New-York. I am disposed to believe, however, that these beds will, for the most part, prove too argillaceous to be successfully used for hydraulic cement.

After passing the first anticlinal axis of the limestone on the south, within the town, the strata gradually descend in that direction; and we have an exposure of the lower strata of this group, resting in the synclinal axis of the nearly horizontal beds of the Leclaire limestone below.

A section of this quarry in detail gives the following beds:

Rough beds with cavities	5 feet.
Thin beds becoming vesicular above	2 – 3½ ft.
Yellowish or bright-buff limestone	5 inches.
Arenaceous limestone	8 inches.
Buff-colored limestone with geodes lined with spar . .	16 inches.
Regularly and even-bedded limestone throughout, each bed having the thickess here given	14 inches. 7 inches. 32 inches. 14 inches. 11 inches.
Buff-colored limestone, with elevations upon the surface of different character arching over masses of clay .	10 inches.
Drab-colored limestone extending to level of river, where there occurs a thin stratum filled with *Spirifer* . .	6 feet.
Thin slaty layers, extending along the river below, being apparently beds of passage from the limestone previously described to the Onondaga-salt group . .	15 feet.
Hard, rough, thin-bedded limestones with cavities : the upper part of the limestone of Leclaire rapids.	

This section, to the base of the sixteen-inch layer, constitutes the quarry from which stones were taken, in part, for the bridge piers at Davenport. The six feet to level of the river, marked by the stratum containing *Spirifer*, etc., is not so distinctly exposed, but, where seen, it is in thin beds. All beneath the fifteen feet of thin slaty layers (below the water level) appertains to the limestones of the Leclaire rapids. The relations of the twe groups are very intimate; the sharp grained, harsh rock below, graduating into the regular and thin-bedded argillaceous limestones which are succeeded by thicker beds.

In this quarry the surfaces of the different layers are very uneven; and there is every evidence that considerable time often elapsed between the final deposition of one bed and the beginning of another. In these instances, the inequalities of the surface of the lower beds are filled by conglomeratic aggregations, in which shaly matter, limestone, fragments of organic remains, and siliceous materials, are often mingled.

Throughout the lower part of this group, fossils are numerous, though in such a condition that their characters cannot well be determined. Great numbers of corals of the Cyathophyllidæ occur upon the surfaces of some of the beds.

From the comparative tenuity of this group, it is not probable that any of its products, such as gypsum and brine springs, will be found in valuable quantity. The fact that the upper beds of this group furnish nearly all the hydraulic cement of New-York should induce an examination and trial of the different beds at various points along its exposure. The more compact and less arenaceous of these layers are those most likely to furnish hydraulic cement.

LIMESTONES OF THE UPPER HELDERBERG MOUNTAINS.

In the western part of the State of New-York, in Canada West, and in Ohio, the strata succeeding the Onondaga-salt group consist of gray and blue limestones, containing much chert or hornstone, and formerly known as the Corniferous limestone. In the New-York Geological Reports, the name Onondaga limestone was applied to the lower gray portion, while the term Corniferous limestone was retained for the upper dark-colored beds. These two members are often well marked and distinctly separate over wide areas, while again they alternate one with the other, and become so incorporated as to present a series of beds indivisible by any well-marked character; and for this reason, as well as for others, the distinctive names have been dropped, and the term Upper limestones of the Helderberg mountain has been adopted.

Extending from the Hudson to the Niagara river, these limestones form a continuous terrace, broken only by ravines, the channels of streams and the outlets of the north and south lakes. The same beds form the rapids in the Niagara river at Blackrock; and stretching thence through Canada West, they reappear in Michigan, and extending by Monroe to the falls of the Maumee, and southwesterly through Indiana, appear in great force at the falls of the Ohio.

In many parts of New-York the higher beds are extremely dark, and the name of the town of *Blackrock*, in New-York, indicates the color of the limestone at that place. Farther west, it gradually becomes lighter; and in many localities in Ohio, a whitish gray is the prevailing color of these limestones.

The limestones succeeding the buff-colored beds of the Onondago-salt group are not exposed along the Mississippi river for some distance below Leclaire. No actual junction of the two formations was seen, though their relative position, with the knowledge we have of the same formations elsewhere, serves to guide the determination. The irregularities in the strata below Leclaire, present several anticlinal and synclinal axes; and there may be one or more faults between this place and Davenport. The strata have been deeply denuded; and the Coal formation, as will be shown, rests upon the irregular surfaces of the different limestones.

A broad bottom land prevents the appearance of the limestones of the age of the Helderberg upon the river bank; but on the road to Davenport, these limestones occur at the level of this bottom land, and rising a few feet higher. On Duck creek the same limestone appears in great force, and sections thirty or forty feet high are exposed. This limestone, together with the shaly limestone of the Hamilton group, continues to Davenport; whence the latter extends for many miles below along the river.

At Davenport, and for two or three miles above, the Upper Helderberg limestone is exposed along the bank of the river, and in the hills at considerable elevation above the water level. The rock is a gray or ash-colored mass, fine-grained and compact; some of the beds subcrystalline, with fragments of organic remains. The bedding is regular, but the beds are often crossed diagonally and irregularly by seams which cause it to split into uneven slabs. The thicker and more compact beds are extensively used for foundation and wall stones.

The lowest beds seen are often concretionary, and sometimes iron-stained and brecciated. These beds are separated by shaly partings, and there is often much shale or clay in the interstices. Large spheroidal masses of greenish clay often interrupt the continuity of the beds, and sometimes these masses are connected with fissures that reach the surface.

The following section on the river bank, one mile above Davenport, shows the mode of occurrence of this limestone:

Thinly laminated limestone	2 – 3 feet.
Irregularly-bedded limestone, with shaly partings, varying from	2 – 4 feet.
Concretionary and irregularly laminated shaly beds, with a harder argillaceous concretionary bed below . .	6 – 8 feet.

Another section, fifty yards higher up the river, gives a greater thickness of strata.

Limestone, gray and ash-colored, three or four feet of the higher beds in regular layers : the middle and part of higher beds remarkably brecciated ; the lower beds rough and concretionary	20 feet.
Obscured by crossing of road	6 feet.
Thin slaty layers, splitting into laminæ from half an inch to two inches in thickness	10 feet.
Irregularly-bedded limestone with green shaly partings,	8 feet.
Shaly and concretionary bed, thinning out	3 feet.
Argillaceous stratum, gradually increasing in thickness,	6 feet.

These limestones present great irregularities in their bedding : the shaly partings, which are often not more than half an inch thick, expand to six inches or more, and again thin out; while a concretionary structure is visible in much of the rock. The limestone is remarkably brittle throughout, and, for the most part, breaks into irregular fragments.

In several exposures of this limestone along the river, the continuity of the strata is interrupted by masses of clay, which are sometimes spheroidal or irregular in shape, and not unfrequently communicating by a narrow fissure with a similar expansion of clay in a lower or higher bed of limestone.

The following section exhibits one of the irregular masses of clay, seen in a section on the river above Davenport :

FIG. 5.— Section near Daveaport.

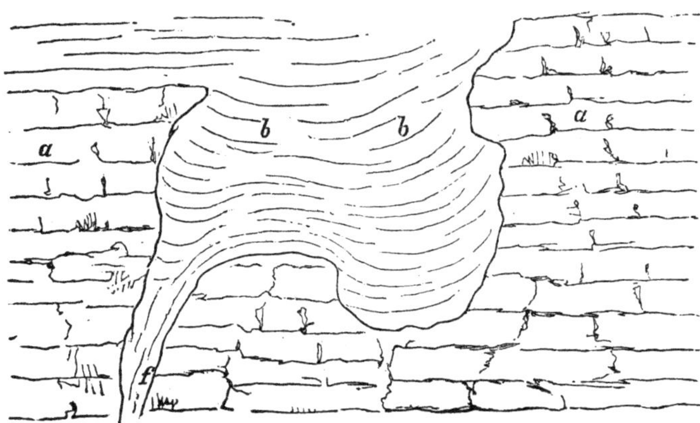

a, a. Regularly stratified limestone.

b, b. Compact greenish gray clay filling a cavity in the limestone, and communicating through the narrow fissure, *f*, with the beds below, where it again becomes expanded into a large mass similar to that above*.

Several other exhibitions of this character occur in the neighborhood of Davenport, some of them penetrating not only these limestones, but also the strata of the Hamilton group above.

The limestone of this age, along the Mississippi, presents no characters to admit of subdivisions into two members. The large amount of shaly matter, either mingling with the material of the rock, or occurring as shaly seams between the beds, would appear to have rendered the condition of the ancient ocean, in a great degree, unfit for the development of animal life. In nearly all the exposures observed, it contains few fossils.

* For farther illustrations of this character, see under head of Coal measures.

HAMILTON GROUP.

The strata succeeding the limestone just described have been designated in the Geological Reports of New-York as the *Hamilton group*. In the more easterly exhibition of these strata, they consist first of a black slate, known as the Marcellus shale; and above this, of more or less argillaceons and calcareous shales and argillaceous sandstones, acquiring altogether a thickness of one thousand or twelve hundred feet. In Eastern and Central New-York this group has a great development in its different members. Farther west, the coarser materials of the sediments become gradually less and less important; and finally in Western New-York the group consists of calcareous shales with bands of limestone, and, rarely, a thin bed which is partially arenaceous.

Over a great part of the area known to be occupied by this group, it is succeeded by a black slaty shale, known as the Genesee slate, and which may be regarded as a part of the same series of beds. The underlying black slate is known throughout Ohio, Indiana, and to some extent in Illinois; but I have not been able to detect its presence on the Mississippi river.

In following this group westward, we find that its calcareous character becomes more decided, with a gradual diminution of the shaly matter and a constant attenuation of the whole group; and in Iowa it consists more properly of argillaceous limestones, or highly calcareous shales alternating with bands of limestone.

Thus far no well-marked line of division has been drawn between the limestones below and the Hamilton group, though further examination may determine the line of demarcation at some points. The localities on the Mississippi river are all far separated from the area over which the coarser sediments were deposited; and the conditions of the ocean bed suffered little change from the close of the Onondaga salt period to the termination of the Hamilton group.

On the Illinois side of the river opposite to Davenport, the shales and shaly sandstones of the Hamilton group rest apparently directly upon the limestones above described, without the intervention of the black shale which marks this horizon everywhere to the eastward.

The lower beds of the Hamilton group are highly calcareous, and some of the bands of limestone are sufficiently compact and durable to furnish building materials. These portions consist of irregular alternations of limestone bands with bands of calcareous shale, the latter charged with great numbers of Brachiopoda and other fossils. The shaly portions crumble rapidly on exposure, and form a gray or ash-colored clay.

Both the limestone below and the limestone and shales of the Hamilton group above, are marked by the presence of the greenish gray clay, filling ancient fissures and former cavernous openings in the rock which not unfrequently show direct communication with the surface.

In going south from Davenport, the limestone soon dips beneath the river, and is last seen at a quarry just below the city. At Rockingham, the shales and limestones of the Hamilton group are seen at two or three exposures.

In the next ravine south, the same shales and limestones are visible ; and from this point the outcrop is traced in the face of a hill for a quarter of a mile, and, descending into a deep ravine, the shale and shaly limestone of the Hamilton group is seen to be succeeded by the Encrinal limestone of the same group, giving a section of fifty or sixty feet, as below:

Encrinal limestone	10 – 15 ft.
Shales and shaly limestones of the Hamilton group, containing *Spirifer ligas*, *Strophodonta demissa*, *Orthis*, etc.	50 feet.

The surfaces of the lower division weather to an ashen hue, and crumble somewhat rapidly on exposure to the air.

In another ravine about one mile north of New-Buffalo, we find the same series of beds, with the Encrinal limestone at the upper part having a thickness of fifteen or twenty feet. The higher beds are sometimes iron-stained, from the decomposition of iron pyrites.

At New-Buffalo, in the bank of the river, and in the ravines west of the town, the shales and shaly limestones of the Hamilton group are better developed than observed at any other point along the Mississippi. The peculiar fossils of the group are very numerous, though mostly in separate valves, or broken specimens, indicating that they were drifted before being imbedded. In some of the beds, however, the specimens are more perfect; and the nature of the calcareous shales would indicate a favorable condition for the development of organic existences. Among the fossils from this locality are two species of *Fenestella*, *Retepora* and *Stictopora*, a species of *Pentremites*, numerous fragments of crinoids and crinoidal columns, *Favosites gothlandica*, *Cystophyllum*, *Cyathophyllum*, *Orthis iowensis*, *Strophodonta demissa*, *Atrypa reticularis*, and *A. aspera*.

The rocks of this group appear at intervals along the river, and in the ravines for some distance below New-Buffalo. About two miles above Pine creek, the Hamilton group is succeeded by the shales and soft sandstones of the Chemung group. The junction, though somewhat obscure, presents the following beds:

1. Yellowish sandstones.
2. Sandy beds with *Spirifer*.
3. Green shale, thickness not ascertained.
4. Shaly limestones of Hamilton group.

On Pine creek, nearly a mile above its mouth, the higher beds of the Hamilton group are of brownish siliceous limestone, showing a passage to the sandstone of the group above, without any visible shaly beds. The strata of this place have a decided dip to the southwest.

At Fairport, three miles below Pine creek, and at points between these places, the Hamilton group is exposed along the river. The higher beds are intermingled with yellow sandstone and greenish shaly matter, indicating the beds of passage to the next group. The strata of this group continue in view along the river for some distance below Fairport, when they dip beneath the river, but reappear about two miles above Muscatine, where the upper limestone of the Hamilton group is exposed for some distance along the river bank, and is quarried for burning into lime.

The presence of the limestone at this place is marked by abundance of *Stromatopora*, which often forms masses of several feet in extent. This is the more interesting, since the waters of the period were very turbid, and an influx of mud has often checked the growth of the coral at one point, or over some of the numerous prominences which the surface presents; while at other points it has gone on increasing, and finally has again extended over and covered the portion destroyed by the influx of mud.

This group is likewise developed in the neighborhood of Iowa city, and for some distance to the south we find the same strata.

CHEMUNG GROUP.

The gray and yellow sandstones, with shaly admixrures and shaly partings, which exist at numerous points on the Mississippi river below Davenport, at Burlington, and again below the Lower rapids in the States of Illinois and Missouri, are referable to the age of the Chemung group of New-York.

In some localities there is a considerable thickness of green shale at the base of these sandstones, which may represent the Portage group of New-York; but this rock is not constantly present.

On descending the Mississippi river, the sandstones of this group were first observed above the mouth of Pine creek. Some of the beds are partially calcareous; but the prevailing character is that of a yellowish friable sandstone, argillaceous in character, and sometimes becoming shaly. Fossils are often abundant in some of the beds, while other beds are almost entirely destitute of them.

At the mouth of Pine creek, and a short distance above on that stream, a section of fifteen or twenty feet may be obtained. Along the river for two miles above this, only from two to four feet in thickness were visible at the stage of water then prevailing.

The best section of these beds was seen at Burlington, where the Burlington limestone succeeds the sandstones of the Chemung group, in the lower part of the town. The green shale of this section, which measures thirty feet to the river level, appears to be the same which is but a few feet thick at Pine creek, and in another locality has no visible existence.

Section of Rocks at Burlington, Iowa.

CARBONIFEROUS LIMESTONE.	Burlington limestone; an encrinal limestone, brown or greyish brown in color: higher beds white and subcrystalline .	72 feet.
	Cherty beds near the base of limestone, varying from 6 to 10 feet in thickness, and increasing to the southward . . .	4 to 10 ft.
	Beds of passage, consisting of calcareous and argillaceous layers*	20 inches.

* In another quarry there were no visible beds of passage, the oolitic beds coming directly below the well-marked Burlington limestone.

CHEMUNG GROUP.	5.	Oolitic bed (often absent); its greatest thickness	4 feet.
	4.	Argillaceous sandstone with fossils as below, of Chemung species	6 feet.
	3.	Limestone, irregularly-bedded, concretionary and rarely brecciated, with shaly interlaminations; compact, brittle, ash-colored, apparently silicious. Higher beds more regular and arenaceous : near the base, a thin band of limestone charged with *Chonetes*	10 feet.
	2.	Fine-grained, siliceous and argillaceous sandstone, with bands of shale, highly fossiliferous : lower half much softer and more argillaceous than the upper part (often shaly)	25 feet.
	1.	Soft green shale like that of Portage group, to level of river	32 feet.

The green shale at the base of the section holds the place of the green shales and sandstones of the Portage group in New-York. At Burlington, there is a much greater thickness than at any other point examined on the Mississippi river. So far as observed, it is destitute of fossils, decomposes rapidly on exposure, and produces an unctuous clay. The beds No. 2 and 4 are charged with fossils, some of which are Chemung species, leaving no doubt of their true position in the series; while at the same time we have the collateral evidence of superposition in the sections upon the river above Muscatine. The concretionary beds No. 3 of Section are destitute of fossils, except a thin regular layer at the base, which abounds in *Chonetes*.

The Oolite bed, No. 5, contains fossils which ally it more intimately with the Chemung group than with the Carboniferous limestone above; and it is sometimes separated by a few inches of beds of passage which contain no fossils, and at other times there are no beds of passage. The principal fossils of the oolitic bed are the large *Gyroceras burlingtonensis*, figured and described by Dr. OWEN, a species of *Euomphalus*, an *Avicula* and a species of *Orthis*; but they are usually not in a condition to give good specimens for study.

In this section, therefore, which is the most complete that I have examined, the passage from the Chemung (Devonian) to the Burlington limestone (Carboniferous) is so gradual, both in physical aspect and in the generic and specific characters of the fossils, that it forms no greater change than is observed between any of the subordinate groups; and is far less strongly marked than the change from Lower to Upper Silurian, and not more strongly than between the Hamilton and Chemung groups. The Chemung group, together with the Portage group, in their more easterly extension in the State of New-York, have a thickness of at least two thousand feet, and in some places probably twenty-five hundred feet. In tracing these strata to the westward, there is a very perceptible attenuation; and on their northwestern exposures in the Mississippi valley, no section gives a thickness of one hundred feet, and rarely one gives more than half that amount.

In Missouri, according to Professor SWALLOW, the strata appertaining to the Chemung group have a thickness of two hundred feet or more; but these strata will probably be found to include a portion of the Hamilton group, leaving the Chemung and Portage rocks to be represented by not more than one hundred feet in the Mississippi valley.

These conditions are also in accordance with what has already been shown in reference to the Hudson-river group; and thus those formations, which have furnished the immense deposits of sediment composing the Green and White mountains and the Appalachian chain, have a maximum thickness in the Mississippi valley scarcely exceeding three hundred and fifty feet, and in many places hardly reaching two hundred feet.

These differences in the physical condition of the ancient ocean bed have given origin to differences in the organic remains, which will be more fully treated of hereafter in the Report upon the Palæontology of the State.

CARBONIFEROUS LIMESTONES.

BURLINGTON LIMESTONE.

ENCRINITAL LIMESTONE OF DR. D. D. OWEN AND PROF. SWALLOW.

In the order of succession among the strata, the limestone of Burlington succeeds the sandstones and beds of limestone of the Chemung group already described. The most northerly point at which this rock was observed along the Iowa river, is about nine miles south of Iowa city. It has subsequently been traced much farther to the northward. In the Mississippi river section this limestone does not appear till after passing the mouth of the Lower Iowa river, and only acquires its greatest development in the neighborhood of Burlington and along the river above and below that city. Its thickness is not much less than one hundred feet along the river; and having here suffered denudation, it is probably much thicker in the interior of the State*.

This limestone continues to form the river bluff for about five miles below Burlington to the mouth of Skunk river, when it terminates abruptly, and no rocks are again visible on the Iowa side of the Mississippi for several miles, or till we reach Montrose, while the Burlington limestone does not again appear above the river level within the State of Iowa. Dipping to the southwest, it passes beneath the river before reaching Keokuk; and making a broad and gentle synclinal, rises again above the river level, and is seen in the cliffs at Quincy in Illinois and Hannibal in Missouri, where it appears as at Burlington, resting on the Chemung group†.

* In the Geological Report of Missouri this limestone, under the name of Encrinital limestone, is given as five hundred feet in thickness. The successive members of the group of limestones, designated as Lower Carboniferous limestones, all diminish towards the north, while they increase in thickness towards the south for a certain extent, and then diminish again, so that in Alabama the Burlington limestone has nearly disappeared, while some of the higher members which are extremely thin or absent altogether in Iowa become much augmented in thickness.

† The argillo-calcareous group of Evans' Falls, Owen's section.

In the Report of Dr. D. D. Owen, the "Encrinital group of Burlington", Iowa, and the "Encrinital group of Hannibal", Missouri, are given in the section as distinct groups; but a careful examination of the two localities shows no reason for considering the limestones as distinct : on the contrary, they are clearly identical.

The Burlington limestone* is subcrystalline in texture, gray or brown and in some parts nearly white in color, often quite friable, and largely constituted of the remains of crinoideæ. It is throughout an encrinital limestone; the separated joints of the columns are often packed together, with scarcely enough of finer material to cause the mass to cohere. Upon the weathered surfaces of these beds, and in the decomposing material of the mass, there occur large numbers of more or less perfect individuals of several genera and many species of this family of fossils. Even the more compact portions of the rock, when weathered, show that the mass is largely constituted of these remains.

Near the base is a bed of white or light-colored chert, with cavities containing much oxide of iron, and the rock is often highly colored from this source. The color, however, is mostly external, derived from decomposition in the fissures and cavities. The limestone becomes gradually more compact in the higher beds, and the crinoidal remains are there less abundant and characteristic. Some of the upper beds are nearly white, and contain large numbers of *Spirifer*, *Productus*, etc.

From its outcrop on the Mississippi, this limestone trends to the northwest, and is known to occur about nine miles south of Iowa city, and has been traced thence through the westerly part of Iowa, Talma and Grundy counties.

* The name "Encrinital limestone" alone can scarcely be sustained as designating any particular group of strata, since this character is a common one among limestones of different ages. The name *Burlington limestone* is proposed from the city of Burlington in Iowa, where this rock is better developed than elsewhere in the State. and is one of the best known localities of the rock in the West.

KEOKUK LIMESTONE.

ARCHIMEDES LIMESTONE OF OWEN.

This limestone and its associated cherty beds succeed the Burlington limestone. On the Iowa side of the Mississippi river, the rock is not visible in the river section before reaching Montrose. From Montrose it is continuous along the river as far as Keokuk, and disappears near the mouth of the Des Moines river. On the Illinois side of the Mississippi river it appears at Dallas, at Appanoose, and opposite Fort Madison, and thence to Nauvoo and Warsaw.

This rock, in its full development, consists of a gray or bluish-gray compact encrinal limestone, in beds separated by shaly partings; while bands of shale or marl of considerable thickness sometimes occur. Some of the beds are thinly laminated, and readily separate in quarrying.

At the base of this limestone series lies a succession of cherty beds, which consist of thin alternating layers of chert and of encrinal limestone, and sometimes an intimate intermixture of both.

These beds, from their indestructible character, have resisted denudation, and now form the river bed above Keokuk, producing the rapids so well known in the navigation of the Mississippi river. At this point they have a thickness of sixty to seventy feet, but, farther to the south, become greatly augmented, and produce the series of beds known in Tennessee as the "Siliceous group".

The thickness of the limestone visible in the river section at Keokuk, above the cherty beds, may be estimated at forty to fifty feet.

This rock gradually thins to the northward, and towards its margin presents alternations of argillaceous and arenaceous beds with the encrinal limestone, the latter being quite subordinate. The same character is seen to some extent at Appanoose in Illinois; but it is more extreme in the neighborhood of Mount Pleasant, Iowa, where some of its exposures present only argillaceous and arenaceous beds. On the Asylum farm at this place, the following beds were seen in the quarry near a small stream :

Argillaceous limestone, in some thin irregular beds : surface of quarry.	
Argillaceous limestone, somewhat harder than that below,	2 feet.
Argillaceous and calcareous bed, with nodules of chert,	$1\frac{1}{2}-2\frac{1}{2}$ ft.
Magnesian bed	$1\frac{1}{2}$ feet.
Arenaceous limestone, slaty at top.	

The crinoidal beds are not represented here, though the beds exposed in this quarry are elsewhere seen in connexion with the compact encrinal limestone which lies at a lower level, and sometimes alternates with argillaceous and magnesian beds. Other quarries in the same neighborhood exhibit numerous beds of argillaceous and magnesian limestone: these are finally succeeded by a light-colored limestone, which is sometimes in heavy beds and often brecciated throughout.

At Sipes quarry, two miles north of Mount Pleasant, the following beds are seen :

Greenish clay	1 – 2 feet.
Band of limestone	0 – 1 foot.
Green shaly clay	1 foot.
Encrinal limestone in two unequal layers	3 feet.
Encrinal limestone	7 inches.
Shale or clay, thickness unknown.	

The dip of strata is to the southwest.

A section of the same outcrop at M'Mahons quarry gave the following beds :

Clay or shale, weathering to ash-colored . . . . . 3 – 6 feet.

Encrinal limestone, bluish, weathering to ash-colored, in beds from 6 to 18 inches, about . . . . . . 6 feet to base of working.

The compact crinoidal layers furnish excellent building materials, and, where free from shaly seams and iron pyrites, can be relied upon as a durable stone. The argillaceous and arenaceous beds sometimes associated with this rock are not good in this respect.

This limestone formation, in its lower cherty beds forming the rapids of Keokuk, and in its higher beds of encrinal limestone and shale forming the rock upon which the town of Keokuk is situated, may be designated the *Keokuk limestone.*

A farther experience of this stone in some of the quarries has proved that the blocks will split along the line of lamination, though there be no visible shaly matter present, simply from want of cohesion among the particles. This character has been more particularly observed towards the northern outcrops of the rock. At Keokuk and vicinity the limestone is heavy bedded, and much more compact than in some of the more northerly exposures, and forms a beautiful and durable building stone.

"*The Geode bed.*" The limestone of Keokuk is succeeded by a bed of forty feet of calcareous shale or marl, containing numerous geodes of quartz, and chalcedony; the cavities likewise often filled with calcareous spar, zinc blende, etc. This mass is well known as the geode bed, or geodiferous bed in the limestone series of the Mississippi valley, and forms in Southern Iowa a well-marked upper limit for the Keokuk limestone.

WARSAW, OR SECOND ARCHIMEDES LIMESTONE.

Succeeding the "Geode bed" we find a mass of magnesian limestone; and to this succeed beds of shaly limestone, with partings of shale or marl rapidly decomposing on exposure. The limestone is sometimes arenaceous, and usually separates in thin laminæ. In its fossils it is conspicuously marked by the presence of the spiral axis of a large species of *Archimedes*, or *Fenestella*, and by a great abundance of reticulated Bryozoa. To the shaly limestone succeed some beds of yellow, coarse, calcareous sandstone, which in some places contain small pebbles of quartz.

These different strata together constitute a single group; of which the central member is more persistent, and the lower and higher portions become merged in the mass, as the whole assumes a more homogeneous character. This formation, though seen in the cliffs above and below Keokuk, is much better developed at Warsaw on the opposite side of the river, and the name *Warsaw* or *Second Archimedes limestone* is adopted to designate the group.

In tracing the formations northward, the beds of this group appear in the neighborhood of Mount Pleasant. To the south and east its characters become better defined, and the coarser arenaceous layers and the magnesian beds have disappeared. The rock is every where marked by the presence of large numbers of Bryozoa, and numerous species of other fossils. In descending the Mississippi river, the beds of this group are distinguishable below the limestone of the cliffs at Alton, Illinois. On the eastern margin of the Illinois coal field, the same beds reappear at Bloomington and Spergen hill, and also at Clear creek in Monroe county, Indiana.

Although this group attains no very great thickness, so far as known at the present time, yet the constancy of its characters, and the occurrence of the same species of fossils in its beds over an area of two or three hundred miles, entitles it to the rank of a subordinate group in the great series of Carboniferous limestones.

ST. LOUIS LIMESTONE, OF PROF. SWALLOW;

CONCRETIONARY LIMESTONE, OF DR. D. D. OWEN.

The "Concretionary limestone" cited by Dr. OWEN as occurring near the mouth of the Des Moines river, consists generally of a breccia composed of fine, compact, ash-colored limestone in fragments of various sizes, having the interstices filled with a subcrystalline, yellowish, granular, calcareous material, which is sometimes quite pulverulent and rarely very compact.

The rock, as it appears at Keokuk and at points above this on the river, as well as at Mount Pleasant and elsewhere, appears like the attenuated margin of a more important formation, presenting the usual fractures of the thinning out of a limestone, viz. a brecciated and concretionary structure. This presumption proves to be true; for as we trace the rock southward beyond the State, it presents other aspects, gradually losing its concretionary and brecciated character, and becoming an important limestone formation.

This rock can be traced along the river as far north as opposite Fort Madison, where it has a thickness of a few feet; and it is likewise seen at Mount Pleasant, succeeding the yellow and brown magnesian limestones of that locality. It appears not always brecciated and concretionary, but sometimes as a compact grey limestone, in thin diagonally laminated layers, and also as a fine, compact, ash-colored limestone. It presents both these characters in different localities in the vicinity of Mount Pleasant; and some of the beds are often of sufficient thickness to furnish a good building material.

In tracing these higher members of the series to the northward, the limits of the groups become less and less distinctly defined; and the increase of coarser sedimentary matter gives a different aspect to the whole mass.

In the vicinity of Mount Pleasant the brecciated limestone forms the higher beds, and the strata intermediate between this and the Keokuk limestone are extremely variable. At Hartnet's quarry, one mile southwest of Mount Pleasant, the following beds represent the higher members of the series.

8. Limestone in a single heavy bed with dividing seams .	2 feet.
7. Shaly limestone	18 to 20 in.
6. Argillaceous limestone, with nodules of chert; upper part shaly	2 feet.
5. Limestone, fine grained and compact	1 foot.
4. Argillo-calcareous sandstone, with calcareous bands; shaly below	20 inches.
3. Fine sandstone with nodules of sandstone.	
2. Limestone in two layers with green shaly partings . .	12 to 18 in.
1. Argillo-calcareous sandstone in a single massive bed .	2 feet.

The two higher beds here represent the St. Louis or brecciated limestone; and those below, the Warsaw limestone, with the arenaceous, argillaceous and magnesian limestone.

In another quarry on the same stream, half a mile below the last, we find the following succession of beds.

8. Brecciated and fragmentary limestone, clay, etc. (succeeded above by shale)	4 to 6 ft.
7. Brown limestone in irregular layers	14 inches.
Clay	6 inches.
6. Limestone beds as in quarry above	2 feet.
5. Argillaceous limestone becoming more calcareous below,	20 inches.
4. Limestone in beds of 4 to 12 inches, brownish in the upper half; the lower part furnishing flagstones, with arenaceous partings	4 feet.
3. Yellowish earth with nodules of limestone.	
2. Limestone	1 foot.
1. Argillo-calcareous sandstone, as at the base of the former quarry.	

The change in the character of the strata in so short a distance is very remarkable; and the only rock which affords a guide to the position, is the brecciated limestone, which, though varying in some degree, is usually recognizable. All the beds, with the exception of the brecciated mass, are non-fossiliferous; and the only fossil observed in that rock was the *Lithostrotion floriforme* of OWEN. This fossil occurs in large masses, usually silicified and well preserved.

In the valley of the Mississippi river, opposite to Fort Madison, the section of the strata is as follows:

Brecciated limestone with green clay, and a layer of darker magnesian limestone at the base.	
Magnesian limestone in unequal layers, mostly thickbedded (quarried for use at Fort Madison)	20 feet.
Shale of "Geode bed"	20 to 25 ft.
(Space across river bottom, no rocks seen.)	
Compact encrinal limestone at river bank.	
The Keokuk limestone with arenaceous and magnesian beds intercalated, forming cliffs about	20 feet.

The Keokuk limestone formation, the Geode bed, and the Magnesian limestone at the base of the Warsaw limestone formation, are here well defined; but the shaly limestones of Warsaw appear to be represented by shales or green clay, which is not here distinctly separated from the brecciated limestone above.

With the brecciated limestone, terminates the series of Carboniferous limestones in Iowa. The Coal measures rest directly upon the brecciated limestone at the southern limits of the State, as shown in a section of the cliffs near Keokuk.

Section of Rocks in detail, in the neighborhood of Keokuk, in the descending order.

Formation	Strata	Thickness
	Superficial soil.	
	Coal and coal shales. (Coal 1 foot in old working below Keokuk.)	
	Sandstone of Nassau slough, and top of bluff at Nashville, above Keokuk	10 or 12 ft.
St. Louis limestone.	Brecciated and concretionary limestone, sometimes of a yellow color for a small extent .	20 feet.
Warsaw limestone.	Coarse calcareous yellow sandstone, in thick heavy beds, quarried for building.	
	Argillaceous limestone with shaly partings, containing abundance of large *Archimedes* and other Bryozoa : thickness at Warsaw . .	25 feet.
	Magnesian limestone of variable thickness, and sometimes absent.	
	Calcareous shale and marl with geodes; the "Geode bed" not often exceeding twenty-five feet : greatest thickness	40 feet.
Keokuk limestone.	Encrinal limestone, often in heavy beds with shaly partings (the Keokuk or lower Archimedes limestone proper)	40 feet.
	Cherty beds alternating with beds of encrinal limestone, forming the Rapids above Keokuk: thickness 20 to 50, and sometimes . . .	100 feet.
	(These form the beds of passage to the Burlington limestone below.)	

This succession has, heretofore, been regarded as the true order and sequence among the strata, from the Carboniferous limestone to the Coal measures. Prof. Swallow, however, in his report, has shown that an important sandstone comes in above the St.Louis or brecciated limestone, and between that rock and the Coal measures proper, in Missouri. This sandstone is not a part of the Coal measures, but is regarded very properly by Prof. Swallow as forming a part of the Carboniferous limestone series.

With a view to determine this point in a satisfactory manner, and also to resolve some questions relative to the limestones already examined, after the close of the working season in Iowa, we proceeded southward along the Mississippi, and examined in succession the exposures of rocks almost continuously, to the mouth of the Ohio river. Since these examinations were made with a view to their interest and importance, in connexion with the Geological Survey of Iowa, and as they may enable us to arrive at a more correct understanding of the Carboniferous limestone series in its geographical distribution and relations to the Coal measures, a sketch of the results is here introduced.

For purposes of comparison and reference, the sections which Prof. OWEN and Prof. SWALLOW have given of the same formations are here introduced.

The following table expresses the measurements and succession of rocks as contained in the section of Dr. OWEN.

COAL MEASURES.

20 feet.	Upper concretionary limestone.
10 feet.	Gritstones.
30 feet.	Lower concretionary limestone.
10 feet.	Gritstones.
10 feet.	Magnesian limestone.
30 feet.	Geodiferous bed.
50 feet.	Archimedes limestone.
15 feet.	Shell beds.
15 feet.	Keokuk cherty limestones.
70 feet.	Reddish brown Encrinital group of Hannibal.
55 feet.	Encrinital group of Burlington.
75 feet.	Argillo-calcareous group, Evans falls. [Chemung group.]

Prof. SWALLOW, in his Report on the Geology of Missouri, gives the following as the series from the Coal measures to the Chemung group.

CARBONIFEROUS OR MOUNTAIN LIMESTONE.	E.	Lower Coal measures	140 feet.
	F.	Ferruginous sandstone	195 "
	G.	St. Louis limestone	250 "
	H.	Archimedes limestone	200 "
	I.	Encrinital limestone	500 "
CHEMUNG GROUP.	J.	Choteau limestone	70 feet.
	K.	Vermicular sandstone and shale	75 "
	L.	Lithographic limestone	60 "

The numbers J, K and L constitute the Chemung group, as shown in the section, at Burlington, Iowa; and correspond to the argillo-calcareous group of Evans' falls, in Dr. OWEN'S section. In both the sections given above, the Burlington or Encrinital limestone succeeds to that group.

In Prof. SWALLOW'S section, the two encrinital limestones of Dr. OWEN'S section are given as one mass; and the "Keokuk cherty beds," and the "shell beds" are united with the "Archimedes limestone" as a single formation.

Continuing our observations southward, beyond the limits of Iowa, we find the limestones dipping to the southward for some distance, when there is again a gentle ascent in the same direction; and at Quincy, Illinois, we find the Burlington limestone, the cherty beds of the Keokuk rapids, and the Keokuk limestone, exposed in the river cliffs and quarries, and along Bear creek which joins the river a short distance above the town. The strata still continue to rise, and at Hannibal, Missouri, the Burlington limestone forms the top of the hills near the town, while the lower portions of the same consist of the Chemung group, and the lithographic limestone of the Missouri Reports.

Below this point, the limestones of the Carboniferous period gradually rise in the cliffs, and recede from the river, while lower strata continue to emerge as we go southward. The Burlington and Keokuk limestones still cap the hills at Louisiana and Clarksville, while the shales of the Hudson-river group are seen at the river level.

At Hamburg, on the Illinois side of the river, the Burlington limestone forms the higher part of the cliffs, while the slope below is over Chemung and Hamilton groups, and the Niagara limestone is the lowest rock visible.

In pursuing the examinations still farther south, the Trenton limestone group gradually ascends, forming a high cliff before reaching Cap au Grès, and from beneath it rises the lower sandstone in a bold promontory, which gives origin to the name. On the southern side of this promontory, the rocks have been thrown down, and we find the strata of the Burlington limestone standing vertically in the river bank*. Southward, and within a short space, they pass from vertical and highly inclined strata to those with a gentle southerly dip, so that the entire series from the Burlington limestone to the Coal measures is repeated in the hills within a short distance below Cap au Grès. The higher beds of the Carboniferous limestone series (the St. Louis limestone) continues along the river bank to Milan, within four miles of the mouth of the Illinois river.

The line of the fault before mentioned is nearly parallel to the course of the Mississippi river, from the mouth of the Illinois to the junction of the Missouri; and a small outlier of the Carboniferous limestone which is thrown down, lies in the bend of the Illinois on the east side, a short distance above its junction with the Mississippi river.

* This point on the Mississippi marks the line of a fault which has occurred from the breaking or tearing of the strata in the elevation of a low anticlinal axis; and while the northern half remains, the southern has gone down, allowing the Carboniferous limestones to come in upon the same horizon as the sandstone below the Trenton limestone.

This fault has been traced by Mr. WORTHEN, in his investigations in the Illinois survey, across the country intervening between the Illinois and Mississippi rivers, and still farther to the southeast within the State of Illinois.

The southwesterly outcrop, therefore, of the northeastern half of the axis, is continued along the east bank of the Mississippi at the mouth of the Illinois, and for some distance below; when it declines by a rapid dip, interrupted by one or more transverse faults. The lowest beds examined at Mason's landing (mouth of the Illinois river) are of the Niagara limestone; but there is a slope from the base of the hill, which, with the bottom land, may be about seventy-five feet to the river level; and this is probably occupied by shales of the Hudson-river period.

The Carboniferous limestones soon come in below Mason's landing, and we have the series repeated from the Burlington through the Keokuk and Warsaw limestones, until we find the cliffs capped by the St. Louis or concretionary limestone. The latter rock forms the line of cliffs for several miles above Alton, and continues below that place, as the river makes a westerly bend, leaving the limestone bounding the broad bottom land.

This limestone, including some beds not seen in the river section, corresponds to the brecciated limestone of Southern Iowa; but with its increased thickness, the brecciated character is nearly lost, and only appears at intervals, often beginning and ending abruptly, while the intermediate portions, including a large part of the rock, are heavy bedded, more or less diagonally laminated limestones, of a light grey color and often nearly white.

The higher limestones of the series continue for some distance below St. Louis, when they are interrupted by the elevation of the older rocks in the neighborhood of Selma. Below this place the strata again decline, and the brecciated limestone, with characters similar to those which it presents in the cliffs above Alton, comes to the river level at St. Genevieve in Missouri, and forms the cliffs along the American bottom above and below Prairie du Rocher, upon the Illinois side of the river.

Although not traced continuously below St. Louis, I conceive there can be no hesitation in adopting the conclusions here expressed in relation to these rocks. In following the river bank from St. Genevieve northward, we pass, within a few miles, over all the strata from the St. Louis limestone to the unequivocal Burlington limestone. The intermediate beds have expanded in thickness, and have assumed some different characters beyond those observed in their more northerly extension; containing, moreover, a greater number of species, and some new forms of fossils.

At Prairie du Rocher the limestone (St. Louis or concretionary limestone) contains *Lithostrotion floriforme* (of OWEN), which every where marks its presence from Southern Iowa to this place, over an extent of more than three degrees of latitude. The rock is for the most part heavy bedded, and forms an abrupt cliff bounding the low prairie on the east. It has a gentle southerly dip, and the ferruginous sandstone soon comes in on the south, forming a part of this cliff. The limestone disappears beneath the general level of the bottom land about two miles south of Prairie du Rocher; and from this point the sandstone continues gradually declining to about half way between Prairie du Rocher and Kaskaskia, where it disappears. This is in turn succeeded by a limestone, which being well characterised and in great force at Kaskaskia, may be named from that locality.

KASKASKIA LIMESTONE.

Archimedes limestone of OWEN, SWALLOW et al.; "*Pentremital limestone*".

This rock forms the cliff bordering the American bottom from Kaskaskia to Chester, and thence southward, having a continuous exposure of more than ten miles. The lower part is a compact, arenaceous and coarse textured limestone, with shaly partings, and containing numerous fossils. In its central and upper portions it includes a thick bed of sandstone, and the limestone beds are separated by shaly partings which often equal the calcareous strata in thickness. Towards the higher part there is a mass of green shale or marl sixty feet thick, and this is again succeeded by some heavy beds of limestone containing *Spirifer*, *Allorisma* and a species of *Pinna*.

Among the characteristic fossils, are several species of *Fenestella* (*Archimedes*), and other forms of this family; *Pentremites florealis*, *P. pyriformis*, *P. sulcatus*, and others; several species of *Terebratula*, *Spirifer*, *Productus*, etc., all or nearly all of which are distinct from the species observed in the limestones farther to the north, and in lower positions.

This limestone is far more prolific in the spiral axes of *Archimedes* than either the Keokuk or Warsaw limestone; and containing species all quite distinct from those in the lower beds, it is equally or better entitled to the name of "*Archimedes limestone*." Indeed, I believe it to be this limestone on the Ohio river, and in Illinois and Indiana, to which that name was first applied; while the occurrence of the axes of other species in the Keokuk limestone, and in the Warsaw limestone, which were not distinguished as different from those in the Kaskaskia limestone, first suggested the identity of the limestones of Southern Iowa with those of

Southern Illinois, Indiana, Kentucky, Tennessee and Alabama.

In the limestone under consideration, *Pentremites* occur abundantly; and from this circumstance it has also received the name of "*Pentremital limestone*", which is, indeed, a far better distinctive name than "Archimedes limestone", since *Pentremites* are more abundant in this formation than in any other rock in the West, and species of this genus are, for the most part, comparatively rare in any of the lower members of the Carboniferous limestones*.

Regarding the observations detailed above as correct, it becomes necessary to extend the nomenclature of Carboniferous limestones, and to include another member above the ferruginous sandstone of Prof. SWALLOW's section. The series thus extended, including those before enumerated as occurring in Southern Iowa, will give the following section:

* In the Mississippi valley, species of the Genus *Pentremites* first appear in the limestone of the age of the Upper Helderberg group of New-York, and also in the shales of the Hamilton group which succeed this limestone.

From the Burlington limestone, the following species have been described by Messrs. OWEN and SHUMARD in the Report upon the Geology of Wisconsin, Iowa and Minnesota, viz. *Pentremites norwoodi*, *P. melo* and *P. stelliformis*. In the Geological Report of Missouri, Dr. SHUMARD has described two other species from the same limestone, the *P. elongatus* and *P. sayi*. These are all different from the prevailing forms in the higher members of the series, and may with propriety constitute a distinct section of the genus.

Two species are known in the Warsaw limestone, *P. konincki* and *P. conoideus*, HALL; while in the Kaskaskia limestone we have *P. florealis* and *P. pyriformis* of SAY, *P. globosus*, TROOST = *P. sulcatus*, RŒMER?; *P. laterniformis*, OWEN and SHUMARD, and *P. curtus*, SHUMARD.

It is the great profusion of the individuals of the three first named species, that gives to this last named member of the series the character of a Pentremital limestone.

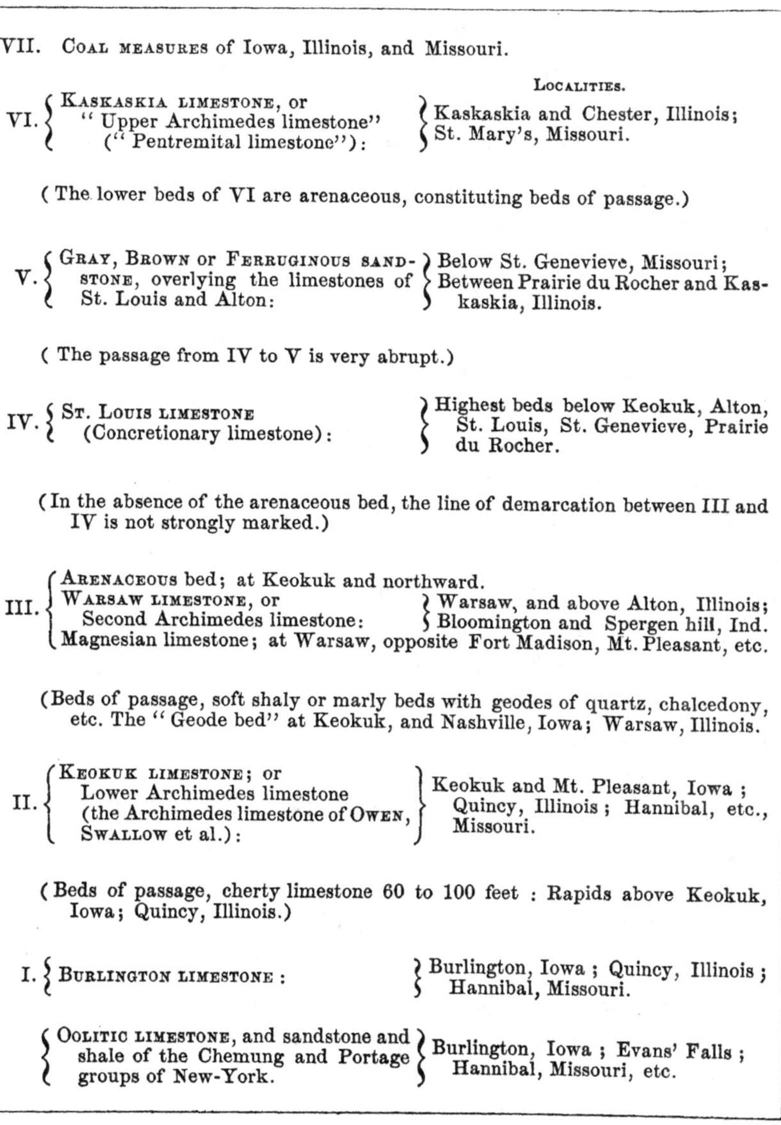

VII. Coal measures of Iowa, Illinois, and Missouri.

		Localities.
VI.	Kaskaskia limestone, or "Upper Archimedes limestone" ("Pentremital limestone"):	Kaskaskia and Chester, Illinois; St. Mary's, Missouri.

(The lower beds of VI are arenaceous, constituting beds of passage.)

V.	Gray, Brown or Ferruginous sandstone, overlying the limestones of St. Louis and Alton:	Below St. Genevieve, Missouri; Between Prairie du Rocher and Kaskaskia, Illinois.

(The passage from IV to V is very abrupt.)

IV.	St. Louis limestone (Concretionary limestone):	Highest beds below Keokuk, Alton, St. Louis, St. Genevieve, Prairie du Rocher.

(In the absence of the arenaceous bed, the line of demarcation between III and IV is not strongly marked.)

III.	Arenaceous bed; at Keokuk and northward.	
	Warsaw limestone, or Second Archimedes limestone:	Warsaw, and above Alton, Illinois; Bloomington and Spergen hill, Ind.
	Magnesian limestone; at Warsaw, opposite Fort Madison, Mt. Pleasant, etc.	

(Beds of passage, soft shaly or marly beds with geodes of quartz, chalcedony, etc. The "Geode bed" at Keokuk, and Nashville, Iowa; Warsaw, Illinois.

II.	Keokuk limestone; or Lower Archimedes limestone (the Archimedes limestone of Owen, Swallow et al.):	Keokuk and Mt. Pleasant, Iowa; Quincy, Illinois; Hannibal, etc., Missouri.

(Beds of passage, cherty limestone 60 to 100 feet: Rapids above Keokuk, Iowa; Quincy, Illinois.)

I.	Burlington limestone:	Burlington, Iowa; Quincy, Illinois; Hannibal, Missouri.
	Oolitic limestone, and sandstone and shale of the Chemung and Portage groups of New-York.	Burlington, Iowa; Evans' Falls; Hannibal, Missouri, etc.

By a comparison of this section of strata with those of Prof. OWEN and Prof. SWALLOW, some differences will be observed; but these are such as appear to be warranted by the examinations detailed above, and we believe this expresses the true order and sequence among the different members of the Carboniferous limestones, not only of the Mississippi valley, but also in their extension to the east and south.

There is essentially a complete agreement of the sections at the base, a single mass of encrinal limestone being recognized in each. The remarkable and wide spread cherty beds of the Lower rapids mark the passage to the next member of the series, the Keokuk limestone, which is recognized in its typical localities, by Dr. OWEN, under the name of "Archimedes limestone"; though other localities are cited in his descriptions, which in our view hold a higher position in the series. The Archimedes limestone of Prof. SWALLOW'S section, in the localities of Clark, Lewis, and Marion counties is a continuation of the Keokuk limestone; but I am unable to recognize the identity of the rock in these localities with that of Perry county, cited in Prof. SWALLOW'S section as the same.

The "geode bed" in Southern Iowa and the adjoining parts of Illinois, shows a cessation of the conditions producing limestone deposits for a considerable length of time; and the recurrence of these conditions gives origin to a set of Calcareous beds quite different in their character and organic remains from those below, viz. the *Warsaw limestone.* This is recognized as occurring between the Keokuk or Archimedes limestone and the St. Louis or Concretionary limestone, which both Profs. OWEN and SWALLOW place in direct succession in their sections.

The Ferruginous sandstone of Prof. SWALLOW is recognized in this section in the same order, succeeding the St. Louis limestone; but above this rock is distinguished an important limestone formation, the *Kaskaskia limestone*, which along the Mississippi river appears to hold unequivocally this order of superposition.

The difficulties which have occurred in the way of reconciliation of the views of western geologists, as expressed in their several Reports, have arisen in part from the fact that these different limestones have not an equal geographical distribution; there being no point on the Mississippi within our knowledge, where a transverse section of this valley will embrace, within a moderate distance, all the beds here enumerated. The limestones likewise change their characters when examined in a north and south direction, owing to causes which will be explained. The fossil forms which have mainly been relied upon for establishing divisions have been mostly of generic value only, and specific differences have not always been ful y appreciated.

The lowest of the series, the Burlington limestone, has, as already shown, a greater extension northward than either of the succeeding groups; and its gradually thinning edges stretch far towards the northern limits of Iowa. Near this latitude was the northern boundary of the ancient ocean, or at least the limit of its fauna. Considerably to the southward of this we first find the attenuated northern edges of the Keokuk limestone, mingled with much earthy sediment, and often consisting of a few thin beds of Encrinal limestone intercalated among other beds of shale and clay. It is only farther south, in the neighborhood of Nauvoo and Keokuk, that this limestone first exhibits decidedly its characteristic features. The limits of the ocean, which admitted of rock deposition and the support of animal life at this period, apparently never extended so far north by many miles as in the period of the Burlington limestone.

The Warsaw limestone and its associated beds of Magnesian limestone and Calcareous sandstone, appear to have been nearly coextensive in a northerly and easterly direction with the limestone below, so far as known at present. The northern extensions of this group, however, are shaly and arenaceous, and apparently destitute of organic remains.

The St. Louis limestone extends nearly or quite as far north as the groups below, but only as a thin brecciated or conglomerated mass; and it is only when we go southward, in the neighborhood of Alton, Illinois, that we find this rock in any considerable force. In the Missouri section, this limestone is given as two hundred and fifty feet thick, while in Southern Iowa it is less than fifty feet. The "Archimedes limestone" of the same section, corresponding with and including the Keokuk and Warsaw groups, has a thickness of two hundred feet; while in its more northerly outcrops its entire thickness does not exceed fifty feet, and is less than this in many places.

The Burlington limestone, which does not exceed one hundred feet at Burlington, Iowa, is given in the Missouri section as five hundred feet thick.

Nor is the augmenting thickness the only evidence of deeper seas and more quiet waters; for as we go southward, the coarser sediments and mixtures of shale and sandstone, prevailing on the northern outcrop, disappear in great part or entirely, and the whole series has a calcareous character.

In the geographical distribution, and the changes of lithological characters at different points, we have yet much to learn from careful local investigation and comparison. The facts here recorded, which are a small part only of those collected during these examinations, show that the thinning margins of the formations are upon the north, each one in succession being less and less extended in that direction; and that each augments in thickness and becomes better defined towards the south.

These facts warrant the conclusion that the entire series of the Carboniferous limestones were successively deposited in an ocean, the limits of which were gradually contracting upon the north, while at the south the conditions were becoming more and more favorable to the development of this kind of deposition, and to the support of the fauna which abounded throughout this period, until both culminated in the great limestone formation of Kaskaskia. This rock is known for its abundance of fossils throughout Kentucky, Tennessee, and Alabama; while it has not been found to extend so far north as the Burlington limestone, by four or five degrees of latitude.

The centres of greatest development, both of deposition and of animal life, were constantly being transferred farther to the south at each successive epoch here indicated; and while the greatest development of the Burlington limestone is to the north of, or about the latitude of St. Louis, that of the Kaskaskia limestone is on the south of the Ohio in Tennessee and Alabama.

To these limestones just noticed succeeds the "Ferruginous sandstone", which, in the Mississippi valley, thins out entirely, or becomes extremely attenuated, before reaching the mouth of the Des Moines river on the north; while the succeeding Kaskaskia limestone only acquires considerable force in the neighborhood of the Kaskaskia river, and is known, in the interior, extending in its thinning northern margins, as far north as Prairie de Long. This limestone increases in force as we go southward; and in Kentucky, Tennessee, and Alabama, it constitutes the greatest part of the rock designated as "*Carboniferous limestone*" or "*Mountain limestone*". In Tennessee, its thickness is estimated by Prof. Safford at twelve hundred feet.

Some sections of the rock in Alabama, measured by Mr. Worthen, gave a thickness of more than nine hundred feet.

The following sections will furnish the means of comparison of the successive groups, and of the several members of the same at different and distant points:

*Section of the Strata exposed in Monte Sana near Huntsville, Alabama**.

COAL MEASURES.	Ferruginous sandstone	30 feet.
	Slate and impure coal	4 feet.

1. Light bluish gray compact limestone, containing teeth of *Psammodus*, *Bellerophon bisulcus?* *Pentremites globosus* and *P. florealis*, *Archimedes*, etc. . . . . . 50 feet.

2. Shaly limestone, somewhat cherty, and weathering to a buff color; its outcrop usually hidden by a slope covered by the debris of the overlying rocks: contains *Spirifer incrassatus?* and *Terebratula* . . . . . 100 – 120 ft.

3. Compact bluish gray limestone, semioolitic in part; comparatively poor in fossils, but containing, somewhat rarely, *Pentremites globosus*, *P. florealis* and *P. pyriformis*, *Archimedes*, etc. . . . . 250 feet.

4. Ferruginous sandstone . . . . 10 – 15 ft.

5. Compact gray limestone, with *Archimedes* and *Pentremites* in great numbers, *Cyathocrinus crateriformis*, *Poteriocrinus gracilis*, *Zeacrinus magnoliaformis*, *Agassziocrinus conicus*, *Productus elegans?* *P. semireticulatus?* etc. . . . . 200 feet.

6. Decomposing cherty layers . . . . 4 feet.

7. Gray cherty limestone with one or two oolitic beds, containing *Lithostrotion floriforme*, *Spirifer striatus?* and joints and plates of crinoideæ; the cherty beds containing *Productus cora?* and *P. semireticulatus* . . . 150 – 200 ft.

8. Dark bluish gray siliceous rock, weathering to a shale in some localities, and containing fossils similar to those above, except the *Lithostrotion* . . . . 100 feet.

Section of the Strata of the Kaskaskia limestone exposed in the Cliff at Chester, Illinois.

The section above the town, and one made a mile below the town, differ in the thickness of some of the members.

1. Compact limestone in irregular beds with shaly partings and sometimes shaly limestone, containing *Pinna*, *Spirifer incrassatus?* *Productus* and *Terebratula*, Bryozoa, etc. . . . . 30 – 40 ft.

2. Soft green argillaceous shale, with calcareous seams near the base, about . . . . 60 feet.

* This section was made by Mr. A. H. WORTHEN, Geological Assistant in the Iowa Survey, lately appointed State Geologist of Illinois.

3. Limestone with shaly partings, containing numerous Bryozoa, as *Archimedes*, etc., *Spirifer*, *Terebratula*, and *Productus*, *Pentremites*, etc. . . . . 20 feet.

4. Fine-grained, sometimes argillaceous sandstone, of a yellowish color, often forming a terrace . . . . 8 feet.

5. Shale and shaly limestone, graduating into dark shale at a distance of five or six feet from the top, and, at ten feet from top, becoming a thin-bedded limestone with shaly partings, which is more compact and heavy bedded at the river level : contains great numbers of *Archimedes*, *Pentremites*, etc. Entire thickness unknown : to river level . . . . 70 feet.

A comparison of the members of these two sections shows a great similarity in general character and organic contents.

No. 1 of the Monte Sana section corresponds with the upper limestone of Chester. The green shale No. 2 of the Chester section is subject to much variation, and is often highly calcareous : this probably corresponds to No. 2 of the Monte Sana section, which is a shaly and sometimes cherty limestone.

The beds No. 3 are similar in the two sections, and contain fossils of the same species.

The sandstone No. 4 in both the sections is of similar character.

The upper part of No. 5 in the Chester section is shaly, and consists of alternations of shale and limestone, becoming more compact below ; while some lower strata, not seen in the section at Chester, but exposed farther to the north, between Chester and Kaskaskia, are heavy-bedded subcrystalline gray limestones. Many of the fossils in the two localities are of identical species.

By reference to the general section, we find that the Ferruginous sandstone lies below these limestones of Chester and Kaskaskia, and below this the St. Louis limestone containing *Lithostrotion*. At Monte Sana we have in the place of the sandstone some cherty layers of No. 6, while No. 7 represents in its lithological character and fossil contents the St. Louis limestone.

No. 8 of the Monte Sana section, which represents a portion of the "Siliceous group of Tennessee and Alabama", is apparently a continuation of the cherty and siliceous beds which form the rapids at Keokuk, Iowa, and constitute the beds of passage from the Burlington to the Keokuk limestone.

In two other sections, one made near Tuscumbia and the other in the vicinity of Buzzard's Roost, Alabama, the gray cherty limestone with *Lithostrotion* is succeeded in one case by 15 to 20 feet of shaly non-fossiliferous sandstone, and in the other by 30 feet of shale entirely destitute of fossils; and in both these instances, this non-fossiliferous bed is succeeded by limestones containing *Pentremites* and other fossils similar to those of Kaskaskia and Chester.

It is certainly desirable that a larger number of sections, and more extensive collections of fossils, should be made, before we rely implicitly upon these comparisons; but the *Lithostrotion floriforme*, which holds a very definite horizon along the Mississippi valley above the mouth of the Ohio, is found in Tennessee and Alabama, underlying the limestones which hold such numbers of *Pentremites* and *Archimedes*, of species identical with those of Chester and Kaskaskia.

Although the Burlington limestone is scarcely recognizable in Tennessee and Alabama as a distinct formation, there are, nevertheless, sometimes cherty crinoidal beds at the base of the "*silicious group*", which may perhaps be regarded as of the same epoch as the crinoidal limestone of Burlington, Quincy and other places.

Some very interesting enquiries are suggested by these facts, and at the same time they afford, in some degree, the solution of a difficulty which has heretofore been unexplained.

It is well known that no limestones of the age of these here described occur upon the west side of the Appalachian coal field on the north of the Ohio river, nor upon the eastern side of the same field to the north of the central portion of Virginia. The same is true of the coal fields of Nova-Scotia and New-Brunswick, according to Prof. DAWSON, the northern sides exhibiting no underlying limestones; while such rocks do appear coming out from beneath the Coal measures on the southeastern side. The same phenomena occur also with regard to the coal fields of Iowa and Illinois. The northern and northwestern margins of all these Coal measures extend beyond the limits of the Carboniferous limestones. At the same time I have ascertained, in the most satisfactory manner, that the coal fields of Iowa, Missouri, and Illinois, rest unconformably upon the strata beneath, whether these strata be Carboniferous limestones, Devonian, Upper Silurian or Lower Silurian rocks.

It would appear, that at a period long preceding the commencement of the Carboniferous limestone deposits, the ancient ocean began to contract its area; that this contraction was consequent upon the uplifting of the older rocks upon the north; and that this state of things continued throughout all the period of the limestone deposits. Furthermore, we have evidence that during this period, or at its close, and previous to the deposition of the Coal measures, the older strata, which had long previously been raised into numerous anticlinal axes with corresponding depressions and along some lines broken by faults, and dipping at various angles, had to some extent been worn down by denudation, which also produced other inequalities of the surface; and that afterwards the Coal measures were spread out over the thinning and slightly inclined edges of the Carboniferous limestone beds, and the edges of the more highly inclined rocks of the preceding periods.

Facts indicate very clearly, as we conceive, that the area of the ancient ocean, which had been contracting up to the Coal period, was then extended in this part of the country by the sinking of the land on the north, allowing the deposits of the Coal measures to be spread over much wider areas, particularly in that direction, than the preceding formations of the Carboniferous limestones. This will explain, in a very satisfactory manner, the cause of the absence of the Carboniferous limestones on the northern margins of all the coal fields of the West, and at the same time suggests an explanation of the greater accumulation of conglomerates and coarser materials in the same relative position.

Should the Carboniferous limestones of Nova-Scotia prove to be of the same age as the Carboniferous limestones of the West and Southwest, their occurrence so far to the northward of the northern limits of the Appalachian coal field may still be explained, by supposing the line of ancient coast, or the line of coral reefs, to have had an irregular direction from the southwest to the northeast, following the undulations caused by unequal depression and elevation; and it may have been interrupted by the elevation of the Green mountain and Appalachian chain, which, if not entirely cutting off the continuity of the Carboniferous sea, must have deflected the course of the limestone deposits very far to the southward. The supposition of this former continuity will furnish at the same time an explanation of those limestones areas in Rhode-Island and Massachusetts, which have been, with hesitation, referred to the Carboniferous period*.

* That the limestones of Nova-Scotia may be different from those already described, will not of itself afford an argument against the correctness of the views advanced above. The age of the Carboniferous limestone of Virginia has not yet been established, so far as I know; for to be simply "*Carboniferous limestone*", it may be either one of the five very distinct groups already described, or it may be a group different from either of these(1). The great difference of fossils at distant points, often referred to climatic influences, I conceive to be only the different expression of life in distinct epochs of the Carboniferous limestone period; and with our present knowledge, it seems more reasonable to conclude that the Nova-Scotia Carboniferous limestone is of a different epoch from those of the Mississippi valley.

(1) Profs. W. B. & H. D. Rogers have announced the discovery of this Carboniferous limestone in Virginia : the former places it as an intercalation between the upper and lower red shale formation, No. XI, wedging out to the northward, but containing "myriads of characteristic carboniferous fossils".

It is not improbable that this may have been the direction of the coast line at that period, since we know that at the west its course was irregular, extending farther to the north in some points than in others. Thus we have in Iowa the Carboniferous limestone reaching to the north of latitude 42° 30′; while from this point it trends to the southeast, as is seen by following its outcrop through Iowa, Illinois, and Indiana.

Beneath the Appalachian coal field, I am not aware that the Carboniferous limestone has been traced far to the north of latitude 38°, though its existence has been indicated somewhat farther in the same direction.

It is quite evident, therefore, that a broad deep sinus has existed in the outline of the Carboniferous limestones; or, in other words, that a broad extension of land (or of sea too shallow for coral reefs) stretched from the north into the ocean of the Carboniferous limestone in the position and in the direction, very nearly, of the present Cincinnati axis; while on the west of that line, the Lower Carboniferous limestones make a northerly bend, as if at that period the area of the present valley of the Mississippi admitted of a more northerly extension of the coral reefs.

The high elevation of the older strata, and the inequalities of surface on which the western Coal measures rest, prove conclusively that extensive denudation had taken place previous to the coal period; and these facts should suggest a caution in our conclusions regarding the vast influence of modern denudation upon the surface of the globe.

COAL FORMATION, OR COAL MEASURES.

The most important and permanent source of mineral wealth in the State of Iowa will be found in the Coal measures. In the geological reconnoissance of 1855, examinations were made along all that part of the series which outcrops along the Mississippi river. During the season of 1856, the same formation was examined throughout the valley of the Des Moines river, by Mr. WORTHEN, who followed out its extent in a northwesterly direction from the southern limit of the State to Fort Dodge.

The field work of 1857 has been divided between the detailed exploration of the Coal measures in the southern counties, and in tracing the limits of the lower formations towards the north line of the State.

The narrow area occupied by the Coal formation on the Mississippi river seems more nearly connected with the Illinois coal field than with the Iowa coal field, if we regard the two as distinct. The separation, however, appears to have been, in part, effected by modern denudation, as well as by causes, operating at the time of the formation, which prevented the continuity of the deposition between the Mississippi and Des Moines rivers. The outliers of Coal measures below Leclaire, and thence to Muscatine, are very clearly but continuations of the measures seen upon the east side of the river, the valley of which is here comparatively narrow. The vallies of the Red, Cedar and Iowa rivers have denuded this formation from a broad space, which separates these outliers along the Mississippi, farther from the coal on the west than from the same formation in Illinois.

The coal field of Illinois differs in no respect from that of Iowa, and is only separated from it by the valley of the Mississippi, which is a valley of denudation; and the coal of Iowa, at Nashville and below Keokuk, is separated from the outcrops on the Illinois side at Montebello only by the river channel. It is quite evident that the coal on the two sides of the river were once continuous beds; the strata of sandstone, shale and coal corresponding in character and thickness, and the lower coal seam on one side agreeing in all respects with the lower coal seam on the other side of the river.

It has been stated that the course of the Mississippi river is along the line of an anticlinal axis, and that this axis separates the two coal basins; but we have not been able thus far to find evidence of the existence of such an axis.

In descending the Mississippi river, from the north line of the State, the Coal measures first appear in some small outliers below Leclaire, coming down to the river level. The strata exposed above the water consist of sandstones, shales and argillaceous iron ore. These strata rest in a horizontal position upon upturned strata of the Silurian limestones; and the outcropping edges of the latter, on either side, are not due to faults, but to the original condition of the beds which were inclined and denuded before the deposition of the shales and sandstones of the Coal measures. In no instance did we observe phenomena of this kind which could be attributed to dislocation by faults of an origin subsequent to the period of the coal, though such faults may occur.

The relative position of these outliers of the Coal formation below Leclaire are illustrated in the following diagram.

FIG. 6.— Section below Leclaire.

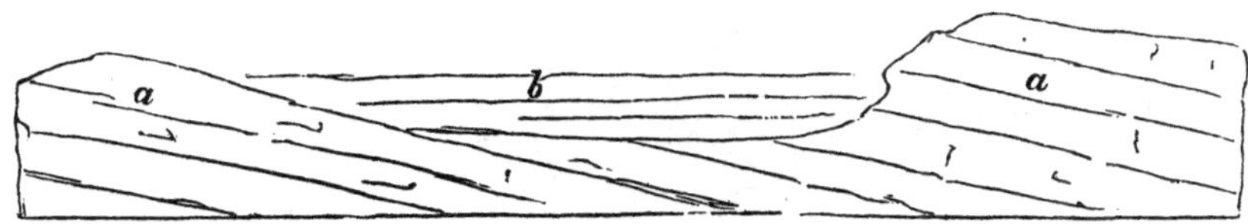

a, a. Silurian limestone, as seen above the level of the river.

b. Coal shales and sandstone, with argillaceous iron ore, resting horizontally upon the upraised edges of the limestone.

The strata of Upper Silurian limestone here dip to the northwest, as described in the preceding pages, under the head of Leclaire limestone.

In ordinary stages of water, the base of the shales cannot be seen, and at the time of this examination the actual contact was not visible. In a similar position on the Illinois side of the river, I examined a mass of coal and coal shale, having but a few yards of extent, and resting in a depression of the limestone which had been excavated by previous denudation; while on three sides of the horizontal layers of coal shale, the limestone was to be seen, dipping at an angle of 30°, and rising above the level of those beds, precisely as seen in the section on the Iowa side of the river, only in a more extreme degree.

There are at least two such outliers on the river bank below Leclaire; and in one place excavations for coal had been made, but judging from the materials thrown out, the experiment was not successful. Farther back from the river margin, the coal strata lie at a higher elevation; and the river section illustrates the relations of the rocks below to the base of the formation, the extent or conditions of which cannot of course be determined from what is seen upon the surface, or where no deep excavations exist.

In a ravine some distance farther down the river than the point just noticed, the relative position of the Coal measures and the limestone below are as follows :

FIG. 7.—Section below Leclaire.

a, a. Axis of Silurian limestone.

b. Shales and sandstones of the Coal measures.

The latter beds were traced continuously to within three feet of the limestone, this interval being obscured by debris. There is here no bending upwards of the horizontal strata at the junction of the rocks, as if participating in the movement which elevated the limestones below : on the contrary, there is the most satisfactory proof that the Coal formation was deposited subsequently to this elevation of the limestones.

Although there are indications of the occurrence of the Coal formation at several points between Leclaire and Davenport, I did not learn that any workings had been successfully carried on. The trial openings appear to have been abandoned without penetrating far into the solid strata, and, indeed, some of them have probably reached only the broken outcrop.

The indications of permanent workable seams of coal, in this region, can scarcely be regarded as at all encouraging. The original inequalities of the floor upon which these beds were deposited will render their extent and continuity very uncertain. These outcrops are also near the most northerly limit of the coal field, and liable to thin out at any point, as well as to be interrupted by the rocks below.

South of Davenport, in the vicinity of New-Buffalo, there are several openings made upon the lower coal seam, and worked to a greater or less extent. This seam varies from $1\frac{1}{2}$ feet to $2\frac{1}{2}$ feet in thickness. Below what is generally known as the lower coal seam, there is a bed of shale, in which sometimes occurs a bed of cannel coal from 1 foot to $1\frac{1}{2}$ feet thick. This is, however, not constant, and, at no point where I have examined it, does it give promise of a workable seam.

Among the openings examined in the lower coal seam proper, Hall's coal bed gives the following sections :

Sandstone and sandy shale.

Coal . . . . 2½ feet.

Fire clay.

A space of a few yards between the two openings.

Black slaty shale . . . . . . Cannel coal, 1½ feet . . . . Black slaty shale	This is a single mass with cannel coal in the middle, sometimes becoming slate.

Hiatus of a few feet.

Brown limestone, and grey limestone and shales of the Hamilton group.

The actual contact of the coal shales and the limestone of the Hamilton group was not seen at this place, though only a few feet intervene between the two formations.

In a ravine south of New-Buffalo, the following section is presented :

Lower coal seam . . . . 1½ feet.

A few feet where no rock is visible.

Limestone and shales of the Hamilton group.

The following section is seen at Havil's near New-Buffalo.

Coarse sandstone.

Ferruginous shaly sandstone . . . . 3 feet.

Shale . . . . 2 to 2½ feet.

Slaty cannel coal . . . . 1 foot.

Shale . . . . 1½ feet.

On the opposite side of the ravine and at a higher level, the following section is visible:

Clay and soil.	
Shale and clay	4 feet.
Bituminous coal	1 foot.
Dark-colored sandstone	1 foot.
Soft shale	3 feet.
Fire clay	1 foot.

The sandstone under the coal contains *Stigmaria;* and in some places it becomes argillaceous, passing into an underclay.

Continuing up the same ravine from the cannel coal opening, and at a higher level, there is an opening upon the lower coal seam, which is now worked. The following section is visible at the working:

Black and shaly sandstone	4 to 5 feet.
Bituminous coal	2 feet 4 inches.
Fire clay.	

A short distance down the ravine below this point, the cannel coal has been opened, having a thickness of one foot. The relative position of the beds is uniformly the same; and the shale with cannel coal appears to be a constant accompaniment of what is known as the lower coal seam of the Iowa and Illinois Coal measures.

From all the examinations made in this region, no evidence was obtained of the second coal seam. There are seldom more than twenty or thirty feet of strata above the lower seam, and often less; while the second seam lies some seventy or eighty feet higher than the first.

Between Pine creek and Fairport there are several coal workings at considerable elevation above the river level. Three miles below Fairport the coal shales and sandstones are at the river level, rising in a bluff of thirty to forty feet; and from this, receding twenty to forty yards, is a second escarpment of equal elevation, making the whole thickness at this place eighty feet or more.

At Muscatine the sandstones and shales of the Coal formations are exposed in the railroad cutting, a short distance below the town. The entire thickness of the strata is about sixty or seventy feet from the river level to the summit.

The series at this place is very interesting, showing the variable character of the beds exposed along the excavation for the railroad. At one point the vertical section presents the following :

Thin-bedded sandstone with shaly layers	10 feet.
Massive sandstone with large concretions	10 feet.
Seam of coal or shaly coal with underclay	4 feet.
Shaly sandstone with shaly partings, more shaly in the lower part	8½ feet.
Thin-bedded sandstone with shaly partings	5 feet.
Heavy-bedded sandstone	6 feet.
Green shale	3 feet.
Distance to level of river (covered)	18 or 20 ft.

A little farther to the northward, the coal seam has entirely thinned out ; and the sandstone above and below it come together, occupying a thickness of twenty feet, and diagonally laminated throughout.

The strata present evidence of contrary currents, and there is a much larger proportion of arenaceous matter than is usual in the lower part of the Coal measures. The conditions here observed do not indicate, with any degree of certainty, a large amount of workable coal.

From the direction and dip of the strata below the coal, and from all other evidence which could be obtained, it seems very well determined that the Coal measures, exposed from below Leclaíre to Muscatine, occupy a narrow belt along the river, never extending far to the westward, and cut off towards the south by the valley of the Iowa river.

This narrow belt of Coal measures, as has been shown, rests, towards its northern limits, upon the Silurian limestone, often filling depressions in the surface of the rock which appear to have been worn by ancient denudation. Farther south, it rests unconformably upon the lowest Devonian limestone, and in many places npon the Hamilton group, while the localities at and below Pine creek are upon the Chemung group. There are also one or two outliers resting upon the Burlington limestone at some distance from the river; and, finally, those of Nashville and below Keokuk rest on the St. Louis limestone, which is the highest member of the Lower Carboniferous limestones known in Iowa. Farther to the south, the Coal measures rest upon the ferruginous sandstone; and still farther in the same direction, upon a higher member of the Carboniferous limestone series, the Kaskaskia limestone.

In Illinois, the Coal measures in some places lie unconformably upon the Lower Silurian rocks, as the Trenton limestone and Calciferous sandstone. Thus we have Coal measure rocks resting directly and unconformably upon strata of the Lower Silurian, Upper Silurian, Devonian, and Carboniferous limestone periods, as shown in the following diagram*:

* We have heretofore had information showing that some one or more small outliers of coal occur in the State of Wisconsin; and Mr. S. W. Hill of Eagle Harbor, Lake Superior, has lately informed me that he has examined an outlier of this character near Janesville in that State.

Section showing the relations of the Coal measures of Iowa, Illinois, and Wisconsin to the subjacent strata.

FIG. 8.

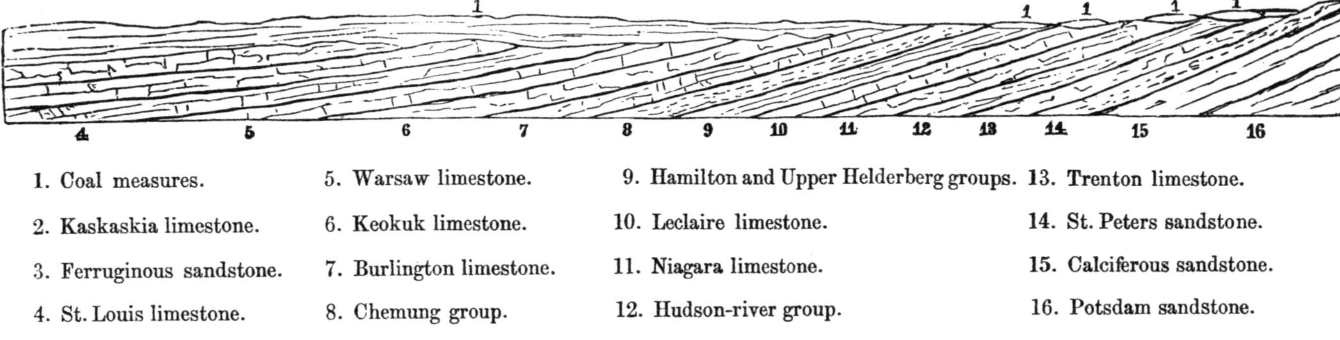

1. Coal measures.	5. Warsaw limestone.	9. Hamilton and Upper Helderberg groups.	13. Trenton limestone.
2. Kaskaskia limestone.	6. Keokuk limestone.	10. Leclaire limestone.	14. St. Peters sandstone.
3. Ferruginous sandstone.	7. Burlington limestone.	11. Niagara limestone.	15. Calciferous sandstone.
4. St. Louis limestone.	8. Chemung group.	12. Hudson-river group.	16. Potsdam sandstone.

The figures 1, 1, 1, 1, towards the right hand of the section, show the relations of certain small coal basins to the strata of Lower and Upper Silurian and Devonian age.

Under these circumstances, we might expect to discover evidences of the ancient denudation still more palpable than these inequalities of surface filled with coal strata. Nevertheless, although the range of subjacent rocks is so extensive, they are chiefly such as cannot long withstand the wearing action; and the sandstones are so friable that they would scarcely produce pebbles or conglomerates.

Beyond these inequalities of surface there are cavities in the limestone of the Upper Helderberg period, which are filled with greenish-gray clay, like the underclay of coal seams. These are so numerous and decided in their character, as to leave no doubt that they are ancient enlarged fissures and cavernous openings made by running water and afterwards filled with clay, during the deposition of the Coal measures. One of the most remarkable exhibitions of this kind occurs in the vertical face of a quarry at Rock island. The strata consists of shales and shaly limestones of the Hamilton group, and some beds of the limestone of the Upper Helderberg. The surface of the rock beneath the superincumbent soil presents a depression which deepens into a broad funnel-shaped cavity, gradually narrowing below till within ten feet of the bottom, when it spreads out on one side with an irregularly arching roof and an unequal floor. It is filled from top to bottom with hard clay, similar to the underclay of coal seams. At the top of the funnel, this clay is of a reddish-brown color, due to the infiltration from the ferruginous soil above; but below it soon becomes of the ordinary gray color. The laminations of this clay conform to the curvatures and irregularities of the roof and floor of the ancient cavern, and exhibit the appearance of having flowed in while in a semifluid condition, while the hydrostatic pressure of the mass above, acting through the deep funnel, had forced the soft mass againt the walls and roof of the cavity, causing it to assume in its lamination the same contour.

In the midst of this clay was the impression of a large *Euomphalus*, distinct from any known in the surrounding rock, and very similar to a carboniferous form. The shell itself was not seen : with this exception, no remains of fossils were observed in the clay at this locality.

The following diagram illustrates the cavity described above : its extension to the left had been cut off in quarrying at the time of the examination.

FIG. 9.— Section at Rock island.

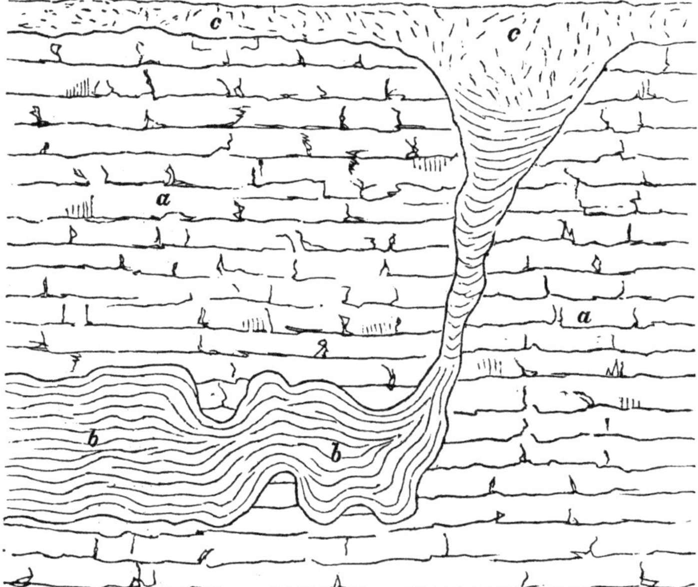

a, *a*. Limestone of Devonian age.

b, *b*. Ash-colered clay, like the underclay of coal seams.

c, *c*. Gravel and yellowish loam.

The conclusion seems, therefore, irresistible, that subsequent to the uplifting of these rocks, the denudation of their surfaces and the wearing into caverns, the materials of the Coal measures were deposited, filling these cavities, and resting in successive members upon the surface of the older rocks.

If anything were wanting to complete the chain of facts, and carry the most conclusive evidence, it is found in a section near Iowa city; where, in a cliff of limestone of the Hamilton group, we have the following phenomena. Between beds of nearly horizontal limestone, appears a black band extending thirty or forty feet : this consists of black carbonaceous mud, the upper part having the character of cannel coal, and the lower part a slaty carbonaceous shale. Beneath this, and less extended, a thicker layer of clay precisely like that which is found in the cavities before described, and of the character of underclay, fills the upper and broader part of the cavity; while below this, and occupying the deepest parts, is a coarse sandstone, which follows, in its lines of lamination, the curvatures of the limestone upon which it lies.

The following diagram illustrates this description :

FIG. 10.— Section near Iowa city.

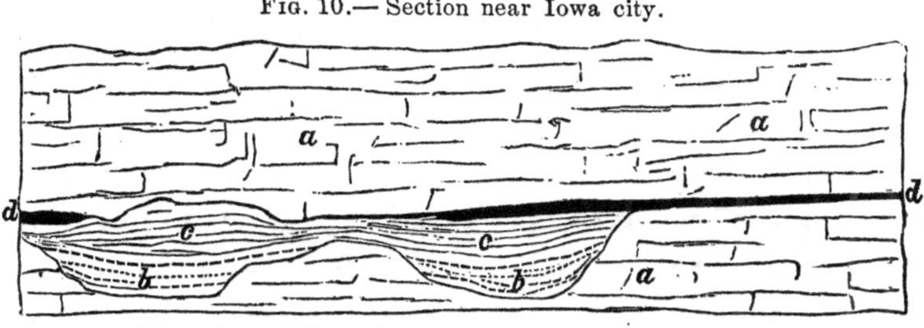

a, a. Limestone of Devonian age.

b, b. Coarse sandstone in curved laminæ.

c, c. Ash-colored and greenish underclay.

d, d. Coal seam; the lower part shaly, and containing fish teeth.

Here we have all the phenomena attending a true Coal measure seam of coal : the sandstone, the underclay, and the coal seam resting upon it; and to complete the analogy, the slaty portion of the seam contains *fish teeth* of carboniferous character. All this is enclosed in limestone, which, in the State of New-York, where the series is more complete, lies at a depth of more than five thousand feet below the Coal measures.

The explanation is obvious. This instance corresponds with the preceding, being only a little more complete in its series of members, while the aperture of admission is not visible in the exposure. The coarse and fine sand were first transported, and, entering some fissure in the rock, continued in deposition in this cavity, while a bed of similar sandstone was being formed outside and upon the bottom of the sea. This ceased, and then came the clay, which was continued in like manner, while the underclay of an exterior coal bed was in process of deposition. Lastly, the carboniferous mud, derived from the materials of a coal seam, was filtered through the fissure, filling the remaining space, and spread out in the narrow seam beyond.

There is no mingling of the materials, as if resulting from the breaking up of a coal seam at a later and modern period. Every part is as distinct as in the Coal measures elsewhere; and this could only have resulted from a participation in the causes then operating to produce those extensive beds of sand, clay, shale and coal which make up the Coal measures*.

It must be observed, also, that this point is near the north-eastern margin of the coal basin, and beyond the limits of any known productive coal seams; a few isolated patches of sandstone and shale being all the remaining evidences of the extension of the series in that vicinity.

An example of the outlying Coal-measure sandstones, without visible coal seams, may be seen in a quarry on the river above Iowa city, lying apparently in a valley of denudation in the Devonian limestone. The phenomena might indicate the existence of a fault, by which the higher rocks are thrown; but from similar examples we infer that it is

* The fissures and caverns occupied by the lead ores in Iowa, Wisconsin, Illinois and Missouri, are apparently of similar character and origin; the period of their formation, and the manner in which they have been filled with the sulphurets of iron, zinc and lead, being a subject for discussion and investigation.

due to denudation of the limestone, and the subsequent deposition of the shaly sandstones.

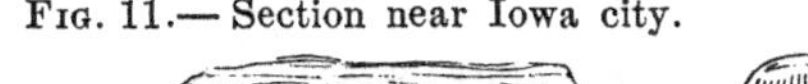

Fig. 11.— Section near Iowa city.

a, a. Limestone of Devonian age.
b. Shaly sandstones of the Coal measures : about thirty feet exposed.

This unconformability of the Coal measures in Iowa to the strata below, renders it the more difficult and laborious to follow out and determine the boundaries of the workable coal beds. The formation, in its general direction and outcrop, does not correspond to the general direction of the inferior groups, nor has it participated in the great movements which disturbed and elevated those lower strata : consequently no outline of any one of these, however carefully traced, will aid in determining the limits of the Coal formation. Its outcrop may lie transversely or irregularly across the outcrop of one or several of the formations below ; and it will require much time, and patient investigation, to determine accurately the limits of the outliers which occupy circumscribed areas of depression or inequalities in the surface of the older rocks. For the same reason it becomes more important that the Coal formation be made a special object of investigation, and its limits accurately determined and defined.

It will probably be found that towards the northern margin, the measures are barren of workable coal seams, while other indications of coal may exist. From these circumstances, and from the nature of the country, which is deeply covered with drift and later deposits, examinations will be more satisfactorily carried on from the central or southern part towards the northern and northwestern margins, by following up the channels of the streams in that direction.

In concluding this sketch of the Palæozoic formations of Iowa and the Upper Mississippi valley, it becomes necessary to notice the occurrence of the important limestone formation every where associated with the Coal measures of the West.

In Northern Ohio (and probably extending into Pennsylvania) there are thin bands of limestone associated with the Coal measures. In several localities examined, these beds are more or less shaly in character, often separated by wide vertical joints, and weathering to a brown or greyish-brown color. These calcareous and shaly beds are always highly fossiliferous.

In Southeastern Ohio, and the adjacent parts of Virginia and Pennsylvania, fossils similar to those characterizing the calcareous bands of that part of the series regarded as the Lower Coal measures, mark the Siliceous or Buhrstone formation of the central portion of the Coal measures, and also the shaly calcareous beds in the same position. Although recognized at numerous points, I am not aware that these beds have been regarded as parts of a continuous formation, or that their position in the eastern coal fields is known to be constant.

A comparison of fossils from numerous localities in the Coal measures of the West show very conclusively that one or more of these limestone bands are continuous; or, at least, that the same association of fossil species occurs at so many points, as to leave no doubt of a similarity in the conditions of the ocean bed over a wide area now occupied by the Coal measures.

Drawing onr conclusions from the occurrence of the same species of fossils, and from the constancy of their association, we infer that one of these bands of limestones exists over a large area in Northern and Northeastern Ohio, and that the same can be recognized on the west side of the Cincinnati axis, and traced through Indiana, Illinois, Iowa, Nebraska, Missouri, and Kansas, every where marked by the same species of fossils.

Limestones of the character here described, and containing the same association of fossil species, are largely developed on the Missouri river and other places within the State of Missouri. In his Geological Report of 1855, Prof. SWALLOW has placed these fossiliferous limestones and calcareous shales in the Upper Coal measures, and has shown them to have a much greater development than in any of the more eastern localities. In the cliffs at Weston, Missouri, he has given a section of limestone bands, shale and marl, with some thin bands of sandstone and seams of coal, altogether of more than two hundred feet. From these facts, and from others derived from Illinois and Iowa, it appears that there is a constant increase in the thickness and importance of these calcareous formations of the Coal measures as we pass westward; while there is a palpable diminution in the thickness of the sedimentary portions, or the shales and sandstones of the same formation. Measurements made at numerous points, over a large part of the western coal field, show altogether scarcely more than one-tenth of the thickness of the Coal measures of Pennsylvania, and in many places they are even less than in this proportion*. We must, therefore, be prepared to find ultimately that the Coal measures, or at least the productive portions of that formation, thin out in great part or entirely in that direction; while the calcareous portions, which are of marine origin, will be found increasing in force.

The prevailing fossil species which mark the occurrence

* Prof. H. D. ROGERS estimates the Coal formation of Pennsylvania at 6750? feet, and the underlying conglomerate at 1400 feet; while Prof. SWALLOW, in his Geological Report of Missouri, has given 640 feet as the thickness of the Coal measures. In Iowa, no measurements have yet reached five hundred feet. Therefore reducing our estimate of the eastern measures to 5000 feet, the western measures give only about one-tenth to one-eighth. It is quite probable, however, that we shall yet find a greater thickness in some portions of the western coal field, though we can scarcely expect one thousand eet in those portions examined.

of these calcareous bands are *Spirifer cameratus*, *S. lineatus*, *Terebratula subtilita*, *T. millepunctata*, *Productus rogersi*, *P. semireticulatus*, *Allorisma* and other fossils. These species are almost always associated in the localities examined over the wide area where this formation extends. In all the collections of Carboniferous fossils brought from the far west by several exploring expeditions : those made by Capt. STANSBURY in his route to the Great Salt Lake; by the Pacific Railroad explorations and surveys, by the United States and Mexican boundary surveys, by Dr. RŒMER from Texas, and from other sources, all or several of the species cited above, as well as others, have been identified. At the same time all the collections which have fallen under my observation have not afforded any characteristic species of the Lower Carboniferous limestones, or from those of the age of the limestones of the Mississippi valley, previously described. Notwithstanding, therefore, that the Lower Carboniferous limestone has been citėd as occurring in the region of the Rocky mountain range, there appears thus far no evidences of its existence in that region*.

From a comparison of the fossils, we must conclude that the great limestone formations which are known at numerous intervals, and extending for long distances continuously in the Rocky mountains, and which extend not only from the northern limits of the United States, but from the shores of the Great Northern Ocean to the Gulf of Mexico, are of the same age, and are parts of the same formation which in the Coal measures of Ohio is marked by a band of limestone of a few feet in thickness.

* The *Productus semireticulatus*, and a few others which are species known to have a wide geographical range, have been brought, with other fossils characteristic of the higher Carboniferous limestones, from some localities near the Rocky mountains. This fact shows that these species have a greater geological range than most of the Lower Carboniferous forms, or that the Lower Carboniferous strata occur in the same neighborhood. The same species have also been cited, on good authority, as occurring in the Coal measures.

The limestone of the Rocky mountains is represented by Capt. STANSBURY, and others, as forming the greater part of mountain ranges which have an elevation of three thousand feet above the plain; and similar observations have been made along the line of the Boundary Survey in Mexico. This limestone, which has been identified by its fossils as occurring near Fort Laramie and in the neighborhood of Great Salt lake, is known in like manner from collections made near Santa Fe, New-Mexico; at the Pecos village; the Mogollan mountains; at El Paso on the river San Pedro; and in the Guadaloupe mountains, and other localities: and from the massiveness and compact texture of many specimens, and the subcrystalline character of others from the southwest, we are prepared to find that this rock has become much more extensively developed in that direction. The shaly beds which accompany the limestone in the more northern and eastern localities, and are there often more conspicuous than the limestone itself, have so far diminished that they form no striking feature in the topography of the region. We have no information that coal has been found in this connexion; and it is probable that both the coal and the shaly and arenaceous materials associated with it have thinned out in that direction, or become of such tenuity as to be of no importance.

In connexion with the description of these formations, may properly be introduced the following remarks on the same subject*.

"The relations of this limestone to the Lower Coal measures, in the States bordering the Mississippi river, render its occurrence a subject of interesting economical enquiry. Since we know that the most extensive and valuable beds of coal in the West are of the Lower Coal measures which lie beneath the upper limestone, they may still be found to

* Report on the Geology and Palæontology of the Mexican Boundary Survey, by JAMES HALL, p. 124.

underlie the Carboniferous limestone of the Rocky mountains, as they do the same limestone in Kansas, Missouri, Iowa, Illinois and Indiana. Thus far I am not aware that any inquiries of this kind have been instituted in the explorations and surveys already made.

" Having thus briefly described the range of the Upper Carboniferous limestone, we may now take a comprehensive view of its conditions and extent. We find that during the Coal period, in the States east of the Mississippi river, thin strata of limestone, or calcareous shale, were deposited. These are charged with brachiopoda of genera characterizing the Carboniferous limestone below the Coal measures, but of species which are, for the most part, distinct and peculiar. So thin and insignificant is this formation, that we can scarcely regard it as the product of a wide and deep ocean. Tracing it westward, however, its importance increases, and from being entirely subordinate to the Coal measures proper, it becomes a characteristic mass ; the calcareous mud mingles with the coal, and the latter becomes subordinate to the limestone and calcareous shales. Still farther west it is a vast limestone formation, next in importance to the great calcareous formation below the coal, or Lower Carboniferous limestone.

" The conditions favorable to the production of an extensive deposit of marine limestone are not such as usually accompany the production of coal. In the present instance, the ocean, depositing the great limestone formations previous to the Coal period, occupied to a great extent the present area of the Coal measures which succeeded in the valley of the Mississippi. Land plants in excessive growth, estuary or shallow-water shells, attend the production of coal and its associated strata. We begin thus to comprehend the truth, that during the period of the great Coal formations of the West, in which these calcareous deposits were in course of formation — that during the oscillations which we know to have occurred throughout the Coal period, there was a time when the whole area became depressed so as to allow the waters of the western ocean to flow over all the Coal-measure region, or, at least, as far northward and eastward as the northeastern part of Ohio; and from hence is derived the limestone under consideration. The calcareous bands deposited along the northeastern margin of this ocean we now find interstratified with seams of coal, and beds of shale and sandstone containing land plants; while, as the waters deepened towards the west and southwest, the formation exhibits the differences of character which we would necessarily expect to find in an ocean deposit.

"The evidences of the existence of this ocean in the far west and southwest during the Coal period amount to almost a proof that the conditions of that area, which now constitutes a part of the continent, were never such as to admit of the production of coal plants and the deposition of such materials as make up the coal measures, at least during the latter part of the Coal period. In regard to the earlier part of that period, or the time in which the lower coal measures were formed, we have not, at present, as I conceive, the means of fully deciding what were the conditions in the central and soutwestern part of our continent."

These facts, the result of so many observations, and coincident over so vast an area in the west, confirm conclusions drawn from other sources, that the dry land and land plants first appeared in the eastern part of the continent. Indeed we have good reason to believe that dry land existed in proximity to our present continent on the east from the earliest geological time, as shown in the vast accumulation of materials in the Laurentian and Huronian periods.

The Potsdam sandstone, it is true, seems to be almost equally spread out over the entire breadth of the country, from the slopes of the Rocky mountains, to the Atlantic;

and judging from its augmenting thickness in many western localities, we may expect to find it, either in its normal condition or as a metamorphic rock, strongly developed in some parts of the Rocky mountains*. Subsequent to this period, however, every sedimentary formation indicates the proximity of land on the east. The great thickness of strata, coarse materials, and numerous fucoids of the Hudson-river group in its eastern extension, indicate proximity to land, or the course of strong currents; while in the west the formation dies out in some inconspicuous fine shaly and calcareous beds, which, both in the nature and condition of the material and in the fossil contents, indicate great distance from land and a quiet ocean. The Clinton group, in like manner, in its coarse materials and abundant fucoids, points to a littoral condition of its area of deposition in the east; while it gradually diminishes in its westerd extension, and is finally altogether lost in that direction.

In the sedimentary rocks of the Devonian period, including the Hamilton, Portage, Chemung and Catskill mountain groups, we find in Canada and Eastern New-York the first appearance of land plants, some of which closely resemble plants of the Coal period; and it was at that time that this peculiar vegetation began its existence on this continent, where we now find its remains in strata of these several groups.

Notwithstanding this great accumulation of land-derived material with its marine shells, gradually decreasing westward as calcareous deposits increase — its numerous fucoids and land plants, the whole series has diminished to less than two hundred feet of marine sedimentary deposits in the Mississippi valley, and is there marked by marine fossils only.

We cannot expect that the Coal formation, with its land-derived materials and its abundant land plants — far more

* See Note on page 145.

abundant in the east than in the west — will prove an exception to this general rule; and when we find that these strata have a thickness of more than fourteen thousand feet in Nova-Scotia, according to the measurements of Sir W. E. Logan; that the productive coal measures in Cape-Breton are estimated by Mr. Brown to exceed ten thousand feet; and that in Pennsylvania, the coal measures, including the conglomerate, may be about eight thousand feet, and in the Mississippi valley one thousand feet, we are forced to the conclusion already suggested of the ultimate disappearance of the Coal measures in that direction.

It would therefore appear, that from the earliest Silurian times, the Great West, or the region of the Rocky Mountains, has been an ocean, which successively received the finer sediments derived from eastern lands, or which produced within its own area the calcareous deposits, but ever an ocean, not only to the close of the Carboniferous period, but still later through the Permian, Jurassic and Cretaceous periods; showing apparently no evidences of dry land till about the beginning of the Cretaceous era, or perhaps a little earlier; while in later Tertiary periods, the continental fauna and flora have been remarkably developed over the same area.

Thus while the older Palæozoic formations have been largely accumulated in the east, in successive beds, having altogether a thickness of several times the height of our highest mountains, they have greatly diminished in the west. At the same time, while the Post-palæozoic formations are very thin or often absent in the east, they have accumulated in vast amount along the line of the Rocky mountains, from one end of the continent to the other.

SUPRA-CARBONIFEROUS FORMATIONS OF IOWA.

Although there have been no careful examinations in the western part of the State of Iowa, we are nevertheless prepared from previous information to find geological formations of newer date than the Coal period*.

The Gypsum beds of the Des Moines valley, which are placed by Dr. OWEN in the Coal measures, appear, from some examinations already made, to be but doubtfully connected with that formation, and to hold a position intermediate to that and the Cretaceous formation above.

In the early part of 1857, Mr. WORTHEN placed in the hands of the writer some peculiar fossils, collected several years since in Illinois, and supposed to be from the Coal measures. These, however, were at once recognized as of peculiar forms differing from Coal-measure fossils; and a farther examination proves them to be of Permian types, and closely allied to British species†. From these and other facts, we infer the existence of the Permian system in the southeastern part of Illinois, while we have also some evidence of the occurrence in Western Iowa of the same formation, with which we have reasons to suppose the gypsum beds are intimately related. These facts increase the interest of geological investigations in the west, and show the existence of the

* The occurrence of the Cretaceous formation in Iowa and the adjoining territories had been made known by the previous explorations of several parties, and is shown upon the geological map accompanying the Report of Dr. D. D. OWEN as low down on the Missouri as the mouth of Sioux river (Memoirs of the American Academy of Arts and Sciences, Vol. v, New series; Geological Report of the United States and Mexican Boundary Survey). See also SILLIMAN'S American Journal of Science and Arts, Vol. xxiv, 2d series, July 1857; and Proceedings of the Academy of Natural Sciences, Philadelphia, etc., for Notices of the Cretaceous strata of the United States.

† They are of the Genera *Pleurophorus*, *Mytilus*, *Monotis*, and *Pecten*. A farther notice of these fossils will be found under the head of Palæontology in the subsequent pages of this Report.

entire Palæozoic series in this discovery of its most recent member*.

We have not yet sufficient knowledge of the relations between the beds containing Permian fossils and those of the Carboniferous period, to speak with certainty of the character of this sequence, or whether the two are conformable with each other in their stratification, though we infer a want of conformity.

The higher beds of the Coal measure-limestones are sometimes of a reddish or brownish color, corresponding in this respect to the limestone mentioned by Mr. SALTER as brought from Albert land, in North latitude 78°; and we infer from the fossils cited as occurring in this and other northern localities, that the limestone there termed "Carboniferous limestone" is in truth a continuation of the limestone of the Rocky mountains, or the Carboniferous limestone of the Coal-measure epoch. This limestone, in its more northern localities, presents in its higher beds much variation in color and texture; and we shall not be surprised to find a close similarity of character, if not an absolute continuity, between the beds of Carboniferous age below and the Permian above. The Illinois fossils referred to Permian types are, however, in a micaceous sandstone, not unlike a true Coal-measure sandstone, so that we have already evidence of considerable variety of composition in the materials referred to Permian age.

The great development of the lower member of the Cretaceous formation in Western Iowa and the adjoining Territories of Kansas and Nebraska, and its extension below the

* While these pages are passing through the press, Prof. SWALLOW has published in the American Journal of Science a notice of the discovery of Permian fossils by Mr. F. HAWN in Kansas, during the present year; and almost at the same time, March 2d, Messrs. MEEK and HAYDEN have read a paper before the Albany Institute, upon some Permian fossils sent from Kansas by Mr. HAWN, and others collected by Dr. HAYDEN in Nebraska, and by Dr. J. G. COOPER in Kansas; so that the Permian system is now known at several points over an extent of more than ten degrees of longitude and at least four degrees of latitude.

line where any well marked cretaceous species have been found, suggests very strongly that we shall yet find lower geological formations, or those of the age of the Jura, or Oolite of Europe. The discovery by Dr. HAYDEN of a species of the Genus HETTANGIA (which is regarded in Europe as of Jurassic age), at the mouth of the Judith river on the Upper Missouri, though associated with other unmistakable cretaceous fossils, points to the probable discovery of strata of Jurassic age in this region. The discovery of Oolitic or Liassic rocks in Exmouth island by Captain BELCHER, referred to by Mr. SALTER* in the paper previously cited, is very significant. He also mentions the discovery by Capt. M'CLINTOCK in Prince Patrick's land, lat. 76° 30′, long. 117° W, of Oolitic or Liassic fossils, *Ammonites*, *Spirifer*, *Pecten*, etc. These localities correspond to the northerly trend of the Carboniferous limestone of the Rocky mountain region, and the accompanying supra-carboniferous formations.

The great thickness of sandstones and marls shown by Mr. MARCOU in his section of Pyramid mountain, an outlier of the Llano Estacado, below any well marked cretaceous fossils, when taken in connexion with the facts above stated and others lately brought out by collections made much farther to the south, indicate the probable occurrence of lower fossiliferous rocks, or those of the Jurassic age, along the whole length of the Rocky mountains, and probably coextensive with the lower member of the Cretaceous system.

Thus far the collections made in the explorations across this western country have brought us no true Jurassic fossils, and it is only in the far north, and upon the Pacific coast, as well also as in the southern extremity of the continent, that we have the evidences of the existence of these rocks below the Cretaceous formation.

* "On some additions to the Geology of the Arctic Regions", by J. W. SALTER, F.G.S. See Report of the British Association for the Advancement of Science for 1855.

It should not be forgotten, moreover, that in the sections made along the eastern slope of the Rocky mountains and upon the Missouri and its tributaries, no absolute continuity has been traced, and the hiatus which is admitted between the Carboniferous limestones of the Coal-measure epoch and the true Cretaceous deposits is great enough to allow of the existence of all the intermediate formations.

The investigations of these formations, including the completion of the examinations in the coal field, will form the subject of a subsequent volume.

The geological formations of greatest economical importance in the State of Iowa, are the Galena or lead-bearing limestone, the Coal formation, and the Gypsum formation. All the intermediate rocks are more or less calcareous, affording abundance of lime and ordinary building stone, and some of them hydraulic cement.

The formations throughout the southern, eastern and central parts of the State, are all of such a character as to produce soils of immense agricultural capacities; and the geological structure of the State clearly indicates that her agricultural products, her coal mines, and beds of gypsum, will constitute her greatness of resourses and her future wealth.

NOTE REFERRED TO ON PAGE 140.

The Reports of Messrs. FOSTER and WHITNEY, and of Dr. D. D. OWEN, on the Lake Superior District, as well as several Mining Reports by S. W. HILL, esquire, and others, of parts of the same district, show an enormous accumulation of material in that region during the period of the Potsdam sandstone formation. Not only from the measurements there made, but from the phenomena accompanying the deposition of the sandstone and associated shales and conglomerates, I infer that the greatest thickness of this rock will be found in that district. At the same time the measurements made farther to the west, together with the occurrence of similar phenomena to those upon Lake Superior, show that the same formation maintains a great thickness far to the west of the Mississippi river.

GEOLOGICAL MAP AND SECTIONS.

The preceding descriptions of the geological formations are illustrated by a geological map of the eastern half of the State, showing the extent of these successive formations as far as they have been traced into the interior. Some of these have not been traced to the northern limits of the State, and this condition of the investigation is indicated by the absence of color in those parts of the map. In a few instances the great accumulation of drift and prairie formations has so completely obscured the line of junction of two formations, that the limits cannot be safely indicated until more detailed observations have been made : these parts are likewise left uncolored.

Several outliers of the Coal measures are shown beyond the general northeastern limits of the formation, resting unconformably upon the Carboniferous limestone, the Devonian and Silurian formations as already described. Some portions of the Coal formation in the southern part of the State have been examined only in a general manner, sufficient to determine the occurrence of these strata as colored upon the map.

The geological sections embrace the results of an examination of the rocks along the Mississippi valley, from the north line of the State, to the mouth of the Des Moines river ; and in order to show the entire series of the Carboniferous limestones as they occur farther down the river, the section (with some interruption) has been extended so far as to include the limestones of Chester and Kaskaskia.

CHAPTER IV.

GEOLOGY OF THE DES MOINES VALLEY.

REPORT OF A. H. WORTHEN,

ASSISTANT GEOLOGIST,

FOR THE YEAR 1856.

TO PROF. JAMES HALL,

STATE GEOLOGIST.

SIR : I herewith submit the result of my examinations during the past season in the Valley of the Des Moines, and along the eastern border of the Iowa coal field, made with a view of determining the number, thickness, and relative value of the different coal seams outcropping in that part of the State.

A. H. WORTHEN, *Assistant Geologist.*

Warsaw (*Illinois*), *December* 1856.

THE first work done was a section from Burlington to the nearest outcrop of coal on Skunk river. Going west from Burlington on the Augusta road, the first rocks seen in place, are exposed on a small branch of Long creek, about two and a half miles northeast of Augusta and about three-quarters of a mile in a direct line north of Skunk river.

At this point I found the Lower Archimedes or Keokuk limestone exposed about sixteen feet in thickness, and overlaid by twelve feet of blue marly clay containing geodes.

One and a half miles below Augusta, at the mouth of Long creek, I found the Burlington beds in place, giving the following section :

	Brown and gray crinoidal limestone	52 feet.
CHEMUNG GROUP.	Light gray limestone	1 foot.
	Oolitic band	2 feet.
	Unexposed	35 feet.

On the south side of Skunk river, opposite the town of Augusta, the Burlington limestone forms a bluff eighty feet in height, composed of gray and brown limestone, with cherty bands intercalated, and rich in fossil remains, among which the following species were identified. *Actinocrinus verneuilianus*, *A. rotundus*, *A. pyriformis*, *A. christyi*, *A. unicorni*, *Platycrinus planus*, *P. corrugatus*, *Pentremites elongatus*, *P. melo*, *P. norwoodi*, *Spirifer sowerbyi*, *S. ventricosus*, *S. forbesi*, *Terebratula lamellosa*, and several species of corals. In the upper part of the bluff at this point, and about twelve feet from the top, a thin band of limestone is seen densely filled with remains of fishes, consisting of jaw and palate teeth and spines. This seems to be identical in position with the fish bed previously observed at Quincy and on Honey creek in Illinois, and is the lowest of the three already known in the mountain limestone of this region.

One mile above Augusta, on the north side of Skunk river, following up a small creek, the following section was made :

Brown slaty limestone	6 feet.
Concretionary limestone	18 feet.
Magnesian limestone	5 feet.
Blue and yellow marlites with geodes	40 feet.
Grey cherty limestones, containing the fossils common to the lower beds at Keokuk	50 to 60 ft.

From the foregoing sections it will be seen that the whole series of mountain limestone beds, from the base of the Burlington crinoidal to the concretionary limestone, are found *in situ* within one mile of Augusta, but thinned out so that the whole series does not occupy a stratigraphical thickness exceeding two hundred feet. Detached blocks of quartzose sandstone were observed in this vicinity, undoubtedly belonging to a higher bed, and which probably appertains to the Coal measures.

Five miles above Augusta at Wilson's mill on Skunk river, the Keokuk limestone crops out in the river bluff from ten to fifteen feet in thickness, and is overlaid a short distance back from the river by the geode bed, which is only partially exposed. Isolated blocks of the concretionary bed were also abundant, indicating its presence, though it was not seen in place here.

On the northeast quarter of Section 14 in Township 69, Range 5 (Pleasant-ridge), a thin seam of coal has been opened at several points, the coal varying from 10 to 14 inches in thickness. This is overlaid by a slaty clay resembling a fire clay, and is underlaid by about six feet of bituminous shale and shaly sandstone, the latter resting directly upon the limestone. The upper layers of this limestone are regularly bedded in strata from four to eight inches thick, compact, and of a light grey color, affording an excellent building material as well as lime of superior quality.

At Lowell, just below the mill-dam, the upper layers of the Keokuk limestone may be seen at low water; and from the loose material thrown out in constructing the mill-race, I obtained several fish teeth, as well as the small *Spirifer* so common in the Keokuk beds. About half a mile below the town, at the mouth of the creek, the following section was made :

Light grey compact limestone	12 feet.
Buff-colored magnesian limestone	16 feet.
Brecciated arenaceous limestone	24 feet.
Unexposed	15 feet.
Blue marlites of the Geode bed extending to the river level .	26 feet.

The two upper beds in the foregoing section afford very good building material, the upper limestone being pretty regularly bedded in layers from four to twelve inches thick, while the magnesian bed affords strata from fifteen to eighteen inches in thickness. Overlying these beds were indications of the presence of the quartzose sandstone, though it was for the most part hidden under the drift deposits.

From this point I went out to the neighborhood of Salem, to examine a seam of cannel coal reported to have been recently opened there. At the crossing of Pilot creek on the road to Salem, and four miles from Lowell, I found the beds in the foregoing section outcropping in the bluffs of the creek. The next exposure of rocks seen in place was on Cedar creek, three miles west of Salem, near the bridge, where the following section was made :

Light grey regularly-bedded limestone	10 feet.
Magnesian limestone in layers from 6 to 12 inches thick,	9 feet.
Shaly magnesian limestone	8 feet.
Green argillaceous shale	6 feet.
Band of limestone	1 foot.
Geode bed extending below the level of the creek . .	17 feet.

One mile west of Cedar creek, on the lands of Drs. Eaton and Rodgers, I found the seam of cannel coal above refered to. The best exposure to be seen at this time showed the following beds. First, black slate five to six feet thick, with a thin seam of cannel coal from four to five inches in thickness, intercalated in the slate. This was underlaid by a band of Ferruginous sandstone about one foot thick, and the whole resting upon a bed of gray shale of which about six feet only was exposed, as shown in the following section :

Black slate . . . . Cannel coal 5 inches . Black slate	. . . . 6 feet.
Ferruginous sandstone	1 foot.
Grey shale	6 feet.

Two miles southwest of Salem, on Little Cedar, the limestone equivalent to the upper bed in the foregoing section on Cedar creek, is quarried extensively for building purposes and for lime. Here it is a compact light grey limestone, breaking with a smooth conchoidal fracture ; regularly bedded, in layers from four to six inches thick. Between the layers of limestone are marly partings, which contain one species of *Spirifer*, two or three species of *Terebratula* and a *Productus*, all in a fine state of preservation.

Three and a half miles northwest of Hillsborough on the lands of Mr. Martin, an interesting exposure of coal may be seen in connection with the following beds :

Fig. 12.

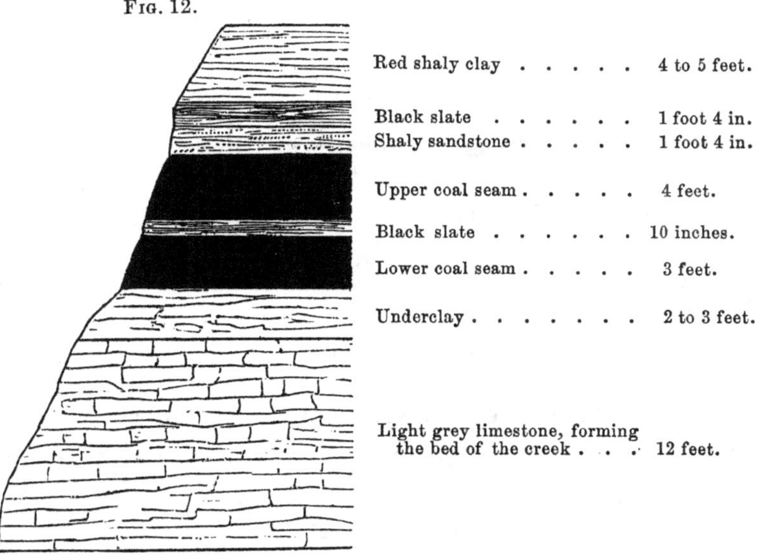

These two coal seams approach so near together that they may be wrought as one; and a drift has been made into the hill in a westerly direction by the present owner, and a sufficient amount of coal has been taken out each season to supply the demand of the neighborhood. Being away from any navigable stream or line of railroad, the demand for coal is not so great as to justify the working on a large scale.

At the time of my visit, the drift was partially filled with water and consequently inaccessible, and I was unable from this cause to obtain specimens of this coal; but through the kindness of Mr. Martin, specimens for the State Collection and for analysis have since been received through Messrs. Chittenden and M'Gavic of Keokuk.

Agreeable to your instructions, the next work undertaken was a section up the Des Moines river.

Crossing the Mississippi at Warsaw and ascending the Des Moines, the first rocks seen in place are found at St. Francisville, on the south side of the Des Moines river, where the following section was made:

Light grey regularly-bedded limestone containing *Lithostrotion*	14 feet.
Impure concretionary and siliceous? limestone	10 feet.
Brown arenaceous limestone, with veins of calcareous spar	2 to 4 feet.
Argillaceous and siliceous rock, brecciated and concretionary, without fossils	24 feet.
Regularly-bedded magnesian limestone	5½ feet.
Argillaceous and marly bed, with bands of impure limestone containing geodes of quartz crystals, calcareous spar and chalcedony	40 feet.
Keokuk limestone, with *Archimedes oweni*, fish teeth, etc.	15 to 20 ft.

The lower part of the Geode bed is here quite calcareous, and passes almost imperceptibly into the Keokuk limestone below. The upper part is very argillaceous, and is filled with geodes, many of which contain magnificent crystals of calcareous spar or dolomite, and occasionally, minute crystals of zinc blende and sulphuret of iron. The magnesian limestone bed is quite thin in the immediate vicinity of the town of St. Francisville; but one mile above, it is from ten to twelve feet thick, and has been quarried extensively for the construction of the locks and dam at this place. As this rock usually hardens on exposure to the weather, and can be obtained in blocks of suitable thickness, it is well adapted to works of this kind where strength and durability are the great ends sought.

The bed overlying the magnesian limestone occupies the place, and is undoubtedly the representative of the Warsaw Archimedes limestone, and yet very dissimilar in aspect and in constituent material at these two localities, though only some seven or eight miles apart.

At Warsaw, this bed consists of bands of blue marly clay, with intercalations of limestone, and the whole filled with fossils in the greatest abundance, especially corals. At St. Francisville, we have a rough siliceous rock, brecciated and concretionary, without regular lines of bedding, utterly worthless for all economical purposes, and entirely destitute of fossil remains. Here we have a striking example of the changes that may take place in the lithological characters of the same bed in the distance of only a few miles.

Crossing the Des Moines at St. Francisville and ascending the river on the north side, the first rocks seen in place were found at the crossing of a small creek four miles above the ferry. This was an outcrop of a portion of the concretionary limestone, but not sufficient to afford a good section. The outcrop seen was some thirty or forty feet above the bed of the river.

At Belfast, where Dam No. 2 was in process of construction, extensive quarries have been opened in the magnesian bed, and the rocks at this point afford the following section :

Concretionary limestone, partially exposed	25 to 30 ft.
Thin-bedded gray limestone	10 to 12 ft.
Massive magnesian limestone, some layers very arenaceous .	14 feet.
Unexposed	25 feet.

The gray limestone overlying the magnesian bed in the foregoing section, is thin-bedded in layers of from one to six inches.

The magnesian bed is tolerably massive, affording layers from sixteen to twenty-four inches thick, and is used for constructing the lock and dam at this point. In the bed of the creek just above the dam, the blue argillaceous marlites of the geode bed crop out at the base of the bluff, and undoubtedly occupy the lower twenty-five feet in the above section. Three miles above Belfast the magnesian bed is found in place, only ten feet above the river level.

In the bluffs at Croton a good section may be seen of the beds overlying the magnesian bed, presenting considerable variety in their lithological characters, as may be seen by the following section :

Massive quartzose sandstone	6 to 8 ft.
Green and yellow shale	1 ft. 3 in.
Fine-grained gritstone	6 inches.
Coarse ferruginous sandstone	1 ft. 6 in.
Ferruginous shale	8 inches.
Cherty band	6 inches.
Compact sandstone	2 ft. 2 in.
Regularly-bedded gray limestone, in layers 6 to 12 inches thick, the upper part having an oolitic structure . . .	10 ft. 8 in.
Brecciated and concretionary limestone	12 to 15 ft.
Brown arenaceous band	4 ft. 6 in.
Slope unexposed	36 feet.

The material for the construction of the Lock and Dam No. 3 have been mostly obtained from the regularly bedded gray limestone of the above section, and the compact sandstone resting upon it. At one point in the quarry, the concretionary character of the lower bed was observed to extend quite up to the sandstone, rendering the whole mass, for a distance of ten to fifteen feet, entirely worthless for building purposes, and appearing like a dike of concretionary limestone replacing the regular layers above.

In the bluffs on the south side of the Des Moines, just above the town of Farmington, a drift has been made into the hill-side for coal, and the following section was made at this point:

FIG. 13.

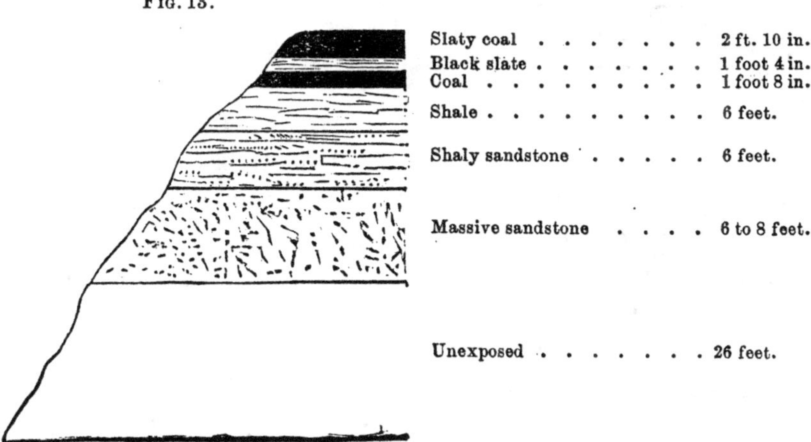

The coal in this section was slaty and poor; and from the fact that the work has been abandoned, it is presumed the quality did not improve on penetrating farther into the bluff.

About two hundred yards higher up the river, the bluff is composed entirely of limestone; and I was at first inclined to believe that there was a fault in the beds, by which the coal had been thrown down; but after a very careful examination, I became satisfied that this state of things was not caused by a fault, but by an irregularity in the limestone deposit, which here forms a trough or basin into which the Coal measures were afterwards deposited. This depression in the limestone appears to extend along the river for two or three miles, in a direction nearly north and south. On the north side of the river, coal is obtained in two localities in this basin: at Williams's, one mile northwest of Farmington; and at Johnson's, one mile below.

FIG. 14.— Section at Williams's coal bank

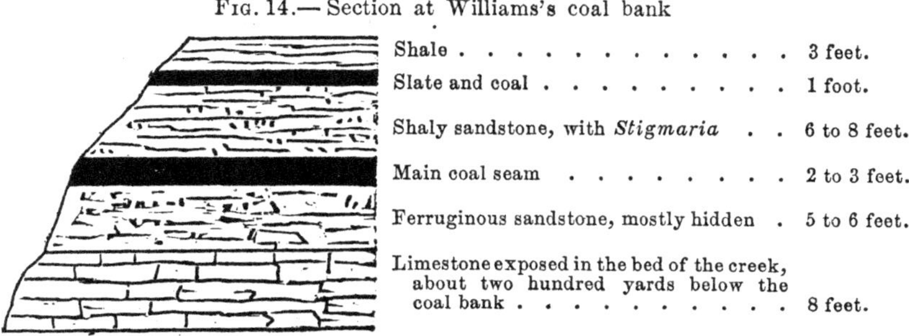

Dr. OWEN, in his Report on the Survey of Iowa, Wisconsin and Minnesota, constructs a section at this point (see his Report, page 107), exhibiting five coal seams in regular order one above the other. A careful examination at this locality gave me no evidence of the existence of the rocks represented in that section.

At Mr. Johnson's coal bank, one mile below Farmington, the seam is about two feet in thickness, and rests upon ferruginous sandstone, and is overlaid by a black slate which was only partially exposed. Up to this time, the coal at this locality has been obtained by stripping the seam of the overlying slate and clay; but Mr. JOHNSON informed me that he was making preparations to drift into the hill, for future supplies.

Three miles above Farmington, and from half to three-quarters of a mile from the Des Moines river at Slaughter's, a coal seam has been opened, and a considerable amount of coal obtained by stripping the seam of the overlying beds.

A section from the river to this point shows the following beds :

Shaly clay not measured.	
Coal	1 ft. 8 in.
Shale and shaly sandstone	4 to 6 feet.
Concretionary limestone : the upper part compact and fine-grained, in regular layers from four to twelve inches thick ; the middle and lower part concretionary and arenaceous, some of the lower layers approaching a fine-grained sandstone	72 feet.
Arenaceous magnesian limestone	6 feet.
Marlites of the Geode bed, extending to the level of the Des Moines river at the mouth of the creek	25 to 30 ft

The Concretionary limestone attains a greater thickness here, than at any point where it has fallen under my notice, and affords an excellent and abundant building material.

Ascending the Des Moines river from Farmington, there is an undulation in the dip of the rocks which brings the lower limestones to the surface ; and at the lime kilns, a half mile below Bonaparte, the rocks afford the following section :

Ferruginous quartzose sandstone	8 feet.
Concretionary limestone	12 feet.
Thin-bedded magnesian limestone	12 feet.
Geode bed but partially exposed	30 feet
Grey cherty limestone with seams of marlite, the equivalent of the Keokuk or Lower Archimedes limestone	66 feet.

These lower beds did not appear to be as rich in fossils at this point as at Keokuk ; but a few very characteristic ones were obtained, among which were the large *Orthis* referred by Dr. OWEN to *O. umbraculum*, *Spirifer striatus*, *S. imbricatus*, *S. ovalis*, and the tail of a *Phillipsia*.

The building material at Bonaparte is obtained from these lower lay rs, which afford a regularly bedded rock of good quality. The upper layers, which furnish the material for all the locks and dams below this point, are here of a very inferior quality, and the beds much thinner than at the points below. These limestones form the bluffs on the north side of the Des Moines to Bentonsport, where the following section is made :

Section at Bentonsport.

Quartzose sandstone	6 feet.
Outcropping of cherty nodules, with *Lithostrotion* . . .	4 – 6 ft.
Brown magnesian limestone in strata from 6 to 20 inches thick,	8 – 10 ft.
Slope hidden. Geode bed in part?	43 feet.
Yellowish marly limestone with cherty seams, and geodiferous,	14 feet.
Regularly-bedded bluish-grey limestones with marly partings, the strata varying from four to twenty inches in thickness,	16 feet.
Light-grey cherty limestones exposed about one mile below the town, and extending below the river level . . .	44 feet.

The lowest bed in the above section presents a similar appearance, and is undoubtedly equivalent, to the cherty beds at Nauvoo and on Hyde's creek three miles above Warsaw, Illinois. These beds underlie the Lower Archimedes or Keokuk limestones, and form the beds of passage into the Burlington crinoidal limestones below.

The bed overlying this is the one from which the building material is mostly obtained at this point; and it presents here nearly the same lithological characters as at Keokuk, as well as the same fossils. From a comparison of this section with the one made at Slaughter's, three miles above Farmington, it will be observed that the concretionary limestone, which is there seventy-two feet in thickness, is here represented by only a few feet of chert and hornstone, but preserving its identity in the fossil coral, the *Lithostrotion*, which seems to appertain almost everywhere to this bed.

At several points in the vicinity of the town, a thin seam of coal has been opened immediately above and usually resting upon the sandstone of the foregoing section.

Crossing over to Vernon on the south side of the river, the same beds were found in place, with the sandstone capping the hill.

Four and a half miles above Bentonsport, the magnesian and concretionary limestone forms a cliff from forty to fifty feet in height, overlaid by the sandstone of the foregoing section.

A mile below Keosauqua, the massive layers of the Magnesian limestone crop out in the bed of the river, in strata from one to two feet in thickness.

Section of the Rocks exposed in the vicinity of Keosauqua.

Black slate	4 feet.
Slaty coal	2 feet.
Shale and shaly sandstone	4 to 6 ft.
Compact grey limestone tolerably regularly bedded in layers from six to sixteen inches thick, with seams of green and blue argillaceous matter	25 – 30 ft.
Concretionary arenaceous bed	20 feet.
Magnesian limestone one mile below the town, at the river level,	6 – 8 feet.

The upper limestone in the above section is by far the most important in an economical point of view, affording an excellent building material for the construction of the lock and dam at this place. The thin argillaceous partings between the layers of limestone were crowded with the fossilized remains of mollusks, affording several species, and a great number of individuals in a very fine state of preservation. The coal in the seam outcropping on the south side of the river is of an inferior quality, and too thin to pay for extensive working.

From Keosauqua to Philadelphia, the road leaves the river; and no rocks were seen, until at the latter point, where the following section was made at the mouth of Lick creek:

Ferruginous shale	6 feet.
Black slate and coaly matter	2 – 3 feet.
Shale and shaly sandstone	6 – 8 feet.
Grey concretionary limestone	20 feet.
Brown magnesian regularly-bedded limestone .	24 feet.
Unexposed	20 feet.
Slaty limestone and marlite, with geodes . .	22 feet.

The upper part of the concretionary bed is at this place quite slaty and arenaceous; the lower part, brecciated and concretionary, rendering the rock comparatively worthless as a building material. The magnesian bed would, however, afford here an abundant supply of "dimension rock" for heavy masonry.

About two miles above Philadelphia, a quarry has been opened in the concretionary limestone, and it affords here a tolerable building stone in layers of six to twelve inches thick. It is, however, quite irregularly bedded, and presents the cross lines of deposition which are characteristic of this bed in the vicinity of Alton (Illinois) and St.Louis (Mo.).

Opposite the town of Portland and about one mile back from the river, a coal seam crops out on the lands of Mr. Harrington, in connection with the following beds:

Fig. 15.

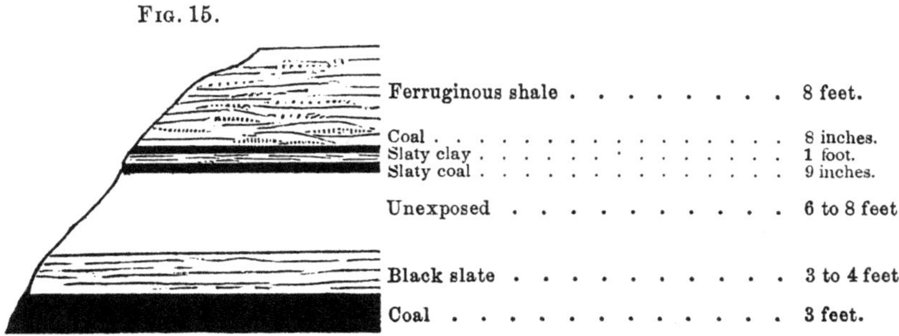

Just below this exposure is a stratum of dark blue limestone resembling a hydraulic limestone, about two feet in thickness.

The coal seam in the above section has been opened at several places in this vicinity. On the opposite side of the river, the concretionary limestone forms a low bluff from twenty to thirty feet above the river level.

Two miles below Iowaville, on the south side of the river, at Manhard's coal bank, the following section was made :

FIG. 16.

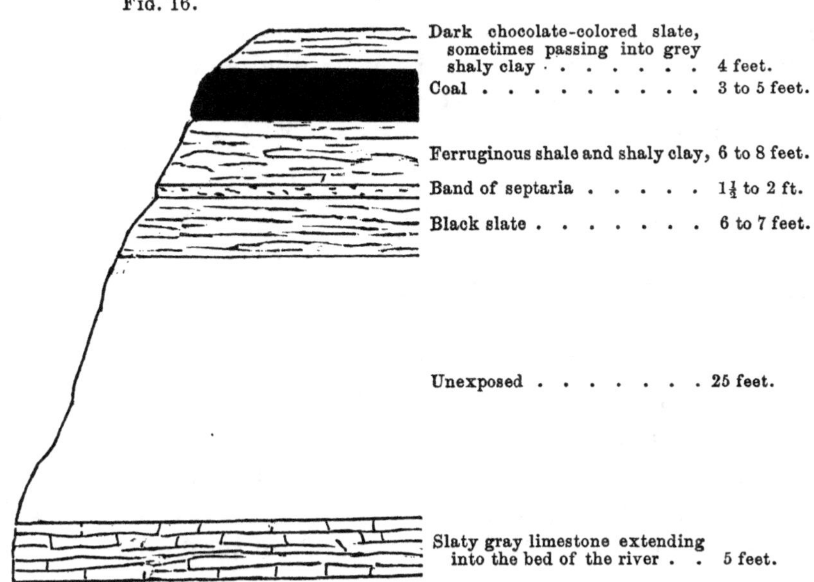

This coal seam has been opened at several places along the river bluff within a distance of one mile, and presents considerable variation in its thickness; being at some points only about three feet thick, and at others nearly or quite five feet. At Iowaville, this coal seam, with the underlying beds, passes beneath the river level, but only for a short distance : the concretionary limestone comes to the surface again one mile above Iowaville, and a quarry has been opened, exposing from six to eight feet of the upper portion.

Crystals of sulphuret of iron, of a bright yellow color, are thickly disseminated through some layers of the limestone at this point. It also contains the same species of *Spirifer* and *Terebratula*, so abundant at Keosauqua.

At the base of the quarry there is a seam of "cone in cone", or *tutenmergel*, about three inches thick, intercalated in the limestone.

After leaving this quarry, the limestone disappears; and the next rock seen in place was a band of brown arenaceous limestone about two feet in thickness, which first makes its appearance about three miles below Dam No. 11, and about ten feet above the river level. A half mile below the dam, this rock has been extensively quarried for the construction of the lock at this point. Among the fossils obtained were species of the Genera *Nautilus*, *Bellerophon*, *Macrocheilus*, *Allorisma*, and *Productus*; all characteristic coal fossils, and most of them specifically identical with those already known from the Coal measures of Illinois and Missouri.

This limestone is underlaid by a bed of fire clay, of which only about one foot of the upper portion was exposed. On the surface of some of the blocks of limestone taken from this quarry, stems of *Stigmaria* and fragments of fossil wood are seen, imbedded with the marine shells and corals. The rock itself is filled with small cavities, which seem to have been formed by the decomposition of crystals of sulphuret of iron.

Just at the dam, a quarry has been opened in a soft quartzose sandstone from three to four feet in thickness, which probably overlies the abovementioned limestone. This sandstone was so soft and friable that it was with some difficulty that a good hand specimen could be obtained, and it is entirely unfit for the construction of any permanent work.

A half mile above the town of Alpine, a bluff of sandstone juts into the river, presenting the following section :

Section half a mile above Alpine.

Regularly-bedded micaceous sandstone; the lower part in strata from six inches to two feet thick, and passing upward into shale	55 feet.
Irregularly-bedded sandstone, with seams of slate and coaly matter	30 feet.
Sandstone mostly hidden	13 feet.

In the upper bed, some of the layers were concretionary in structure and exceedingly hard.

About fifty yards below this point, the irregularly bedded sandstone was replaced by black slate and shale, overlaid by a thin band of slaty limestone, somewhat resembling that below the dam.

Finding no road along the Des Moines from this point to Ottumwa, I went by the way of Agency city. The next exposure of rocks seen was on Sugar creek, about one mile from the Des Moines, where the following section was made:

Sandstone	6 feet.
Shale	12 feet.
Black slate	6 to 8 feet.
Coal	1 foot.
Shaly clay	4 to 5 feet.
Slate	2 feet.

Just below this point, coal is obtained on the land of Mr. HARRELL, by stripping the seam along the banks of the creek. The coal is only eighteen inches in thickness, and may be the same seam shown in the above section. Underlying this coal, and outcropping in the bed of the creek, is a band of septaria about two feet thick.

About half a mile below Harrell's, the concretionary limestone makes its appearance in the bed of the creek, overlaid by fifteen to twenty feet of shale and black slate. This creek empties into the Des Moines about two miles below Ottumwa; and at the town it is exposed about twenty-five feet above the river level, and extends across, forming the rapids.

Ascending the creek, the following section may be seen:

Shale	10 to 15 feet.
Sandstone	1 to 2 feet.
Concretionary limestone	25 to 30 feet.

By request of Col. FOSTER, whom I met at Ottumwa, I went out with him to M'Cready's coal bank on Bear creek, four miles west of that place. About two and a half miles from Ottumwa on the Alba road, I found a thin stratum of siliceous limestone and septaria forming the bed of a creek. From this bed I obtained a few shells very much like those in the limestone at Dam No. 11, and it is quite probable the beds hold the same stratigraphical position.

M'Cready's coal bank is on Sec. 20, T. 72, N.R. 14 west; and the beds in connexion with the coal exhibit the following order:

FIG. 17.

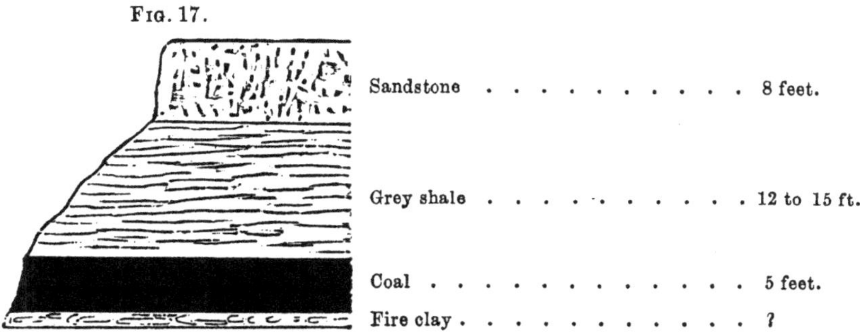

The coal at this point is quite free from sulphuret of iron, and appears to be fully equal or superior to any thing yet found in the State. It is also favorably situated for working; and being on the line of the Burlington and Missouri river railroad, cannot fail of becoming a source of wealth to the owners.

From Ottumwa to Eddyville, the concretionary limestone crops out in the bluffs of all the small creeks flowing into the river from the north, frequently forming a low bluff from fifteen to twenty feet in height. The Des Moines bluffs are only low sloping ridges, with no outcrop of the beds overlying the limestone.

On the south side of the river, nearly opposite Eddyville and about a mile from the town, a coal seam is wrought by Mr. ROBERTS, near the top of the bluff; and at this point I made the following section :

FIG. 18.

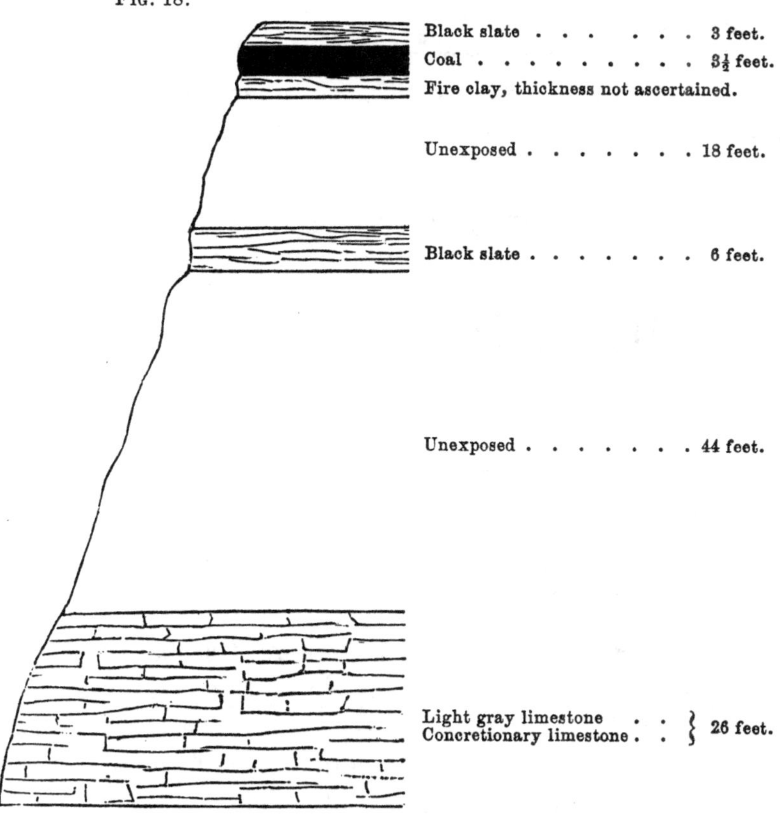

The limestone forming the base of the section at this point is quite regularly bedded, the strata varying in thickness from two to eighteen inches: it is a fine-grained compact nearly white limestone, breaking with a smooth conchoidal fracture, and is well adapted for building purposes as well as the production of a superior quality of lime. The coal in the seam opened by Mr. ROBERTS appears to be of a fair quality, and is obtained by drifting into the hill. I have very little doubt that another seam exists between this and the limestone at the base of the foregoing section; which fact may be determined by boring, at a very small expense.

From Eddyville the road leaves the river, and winds along the highlands until within two miles of Bellefountain, when it again strikes the river.

On the southeast quarter of S. 11, T. 74, R. 16, the following section was made, showing the exact relative position here of the lower coal seam and the limestone:

FIG. 19.

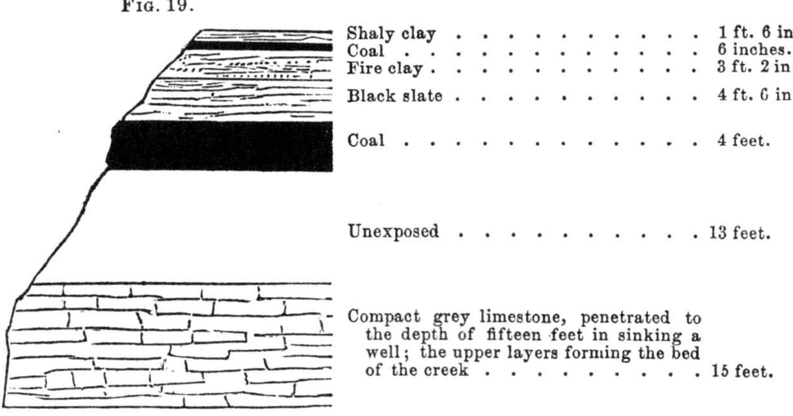

The coal seams in the above section most probably underlie that opened by Mr. ROBERTS opposite Eddyville; as it is hardly possible the strata between the limestone and the coal could have thickened, in the distance of seven or eight miles, from thirteen to near seventy feet.

At Bellefountain, on the south bank of the river, the limestone forms the base of the bluff, and, about one hundred yards above the ferry landing, is twenty-five feet in thickness. It is here concretionary and arenaceous, and nearly valueless for economical purposes. The slope of the hill just above the limestone exhibits masses of quartzose sandstone ; and above this, in sinking wells in the upper part of the town, bituminous slates and shales were passed through to the depth of twenty-five or thirty feet. It is quite probable that one or both of the lower coal seams may be in place in this hill, but covered by a heavy deposit of drift clay and gravel. By boring from the top of the hill down to the limestone, this point could be decided.

At Coalport, on the southwest quarter of S. 14, T. 76, R 19, on the south side of the river, a heavy coal seam outcrops in the face of the bluff, in connection with the following beds :

Fig. 20.

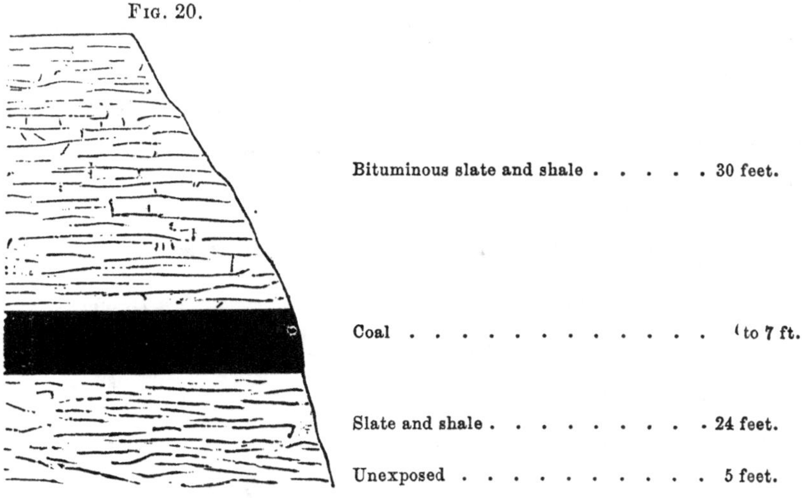

The coal in this seam appears somewhat slaty, especially in the upper part ; but it has only been penetrated for a few feet, and it is probable the quality may improve after reaching a point beyond the influence of atmospheric agencies.

Mr. Welch, the owner of this bank, informed me that another coal seam is sometimes exposed in the river bed, below the rocks in the above section; but at this time it was entirely hidden, either by the water or the debris from the overlying beds.

A half a mile above Amsterdam, the concretionary limestone crops out in the bluff on the north side of the river, at an elevation of twenty to thirty feet above the river level.

Section five and a half miles below Red-rock.

Outcroppings of ferruginous shale and shaly sandstone, partially exposed	20 to 25 ft.
Soft calcareous ? sandstone	8 feet.
Grey arrenaceous limestone, with oolitic bands	14 feet.

A coal seam had been opened near where the above section was made, but being now abandoned, its position with regard to the lower beds was not ascertained.

Within about two miles of Redrock, a bed of sandstone crops out at the base of the bluffs, at first only appearing a few feet in thickness, but rapidly increasing, until in the vicinity of the town it forms a bluff more than one hundred feet in height.

Section of the bluff three-quarters of a mile above the town of Redrock.

Thinbedded ferruginous sandstone	15 feet.
Massive varigated red and yellow sandstone	30 feet.
Hard grey sandstone	5 feet.
Massive brown limestone with nodules of iron ore . .	52 feet.
Concretionary sandstone	6 feet.

The deep brick-red color of a portion of the upper layers of this bluff makes it a striking landmark on the river, and has given name, not only to the village near by, but to the township in which it is situated. It is probable that much of this sandstone will withstand the action of the weather;

and if so, this locality is capable of furnishing sufficient material for all the locks and dams from this point to the mouth of the river. Two miles above, this bed of rock entirely disappears, and is replaced by shales and shaly sandstones ; inducing the opinion that this sandstone is a local deposit, not extending over any great surface of the country, and that it rests directly upon the Concretionary limestone, and occupies the position of the lower coal seams, with thin slates and shales, or perhaps intercalated between them and the limestone below. The limestone outcrops in the bed of the river about two miles below the town of Redrock.

Section at the mouth of Dick's creek, two miles above the Town of Redrock.

Grey shale	8 feet.
Band of septaria in concretionary masses,	1 foot 6 inches.
Impure coal	8 inches.
Shale and shaly sandstone	18 feet.
Black slate, with *Lingula*	1 foot.

The beds in the above section extend down to the level of the Des Moines river, at an ordinary stage of water. On the creek, in Section 21 in Redrock township, the following beds are seen in connection with a four and a half foot seam of coal :

Fig. 21.

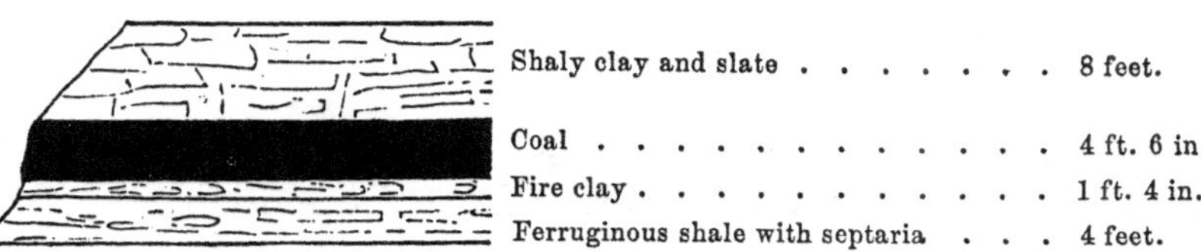

The coal seam in the mouth of the drift dips W. 20° S. at a slight angle. The lower 18 inches of the coal is compact, and appears to be of good quality, while the balance is slaty and poor.

From this point to Bennington, no rocks were seen in place.

Section in the river bluff a quarter of a mile above Bennington.

Ferruginous shaly sandstone, passing upward into shale: some of the lower layers with almond-shaped cavities coated with brown hematite	30 feet.
Black slate	10 feet.
Coal	1 ft. 8 in.
Grey shale and shaly clay, extending below the river level .	12 feet.

From Bennington to Lafayette there is no road along the river, and on the ridge no rocks are seen. A half mile below Lafayette, on the south side of the river, the following section was made.

Loess: marly clay, with land and freshwater shells,	20 feet.
Unexposed	12 feet.
Shaly micaceous sandstone	22 feet.
Blue shale, with limonite	3 feet.
Shale	16 feet.
Shaly sandstone	2 feet.
Bluish grey shale	14 feet.
Unexposed	14 feet.
Hard grey sandstone	1 foot.
Bituminous shale	4 feet.

Finding it impracticable to get along the river with a vehicle, I took the bluff road to Fort Desmoines. At Dr. Brooks's quarry, one mile east of the city, a bed of sandstone is exposed about twenty feet in thickness, and of a somewhat soft texture. A portion of the bed, however, is concretionary; the concretions exceedingly hard and compact, and some of them from ten to fifteen feet in diameter. Nearly all the building rock used at Fort Desmoines is obtained from this bed of sandstone, which has been opened at various places in the neighborhood.

FIG. 22.— Section at J. M. Todd & Co.'s mill, at the upper end of the city of Desmoines.

Soft micaceous sandstone	8 feet.
Compact concretionary sandstone	1 ft. 6 in.
Grey shale and shaly sandstone	10 feet.
Bluish shaly clay	2 feet.
Coal	10 inches.
Sandstone	6 inches.
Slate	6 inches.
Coal	1 ft. 4 inches.
Slate	1 inch.
Coal	1 ft. 6 inches.
Shaly clay	1 ft. 3 inches.
Coal	10 inches.
Shaly clay	5 feet.
Bituminous slate and shale, mostly hidden,	12 feet.

The coal in the above section is rather slaty and poor, though it serves for steam and ordinary purposes tolerably well. A good supply of a much better quality may undoubtedly be obtained by sinking a shaft to the lower seams, which are probably not more than two or three hundred feet below those in the above section. This coal is in a series of four seams, which crop out on the east side of the river a half mile above the town : they are also seen in the bluff on the south side of the river, two miles below.

Two miles above the city, on the east side of the river, a bed of fire clay crops out at the water level, overlaid by a thin band of sandstone containing roots of *Stigmaria.* At the base of the drift deposit here is seen a bed of ferruginous conglomerate about three feet in thickness. Above this, no good exposure of the rocks were seen until we reached Elk rapids, about twenty-five miles above Fort Desmoines.

Section near the mouth of the creek emptying into the river from the west, at Elk rapids.

Grey shale and shaly sandstone	20 feet.
Ash-colored marl, containing *Orthis*, *Productus*, *Chonetes*, *Terebratula*, and joints of crinoids	6 feet.
Grey shale	15 feet.
Dark blue shale	8 inches.
Marly limestone, with *Productus*, *Chonetes*, etc.	10 inches.
Ash-colored shaly clay	4 feet.
Buff-colored arenaceous limestone	4 ft. 6 in.
Unexposed	18 feet.

The uppermost bed in this section contains marine shells in great profusion and in a most perfect state of preservation.

Three miles above Elk rapids, at a mill on the small creek which flows into the Des Moines from the east, the rocks were exposed, giving the following section :

Compact grey sandstone	2 feet.
Grey shaly clay	4 feet.
Massive sandstone	6 feet.
Grey shale	8 feet.
Ferruginous shale	4 feet.
Dark blue slate	4 feet.

These beds were overlaid by a very heavy deposit of drift, forming hills at least one hundred feet in height.

Section at Milford, two and a half miles north of Boonsborough.

Sandstone	4 feet.
Unexposed	6 feet.
Bituminous slate, containing *Lingula* and fossil wood,	8 feet.
Coal	1 foot.
Unexposed	21 feet.
Coal in the bed of the river	1 foot.

The bituminous slate in this section contains large concretions of septaria; one of which, on being broken, was found to contain fish spines and a small species of *Orbicula*.

Most of the coal obtained in this neighborhood is taken from the bed of the stream, where the seams have been laid bare by the current of the river. Along the bluffs the strata are entirely hidden by the heavy deposit of drift clay and gravel, which has been spread in great profusion over the rock strata in this portion of the State.

The next exposure of rocks seen in place was on Deception creek, on the west side of the Des Moines, near the mouth of the creek, and about five miles above the mouth of Boon river.

Section on Deception creek.

Very hard compact sandstone . .	4 feet.
Soft sandstone	8 feet.
Ferruginous shale	10 feet.
Dark blue slate	3 feet.
Coal	10 inches.
Shaly clay	5 feet.

A short distance up the creek, on the other side, a slide had taken place in the drift deposit overlying these beds; exposing about twenty-five feet of the lower part of that formation, which was found to consist here of ten feet of sand, with intercalations of thin irregular masses of sandstone overlaid by fifteen feet of clay and gravel.

On Crooked creek, near the mouth, on the southeast quarter of S. 13, T. 88, R. 28, the following sections were made :

FIG. 23.

Coal	1 ft. 6 in.
Shaly sandstone	7 feet.
Black slate	8 feet.
Coal	1 foot.
Unexposed	12 feet.

A half mile higher up the creek, a bed of shaly clay was exposed by a slide, showing three thin seams of coal, one above the other, as exhibited in the following section:

FIG. 24.

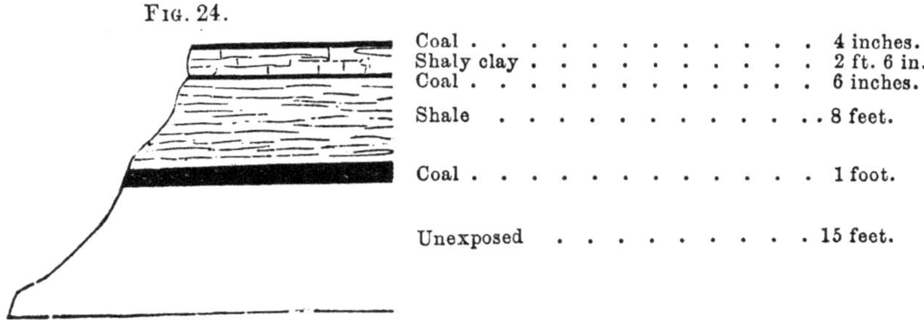

It is probable that the lower seam in this section is equivalent to the upper one in the section above. The coal in the three-feet seam in the first section appears to be of a fair quality, and is favorably situated for mining; the outcrop being sufficiently elevated above the bed of the creek, to allow of thorough draining at a small expense. In the bluffs of the Des Moines, on the east side, nearly opposite the mouth of Crooked creek, a heavy bed of black slate outcrops in connection with a coal seam, which is probably the equivalent of the three-feet seam in the above sections.

On the southeast corner of the northeast quarter of S. 18, T. 88, R. 28, a coal seam, from four and a half to five feet in thickness, outcrops in the bed of a small creek, and is overlaid by a few feet of black slate. The coal contains rather more than an average amount of sulphuret of iron. A short distance down the creek a bed of soft massive sandstone outcrops at apparently a higher level than the coal, and was exposed from ten to fifteen feet in thickness.

Five miles below Fort Dodge, in a ravine on the west side of the Des Moines, the gypsum beds were first met with in the following connection :

Fig. 25.

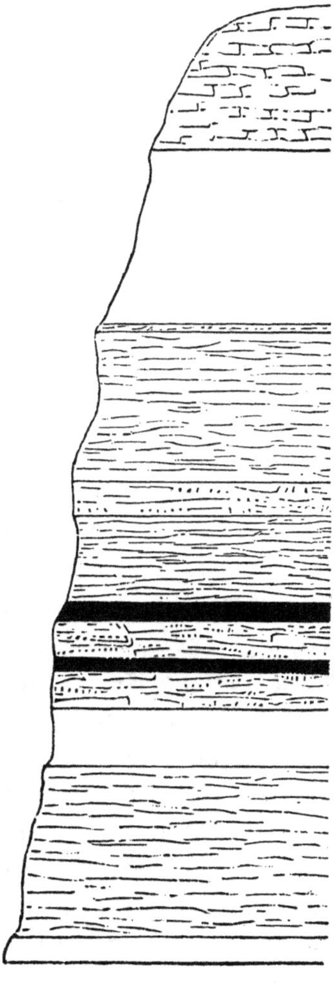

Massive gypsum of a light-grey color, sometimes nearly white	15 feet.
Unexposed	20 feet.
Band of pink shale	10 inches.
Gray shale	16 feet.
Yellow shaly sandstone	4 feet.
Bituminous slates	10 feet.
Coal	1 ft. 6 in.
Shaly sandstone	5 feet.
Coal	1 foot.
Shaly sandstone with stigmaria	4 feet.
Unexposed	8 feet.
Dark blue slate	18 feet.
Unexposed	6 feet.

This section exhibits all the beds from the gypsum down to the level of the river. Overlying the gypsum was a heavy deposit of drift clay and gravel, forming the upper slope of the bluff, and estimated at from forty to fifty feet in thickness.

In the ravine about three hundred yards north of Fort Dodge, a quarry has been opened in the limestone, affording the following section :

Marly clay with nodules of limestone	4 feet.
Compact gray limestone : single stratum	2 ft. 6 in.
Marly clay	2 in.
Soft yellow sandstone	7 feet.
Band of magnesian limestone	2 feet.
Arenaceous limestone : single stratum	1 ft. 6 in.
Compact gray limestone in strata from 4 to 16 inches thick,	4 ft. 6 in.
Arenaceous limestone : single stratum	2 feet.
Unexposed	6 feet.

This is undoubtedly the concretionary limestone bed so frequently met with on the Lower Des Moines; and consequently Fort Dodge occupies exactly the same geological horizon as Ottumwa, Eddyville and Keosauqua. At this quarry no fossils were obtained; but near the mouth of Lizard creek, on the opposite side of the river, the marly clay overlying the limestone is filled with *Spirifer* and *Terebratula*, identical with those obtained at Ottumwa and Keosauqua.

This limestone is well adapted to economical purposes, and these quarries are capable of yielding an inexhaustible supply of excellent building material. The manufacture of lime must at no distant day become a source of profit to this place; as the whole region bordering on the Des Moines, from this to Redrock, appears to be entirely destitute of good limestone. Overlying this limestone at the quarry was a heavy deposit of drift, forming a slope from sixty to eighty feet in height, and entirely concealing the overlying strata. Between this quarry and the mouth of the creek, large blocks of gypsum were observed lying in the bed of the stream, which had probably fallen down from the hill above.

About one mile above Fort Dodge, this limestone crops out along the river bank, and is overlaid by the following beds :

Gypsum	6 feet.
Unexposed	6 feet.
White and ferruginous sandstones .	25 feet.
Dark blue slate	20 feet.
Ferruginous sandstone	5 feet.
Unexposed	4 feet.
Limestone	15 feet.

From a comparison of the above section with the one made five miles below Fort Dodge, where the gypsum beds were first seen, it will be observed that the gypsum is not conformable to or intercalated in the Coal measures, but rather overlies them; and the very interesting question suggests itself at once, as to the age or formation to which it properly belongs. Lying as it does at the base of the drift formation, it has suffered materially from the denuding influences of that period; and the superincumbent strata, if any were originally deposited, which would give a clue to its true position, have been entirely swept away, and the record obliterated. Nevertheless it is to be hoped that a more extended examination over the region occupied by this interesting formation will throw sufficient light upon the subject, to enable us to determine its age with some degree of certainty. As no attempt has been yet made to determine the extent of this gypsum deposit, it may perhaps be considered premature to speak of its value in an economical point of view; but from what is already known, there is very little doubt but that Iowa contains gypsum enough to supply the whole Mississippi valley for centuries to come.

Nearly opposite Fort Dodge, on the opposite side of the river, the limestone disappears with a southwesterly dip, and is overlaid by the rocks of the Coal measures, giving the following section:

Fig. 26.

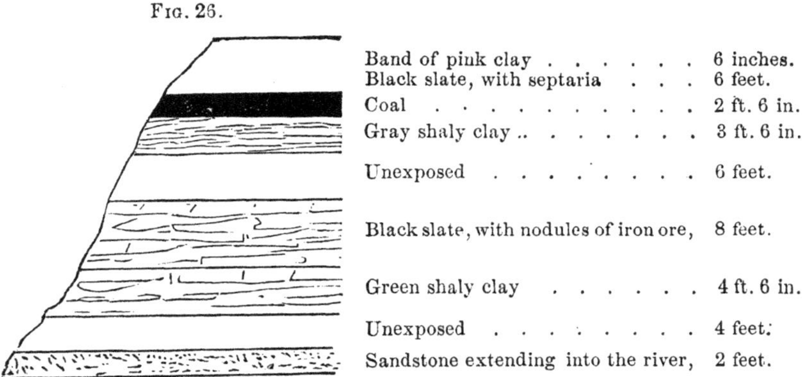

About two hundred yards below this point, the coal seam is thrown down by the dip of the beds within a few feet of the river level, and a drift had just been commenced in it by Mr. Colburn. The coal in the mouth of the drift was from twenty-eight to thirty inches thick, with a band of slate four inches thick near the middle of the seam. Over the coal is a band of cannel coal about two inches thick, which is overlaid by about two feet of black slate approaching cannel coal in its appearance. The coal dips here to the southwest at a slight angle.

The septaria in the black slate of the above section closely resembles a hydraulic limestone in its appearance, and contains a few fossil shells and joints of Crinoidea.

Along the bed of Lizard fork, for half a mile above the mouth, the limestone and overlying marl forms a bluff twenty-five to thirty feet in height. A thin band of hornstone is intercalated in the limestone here, containing casts of *Nucula*, *Productus* and *Bellerophon*. The marl bed above contains three or four species of *Terebratula*, a *Spirifer*, and the tail of a trilobite.

In these examinations on the Des Moines river, from its mouth to Fort Dodge, I have been unable to detect any evidence of the numerous faults and dislocations of the strata, which Dr. OWEN, in his Report on the Geology of the Northwest, remarks as characteristic of the rocks in this region. Indeed I have seen no evidence of the occurrence of a single fault, either in the beds belonging to the Coal measures, or in the underlying limestones. On the contrary, I am constrained to believe that the differences of level at which the same beds appear at various localities are not due to faults or dislocations of the strata, but rather to the undulations of the underlying limestones, and the consequent irregular surface upon which the Coal measures have been deposited.

The concretionary limestone, which everywhere in this region underlies the coal, seems to have been a very irregular deposit, its surface in many cases forming troughs or depressions in which the Coal measures were afterwards deposited; and it is quite probable that all the coal on the north side of the Des Moines river occurs in this way in detached isolated patches or basins, some of them at least of very limited extent, and bounded by the outcroppings of the underlying limestones. This point, however, can only be satisfactorily determined by a very minute and careful examination of all the exposures to be seen along the streams and water-courses between the Des Moines and the Iowa rivers. The coal seams outcropping on the north side of the Des Moines, so far as they have fallen under my notice, are usually thin, rarely more than two and a half to three feet in thickness, and consequently cannot be profitably wrought in competition with those of greater thickness. The only locality I have seen which may be considered as an exception to this, is Martin's coal bank near Hillsborough, where the two lower seams, one three and the other four feet thick, approach so near as to be wrought as one seam. It is to be hoped, however, that further examinations may bring to light other localities, where coal may be obtained with equal facility : if they should not, then Iowa must depend on the region south and west of the Des Moines for a future supply of mineral fuel.

From Fort Dodge, my instructions were to proceed east on the route towards Dubuque, to meet Mr. WHITNEY, who was expected to leave the latter point about this time, and thus together construct a section from Fort Dodge to the Mississippi.

The first rocks seen in place on this route were on Boon river near Webster city, where the same limestone seen at Fort Dodge was found in place, forming a bluff exposure of fifteen to twenty feet in thickness, and passing upward into a soft sandstone. The overlying beds were concealed in the slope of the hill. From this point, no rocks were seen until reaching the Falls of the Iowa, where the following section was made :

Massive brown arenaceous limestone . , ...	25 feet.
Alternating bands of light gray and brown limestone, the light gray bands semioolitic	14 ft. 6 in.
Compact gray limestone resembling the lithographic limestone,	9 feet.
Unexposed	4 feet.

Overlying these beds on the slope of the hill, a thinbedded arenaceous buff-colored rock is thrown out in digging cellars in the west part of the town. The lower limestone is thin-bedded; the strata varying from one to eight inches in thickness, and without fossils.

The overlying bed consists of four or five bands of light gray and brown limestone, containing a few fossils, among which were a small *Atrypa*, a *Euomphalus*, and a few cyathophylla-like corals. The massive brown limestone at the top of the section, as well as the buff-colored arenaceous rock above, seemed to be entirely destitute of fossils at this point. The two lower beds I am disposed to refer to the Chemung, and the upper one is perhaps the representative of the brown limestone forming the base of the Burlington crinoidal beds. At several points between Iowa falls and Cedar falls, the buff-colored arenaceous rock overlying those in the above section is seen to outcrop along the ridges and in the beds of the streams.

At Cedar falls, the only rocks exposed are in the bed of the river, forming a ripple across the stream at this point. The lowest stratum exposed is a brown arenaceous limestone from fifteen to eighteen inches in thickness, overlaid by some thin strata of buff and gray limestone. No fossils were detected in the rocks here, and the exposure was not sufficient to afford an interesting section.

At Independence on the Wapsipinicon, a bed of gray brecciated limestone is exposed in the bed of the river just below the dam. This bed contains a few fossils, among which were *Atrypa reticularis*, *A. spinosa*, and two or three species of *Spirifer* identical with those found in the Hamilton beds at New-Buffalo and Rock island. The fossils were not regularly distributed through the bed, but the mass seemed to be made up of fossiliferous and non-fossiliferous strata broken up and recemented. In its brecciated character, it bears considerable resemblance to the beds just above Davenport.

At the quarries half a mile east of the town, the rock is more evenly bedded, and is filled with fossils, among which were several species of corals identical with those common at New-Buffalo. This bed was traced east as far as Pine creek, and south to Quasqueton twelve miles below.

Meeting with Mr. WHITNEY at this point, it was, on consultation, thought best that I should proceed south to the Iowa river, and make such examinations as the time would permit of the coal seams outcropping on that stream.

After leaving Quasqueton, for several miles the Hamilton rocks showed themselves at short intervals in the beds of the small creeks, and sometimes even from the sides of the low ridges on the prairies. The Drift deposit, with the exception of surface boulders, seemed to be almost entirely absent over a considerable portion of the country traversed between the Falls of the Iowa and Cedar rapids; and the artificial sections along the way exhibited only a few feet of loose material composed of the debris of the rocks in the immediate neighborhood, rather than of those at a distance.

Two and a half miles below Cedar rapids, on the Iowa city road, a perpendicular cliff of rock forms a bluff on the south side of the river from thirty to forty feet in height. This consists of a brownish gray cherty limestone, resembling in its lithological characters the lower portion of the Burlington limestone, but contained no fossils at this point by which it could be identified. A few miles north of Iowa city, heavy drift deposits of clay and gravel again appear, and continue to form high ridges and hills along the water-courses.

Thursday, November 6, I reached Iowa city; and on the next day, a heavy fall of snow, covering the ground to the depth of six to eight inches, put an end to further operations for the season.

A. H. WORTHEN, *Assistant Geologist.*

CHAPTER V.

GEOLOGY OF CERTAIN COUNTIES.

REPORT OF A. H. WORTHEN,

ASSISTANT GEOLOGIST,

FOR THE YEAR 1857;

EMBRACING THE RESULTS OF HIS EXAMINATIONS IN THE COUNTIES OF LEE, DES-MOINES, HENRY, VANBUREN, JEFFERSON, WASHINGTON, AND WAPELLO*.

TO PROF. JAMES HALL,

STATE GEOLOGIST.

SIR : The following report is respectfully submitted as the result of the detailed examinations, made under your instructions during the present season, in some of the southeastern counties of the State. Although the time allotted for this work did not permit me to visit every locality within the district examined, nevertheless it is believed to be sufficiently minute for all practical purposes.

A. H. WORTHEN, *Assistant Geologist.*

Warsaw (Illinois), November 1857.

* The examinations in Davis county were but partially completed at the commencement of snow, and are not reported upon at this time.

LEE COUNTY.

LEE County is situated in the southeast corner of the State, and occupies that portion of territory lying immediately between the Mississippi and Des Moines rivers; and is bounded on the east by the Mississippi, on the north by Skunk river and Henry county, on the west by Vanburen county, and on the south by the Des Moines river.

It has an area of about five hundred square miles of surface, which is nearly equally divided into prairie and timber, and is well watered; having, in addition to the great water-courses which nearly bound it on three sides, two creeks known as Sugar creeks, one emptying into the Mississippi and the other into the Des Moines, which traverse nearly the whole extent of the county from northwest to southeast. These streams furnish a large amount of water power, especially Skunk river, upon which several mills have been in successful operation since the earliest settlement of the country. The construction of dams on the Des Moines river, for the purpose of improving the navigation, will create an extensive water power at such points; and three of these are now under progress within the limits of this county.

The prairies have a rolling or undulating surface, and are covered by a rich black loamy soil from one to four feet in depth, unsurpassed in fertility by any territory of equal extent in the State.

The timber on the uplands consists of black, white and red oak, linden, hickory and cherry; while upon the bottom lands we find, in addition to those above named, black and white walnut, ash, hackberry, buckeye, sugar and white maple, cottonwood, sycamore, and honey locust.

The following section exhibits the different geological formations exposed in Lee county, with their true strati-

graphical position; and are noted in the order in which they occur, beginning with the upper.

Alluvium.	
Drift or Boulder formation	50 – 185 feet.
Coal measures . . . . / Shale and sandstone with coal seam	30 feet.
Concretionary limestone	40 feet.
Arenaceous limestone	10 feet.
Marly clays and impure limestones, with *Fenestella* (*Archimedes*)	20 feet.
Magnesian limestone	12 feet.
Geode bed	45 feet.
Keokuk limestone	25 feet.
Cherty limestone	40 feet.
Burlington crinoidal limestone	80 feet.
Chemung gritstones and Oolitic limestone . . .	20 feet.

The term *alluvium* is made to include those deposits that have been formed since the present order of things, and which do not contain the remains of extinct species of animals or plants in a fossil state. This includes the soil and subsoil of the uplands, and the deposits along the creeks and rivers termed 'bottoms', and consequently forms the surface everywhere except where it may have been removed by the action of water. Nearly the whole of Greenbay township, in the northeast corner of the county, is composed of alluvial bottom lands, and is by far the most valuable deposit of this kind in the county. This bottom was once subject to overflow at periods of high water; but by a judicious system of leveling, it is now secured from inundation, except in seasons of extraordinary flood; and in point of fertility, it is hardly excelled by the far-famed bottom lands of the Miami.

There are no lands in Lee county, or perhaps in the State

of Iowa, capable of producing as great an amount of human food to the acre as those of the Greenbay bottoms. The inhabitants were formerly subject to periodical attacks of chill and fever; but since the surface has been generally brought under cultivation, and swampy portions cleared out and properly drained, they have enjoyed as good health generally as those living on the high lands adjacent.

Between Fort Madison and Montrose there is a belt of what may be termed high bottoms, or terrace lands from three to four miles in width, which seem to belong to an older period than those just described, and consisting of beds of sand and gravel, the surface of which is from twenty to thirty feet above the present high-water level of the river, and yet bear strong marks of having been deposited by river floods when the bed of the Mississippi was at a considerably higher level than it occupies at present. As an evidence that the river along the rapids once occupied a much higher level, we have the fact that a band of *Uniones* (river mussels) extends on both sides of the river, at an elevation of from fifteen to twenty feet above the present high-water mark, nearly the whole distance from Nauvoo to Keokuk. Just below the Mansion House Nauvoo, this mussel band is twenty-five feet by measurement above the ordinary water level of the river. This band consists of waterworn shells, of the same species with those now living in the river, in many places from twelve to eighteen inches thick; the shells worn perfectly white, and having the appearance of a white belt drawn along either shore. I know of no way to account for this shell band along the rapids, except on the supposition that it marks what was once the low-water level of the Mississippi river.

Some of the ridges on this high bottom are covered with sand, and destitute of soil; but the greater portion is well adapted to the growth of corn, from the great amount of siliceous material contained in the soil.

DRIFT OR BOULDER FORMATION.

This deposit covers all the high lands in the county, and varies in thickness from fifty to one hundred and eighty-five feet. It is mostly composed of clay and gravel with occasional beds of sand, and is deposited without much regularity of stratification, and contains many worn and rounded masses of granite, gneiss, porphyry, hornblende and other primary rocks, together with limestone, sandstone, bits of coal and slate, all of which have been transported from points more or less remote from their present locality. Fragments of galena and native copper have also been found in it; but this should not be regarded as an indication of the existence of any workable bed of these minerals in the vicinity, as it only proves that a portion of the materials composing the drift has been transported from a region where these minerals abounded.

The only materials of economical value to be obtained from the Drift deposits are sands and clays. Sand of an excellent quality, suitable for moulder's use and cement, may be obtained in the river bluffs in abundance; and occasionally beds of clay, sufficiently pure for potter's use, may be procured from this formation.

The best wells of water are to be obtained by sinking to the subterranean streams that percolate through the sandy strata of this deposit. Usually, on the prairies, good water may be reached from twenty to forty feet below the surface.

In the bluffs immediately above Fort Madison, this deposit attains its maximum thickness of one hundred and eighty-five feet above the river level. The lower portion consists of a compact blue clay, containing a few pebbles : this passes into a marly ash-colored clay, which is overlaid by irregular beds of sand, and these by beds of yellowish clay with boulders. These bluffs occupy what seems to have been an ancient basin excavated in the limestone at a period antecedent to the Drift formation, and by causes which ceased to operate before the commencement of the Drift period. The limestones which on the east side of the river form high bluffs extending to the river bank, are entirely absent on the west, and their place is now occupied by the substitution of drift material. The valley thus scooped out of the solid rocks extends from Montrose to the mouth of Skunk river, and is from six to eight miles in width. The eastern portion of this ancient basin, except the bluffs on the river above Fort Madison, is now covered by the alluvial deposits before mentioned, while the western part is occupied by deposits of drift material from one hundred to one hundred and eighty-five feet in thickness. That this valley was formed by ancient currents previous to the Drift period is proved by the fact that a considerable portion of it is now occupied by deposits of that age, and which must have been formed after those currents ceased to act.

Fossils. The only fossils obtained as yet from the Drift formation of this region are a few shark's teeth and a fragment of siliceous wood, which probably belong to a period somewhat older than the drift, and have been transported from some Tertiary or Cretaceous deposit over which the drift has passed.

COAL MEASURES.

The rocks belonging to this formation, occurring in this county, consist usually of a quartzose sandstone at the base, on which rests a thin seam of coal with its underclay : the coal is almost invariably overlaid by black slate, and the whole covered with a bed of grey shale. The following section shows the order of superposition of these strata :

Grey shale, sometimes ferruginous.

Black slate.

Coal.

Underclay.

Quartzose sandstone.

These beds always rest upon the Concretionary limestone, which in this region forms the upper member of the Mountain limestone series. All the deposits of the Coal-bearing period which occur in this county are found in detached patches or outliers from the main coal basin, and are of limited extent, seldom occupying more than two or three square miles of surface ; while the coal seam is too thin to be profitably wrought, and the coal itself of an inferior quality.

The most promising of these coal deposits yet found in Lee county is on Section 16 in Pleasantridge township, on the lands of Mr. Norris. The coal here is said by the workmen to be from twenty-four to thirty-four inches thick ; but at the time of my visit to the locality it could not be examined satisfactorily, as the old diggings were full of water, and in the new they had not yet reached the coal. It is not probable, however, that any thing like a supply of coal can be obtained in this vicinity, except for the use of the neighborhood immediately around it.

Coal has also been obtained a half mile west of Tuscarora in Marion township, and west and southwest of West-point, and within a mile and a half or two miles of the town ; but neither the quantity or quality of the coal justifies the working of the seam at these points.

In the bluffs on the Nassau slough, two miles below Keokuk, an outlier of the same kind occurs ; but the coal is only a few inches in thickness, and valueless for economical purposes.

The upper layer of the bluffs, for a mile below the town of Nashville, consists of the quartzose sandstone which forms the base of the Coal measures, and is here from fifteen to twenty feet in thickness. No coal, however, is at present known to occur in this neighborhood. It is probable this sandstone was once connected with the outliers of coal which exist on the opposite side of the river in Hancock county, Illinois. It appears to withstand the action of frost very well, the rock in the bluff presenting sharp angles where it has been long exposed, and its massive character renders it well adapted to purposes of heavy masonry.

CONCRETIONARY LIMESTONE.

This member of the Mountain limestone series forms the surface rock, when the superficial material is removed, over at least three-fourths of the county, and, hence, in economical value, becomes one of the most important limestone deposits. It forms the upper portion of the bluffs from Croton on the Des Moines to Montrose on the Mississippi; and, in the southeastern part of the county, is an irregularly bedded, brecciated and concretionary limestone of a steel or bluish grey color, passing upward into a regularly bedded, nearly white, compact limestone at the top. It is by far the purest limestone in the county, and hence forms the best resource for the burning of quicklime. Its concretionary character in this part of the county renders it of little value as a building material; but in its more northerly and western extension, it becomes more regularly bedded in strata from two to twelve inches in thickness, and is extensively used in the interior and northwestern portions of the county for building purposes.

In Franklin, Marion, Westpoint and Pleasantridge townships, this rock may be obtained in great abundance on North

Sugar creek and the small tributaries of Skunk river; and in Charleston and Desmoines townships, it is found on the South or Sugar creek of the Des Moines.

In the bluffs of the Des Moines, at the town of Croton, the bed exhibits both its most characteristic features : the lower portion, for fifteen to twenty feet in thickness, is concretionary and brecciated, with irregular seams of green marly clay; while above it becomes a regularly bedded light grey limestone in strata from six to twenty inches in thickness, the upper layers having an oolitic structure. The material for the construction of the lock at this point was obtained from the upper part of this bed and the sandstone above it.

The changes in the lithological characters of this bed, which form one of its most striking peculiarities, probably led Dr. OWEN into the erroneous supposition that there were two distinct beds of Concretionary limestone, which he has represented in his general section with a bed of sandstone between.

FOSSILS. The only fossil obtained from this bed in this county, and the one which may be regarded as most characteristic of it everywhere, is the coral known as *Lithostrotion canadense* of CASTELNAU, or *Lithostrotion basaltiforme* of OWEN, which weathers out from it almost everywhere, and is found in detached masses in the beds of streams where this rock is exposed. From Southern Iowa to Northern Alabama, this fossil forms a well-marked and reliable horizon for the determination of the position of geological strata, making its appearance wherever rocks of this age are to be found.

These corals are always siliceous, and weather out from the limestones in so perfect a state of preservation that those unacquainted with the subject can scarcely believe that they were ever imbedded in the solid limestone strata.

WARSAW ARCHIMEDES LIMESTONE.

This deposit is not very extensively developed in Iowa; disappearing in a northerly and westerly direction shortly after leaving the mouth of the Des Moines river, either by wedging out, or by merging in the concretionary bed above. On the east side of the Mississippi it is a well-marked member of the group, and retains its lithological character for at least one hundred miles, or to near the mouth of the Illinois river.

In the bluffs of the Mississippi just above the mouth of the Des Moines, this bed may be seen in place. The upper portion consists of a massive arenaceous limestone from ten to twelve feet in thickness, underlaid by blue marly clays with irregular bands of impure limestone; and forming a durable material for heavy masonry, the strata in some cases attaining a thickness of from two to three feet.

FOSSILS. The most characteristic fossils of this formation are the screwshaped coral *Fenestella* (*Archimedes*) *wortheni*, *Pentremites conoideus*, *Orthis dubia*, *Rhynchonella subcuneata*, *Capulus acutirostris*; together with many species of Crinoidea, Bryozoa, etc. yet undescribed.

MAGNESIAN LIMESTONE.

Immediately below the beds last mentioned, we find a deposit of brownish gray magnesian limestone, sometimes inclining to a yellowish color, usually deposited in massive strata from one to three feet in thickness.

Although this bed seldom exceeds ten or twelve feet in thickness, it has afforded a large amount of material for heavy masonry: it has been used in the construction of the locks at several points on the Des Moines, and is admirably adapted to works of that kind, where strength and durability are mainly required. When first taken from the quarry, it is soft enough to be cut with facility, but hardens on exposure and becomes exceedingly durable.

This rock may be quarried almost anywhere in the bluffs of the Des Moines below Croton, as well as along the Mississippi from Keokuk to Montrose. Above this point it was not seen presenting its usual characters; and at Judy's mill on Sugar creek, the most northerly point where it was observed, it was represented by about four or five feet of brown shelly limestone. It is probable that it thins out entirely at some point not much north of Skunk river.

FOSSILS. The most conspicuous fossils belonging to this bed are a large *Conularia*, a *Lingula*, and the palate bones of fishes; all of which are at the present time undescribed.

GEODE BED.

Below the Magnesian limestone, we find a deposit of marly clays and argillaceous limestones filled with spherical masses of siliceous material, termed *geodes;* many of which are hollow, and, on being broken, present magnificent crystals of quartz, calc spar, dolomite, zinc blende and iron pyrites, as well as mammillary and botryoid forms of chalcedony.

This bed affords nothing of economical value, and contains no fossils except where there is an intercalation of thin bands of limestone.

KEOKUK LIMESTONE.

The beds of rock to which this name has been given, consist of regularly stratified bluish grey limestones in strata from four inches to two feet in thickness, with seams of chert and blue marly clay between. This has been extensively quarried in the vicinity of Keokuk, and used for building purposes, to which it is well adapted. One stratum, near the base of the quarries, is a semicrystalline light-grey crinoidal limestone, usually quite free from chert : being susceptible of a fine polish, it is well adapted for cutting, and is generally used for caps and sills. A mill was erected some two years since at the lower end of the city, for the purpose of sawing this rock into the various forms required; but the siliceous character of the imbedded fossils, even when the rock itself appears free from chert, renders it unsuitable for that purpose, and the undertaking was soon abandoned.

This bed of rocks forms the base of the bluffs from the mouth of the Des Moines to Montrose, and is also exposed on Lost creek one mile and a half southeast of Denmark, where extensive quarries have been opened on the lands of Mr. M'Niel. It is extensively used in the vicinity of Keokuk for making quicklime; but as a material for that purpose, I regard it as inferior to the Concretionary limestone above it.

Fossils. This rock has sometimes been called Lower Archimedes limestone, from the fact that it is the lowest bed at present known to contain fossil corals of that genus; one species of which, the *Fenestella* (*Archimedes*) *owenana*, is a characteristic fossil of this bed.

Near the upper part of this limestone, a thin stratum is frequently found containing the teeth and palate bones of fishes in considerable abundance. Among the well-known species of fossils may be mentioned *Agaricocrinus tuberosus*, *Actinocrinus mississippiensis*, *Platycrinus saffordii*, *Palechinus multipora?*, *Productus semireticulatus*, *P. alternatus*, *P. cora*, *P. punctatus*, *Spirifer striatus?*; with many undescribed species of Crinoideæ, Brachiopoda and Bryozoa.

CHERTY BEDS.

Underlying the Keokuk limestones, we find a bed some forty feet in thickness, made up of alternations of chert with irregular seams of light grey limestone, usually too thin to be of any economical value.

The siliceous material which forms the greater portion of this bed is not sufficiently free from foreign ingredients to be of value for any of the uses to which silex in its purer forms is usually applied. It is more or less colored with oxide of iron, and, where it decomposes, forms a reddish brown marly clay.

This bed outcrops along the Mississippi river near the water level, from Keokuk to Montrose; also on Lost creek, between Denmark and Wilson's mill; and caps the bluffs at South-Augusta, overlying the Burlington limestones.

Fossils. The fossils of this bed generally agree specifically with those of the Keokuk limestone, except the *Fenestella* (*Archimedes*) *owenana*, which I have not observed in it.

BURLINGTON CRINOIDAL LIMESTONE.

These beds, which form the base of the Mountain limestone series, and which rest directly on rocks of Devonian age equivalent to the Chemung group of New-York, consist of light-grey semicrystalline crinoidal limestone, the strata varying from four to eighteen inches in thickness, with intercalations of chert in seams and lenticular masses.

This bed forms the greater portion of the river bluffs on the south side of Skunk river, from the north line of Greenbay township, to a point about two miles above Augusta, where it is overlaid by the cherty beds abovementioned. It also outcrops on Lost creek at Wilson's mill on Section 12 in Washington township, the most southerly point where it has been observed in this county. The quarries in the vicinity of Augusta are capable of yielding an almost unlimited amount of building material of an excellent quality.

A more extended notice of this limestone, with its characteristic fossils, will be given in the report on Desmoines county, where it outcrops over a much larger surface.

CHEMUNG GRITSTONES AND OOLITIC LIMESTONE.

These beds, which are referable to the Devonian system, outcrop at the base of the bluffs, beneath the Burlington limestone, from the lower end of these bluffs on the south side of Skunk river, to the neighborhood of Augusta, where they dip below the river level and disappear. As their outcrop is so exceedingly limited in this county, and they yield no material of economical value, a more extended notice of them will be omitted for the present.

ECONOMICAL GEOLOGY.

Building and Flagging Stones. Nearly every part of this county is supplied with good building rock, easily accessible, and costing at the present time no more than the labor of quarrying. The northeastern portion of the county is supplied from the beds of crinoidal limestone which outcrop in the bluff on the south side of Skunk river, as well as on Lost creek in the vicinity of Wilson's mill. This rock is usually a soft granular limestone in strata from six to fifteen inches thick, easily wrought, and well adapted for the ordinary purposes for which limestones are required. Some of the layers are semicrystalline and susceptible of a good polish, and may be used as a marble. The Keokuk limestone also furnishes an abundant supply of good building material, and is accessible along the bluffs of the Mississippi from Montrose to Keokuk, and also one and a half miles southeast of Denmark, and at several points on Skunk and Des Moines rivers. The interior portion of the county, however, is mostly supplied from the Concretionary limestone which outcrops on both Sugar creeks, affording an abundant supply for the middle and western portions of the county. This bed also affords an excellent flagging stone in the vicinity of Denmark, where the upper layers are somewhat arenaceous and from two to four inches in thickness.

Quicklime. Quicklime is made from all the limestones above named, though the Concretionary is undoubtedly the best adapted to this purpose. At Keokuk, the city is mainly supplied with this material from the upper layers of the Keokuk limestones. Some layers of this bed, as well as a portion of the Crinoidal limestone, afford a very good lime; but they usually contain too much arenaceous or siliceous material, and require to be selected with considerable care when used for the manufacture of lime.

Clay and Sand. An inexhaustible supply of these materials for the manufacture of brick may be obtained from the Drift or Boulder formation in all parts of the county. The clays are accessible everywhere at a short distance below the surface; and the sands, which are mostly in the middle and lower part of the deposit, may be obtained in the bluffs of the streams and also in their beds. Fire clay, suitable for the manufacture of fire-brick and pottery, may usually be obtained from the underclay of the lower Coal seam, outliers of which are found at several points in this county.

Few counties in the State are more bountifully supplied with all the elements of material wealth, than the county of Lee; having an abundant supply of building stone, timber and water, and a soil of unsurpassed fertility. Although no valuable deposits of mineral wealth have been found within the limits of the county, nevertheless her citizens possess a mine of wealth in the rich soil everywhere overspreading the surface, of far more importance and greater value than the richest mineral deposits, accompanied as such deposits usually are with a barren and unproductive soil.

To those who are desirous of ascertaining whether coal may be found at any particular locality, I would suggest that by simply boring down to the limestone, the question will be definitely settled, as no workable coal seam has ever been found below the Concretionary limestone. From the character of the outliers of coal in this county which have fallen under my observation, it is not probable that they will prove to be of any great economical value.

DESMOINES COUNTY.

DESMOINES County is bounded on the north by Louisa county, on the west by Henry county, on the south by Skunk river, and on the east by the Mississippi. It contains a superficial area of about four hundred and seventy-five square miles, and is well timbered and well watered; having, besides the rivers which bound it on two sides, Flint creek and its tributaries, which traverse the whole extent of the county from northwest to southeast. The surface is nearly equally divided into timber and prairie, and the eastern portion is well supplied with neverfailing springs.

The timber upon the uplands consists of black and white oak, hickory, elm, linden and cherry; while the bottoms sustain a heavy growth of black and white walnut, shellbark and pignut hickory, white and sugar maple, red and burr and pin oak, elm, ash, buckeye, cottonwood, sycamore, hackberry, and honey locust. A more magnificent growth of timber can scarcely be found in Southern Iowa, than may be seen on Flint creek in this county.

Desmoines county is well supplied with building material, having the Concretionary limestone, the Keokuk limestones and the Crinoidal limestones outcropping within the county, and exposed along the bluffs of all the water-courses within its limits. These beds afford always an abundance of good building stone; and the facility with which it may be quarried, renders it the most economical material for building purposes that can be used. Sand and clay suitable for brick-making is also abundant, and accessible at almost every point in the county.

The following section exhibits the different geological formations in Desmoines county, which will be noted in the order they occur:

	Formation	Thickness
	Alluvium.	
	Drift	40 – 60 feet.
	Coal measures	20 feet.
	Concretionary limestone	30 – 40 feet.
	Geode bed	30 feet.
	Keokuk limestone	40 feet.
	Burlington crinoidal limestone	60 – 80 feet.
Devonian.	Oolitic limestone	4 – 6 feet.
Devonian.	Compact finegrained limestone	10 feet.
Devonian.	Ash-colored gritstones	25 feet.
Devonian.	Blue shaly clay	30 feet.

Alluvial bottom lands extend along the Mississippi river from the mouth of Flint to the north line of the county, varying in width from one to six miles. The lower end of this belt is heavily timbered, while the northern portion is mostly prairie, with the exception of a narrow belt of timber along the river. A part of this bottom is subject to overflow from the river; but the northern and western portions are above the usual high-water level, and include some of the best lands in the county. Narrow belts of bottom land also extend along Skunk river and Flint creek, and are heavily timbered, affording the most valuable timber lands in the county.

DRIFT DEPOSIT.

The Drift formation presents no very marked features in this county, differing from those noted in the report on Lee county, except that it does not usually attain a thickness exceeding sixty feet. It consists of partially stratified deposits of clay, sand and gravel, with boulders of primary and secondary rocks irregularly distributed through the mass, though usually most abundant in the lower portion. It yields an abundant supply of water, which may be obtained on the prairie lands usually from twenty to thirty feet below the surface; and where the country is more broken along the streams, the wells are somewhat deeper, varying from thirty to fifty feet. It affords a good supply of sand and gravel, as well as clay suitable for making brick.

This deposit covers all the uplands in the county; hiding the underlying rocks from view, except along the beds of the streams where they have been laid bare by the action of running water.

COAL MEASURES.

An outlier of coal occurs in Danville township on the waters of Cedar creek, which, although it affords no coal of any value, yields an excellent clay suitable for fire-brick and for potter's use. Two pottery establishments are now in successful operation, owned and conducted by the Messrs. MELCHER, whose ware is perhaps equal to any manufactured in the West. The bed of clay, where they have opened it, varies in thickness from three to seven feet, and has afforded an abundant supply for several years without drifting, by stripping off the overlying drift deposit.

The following beds, belonging to the Coal measures, occur on the southeast quarter of Section 30, Danville township:

Fig. 27.

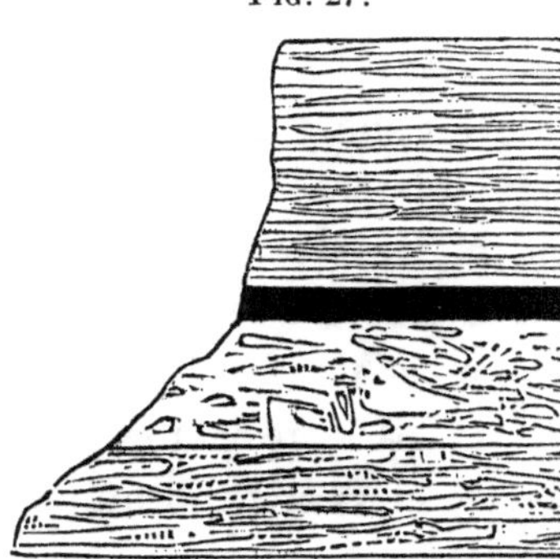

Bituminous slate and shale	. .	10 feet.
Coal	. . . .	6 – 12 inches.
Fire clay	. . . .	3 – 7 feet.
Ferruginous sandstone	. . . .	4 feet.

CONCRETIONARY LIMESTONE.

I include under the above name all the limestones occurring in this county above the Geode bed. No indications of the Warsaw Archimedes beds are seen here; and the Magnesian bed has in a manner lost its distinctive character, and becomes merged in this bed, which is really somewhat magnesian in the lower part.

The principal exposures of the Concretionary limestone in this county are on Long and Cedar creeks. On Long creek, about two miles northwest of Augusta, this bed presents the following characters:

Regularly-bedded light-grey compact limestone in strata from three to six inches thick	30 – 40 feet.
Brown arenaceous limestone	
Concretionary and brecciated limestone	
Massive magnesian layers	

The magnesian layers at the base of this bed form an excellent material for heavy masonry, and constitute a very durable rock. The concretionary and brecciated limestone above may be advantageously used for the manufacture of quicklime, while the upper or light-grey portion of the bed is well adapted to the ordinary purposes for which building rock is required.

GEODE BED.

This bed consists of bluish ash-colored shaly clays, with siliceous geodes containing quartz crystals, calc spar, zinc blende, and chalcedony. It is exposed on Skunk river above Augusta, on Long and Cedar creeks, and also on Little Flint about half a mile above the mouth, the most northerly point where it was observed in this county. It often presents the appearance of potter's clay, but probably contains too much calcareous matter to answer for such purpose. Crystals of sulphuret of iron are also abundant it, sometimes of a bright yellow color, and then frequently mistaken by the ignorant for gold. It is needless to say that mineral wealth will be looked for in vain in the Geode bed.

KEOKUK LIMESTONE.

This rock is exposed on Skunk river, from about one mile above Augusta, to the west line of the county; also on Long creek, two and a half miles northeast of Augusta; and on Brush creek, five miles from Burlington on the lower Augusta road : it likewise outcrops on Little Flint creek, a half mile above the mouth. Its lithological characters in this county are very similar to those presented in Lee county; consisting of alternations of buff-grey and bluish grey limestones, with seams of chert and hornstone often occurring in lenticular masses. It forms a good building material, wherever the strata are sufficiently massive to answer the required purpose. As a resource for the manufacture of quicklime, it is second only to the Concretionary limestone.

Fossils. The same fossils occur in the beds in this county as in Lee. Among those most common here may be mentioned *Spirifer striatus*, *S. imbricatus*, *Athyris lamellosa*, *A. squamifera*, *Productus punctatus*, *P. semireticulatus*, *P. alternatus*; with teeth and palate bones of Ganoid fishes.

BURLINGTON CRINOIDAL LIMESTONE.

This is by far the most important rock formation in this county, inasmuch as it underlies at least three-fourths of its surface, cropping out along the rivers and creeks throughout the northern and eastern portions. It forms the upper part of the river bluffs from Augusta to the mouth of Skunk river, and, on the Mississippi, from the mouth of Skunk to the Iowa, from which point it trends off in a northwest direction to the vicinity of Columbus city in Louisa county. It is also exposed on Flint creek and its tributaries to near the western border of the county. It consists usually of light-grey and brown limestones, alternating with seams of chert, and is termed Crinoidal limestone, because the rock is almost entirely constituted of the remains of the beautiful lily-stars or crinoideans, which once swarmed beneath the waters of the ocean in such profusion that whole formations are composed of their fossilized remains. A large proportion of the Burlington limestone is made up of the calcareous plates and joints of these beautiful creatures, with scarcely enough of mineral matter to cement them together.

In the vicinity of Burlington, the lower twenty feet of this bed contains considerable arenaceous material; and some of the strata, on exposure to the atmosphere, crumble to sand, and thus liberate the beautiful fossils imbedded therein. This character, however, is only local, the whole mass being usually calcareous to the bottom. The upper portion consists of light-grey and brown limestones, semi-crystalline in texture, and sometimes sufficiently massive for all ordinary building purposes, and sufficiently pure and free from siliceous matter to be easily wrought into any desirable form. Towards the top it becomes thinbedded and cherty, and finally passes into the hornstone and chert beds which separate it from the Keokuk limestones above. The

Crinoidal limestone abounds in fissures and caverns, and serves as a natural drain to the surface which it underlies : the water, finding its way through these channels, issues from the base in springs of the finest limestone water. Hence there is no portion of the country where fine springs are so abundant as in the region underlaid by this formation.

Some strata in this bed are susceptible of a high polish, and may be used for the ordinary purposes of marble. The rock may be quarried to advantage almost anywhere along the bluffs of the Mississippi river, affording a good supply of building material to the eastern portion of the county.

FOSSILS. No formation in the West is more important and interesting to the geologist, than the one now under consideration; and Burlington, Iowa, has become a classic ground to the man of science, and is known wherever geology is studied, as one of the richest fields for the collection and observation of the fossil remains of palæozoic life yet found on our continent. A large proportion of the species occurring at this locality are yet undescribed*, but I will enumerate those best known.

Of the Crinoidea, we find here *Actinocrinus verneuilianus*, *A. rotundus*, *A. christyi*, *A. pyriformis*, *A. concinnus* and *A. konincki* of SHUMARD (Vide Report on the Geological Survey of Missouri, Plate A); also *Pentremites elongatus* and *P. sayi* of SHUMARD (Vide same Report, Plate B), *Platycrinus discoideus*, *P. corrugatus?*, *P. planus*, *P. burlingtonensis*, *P. yandelli*, *P. americanus*, *Pentremites norwoodii*, *P. melo*, *P. planus*, *P. stelliformis*, *Dichocrinus striatus*, *D. ovatus*, *Megistocrinus evansii*, *Cyathocrinus cornutus* and *Actinocrinus unicornus* of OWEN and SHUMARD (Vide Report on the Geological Survey of Iowa, Wisconsin and Minnesota, Tab. 5 A and B).

Several species of Brachiopoda are also characteristic of this formation, among which may be mentioned two large

* June 1857.

species of *Spirifer*, which have been referred by Mr. PRATTEN of the Illinois Survey to *S. sowerbyi* and *S. ventricosa* of the European authors. *Spirifer forbesii* of PRATTEN and NORWOOD is also a common fossil in the lower portion of the Burlington limestones; and *Productus flemingii*, *P. semireticulatus* and *P. punctatus* are abundant in the upper part of the bed. An undescribed species of *Chonetes* is common at Augusta and at Bluffdale, in the upper portion of this bed. One or two species of *Euomphalus*, probably undescribed, also occur here, as well as an undetermined *Conularia*.

At Augusta, on Skunk river, fish teeth are abundant in a thin band of limestone which may be seen in place on the south side of the river, near the top of the bluff. This band is not above four inches in thickness, and is filled with the teeth, spines, and palate bones of fishes in the greatest profusion.

In what immense numbers must the crinoids, the mollusks and the fishes have swarmed in the Subcarboniferous era, to have formed whole systems of rocks by the deposit of their bony skeletons! It is hardly possible to obtain a fragment of the Mountain limestone, however small, that does not contain some trace of organic life; and thousands of specimens may be obtained, in which the animal structure may be traced as easily, and studied as correctly, as though they had perished but yesterday.

OÖLITIC LIMESTONE.

Immediately below the Crinoidal beds we find a band of Oolitic limestone usually about four feet in thickness, and deposited in strata varying from four to twelve inches thick. This rock has been used freely at Burlington for curbstones and various other purposes; but it is not a reliable building material, as it yields readily to the action of frost, and consequently should not be used where durability is required.

COMPACT FINEGRAINED LIMESTONE.

This bed is about ten feet in thickness, and consists of thin layers of brownish grey limestone, compact, breaking with a smooth conchoidal fracture, and containing crystals of calc spar in seams and pockets, associated with zinc blende. This is the representative of the Lithographic limestone of Missouri, but is not sufficiently even-textured here to answer the purposes of the lithographer.

ASH-COLORED GRITSTONE.

This bed is composed at the top of tolerably regular-bedded gritstone in strata from four to twelve inches thick, passing downward into ash-colored shale. The bed affords no building rock of any value, the strata generally yielding to the influence of the weather, and crumbling where exposed to atmospheric agencies.

Fossils. Among the fossils common to these beds may be enumerated *Spirifer marionensis* of Shumard, *Chonetes logani* and *C. fischeri* of Pratten and Norwood, together with several species of *Productus*, *Avicula*, *Grammysia*, *Bellerophon*, etc., which appear to be closely allied to, or identical with species common to the Waverly sandstone of Ohio and the Portage and Chemung groups of New-York.

These beds outcrop along the river bluffs from Augusta on Skunk river, to the vicinity of Bluffdale P. O. twelve miles above Burlington, where they pass below the surface and disappear.

BLUE SLATY CLAY.

This bed, which is from twenty-five to thirty feet thick at Burlington, is the lowest rock outcropping in the county, and is only exposed at the base of the bluffs from the mouth of Flint creek to the bluffs on Skunk river. It consists of a dark blue argillaceous slate that weathers to a blue clay, and contains sulphuret of iron in crystals and brown oxide of iron in nodules of clay iron ore.

No fossils have as yet been found in this bed in Desmoines county; but its position and lithological characters would seem to indicate it to be the equivalent of the Genesee slate.

ECONOMICAL GEOLOGY.

Building-rock. The Crinoidal limestone furnishes an abundant supply of building material to the eastern part of the county, being accessible everywhere in the river bluffs from the north line of the county to the mouth of Skunk river, and also up that river to a point about one mile above Augusta. This bed also outcrops on Flint creek, as far as the southwest corner of Yellowsprings township.

The Keokuk limestones are found on Brush creek, five miles southwest of Burlington; also on Little Flint creek a half mile above the mouth, and on Skunk river from Augusta to the west line of the county. The Concretionary limestone also outcrops on Long creek, as well as on some of the smaller streams in the southwest part of the county.

Quicklime. These beds all furnish an abundant supply of material for the manufacture of lime; which, at Burlington, is obtained from the upper beds of the Crinoidal limestone, some layers being nearly pure carbonate of lime.

Sand and Clay. These materials are abundant in nearly all parts of the county; enabling almost every farmer to manufacture his own brick upon his own premises, when he chooses to do so.

Fire-clay. An excellent bed of fire-clay occurs in Danville township, affording an abundant supply for two potteries now in successful operation. This bed forms the underclay to an outlier of coal in this township.

As an agricultural region, Desmoines county is one of the best in Iowa; and from its geographical position and commercial advantages, is destined to be one of the most populous and wealthy counties in the State. The prairies have a soil of unsurpassed fertility; and a considerable portion of the timbered lands, where the growth consists of elm, linden and cherry, possess a soil scarcely inferior to the best prairie lands. Along the river bluffs the soil is admirably adapted to the growth of fruit, especially where it is rendered calcareous by the outcrop of limestones; and the apple and peach orchards planted on such locations are usually more healthy and productive than those upon the prairies. The steep hillsides are also admirably adapted to the growth of the vine, and there are several flourishing vineyards in the county.

The people of the West are hardly yet aware of the fact, that in the production of fruit, the broken lands along the streams will really yield a greater return for the labor expended on them, than can be obtained from the best corn and wheat lands in the country. It is to be hoped that the time is not distant when the slopes of our river bluffs will be covered with vines, furnishing an abundant supply of pure and wholesome wines to supersede the vile compounds now sold under that name.

HENRY COUNTY.

HENRY County lies immediately north of Lee, and is bounded on the east by Desmoines and Louisa counties, on the north by Louisa and Washington, on the west by Jefferson and Vanburen, and on the south by Lee. It has an area of twelve townships or 432 square miles, and is well watered by Skunk river and its tributaries.

Skunk river enters the county near the northwest corner, and, after winding along its western borders for about ten miles, trends off in a southeasterly direction, passing out of the county near the southeast corner. The principal tributaries of Skunk river in this county are Cedar and Big creeks: the former enters it from the west, near the northwest corner of Salem township, and, after a winding course of a few miles, turns due north, and empties into Skunk river just below Rome. Big creek rises in the eastern part of New-London township, and runs northwestwardly through New-London and Marion townships, and then turns south, and finally southeast, emptying into Skunk river about two miles and a half above Lowell.

Water power is abundant on these streams, especially on Skunk river, which affords good millsites at intervals of five to six miles throughout its extent in this county.

Heavy bodies of timber are found on these streams and their tributaries, affording an abundant supply to the whole county. Black and white oak and hickory are the principal growth upon the uplands; while along the streams may be found black and white walnut, red and burr and pin oak, linden, hackberry, white and sugar maple, hickory, elm, ash, buckeye, honey locust, sycamore and cottonwood.

The following section exhibits the geological formations outcropping in this county:

Alluvium.	
Drift	60 – 80 feet.
Coal measures	40 – 50 feet.
Concretionary limestone	30 – 40 feet.
Geode bed	30 feet.
Keokuk limestone	30 – 40 feet.
Crinoidal limestone	10 feet.

ALLUVIUM.

The only deposits of Alluvial bottoms in this county are found on Skunk river, which is skirted by a narrow belt on both sides, seldom exceeding a mile in width. These bottom lands sustain a magnificent growth of timber, and, when cleared and brought under cultivation, are among the most productive in the county. The soil is usually a deep black sandy loam, admirably adapted to the growth of corn, sweet potatoes, and all other products requiring a dry and warm soil. Fruit of all kinds may be raised either on the bottoms or bluff-lands, with more certainty of annual crops than on the prairies.

DRIFT.

Overlying the Mountain limestone and Coal measures, throughout the county, we find a heavy deposit of Drift material, consisting of clay, sand and gravel, with boulders of quartz, granite, gneiss, hornblende, porphyry and sienite as well as limestone, and containing also bits of coal and slate derived from the breaking up of the Coal measures over which the Drift agencies have passed. The appearance of these bits of coal in the beds of streams leads many persons, unacquainted with the circumstances under which the Drift formation has been deposited, to suppose that a coal-seam must necessarily exist wherever such fragments appear; but a careful study of this deposit, and of the circumstances under which it was formed, will soon produce the conviction that no coal-seam, or other extensive deposit of mineral wealth can reasonably be looked for in it.

Native gold has been obtained from the gravel beds of this deposit in Indiana, and may perhaps be found in Iowa or Illinois, but in quantities too small to repay the labor of washing. Fragments of galena and native copper are likewise found in the drift.

Beds of sand and clay are abundant in the drift almost everywhere, and furnish an inexhaustible supply for the manufacture of brick; and wells of good water may be obtained from it on the prairies and uplands, by digging from twenty to forty feet. Where the prairies are quite rolling, good springs occasionally occur, issuing from the sandy portions of this deposit where they rest upon the clay beds beneath.

COAL MEASURES.

Several outliers of coal occur in Henry county, on the east side of Skunk river and Cedar creek; but none of them have as yet yielded a profitable coal-seam, nor is it probable they ever will.

North of Salem and between Skunk river and Cedar creek, a deposit of coal occurs, extending about five miles from north to south, with an average width of about three miles. This has as yet only afforded a seam of indifferent coal, from sixteen to twenty-four inches thick : it however affords considerable deposits of potter's clay, some of which are likely to prove of value.

A deposit of this kind was observed near Trueblood and Hyatt's mill, on Section 28 in Tippecanoe township : it was exposed in some old coal diggings, and was from four to five feet thick.

A heavy bed of bituminous slate overlies the coal in this vicinity, and sometimes takes its place entirely. This slate has been designated *cannel coal* by some parties, and has given rise to expectations of an abundant supply of mineral fuel that will not be realized. The outlier is entirely surrounded by the outcroppings of the underlying limestone, which is exposed everywhere along the bluffs of Skunk river and Cedar creek, and underlies all the coal deposits in Southern Iowa.

On the east side of Big creek in Centre township, on Sec. 26, an outlier of coal occurs in a depression or basin in the Concretionary limestone, which outcrops within fifty yards of the coal diggings, and apparently at a higher level : it has yielded no coal of any value, and the diggings are now abandoned.

The outlier of coal mentioned in the Report on Desmoines county as occurring in Danville township in that county, also extends into the edge of Baltimore township in this county, but is only valuable for the deposit of potter's clay which it affords.

On the west side of Skunk river, above the mouth of Cedar creek, coal occurs under more favorable circumstances, and in a seam averaging two and a half to three feet in thickness. This seems to be an extension of what may be termed the Fairfield basin, which is supposed to occupy the greater portion of Jefferson county.

At Crawford's mill on Skunk river, six miles below Deedsville, coal outcrops in the river bluffs in connection with a bed of shaly clay and iron ore. The exposure here did not admit of a perfect section, but the beds seemed to hold the following relative positions :

Fig. 28.

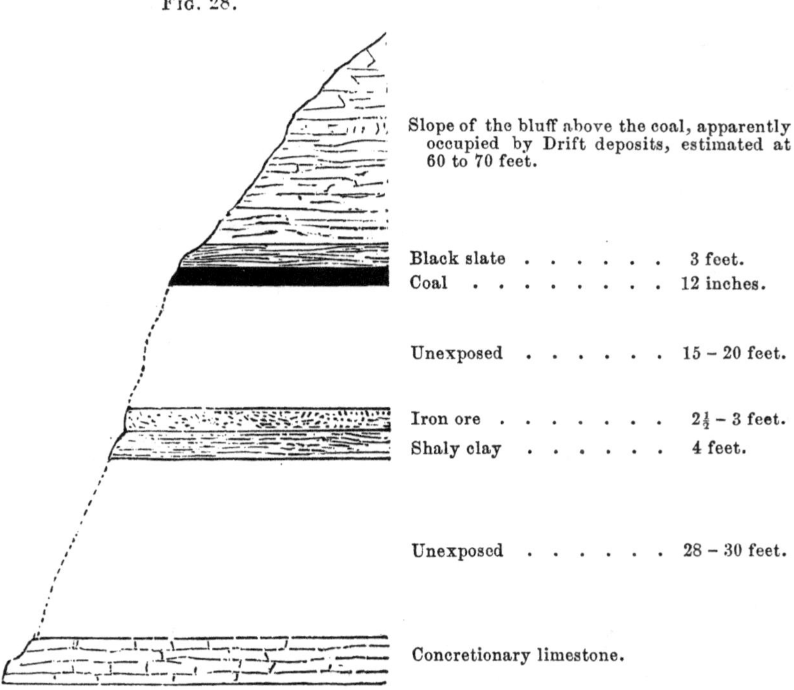

At this point, Messrs. Eaton, Allen & Co. have sunk a shaft some fifty feet in search of coal; commencing on the west bank of the river immediately above the Concretionary limestone, and passing entirely through that bed into the shaly clays of the Geode bed beneath. As, on reaching the limestone, they are below all coal deposits, the farther they penetrate in that direction, the more remote is the prospect of finding a workable coal-seam.

It is quite probable that a coal-seam may be found at this point, between the one already opened and the limestone below; and if the shaft had been commenced at or near the top of the bluff, and carried down to the upper surface of the limestone, the question would have been definitely settled as to the amount of coal to be found at this point.

The Concretionary limestone extends quite across the river here, forming a ripple just below the dam. The bed of iron ore in the foregoing section is from two and a half to three feet in thickness, and appeared to thicken in a wedge-shaped form as it penetrated the hill. The ore itself is a cellular brown oxide of iron, and, if the bed thickens sufficiently to keep a furnace in operation, may prove a valuable acquisition to the mineral resources of the State. Specimens of this ore have been forwarded to the State Chemist for analysis.

On Section 32 in Tippecanoe township, a coal-seam has been opened, which is said to be from three to four feet in thickness; but at the time of my visit to the locality, the roof had fallen in, preventing any satisfactory examination either with regard to the thickness of the seam or the quality of the coal.

On the south side of Cedar creek in the west part of Salem township, this seam has been opened at several points near the county line, and about two miles north of Hillsborough. At Dr. Crail's bank the coal is three and a half feet thick, and is overlaid by about four feet of bituminous slate. The coal here rests directly on the Concretionary limestone, with only a few inches of shaly clay and slate between. The vicinity of Hillsborough now furnishes nearly all the coal used in the southern part of the county.

It will be seen from what has been said, that the only coal lands in Henry county, that promise anything like a profitable coal-seam, are those lying west of Skunk river and Cedar creeks; and for the benefit of those who are disposed to test the question whether coal can be found at a particular spot, let me repeat, that by boring down from a point near the general level of the country to the limestones below, which, in Henry county, may be reached almost anywhere in less than a hundred feet fr m the surface, the question will be settled beyond a doubt, so far as that particular locality is concerned.

CONCRETIONARY LIMESTONE.

This is one of the most important limestones of the county, inasmuch as it outcrops over a greater extent of surface than any other in it, and affords almost everywhere an abundant supply of building stone, as well as an inexhaustible quantity of material for the manufacture of lime.

This bed outcrops in the bluffs of Skunk river and Cedar creeks throughout the county, and on Big creek from the mouth to the point where the Iowa city road crosses it, two miles north of Mount Pleasant. It also outcrops on Crooked creek in Scott township, in the northeast corner of the county, and on Little Cedar creek throughout its extent in Salem township. Its average thickness in this county does not exceed forty feet, and in the northern part is somewhat less.

The lower portion of the bed is usually more or less magnesian and quite massive, affording suitable material for heavy masonry. The rock for the abutments of the railroad bridge across Skunk river was obtained from this portion of the Concretionary bed, four miles below Rome. The middle portion is usually a mass of greenish grey, concretionary, and brecciated limestone without regular lines of stratification, and only valuable for the manufacture of lime. The upper part is usually a thinbedded light-grey limestone in regular layers from two to six inches thick, sometimes arenaceous, and affording good flagging stones.

Fossils. The most characteristic fossil of this bed is the *Lithostrotion canadense*, which is usually found weathered out in the beds of all the streams traversed by this rock. At Trueblood & Hyatt's mill on Cedar creek, this coral is exceedingly abundant; also on Big creek, three miles south of Mount-Pleasant.

Two miles south of Mount-Pleasant and one mile south

of Salem, there are marly partings between the limestone strata, containing *Terebratula*, *Rhynchonella*, *Productus* and *Spirifer*, of species yet undetermined.

GEODE BED.

This bed is well exposed in the vicinity of Lowell, where it attains a thickness of about thirty feet, and consists of calcareo-argillaceous shales, with geodes of quartz crystals, chalcedony, calc spar, etc. In its northern extension it thins out rapidly; and in the vicinity of Mount-Pleasant, it is only represented by a few feet of blue and yellow shaly clay, which separates the Concretionary limestone from the Keokuk beds below.

KEOKUK LIMESTONE.

This limestone forms the bed of Skunk river from Lowell to Rome, and also appears again at Deedsville in the north part of the county: it likewise outcrops on Big creek northeast of Mount-Pleasant, and on Cedar creek northwest of Salem. It consists of layers of buff-grey and bluish grey limestones in strata from four to fifteen inches in thickness, and has been quarried extensively on Big creek, northeast of Mount-Pleasant, for the construction of the Insane Asylum. Not more than twenty feet in thickness was exposed in any of the quarries in this vicinity; and it is quite probable that this, as well as the Geode bed, thins out rapidly towards the north.

The rock quarried in the vicinity of Mount-Pleasant, for the construction of the Asylum, is sometimes traversed by seams of argillaceous matter, which causes it to split on exposure to frost, and renders it unfit for heavy masonry. For this reason, great care should be taken in the selection of the material for so important a work; and none should be used, especially when they are required to be set on edge unless quite free from seams and of an even texture. The bluish grey layers contain iron pyrites, which decompose on exposure to the atmosphere, giving a dingy copperas color to the surface of the rock : for this reason, the buff-grey layers should be preferred.

FOSSILS. These beds do not afford as great a variety of fossils in this county as at points farther south, but enough can be obtained to identify the beds without difficulty. At Willet's quarries I found the large *Spirifer striatus*, *S. imbricatus?*, *Athyris lamellosa*, *A. squamifera?*, *Productus alternatus*; together with several species of *Capulus*, *Pleurotomaria*, etc., common in the same beds at Keokuk. No trace of crinoids, other than a few joints of the columns, were seen here. At Oakland mills on Skunk river, and Trueblood & Hyatt's mill on Cedar creek, the fossils of this bed may be obtained.

CRINOIDAL LIMESTONE.

The only outcrop of this bed in Henry county is on Big creek in the northwestern part of New-London township, on Sections 4, 5 and 6. Only a few feet of the rock is exposed along the bed of the creek, where two or three small quarries have been opened in it. These beds have a slight dip to the southwest, and soon disappear beneath the Keokuk limestone.

ECONOMICAL GEOLOGY.

Building-rock. The Keokuk limestones and Concretionary bed afford an abundant supply of good building stone, which may be procured in the bluffs of Skunk river, on Big creek north and west of Mount-Pleasant, and on Cedar and Crooked creeks and several smaller tributaries to Skunk river. The Keokuk limestone is more argillaceous here than at places further south; and some of the layers are traversed by seams of argillaceous matter, which cause the rock to split where exposed to the action of frost.

The Concretionary limestone of some localities is magnesian and heavy-bedded, affording strata two feet in thickness, and well adapted to heavy masonry. This character is usually restricted to the lower portion of the bed; while the upper part is commonly a light grey or dove-colored compact limestone with a conchoidal fracture, and in layers from four to eight inches thick.

Quicklime. The Concretionary limestone is the only deposit in the county from which a supply of lime can be obtained, the Keokuk limestones being too argillaceous to be used for that purpose. As this bed is accessible on almost every stream in the county, it will afford an inexhaustible supply of material for the manufacture of lime.

Coal. Thin outliers of coal are found in various parts of the county; but the workable seams appear to be restricted to the west side of Cedar creek, along the west line of the county. The coal-seam outcropping here varies from two to three feet in thickness, and is probably the same as that opened in the vicinity of Fairfield in Jefferson county. The southern part of the county is mostly supplied at the present time from the vicinity of Hillsborough.

Iron Ore. Nodules of clay iron ore occur very generally in connection with the lower coal-seams, and are also common in the drift, derived probably from the same source.

At Crawford's mill on Skunk river, about one mile north of Rome, a bed of ore occurs in the Coal measures, as seen in the section at that place. The bed, at its outcrop, is only two to three feet thick, but seems to thicken in a wedge-shaped form as it penetrates the hill.

Potter's Clay. Good potter's clay occurs at Trueblood and Hyatt's mill on Cedar creek, six miles north of Salem, and also at several places in the county where outliers of coal are found.

As an agricultural region, Henry county may be ranked among the very best in the State; having an abundant supply of timber, while the prairie lands are generally rolling and dry, and all susceptible of a high state of cultivation. Building stone is abundant in nearly all parts of the county, costing only the labor necessary to quarry and remove it to the places where it is wanted. An abundance of water may be procured at points remote from the main water-courses, by sinking wells to the depth of from twenty to forty feet. The Burlington and Missouri river railroad, now complete to the western borders of the county, will afford facilities of transportation, such as are enjoyed by but few counties in the State. To the emigrant seeking a home in the West, especially the practical agriculturist, Henry county offers inducements hardly excelled by any portion of the State.

VANBUREN COUNTY.

VANBUREN County is bounded on the east by Lee and Henry counties, on the north by Jefferson county, on the west by Davis county, and on the south by the Missouri line. It embraces a fraction over thirteen townships, or about 480 square miles of surface, and is one of the best timbered counties in this part of the State.

The Des Moines river runs diagonally through the county from northwest to southeast, affording a belt of fine timber from six to ten miles in width. On the south side of the Des Moines are Fox river, and Indian, Chequest, Bear and Holcomb's creeks, each affording a considerable belt of timber and an abundant supply of stock water in ordinary seasons; and on the north side of the river are Crooked, Lick, Coates, Reed and Cedar creeks, each skirted with timber from their source to their outlet.

The prairies are generally small, with a rolling surface, and a soil fully equal to the average of the prairie soils of the west. The upland timber consists of black and white oak, hickory, elm, linden and cherry; while upon the Des Moines bottoms may be found black and white walnut, sugar and white maple, ash, hackberry, cottonwood, sycamore, honey locust and mulberry.

The Des Moines river furnishes a great amount of water power; and five dams are now under process of construction, or finished, within the limits of this county. The command of so great an amount of water power must eventually prove of great advantage to the prosperity and wealth of the county, as a considerable portion of the adjoining and less favored sections of the State will thus be made tributary to the valley of the Des Moines for their mechanical and manufacturing facilities.

The following geological formations outcrop within the limits of this county, and will be noticed in the order in which they are represented in the section, beginning with the upper or newest of the group.

Alluvium.	
Drift	60 – 80 feet.
Coal measures	80 – 100 feet.
Concretionary limestone	40 – 80 feet.
Geode bed	25 feet.
Keokuk limestone and cherty beds .	70 feet.

Narrow belts of alluvial bottoms are found on one or both sides of the Des Moines river, varying in width, but seldom exceeding a half mile. These bottom lands were covered originally with a very heavy growth of timber; but considerable portions have been cleared and brought under cultivation, and, possessing a warm, light and productive soil, are among the very best lands in the State.

DRIFT DEPOSITS.

The Drift formation presents nearly the same features in this county as in those previously examined, and has an average thickness of sixty to seventy-five feet. Along the bluffs and ridges the upper portion, to the depth of four or five feet, presented a strong lithological resemblance to the *Loess*, but contained no shells at the points examined to determine its identity.

On the prairies, good wells of living water are obtained from twenty to thirty feet below the surface ; but along the river bluffs and on the timbered lands generally, considerable difficulty is experienced in procuring good water, and cisterns are in very general use.

The Drift deposit here, as everywhere else throughout Southeastern Iowa, affords an inexhaustible supply of sand and clay suitable for the manufacture of brick, accessible at almost any point in the county where such material may be needed. This fact, taken in connection with the abundance of timber and water power, renders the construction of substantial buildings comparatively cheap, and gives to the inhabitants a decided advantage over less favored portions of the State.

Fossils. The only fossil obtained from the drift in this county was a mass of siliceous wood, procured in the bluff on the north side of Indian creek, about one mile southeast of Mr. Thompkins's place. This specimen presented none of the waterworn characters of a boulder, but the angles were as sharp and well-defined as if it had never been removed from the spot where it was first buried. No remains of the mammoth, mastodon, or other extinct mammalia have as yet been found in Vanburen county, so far as I could learn.

COAL MEASURES.

At least three-fourths of the supérficial area of this county is underlaid by deposits belonging to the Coal formation, but it is not probable that a workable coal-seam will be found to extend over more than one-half or two-thirds of the territory so underlaid.

At least two workable coal-seams outcrop in the county, varying in thickness from two to five feet. The upper one is exposed in the vicinity of Iowaville on the south side of the Des Moines, and at Business-corners and vicinity on the north side of the river. This seam is usually overlaid by a band of hydraulic limestone from two to three feet in thickness; and the coal is less impregnated with sulphuret of iron, and consequently better adapted to mechanical uses, than that from the lower seam.

The following section exhibits the various beds belonging to the Coal formation exposed in this county:

Grey shale and shaly sandstone.

Thin seams of coaly matter separated by shaly clay.

Shale.

Hydraulic limestone.

Bituminous slate.

Second coal-seam . . . . 3 – 5 feet.

Shale and shaly sandstone, with a thin seam of impure coal.

Bituminous slate.

Lower coal-seam . . . . 2 – 4 feet.

Fine clay, sometimes wanting.

Ferruginous sandstone, varying from 3 to 20 feet in thickness.

The entire thickness of these beds probably will not exceed one hundred feet, though no point was seen where the whole was exposed in a single section. The lower seam, where it occurs of sufficient thickness to afford a profitable bed, seems to have been deposited in basins or depressions in the Concretionary limestone. The coal at Farmington, both at Williams's and Johnson's bank, occurs in a basin of this kind.

At Mr. Cox's coal-bank two miles north of Hillsborough, a miniature basin may be seen, which affords a very instructive example of the kind. This basin is of an oval form, and does not exceed fifty paces in diameter in either direction. The limestone has been laid bare by diluvial action on the north, east and west sides of the basin, leaving it exposed from five to six feet in height above the edge of the coal at the present time. The coal dips rapidly from the edge of the basin towards the centre in every direction, and, at the deepest point penetrated in digging the coal, exhibits a depression of about fifteen feet below the surface of the limestone outcropping around the rim of the basin. On the south side the coal extends up into the bluff, following the inequalities of the limestone, and dipping towards the centre of the basin.

At several points in the neighborhood this seam has been opened at a higher level, where it occupies its usual position above the limestone.

Section across the Basin from east to west, at Cox's Coal-bank.

FIG. 29.

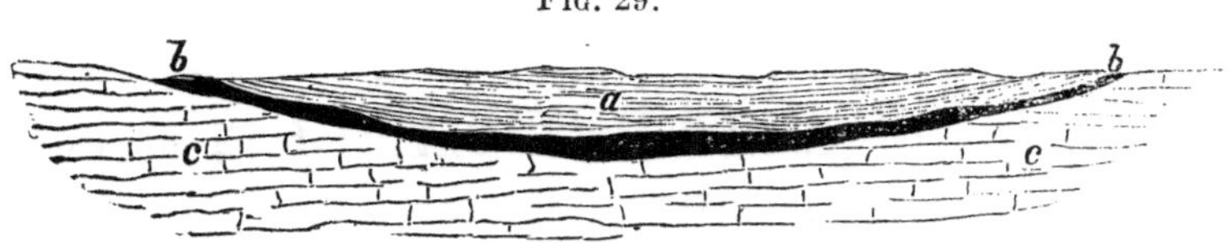

a. Black slate. *b*. Coal, five inches thick. *c*. Concretionary limestone.

The Farmington basin is about two miles in width from east to west, and extends south a half mile beyond the Des Moines river, but its northern boundary is hidden in the bluffs on that side of the river. The coal varies in thickness from two to three feet, appearing to thicken from the borders towards the centre of the basin.

At Thomas's coal-bank on Bear creek, on the southwest quarter of Section 10 in Vernon township, the following beds are exposed

FIG. 30.

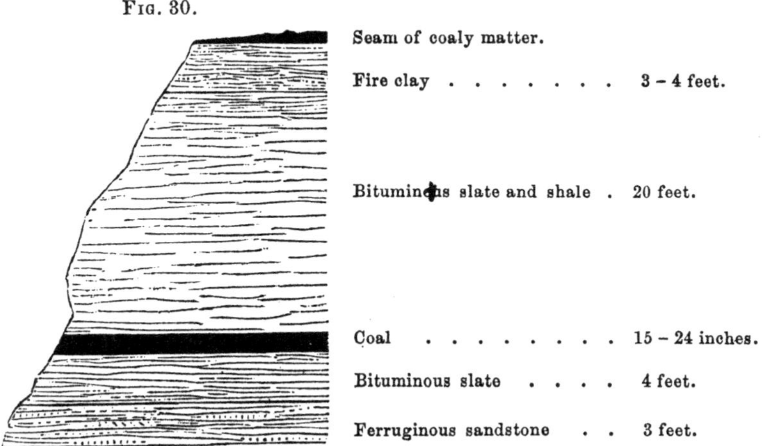

The Concretionary limestone outcrops along the creek, both above and below the point where the beds in the foregoing section were exposed.

Three-quarters of a mile west of Pittsburgh, this seam is opened again for the use of the steam mill in that town. Here the coal is about the same thickness as in the above section, and is underlaid by a bed of fire clay from three to four feet in thickness. Along the bluffs of Chequest creek in this portion of the county, thin outcrops of bituminous slate and shale are frequently met with, but afford no workable coal-seam so far as is known at present.

At Keosauqua the same seam outcrops in the bluffs on the south side of the river, immediately above the limestone. The coal here averages about two feet in thickness, but is slaty and poor, with much sulphuret of iron.

Opposite Portland, coal is said to extend into the bed of the river from the north side; but at the time of my visit to the spot, none could be seen above the water level. The Concretionary limestone outcrops along the bluff on the south side of the river from Portland to within two miles of Iowaville; and if coal occurs at Portland in the position mentioned, it is probably in a depression in the limestone along the southern edge of which the river runs. On the north side of the river, no rocks are exposed in the immediate vicinity; and the occurrence of the second coal-seam in the first exposure on the north side rather serves to give probability to the assertion.

One and a half miles below Iowaville, the second coal-seam has been opened at several points on the lands of Mr. MAUHARD and Mr. M'HUGH. The coal in these openings is from three to five feet in thickness, and of a better quality than the average of the lower seam, containing much less sulphuret of iron. These openings are about fifty-five feet above the low-water level of the river, and from twenty-five to thirty above the limestone. Just above Iowaville on the south side of the river, this seam passes below the river level, being thrown down by a depression in the limestone, and reappears on the north side of the river about a mile above the town.

On the southwest quarter of Section 10 in Village township, on the lands of Mr. WALKER, the second seam is exposed. The coal is here from three to four feet in thickness, and appears to be of a quality similar to that of Mauhard's bank on the south side of the river.

In the neighborhood of Business-corners this seam has been again opened at several points, but presents no essential variation either in thickness or quality from the other localities mentioned. There is about sixty feet of shale and shaly sandstone above the coal at this place, though it is but partially exposed.

At Martin's coal-bank on the northwest quarter of Section 14 in Cedar township, two seams are exposed, separated by a few inches of black slate. It is quite probable that this is a mere local deposit, from the fact that no other outcrop in this vicinity presents a similar section. The two seams average from six to seven feet in their aggregate thickness, and rest directly upon the Concretionary limestone, with only from three to five feet of clay and shale between. Specimens for analysis have been collected from all these localities, and forwarded to Professor WHITNEY the State Chemist.

FOSSILS. The Coal measures of Vanburen county have as yet yielded but few fossils. In the ferruginous sandstone usually underlying the lower seam, stems of *Lepidodendra* and *Sigillaria* were occasionally seen; and in the shaly sandstone above, roots of *Stigmaria* were met with at Farmington and some other localities. The hydraulic limestone overlying the second coal-seam at Business-corners contains a few marine shells, among which were observed *Productus*, *Chonetes*, *Spirifer* and *Terebratula*, but in such a state of preservation as rendered their specific identification somewhat difficult.

CONCRETIONARY LIMESTONE.

This formation is exposed on nearly every water-course in the county; and from the facility in quarrying it, and the extent of surface over which it outcrops, it becomes the most important and valuable limestone deposit in the county. The lower portion of the bed is usually a massive brownish grey magnesian limestone, and has been quarried and used for the construction of several of the locks for the improvement of the navigation of the Des Moines river, for which purpose it is well adapted. The middle portion is always more or less concretionary in structure, and only suitable for the manufacture of lime. Some of the finegrained strata in this portion of the bed are susceptible of receiving a fine polish, and the limestones on Chequest creek have obtained some celebrity as a marble, a block of which was sent by the citizens of this portion of the county to the National Monument at Washington.

The Concretionary limestone outcrops in the bluffs of the Des Moines river, on one or both sides, throughout the county; also on Indian, Bear, Chequest and Holcomb's creeks on the south side of the river, and on Crooked, Lick, Coates, Reed, Cedar and Rock creeks in the north part of the county.

FOSSILS. The lower portion of this bed is characterized by silicified specimens of *Lithostrotion canadense* (*L. basaltica*) of OWEN, which are abundant at almost every locality where the rock is exposed; and on the south side of the river at Keosauqua, they may be seen in place at the base of the bluff just above low-water mark, in the magnesian portion of the rock.

Fossil shells are abundant in the marly partings between the limestones at Keosauqua and at Seigler's mill on Cedar creek; and on Indian creek, near the residence of Mr. THOMPKINS, the limestones are filled with *Productus, Bellerophon, Orthis*, etc. of species yet undetermined, except the *Productus altonensis* of PRATTEN and NORWOOD, which was identified at this locality. Crinoidal joints were common in the marly limestones at Seigler's mill, but no parts of the bodies of these interesting fossils could be found.

GEODE BED.

The argillaceous shales and marlites of the Geode bed outcrop on the Des Moines river from the vicinity of Farmington to three miles below Keosauqua, where they pass below the river level and disappear. The only interesting specimens afforded by this bed are the minerals contained in a crystallized form in the geodes, consisting of quartz, calc spar, dolomite, zinc blende, sulphuret of iron, and chalcedony. Sometimes the lower part of the bed becomes quite calcareous, and contains a few fossils which are usually identical with those from the limestones below.

KEOKUK LIMESTONE.

This formation first appears on the Des Moines river in this county about two miles below Bonaparte, and, gradually thickening in a westerly direction, attains its maximum in the vicinity of Bentonsport, where it reaches an elevation of about seventy feet above the bed of the river. From this point it is gradually depressed, until it finally disappears below the river level about four miles above Bentonsport. The upper portion of the bed is also exposed for a short distance on Indian creek, about three miles from Farmington.

This limestone presents the same lithological characters here as at Keokuk, consisting in the upper part of regularly bedded bluish grey limestone with seams of marlite, while the lower part becomes a thinbedded and cherty rock like the equivalent strata which outcrop along the Lower rapids on the Mississippi river. The upper part of the bed affords good building material in the vicinity of Bentonsport and Bonaparte, where extensive quarries have been opened in it.

FOSSILS. The fossils obtained from the Keokuk limestone at this point appear to be identical, specifically, with those most characteristic of it at places farther east. The *Fenestella* (*Archimedes*) *owenana* of HALL, *Productus semireticulatus*, *P. punctatus*, *Spirifer* identical with those common at Keokuk, and the large *Orthis* referred by OWEN to *O. umbraculum*, are among the most common fossils noticed at these localities. A few palate bones and teeth of fishes were obtained here, but they are by no means abundant. Spines of the *Actinocrinus mississippiensis* of RŒMER were quite common, and one body of this fine species was obtained in the quarries at Bentonsport. The marly seams contain many fine forms of Bryozoa in a good state of preservation, as well as fragments of trilobites.

ECONOMICAL GEOLOGY.

Building-stone. The Keokuk limestones outcrop on the Des Moines river for a distance of about six miles in the vicinity of Bentonsport and Bonaparte, affording an abundance of good building material at those places. The Concretionary limestone, however, must always be the main resource for building-stone in this county, from the fact that it outcrops on nearly every creek in the county, and hence is easily accessible at all points.

Flagging-stones. Some of the upper layers of the Concretionary limestone in this county are suitable for flaggings, and may be quarried in strata from one to three inches in thickness.

Marble. On Chequest creek, the upper portion of the concretionary bed is a finegrained compact limestone of a light grey or dove-color, breaking with a conchoidal fracture, and susceptible of a fine polish. The rock seems well adapted to many purposes for which an ornamental stone is required, and has acquired some reputation as Chequest marble.

Iron-ore. Thin bands of the variety of iron ore known as limonite occur in connection with the lower Coal measures in this county, but have not yet been found in quantities sufficient to justify the erection of furnaces. At Martin's coal-bank, a band of red and yellow ochre, about two feet in thickness, occurs in the shale above the coal.

Coal. Vanburen county is well supplied with coal from the two lower seams, which have been opened in various parts of this county, especially along the Des Moines river.

The best coal yet found in this county comes from the second coal-seam in the vicinity of Business-corners and Iowaville. This seam varies from three to five feet in thickness, and is usually overlaid by a band of hydraulic limestone. It contains less sulphuret of iron than the lower seam, and is consequently better adapted to mechanical purposes.

Potter's Clay. Fire clay, suitable for the manufacture of fire brick and pottery, occurs in several places in this county in connection with the lower coal-seam, as at Thomas's coal-bank on Cedar creek, and in the vicinity of Portland.

Quicklime. The Concretionary limestone furnishes an inexhaustible resource for the manufacture of quicklime, and is accessible on nearly every stream in the county, except Fox river. As some portions of this bed are magnesian and others arenaceous, some care will be requisite in selecting material for burning.

Sand and Clay. These materials are abundant in all parts of the county, furnishing an inexhaustible supply for the manufacture of brick.

With an abundant supply of rock suitable for building purposes, outcropping in almost every portion of the county; stone coal, and timber equally abundant and easily obtained, and water power sufficient for all mechanical and manufacturing uses, Vanburen county stands unrivalled as a desirable field for investment, either to the mechanic, the manufacturer or the agriculturist.

JEFFERSON COUNTY.

Jefferson County is bounded on the east by Henry county, on the north by Washington and Keokuk counties, on the west by Wapello county, and on the south by Vanburen county. It has a superficial area of twelve townships, or about 432 square miles. The surface is generally rolling, and some parts, especially along Skunk river, are somewhat broken.

The prairies in this county are generally small, and the supply of timber abundant. The timber consists for the most part of black and white oak, shellbark and pignut hickory, slippery and red elm, linden, cherry, black walnut, sugar maple, redbud and honey locust.

The principal water-courses in the county are Skunk river and Cedar creeks, with their tributaries. Skunk river enters the county at the northeast corner, and runs south along the county line to about the middle of the county, and then passes out in a southeast direction into Henry county. This stream affords good water power at intervals of four or five miles, which has been improved by the erection of mills at several points in the county.

Cedar creek enters the county from the west near the middle, and runs diagonally through it, passing out near the southeast corner. This stream affords many good millsites, but the supply of water is not sufficient to run them at all seasons of the year.

In addition to these streams, Jefferson county contains several others of smaller size, among which are Walnut and Brush creeks, which afford a good supply of stock water the greater part of the year.

An abundant supply of well-water is obtained on the prairies by digging from fifteen to twenty-five feet below the surface; and on the timber lands, it may usually be found at depths varying from twenty-five to forty feet.

The following section exhibits the geological formations outcropping in Jefferson county, and their relative position.

Alluvium.	
Drift deposits	60 – 75 feet.
Coal measures	75 – 100 feet.
Concretionary limestone	25 feet.
Blue argillaceous and calcareous shales of the Geode bed,	10 – 12 feet.

ALLUVIUM.

Narrow belts of alluvial bottoms occur on Skunk river and Cedar creeks, but not of sufficient extent to form a striking feature in the physical structure of the country, and are only valuable for the fine timber they afford.

DRIFT DEPOSITS.

This formation, consisting of beds of yellow clay, gravel and sand, is spread over the entire surface of the county to the depth of sixty feet or more, except along the streams where it has been partially or wholly carried away by the action of running water. The lower portion of the formation consists of beds of sand and gravel with imbedded boulders of granite, gneiss, porphyry and quartz rock; while the upper portion consists mostly of yellow clay with a few pebbles, sometimes alternating with beds of sand.

No minerals of any value occur in this deposit; and it has as yet, so far as I am aware, afforded no fossils in this county.

A bountiful supply of water is yielded to the wells sunk in this formation, from the underground streams that percolate through its sandy portions.

COAL MEASURES.

At least three-fourths of the surface of Jefferson county is underlaid by rocks belonging to the Coal formation, though workable coal-seams may not be found everywhere over this extent. The beds are so exceedingly variable in thickness, that a seam of coal, three feet thick at one point, may thin out to as many inches in a distance of two or three miles, or perhaps entirely disappear. This is illustrated by the following local sections:

FIG. 31.— Section at Huntsinger's Coal-bank on Cedar creek, 2 miles S. of Fairfield.

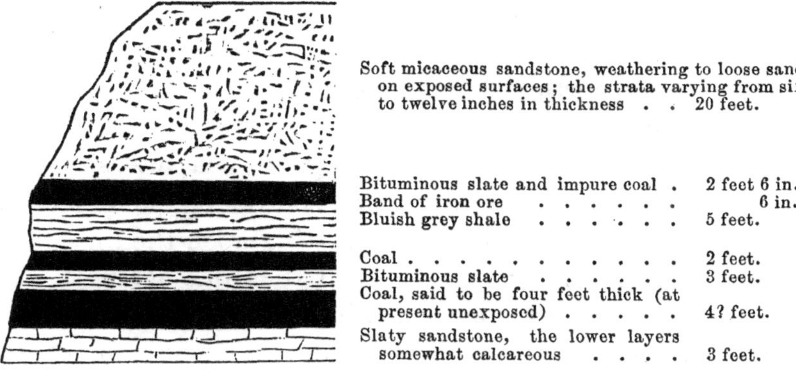

The lower bed in the above section doubtless rests immediately upon and merges into the Concretionary limestone, which outcrops both above and below at no great distance in the bed of the creek.

FIG. 32.— Section at Thompson's Mill on Cedar creek, three miles below Huntsinger's.

Band of limestone	1 feet.
Coal	1 foot 3 in.
Chocolate-colored shale	1 foot 6 in.
Thinbedded sandstone	6 feet.
Grey shale	10 feet.
Bituminous slate	2 feet 6 in.
{ Green marly clay	2 feet.
{ Concretionary limestone	3 feet.

The distance between the points where the two foregoing sections were made does not exceed three miles, and yet the variations in the lithological character of the same strata are very notable. We find the four-foot seam of coal of the first section here represented by two and a half feet of bituminous slate, and sixteen feet in thickness of shale and sandstone interposed between this and the next coal-seam; whereas, at the other locality, they were only separated by three feet of bituminous slate.

The band of limestone at the top of this section afforded a few fossil shells, among which were two or three species of *Productus*, a small *Spirifer*, a *Nautilus*, and the tail of a trilobite. The thinbedded sandstone also contained traces of plants, and a specimen of *Lepidodendron* was obtained in a quarry on the north side of the creek.

The Concretionary limestone, forming the base of the section, presents its usual lithological characters, being brecciated and concretionary, but containing no fossils at this point. The green marly clay resting upon the limestone I have no hesitation in referring to the same age with the limestone, although at this point it affords no fossils.

The following section, made near the mouth of Brush creek on the northeast quarter of Section 36, serves farther to illustrate the point under consideration.

Fire clay	15 feet.
Band of iron ore	6 inches.
Grey marl, with *Productus*, *Spirifer*, *Rhynchonella*, etc.	8 feet.
Concretionary limestone	11 feet.

In the above section we see a bed of fire clay coming in immediately above the limestone deposit, and either replacing the coal or intervening between it and the limestone. The slope of the hill covers whatever beds come in above the clay. The grey marl resting upon the limestone contains the same species of *Productus*, *Spirifer*, *Rhynchonella* and *Cyathophylla* so characteristic of that bed at other localities.

FIG. 33.— Section at Richardson's Coal-bank, two miles west of Fairfield.

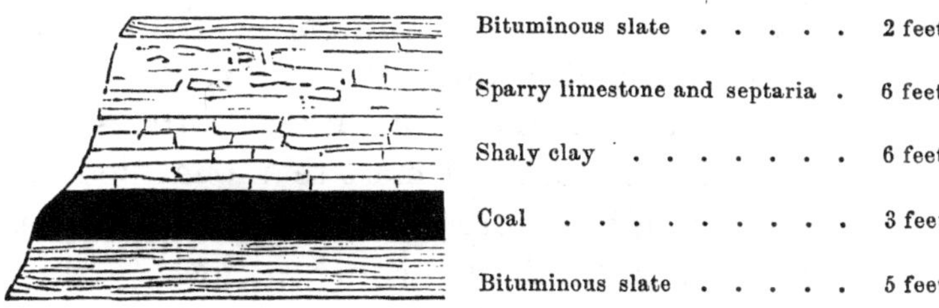

The coal in this section is quite free from sulphuret of iron, and is the best yet found in the county.

Six miles and a half west of Fairfield, the same band of limestone overlying Richardson's coal-seam outcrops on the north side of Cedar creek, on Section 35, T. 72, R. 11. The coal-seam underlying it here is only eighteen to twenty inches thick; showing a thinning out of about one half its thickness in a distance of four miles.

Section at Reed's Mill on Cedar creek, three miles southwest of Fairfield, on Sec. 10, *T.* 71, *R.* 10.

Bituminous slate	2 feet.
Nodular limestone and septaria . . .	3 feet.
Slaty clay	10 feet.
Coal	2 inches
Shaly clay with crystals of selenite . .	13 feet.
Shaly micaceous sandstone with ferns . .	6 feet.
Bituminous slate . . . . . . , . . .	2 feet 6 inches.
Coal	6 inches.
Shaly clay	8 feet.
Bituminous slate	2 feet.
Coal	3 feet 3 inches.

Reed's mill is about one mile and a half in a direct line south from Richardson's coal-bank, and we find this coal-seam dwindled down to a thickness of two inches at this point. The limestone above it, in both localities, appears to be the same. The coal seam at the bottom of this section is undoubtedly the lower one at Huntsinger's, as it holds the same relative position, and the Concretionary limestone outcrops in the bed of the creek not more than one hundred and fifty or two hundred yards from the mill, and at about the same level as the base of the foregoing section.

From a careful comparison of these sections, all of which, except the one at Richardson's, commence at about the same horizon (the Concretionary limestone), it will be seen that the Coal measures of this region are exceedingly irregular. Richardson's coal-seam we find thinning out in a westerly direction to eighteen inches in about four miles, and in a southerly direction to about two inches in a distance of a mile and a half. The lower seam at Huntsinger's, four feet in thickness, is replaced at Thompson's mill, about three miles east, by a two-foot seam of bituminous coal.

The thinbedded micaceous sandstone at Reed's mill contains ferns, and some other plants in a good state of preservation. The shaly clay overlying this sandstone contains crystals of selenite in considerable abundance, though usually of small size.

CONCRETIONARY LIMESTONE.

This is the principal limestone formation outcropping in this county, and is found on Cedar creek as far north as Reed's mill, on Skunk river, and on Walnut creek for two or three miles from the mouth. It has everywhere a brecciated and concretionary structure, which renders it ill adapted to the purposes of building. The lower part of the bed appears to be arenaceous, and may afford some good building material.

Fossils are not very abundant in this formation in this county; but at Reed's mill, and on Brush creek, a few of the most characteristic species were obtained.

ARGILLO-CALCAREOUS SHALES OF THE GEODE BED.

Skunk river, from the northeast corner of the county to a point some two or three miles below Deedsville, runs upon this formation, exposing at intervals thin bands of limestone which may be considered the equivalents of the Keokuk limestones. These are the lowest beds outcropping in the county, and appear to have thinned out very much in their northerly direction, not exhibiting more than ten or twelve feet in perpendicular thickness.

ECONOMICAL GEOLOGY.

Coal. Coal is by far the most valuable mineral product to be found in Jefferson county; and notwithstanding the great irregularity with which the coal seems to have been deposited in this region, there is undoubtedly within the limits of the county an adequate supply for a long period. The lower seam has been opened in almost every township in the county, and is the one mainly to be relied on for future supplies. The upper seam probably underlies but a limited tract of country; and it has nowhere yet been found thick enough to justify being wrought, except in the vicinity of Fairfield. The coal from the upper seam contains less sulphuret of iron than almost any other yet found in the State, and is in consequence much sought after for mechanical purposes.

Iron-ore. Thin beds of iron ore, consisting of red and brown hematite, occur almost everywhere in connection with the lower coal-seams, but has not yet been discovered in quantities sufficient to justify the erection of furnaces.

Fire-clay. Beds of fire clay are found in various parts of the county, in connexion with the coal-seams; and on Brush creek near the mouth, on the northeast quarter of Sec. 36, is a bed about fifteen feet thick, resting on the Concretionary limestone, with a few inches of iron ore between. The lower part of the bed is somewhat slaty in texture, but the upper part seems to be of excellent quality. Should it prove as good as its appearance would indicate, it must become a valuable addition to the resources of that part of the county.

Building materials. Jefferson county is not well supplied with good building stone; her main resource being the sandstones of the Coal measures, which are not very reliable when exposed to atmospheric agencies, and, if used at all, require to be selected with much care. The Concretionary limestone is accessible along the eastern part of the county; but owing to its irregular stratification, it affords but little material for good walls. Some good building stone may probably be obtained from the lower part of this bed, at Harmon's quarries and some other points in the southeast part of the county, where the rock seems to be somewhat arenaceous and more regularly bedded than the purer limestones at the top.

The limestone overlying Richardson's coal-seam is used to a considerable extent in the neighborhood of its outcrop, for rough walls, but, owing to its irregular fracture, is not well adapted to that purpose.

Quicklime. The Concretionary limestone is the main resource for the manufacture of quicklime in this county, and no better article for that purpose need be desired than that afforded by Harmon's quarries. It is also accessible at various localities in the eastern part of the county, on Brush and Walnut creeks, as well as several smaller tributaries of Skunk river.

Clay and Sand for Brick. An abundant supply of these materials is furnished by the Drift deposit in all parts of the county; the clay being accessible immediately below the subsoil, and the sand along the breaks of the streams, where the sand-beds of the deposit have been exposed by the action of the water.

WASHINGTON COUNTY.

WASHINGTON County is bounded on the east by Louisa and Johnson counties, on the north by Johnson and Iowa counties, on the west by Keokuk county, and on the south by Jefferson and Henry counties. It comprises a superficial area of nearly sixteen townships, or about 570 square miles. The surface is generally rolling prairie, with some belts of good timber along the streams.

The principal water-courses in the county are the Iowa, Skunk and English rivers, and Crooked creek. The Iowa river traverses the eastern portion of the northeastern township in the county only. Skunk river runs diagonally through two townships in the southwest part of the county, and English river runs nearly due east through the most northerly tier of townships. Crooked creek traverses a considerable portion of the central and southeastern parts of the county, and empties into Skunk river near the corner of Henry and Jefferson counties.

Skunk and English rivers afford considerable water power, and several fine mills are in successful operation on these streams in this county.

The heaviest body of timber in the county is in the southern portion, on Skunk river and Crooked creek. It consists for the most part of black and white oak, black and white walnut, shellbark and pignut hickory, elm, ash, linden, cherry, white and sugar maple, hackberry, buckeye, sycamore and honey locust. Considerable belts of timber are also found in the north part of the county, on English river and its tributaries; but taken as a whole, Washington county is not as well supplied with timber as some of the adjoining ones.

The streams above mentioned furnish an ample supply of stock water; and upon the prairie, good wells of neverfailing water are obtained at depths of from twenty to forty feet below the surface. Along the banks of the streams the wells require to be deeper, and in some cases a depth of fifty feet failed to afford an adequate supply.

The following section exhibits the various geological formations outcropping in the county, and their relative position:

Alluvium.	
Drift deposits	40 – 60 ft.
Coal measures	15 – 20 ft.
Concretionary limestone	25 feet.
Argillaceous and calcareous shales of the Geode bed . . . Keokuk limestone?	15 – 20 ft.
Burlington limestone	10 – 12 ft.
Gritstones and arenaceous limestones of the Chemung group,	50 feet.

ALLUVIUM.

The deposits strictly referable to this formation in Washington county, are, the soil everywhere covering the surface, and narrow belts of alluvial bottom lands skirting the principal streams: these consist of irregularly stratified deposits of sand, gravel, and decomposed vegetable matter, the whole seldom exceeding ten or fifteen feet in thickness.

DRIFT DEPOSITS.

The entire surface of Washington county is covered with a heavy deposit of drift material, presenting the usual characteristics of this formation, and consisting of irregularly stratified beds of sand, gravel and clay, with an average thickness of from forty to sixty feet. Along the bluffs of the Iowa river, the upper portion of the bed presents the lithological characters of the *Loess*, but no fossils were found to determine its identity.

The drift of this region contains a greater amount of arenaceous or sandy material than is found in the same deposit farther south, which seems to have been derived from the decomposition of the sandstones and shales of the Coal measures in the immediate vicinity. Outliers of these sandstones and shales must have existed over all the northern portion of the county previous to the Drift period, and have been broken up and redeposited by Drift agencies, in beds of loose sand, with boulders of soft quartzose sandstone, which form the base of the Drift formation in this county. Fragments of coal are also quite common in this deposit, and have been derived from the coal-seams previously existing in the outliers above mentioned, but are no evidence of the presence of workable coal-seams in the vicinity.

COAL MEASURES.

Outliers of rocks referable to the age of the coal seem to have been originally spread over a considerable portion of the surface of Washington county, but have to a great extent been broken up and carried away by drift agencies. On the northeast quarter of Section 5 in Brighton township, on the land of Mr. Farrier, coal is obtained from one of these outliers, and the only one yet found in the county that affords a workable coal-seam.

The beds exposed at this locality give the following section :

Fig. 34.

Shaly clay	3 feet.
Coal	$3\frac{1}{2}$ feet.
Slaty clay	2 – 3 feet.
Ferruginous quartzose sandstone, partially exposed.	
Concretionary limestone	10 feet.

Although borings have been made at several points in this neighborhood in the expectation of striking this coal-seam, no coal has been found; and it is probable this is but a very limited deposit, occurring in a depression of the limestone, and covering but a small extent of surface. The coal itself is of a very inferior quality, and contains an amount of sulphuret of iron that renders it unfit for smithing purposes, except a portion of the middle of the seam from six to twelve inches thick, which approaches cannel coal in structure, and is quite free from sulphuret of iron.

Outliers of the quartzose sandstone, forming the base of the Coal measures in this region, were observed in the vicinity of Wassonville in the northwest part of the county, and on Davis creek and Goose creek in the northeast, sometimes resting upon the Burlington limestone, and sometimes on the gritstones and arenaceous limestones of the Chemung group beneath.

CONCRETIONARY LIMESTONE.

This formation underlies all the southern portion of the county, outcropping on Skunk river and its branches, and on Crooked creek to a point about three miles south of Washington. It is here a rough irregularly-bedded white limestone, concretionary in its structure, with green marly seams and partings, the lower portion passing into a soft shaly sandstone which readily decomposes on exposure to the atmosphere.

The lower part of the bed is well exposed in the south bluff of Skunk river one mile north of Brighton, where the following section may be seen:

Concretionary limestone	25 – 30 feet.
Ash-colored sandy layers, easily decomposed and shaly,	15 – 20 feet.
Blue argillaceous marlites of the Geode bed . . .	6 feet.

The ash-colored sandy layers of this bed represent the massive magnesian portion of the formation at points farther south, which forms in the more southern counties so valuable a material for heavy masonry, and is here rendered entirely worthless for all economical purposes by the change which has taken place in its lithological characters. The limestone forming the upper portion of the formation is usually too concretionary in its structure to afford a good building stone; but at some points it becomes locally more regularly bedded, and is sufficiently massive to be a tolerably good material for ordinary building purposes.

Fossils are not so abundant in this rock in Washington county as at points farther south, the *Lithostrotion canadense* being the only one recognized.

KEOKUK LIMESTONE ?

No rocks were seen in Washington county that could be positively identified with the Keokuk limestone ; but as the rocks above and below were found *in situ*, this formation may also exist here, though probably so much reduced in thickness as to be easily concealed beneath the superincumbent Drift material.

BURLINGTON LIMESTONE.

This well-marked subdivision of the Mountain limestone series is exposed at several localities in the county; and although it is only found from four to twelve feet in thickness, and thins out altogether before reaching the north line of the county, it nevertheless presents its usual well-marked lithological and palæontological characters.

The first exposure of this rock seen in the county was on Crooked creek three miles northwest of Washington, at Mac Millan's quarries, where the following section is exposed :

Arenaceous cherty layers	2 feet.
Burlington limestone	10 feet.
Buff-colored arenaceous layers . . .	3 feet.
Unexposed	6 feet.

The limestone in the above section is thinbedded, the strata varying in thickness from three to six inches. It is a light-grey crinoidal limestone with some brownish layers, and scarcely differs in its lithological characters from the same beds where more fully developed in Illinois and Missouri.

The following characteristic fossils were obtained in these quarries : *Actinocrinus rotundus*, *A. verneuilianus*, *A. christyi*, *A. multiradiatus*, *Pentremites elongatus*, *P. norwoodii* and *P. melo*. The large *Spirifer* characteristic of this bed at Burlington (Iowa) and Quincy (Illinois) was also found here, together with *Productus flemingii* and several species of *Capulus*, *Orthis*, *Cyathophylla*, etc.

At Walker's quarries on Goose creek, on Sec. 20, Township 76, N. Range 6 west, the limestone is eight feet thick, and presents nearly the same lithological characters as at M'Millan's quarries.

In the vicinity of Wassonville, as well as at Hawthorne's quarries on Davis creek, on Sec. 31, Township 77 N., Range 6 west, the limestone has thinned out to a thickness of from four to six feet, and is overlaid by the quartzose sandstone of the Coal measures, and here finally disappears in a northerly direction. This is the same limestone which, forty miles above St. Louis, in the bluffs of the Mississippi, is about two hundred feet in thickness.

CHEMUNG GROUP.

The rocks referable to this group consist of soft gritstones and arenaceous limestones, and outcrop on English river from its mouth to the northwest part of the county, about one mile west of Wassonville, where they disappear beneath the Drift deposits.

The following section, made at Wassonville, is the most complete one obtained of these beds in this county:

Slope with outcropping masses of quartzose sandstone,	6 feet.
Burlington limestone	3 – 4 feet.
Massive brown arenaceous limestone	42 feet.
Ash-colored gritstone	2 feet 2 in.
Buff-colored gritstone	6 feet 6 in.

These gritstones bear a close resemblance to their equivalents at Burlington, both in lithological characters and in the fossils they contain. The rock splits in all directions when exposed to the action of the atmosphere, which renders it worthless for building purposes.

The brown arenaceous limestone is tolerably massive ; the strata varying in thickness from six to fifteen inches, and, presenting a bold line of cliffs along its outcrop, it seems well adapted to common use as a building stone. It contains seams and lenticular masses of chert filled with fossil shells, which appear to be identical with those from the Oolitic limestone at Burlington. In its lithological characters, it closely resembles the brown arenaceous layers at the base of the Burlington limestone at Burlington ; but I did not find a single crinoid in it, or any other fossil that could be referred unequivocally to the Mountain limestone period. It contained one species of *Chonetes*, two or three of *Bellerophon*, one of *Euomphalus*, one or two of *Productus*, and a *Spirifer*.

These beds also outcrop on Davis creek and Goose creek, near the east line of the county.

ECONOMICAL GEOLOGY.

Coal. Washington county is but poorly supplied with coal, her resources being confined, so far as is at present known, to the local outlier before mentioned in Brighton township. Although the shales and sandstones belonging to the Coal measures are found at several localities in the county, they have nowhere else afforded a workable coal-seam ; and from the fact that rocks older than the Coal measures are everywhere exposed where the streams cut through the superincumbent Drift deposits, it is not probable that any extensive deposits of coal exist within the limits of the county. A local outlier like the one on Mr. Farrier's place may occur anywhere above the limestones, and their presence can only be determined by boring from the highest level of the country down to the limestone, which everywhere underlies the coal in this region. The fact that these outliers seldom afford a coal-seam more than two or three feet in thickness, and the coal of an inferior quality, is far from encouraging to those who feel disposed to invest money or labor in searching for coal in this region.

Building-stone. In the southern portion of the county, the Concretionary limestone is the only rock exposed, that can be made available as a building material, and, from its uneven bedding and concretionary structure, is not well adapted to the purpose. At some points, however, along Skunk river, the quarries in this bed afford a tolerable material for rough walls. The central portions of the county are supplied with a tolerable building stone from the Burlington limestone, which outcrops on Crooked creek at several points northwest of Washington, as well as on Goose creek and Davis creek in the northeast part of the county. This rock is quite thinbedded, the strata seldom exceeding four or five inches in thickness, but is a durable rock, and answers well for foundation walls. The best building stone is obtained in the north part of the county, from the brown arenaceous limestones of the Chemung group, which are sufficiently massive to afford material for abutments and for heavy masonry, the strata varying in thickness from six to fifteen inches. This rock outcrops on English river throughout the north part of the county, and on Davis creek and Goose creek near the east line of the county.

Material for Quicklime. The central and southern portions of the county are supplied with an inexhaustible amount of material for the manufacture of quicklime, from the Concretionary and Burlington limestones which underlie the whole region. The former is by far the best rock for this purpose, and is the purest limestone in the county. The Burlington limestone contains some arenaceous matter, that affects somewhat the quality of the lime made from it; but as a cement, it answers a good purpose.

Material for Brick. Sand and clay suitable for brick are found in the Drift deposits in all parts of the county : the clay may be obtained immediately below the subsoil, and the sand from the lower portion of the same deposit, or from the beds of the streams. These, in connection with the limestones above mentioned, will always afford an abundant supply of cheap building material to the inhabitants of this county, sufficient for the wants of a dense population.

WAPELLO COUNTY.

WAPELLO County is bounded on the north by Mahaska and Keokuk counties, on the west by Monroe county, on the south by Davis county, and on the east by Jefferson county. It contains a superficial area of twelve townships, or 432 square miles.

The face of the country is sufficiently level to be susceptible of the highest degree of improvement as an agricultural region, although there is but little of what may be termed level land in the county. The prairies are usually small, and quite rolling or undulating, and are covered with a rich black loamy soil from one to four feet in depth.

Wapello county is well timbered, the timbered lands embracing more than one-half the entire surface of the county. These lands, which for the most part lie upon the water-courses, are somewhat broken, but possess a fine soil, though not so deep as that upon the prairies : it is well adapted to the growth of wheat and other small grains, and also produces fine crops of corn, and is decidedly preferable for the growth of fruit to the rich prairie soil.

Wapello county is well watered, the Des Moines river traversing the county from northwest to southeast, and affording fine water power at the several points where dams are now in process of construction for the improvement of the river. Six dams are to be built within the limits of this county. The principal creeks in the county are Cedar and Sugar creeks on the north side of the Des Moines, and Little Soap creek and the two Avery's on the south. These streams afford an abundant supply of water for the use of stock; and upon the prairies, especially those on the north side of the Des Moines, good wells of never-failing water are obtained by digging from twenty to thirty feet below the surface.

On the timbered lands, especially on the south side of the river, considerable difficulty has been experienced in obtaining a supply of water by digging, and in some neighborhoods a resort to cistern wells seems to be the only means of obtaining an adequate supply. This difficulty undoubtedly results from the porous or sandy nature of the underlying rocks, which allow the water to sink to such a depth below the surface as to be beyond the reach of the ordinary well-digger.

The following section exhibits the strata exposed in Wapello county:

Alluvium.	
Drift	40 – 60 feet.
Coal measures	150 – 200 feet.
Concretionary limestone	25 – 30 feet.

ALLUVIUM.

Besides the surface soil, the principal deposits referable to the Alluvial formation are the bottom lands on the Des Moines river and its tributaries. On the Des Moines, these bottom lands form a belt from one to three miles in width. These alluvial deposits are very fertile, and, in their natural state, sustained a heavy growth of the finest timber in the county.

DRIFT.

Very few good exposures of the Drift formation were seen in this county. So far as observed, it appeared to have been derived to a very considerable extent from the sandstones and shales of the Coal measures which have been broken up and redeposited by aqueous action. Occasional boulders of transported material were seen, but by far the greater part of the deposit contained little or no evidence of a foreign origin. Its entire thickness in this county will average from forty to sixty feet, covering up and hiding from view the inferior strata everywhere, except along the water-courses, where it has been removed by mechanical agencies.

COAL MEASURES.

The rocks belonging to the Coal formation, which outcrop in this county, consist of sandstones, shales, bituminous slates, and thin bands of limestone, with two and perhaps three workable seams of coal. Bands of *septaria* and *tutenmergel* also occur in the bituminous slates in this county. The coal-seams vary in thickness from eighteen inches to five feet, and are not persistent everywhere; the coal in some cases giving out entirely, and being replaced with sandstone or slate. An example of this kind may be seen on Sugar creek one mile south of Dahlonega, where a coal-seam is opened on the lands of Mr. COOPER, and the coal is from three to three and a half feet in thickness, with a roof of bituminous slate. About one hundred yards south of this point on the same quarter section, an exposure of the strata may be seen in the bluffs of the creek, giving the following section :

Bituminous slate	2 feet.
Shale	8 to 10 feet.
Sandstone	3 feet.
Bituminous slate	6 feet.
Shaly clay	4 feet.

The lower bituminous slate in the above section occupies the place of the coal, and it is quite probable that a drift into this slate would reach coal again at no great distance from the outcrop. At another point in the same neighborhood, where an opening had been made in this seam, the coal suddenly gave out and was replaced by slate ; but the miners persevered in their work, and at a distance of fifteen or twenty feet the coal again appeared. These facts should be borne in mind by those engaged in the business of coal-mining; as the abandonment of the work after it has been fairly commenced, in consequence of the apparent giving out of the coal, would be attended with far greater loss, than the cost of a persevering effort to reach the coal again.

In the vicinity of Dam No. 11 on the Des Moines river, a notable example of the wedging out and replacement of strata may be seen. About three hundred yards below the dam, a band of dark blue siliceous limestone about three or four feet in thickness has been quarried extensively in the bed of the river, for the construction of the lock at this place. The bed at the quarries seems to lie quite horizontal ; the dip, if any, being too slight to be measured. About half a mile above these quarries this band of limestone is thrown up out of the river bed at an angle of about twenty-five to thirty degrees, and runs up into the bluff to an elevation of thirty to forty feet above the river level, where it passes into an irregular band of septaria, and finally wedges out entirely and disappears. The beds immediately underlying this band of limestone, where it is exposed in the hill-side, consist of bituminous slate from four to five feet in thickness, impure coal four feet, and bituminous slate and shale about twenty feet. These beds all disappear in a distance of fifty yards, and are replaced by a bed of micaceous sandstone nearly one hundred feet in thickness. The following sketch is designed to represent the appearance of the bluffs for a distance of three hundred yards along the river :

FIG. 35.

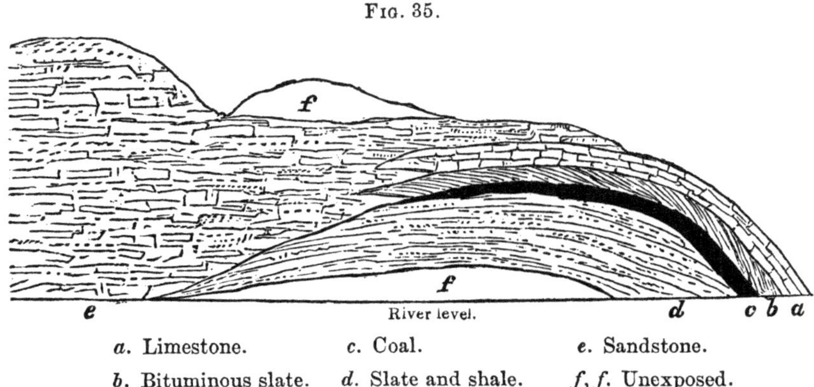

a. Limestone. *c.* Coal. *e.* Sandstone.
b. Bituminous slate. *d.* Slate and shale. *f, f.* Unexposed.

The appearance of the beds at this point would seem to indicate, at the first glance, that there had been a disturbance of the strata, which had thrown up the coal and limestone from beneath the river-bed to their present elevation ; but a careful examination of the locality has produced the conviction that the appearances here presented are not due to any disturbing cause, but have resulted entirely from the irregular deposition of the strata.

The limestone in the foregoing section is rich in organic remains ; and the surface of many of the slabs recently taken from the quarry were literally covered with marine shells, imbedded with *Stigmaria* and other remains of the vegetable kingdom upon the limestone strata.

Among the fossils collected at this locality were two or three species of *Nautilus*, *Productus æquicostatus*, *P. muricatus*, *Spirifer cameratus*, *Macrocheilus* (two species undetermined); together with *Terebratula*, *Orthis*, *Pleurotomaria coronula*, and an undetermined species of *Bellerophon*. A fucoid is also common here, which closely resembles the *F. cauda-galli* of the Devonian beds.

The principal coal banks at present opened on the north side of the Des Moines river are in the neighborhood of Dahlonega and Kirkville, and in the river bluffs four miles below Eddyville. Coal is also taken from the bed of the river at low water, just above the mouth of Soap creek; but the thickness of the seam could not be correctly ascertained. In the vicinity of Kirkville, the seam opened is from four to five feet in thickness; while in the neighborhood of Dahlonega and Eddyville, they vary from three to four feet.

On the south side of the river opposite Eddyville, at Roberts's coal bank, the following section was made:

Fig. 36.

Bituminous slate	3 feet.
Coal	3½ feet.
Fire clay	2 feet.
Hidden	18 feet.
Slate and Shale	6 feet.
Hidden	44 feet.
Concretionary limestone	26 feet.

The thickness of the strata between this coal-seam and the Concretionary limestone, which forms the base of the section, indicates this as one of the upper coal-seams, and renders it very probable that a lower one will be found between the one now opened and the limestone.

Four miles west of Ottumwa, on Sec. 20, T. 72 N., R. 14 west, a fine coal-seam is opened on the lands of Col. FOSTER, where the following section was exposed :

FIG. 37.

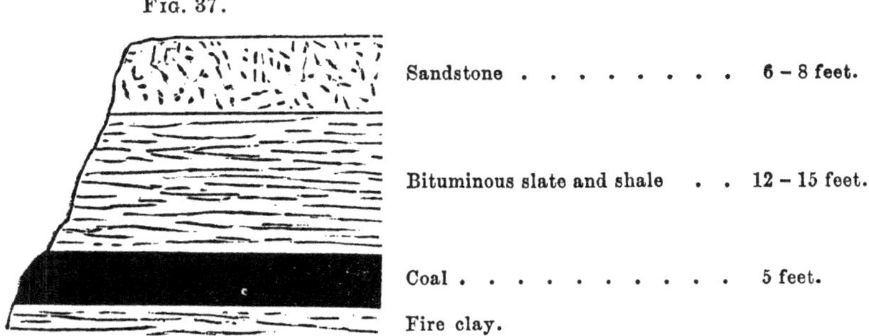

The coal in the above section is of a good quality, light and even-textured, and comparatively free from sulphuret of iron. The sandstone is deposited in regular strata from four to eighteen inches in thickness, and appears to be a durable rock, hardening on exposure to atmospheric agencies. This locality is near the line of the Burlington and Missouri river railroad, which, when completed to this point, will open a desirable and profitable market for the coal of this region.

Outcrops of coal are numerous in the banks of all the creeks on the south side of the river; but owing to the want of a market, very little has been done towards opening even those seams which outcrop at the surface, while no effort at all has yet been made to find those which are not exposed by natural causes.

CONCRETIONARY LIMESTONE.

This formation, which is the oldest rock known to outcrop in Wapello county, forms the bed of the river, from the point where it leaves the county near the southeast corner, to the mouth of Soap creek. Just above the mouth of Soap creek, it passes below the river level, and disappears beneath the Coal measures; coming to the surface again just below the mouth of Sugar creek, and continuing to outcrop along the river from this point to the northwest corner of the county. It also outcrops on both Avery creeks, for several miles from the river. In the vicinity of Ottumwa and Eddyville, this rock is from twenty-five to thirty feet in thickness, and is a regularly-bedded compact grey limestone, the strata varying in thickness from three to fifteen inches. Some of the lower layers at Eddyville are magnesian, and of a light buff color.

This rock is much more regularly bedded in this county than it is usually found at points farther south, and loses almost entirely its brecciated and concretionary structure, which distinguishes it almost everywhere from the other members of the Mountain limestone series. The same fossils, however, *Spirifer*, *Productus* and *Rhynchonella*, which characterize it at other localities, are found here, leaving no doubt of its identity. The *Lithostrotion canadense*, which is one of its most characteristic fossils on the Lower Des Moines as well as in Illinois, was not met with in this county. This coral seems to be most common in the lower portion of the bed in Iowa, although in Illinois it is quite common in the upper layers. It is quite possible that a careful examination will show the existence of two species of this coral, one of which is characteristic of the upper, and the other of the lower portion of the formation.

ECONOMICAL GEOLOGY.

Coal. By far the most valuable mineral product of Wapello county is stone coal, of which it has an abundant supply for the use of a dense population for centuries to come. By a reference to the map, it will be seen that nearly the whole of Wapello county is underlaid by rocks belonging to the Coal measures, and it is quite certain that more than one-half of its entire surface is underlaid by workable coal-seams.

The mining engineers of Europe are said to allow one million tons of coal per square mile for every foot in thickness of workable coal. Allowing one-half the surface of this county to be underlaid by a three-foot coal-seam, we have six hundred and forty-eight million tons of coal as the product of this county alone. This is undoubtedly an under rather than an over estimate of the resources of this county in mineral coal. A considerable portion of the county is underlaid by at least two coal-seams, averaging from two to five feet in thickness each. When railroad facilities shall render coal-mining profitable in this region, these coal-seams will be sought out and opened; and the time will undoubtedly come, when the mining privilege of a large portion of this county will be worth more per acre than the best farming lands are now held at.

The abundant supply of timber in this county has rendered the local demand for coal exceedingly limited; and it will require increased facilities of transportation, and a better market, to fully develop the mineral resources of this region.

Building-stone. Some portions of the county, especially the northeastern and southern parts, are but poorly supplied with good building stone; but along the Des Moines, from the mouth of Sugar creek to the northwest corner of the county, an abundant supply may be obtained from the Concretionary limestone. This bed furnishes a compact regularly-bedded grey limestone in strata from six to twelve inches thick, which is exceedingly durable, and well adapted to all the ordinary uses for which a building rock is required. Some of the Coal-measure sandstones may also be used for foundation walls; but they require considerable care in their selection, if required to withstand the action of frost and moisture.

The band of Coal-measure limestone which outcrops in the vicinity of Dam No. 11 has been quarried extensively for the construction of the lock at that point, and appears to be a durable rock. It contains a good deal of sulphuret of iron disseminated through it in crystals, which disintegrate readily on exposure, leaving cavities in the rock.

Limestones for lime. The only rock in the county suitable for the manufacture of quicklime is the Concretionary limestone above mentioned, which affords an excellent material for that purpose, and in great abundance. Its extent of outcrop is given under the head of Building-stones in the foregoing section.

Iron Ores. The brown hematitic ores of iron occur in various parts of the county in connection with the Coal measures, but no bed has yet been found of sufficient thickness to justify the erection of a furnace.

Hydraulic Limestone. Some of the bands of Coal-measure limestone which outcrop in this county appear to possess hydraulic properties, but they are usually too thin to be of much value.

Fire Clay. Beds of good fire-clay may be found at many points in the county, underlying the coal-seams, and only require a small outlay of capital to become a source of wealth to the county.

Clay and Sand for Brick. These materials are abundant in all parts of the county, and may be obtained at almost any point where circumstances make it desirable to manufacture the article. Good clay for this purpose may be obtained immediately below the soil; and sand is abundant in the lower portion of the Drift deposit, and is accessible on nearly all the streams in the county.

A. H. WORTHEN, *Assistant Geologist.*

CHAPTER VI.

COUNTY GEOLOGY—CONTINUED.

CENTRAL AND NORTHERN COUNTIES OF THE EASTERN HALF OF THE STATE.

The geology of the six counties lying in the southeastern corner of the State, between the Des Moines and the Mississippi rivers, has been investigated by Mr. Worthen with considerable detail, and the results of his examinations are given in the preceding chapter of this Report. As there are about one hundred counties in the State, it is evident that neither the time nor the means at the disposal of the Survey would admit of its being carried on with sufficient minuteness to give the details of the geological structure of each county; and we have therefore endeavored to examine the leading features of the remaining counties, with a view to the establishment of the outlines of their geology, leaving the remainder of the work to be developed, as opportunity is afforded, by future observers. Indeed, the fact that the rocks are, to so great an extent, concealed by the superficial formations, especially through the central portions of the State, renders it impossible that the geological structure of that region should be given with any minuteness of detail; at least not until the number of artificial excavations, exposing the rocky strata, shall be very much greater than it now is. The report of the examinations of the remaining counties of the eastern portion of the State is to be looked npon as containing the results of a reconnaisance of the region described, rather than as a finished work.

Owing to the unexpected shortness of the seasons for field-work in the autumns of 1856 and 1857, a less proportion of the State was minutely examined than had been originally intended, and the counties of Mahaska and Keokuk have hardly been explored at all; although from the general trend of the formations the character of the geology of those two counties is probably laid down on the map with a tolerable approach to correctness, yet a farther examination of them will be requisite before the completion of the Survey. The counties lying along the course of the Wapsipinicon river will also need additional exploration, as they have, thus far, only been hastily passed over.

JOHNSON, LINN, BENTON AND IOWA COUNTIES.

THESE four counties are placed together, on account of the general resemblance in their geological structure, as well as in their physical features. The district which they occupy may be properly called one vast plain, or gently-rolling prairie, almost entirely destitute of trees, except along the margins of the streams, and hardly affording any opportunity to the geologist to become acquainted with the rocks, as they are almost everywhere covered up by the superficial deposits, and only crop out, even in the river vallies, except at a very few points. In such cases, where observations to determine the character of the strata can only be made at great distances from each other, we are obliged to rely chiefly on the regularity of the trend of the formations, to enable us to come to the most probable conclusion with regard to the underlying rocks; and to connect the localities with each other on the geological map of the State, in accordance with what seems to be the general direction of the line of outcrop of the formation, aided by the few certain determinations of the character of the strata made where opportunity offers.

The district comprised by these four counties is watered by the Cedar and Iowa rivers and their very numerous affluents. The Wapsipinicon also runs through the north-eastern corner of Linn. The Cedar furnishes valuable water-power at several points, one of the most important of which is Cedar rapids, where a thriving town has been built up. The course of the Iowa is more winding, and consequently its fall is less rapid and mill power less attainable: the same is true of its tributaries, while those of the Cedar, especially in Linn county, furnish in numerous places sufficient fall for running saw-mills.

The soil of the whole district is, with the exception of a few localities of limited extent, of a remarkably fertile character, and the region is one capable of developing great agricultural resources. The progress of the necessary internal improvements will enable the settler to supply himself at a reasonable rate with those necessaries for building which are not to be procured on the spot, and the fertility of the soil will more than compensate for the absence or scarcity of building materials.

As far as our observations have yet extended, there have been no other rocks actually ascertained to exist over the extended region occupied by these four counties than those of the Hamilton group, excepting some small patches of sandstone, apparently belonging to the Coal measures, which appear to be the remains of a formation which once extended over a considerable portion of the State, and has been removed by denudation. It is not unlikely that strata belonging to lower groups than the Hamilton may exist in the north-eastern corner of Linn, but they have not yet been recognized.

The following exposures of the Hamilton group were

noticed on Cedar river. At Cedar rapids, at the mill near the ferry, and at the lime-kilns a little farther up the river, the beds are thin, not exceeding an inch or two in thickness, and weathering of a light yellow color. About two miles farther down the river, the rocks are exposed along the banks, showing a vertical height of sixty or seventy feet. The beds are quite irregular in thickness, and vary much in their lithological character. The highest rock exposed is a crystalline white limestone, in irregular beds, and with an almost saccharoidal texture. A little farther down the stream, the layers are much disturbed : no regular stratification is visible, but the whole mass is penetrated with ramifications of calcareous spar.

The piers of the new bridge across the Cedar at the Rapids are built of the thin dove-colored layers, which answer a tolerable purpose, being a durable material, although too thinly stratified to be conveniently and economically used. No traces of any fossils could be found in any of the beds at this point, or anywhere in the immediate vicinity of Cedar rapids. There are several localities in this township where the rocks are exposed; but, usually, only a very limited thickness can be observed at any one point, and fossils are very scarce. At Adair's settlement, six miles west of Marion, the strata are thinbedded, white, but not fossiliferous, limestones. The same may be said of the exposure at Blair's Ferry, on the road from Marion to Vinton. At Shellsburg (N.E. corner of Sec. 11, T. 84, R. 9), several characteristic Hamilton fossils were observed, in an argillaceous buff-colored limestone. Among them, *Spirifer mucronatus*, *Atrypa reticularis* and *Orthis iowensis* were the most conspicuous. At Vinton, there is an exposure of from twelve to fifteen feet in thickness, a few rods below the bridge, where a quarry has been opened and worked to some extent. The two lower layers exposed are each eighteen inches thick; the lowest is a soft argillaceous yellowish limestone, irregularly stratified and very much broken up. The succeeding layer is of a bluish color, weathering yellow, and being much tougher than the one below. It is filled with fossils similar to those at Shellsburg. Above this, there is a mass of some ten feet in thickness so much broken up and decomposed, that it would be difficult to say what its original character might have been. At Hare's quarry, one-half a mile east of the town, the rock has been extensively quarried for lime and building-stone. There is a thickness of about forty feet exposed. The rock is a limestone of a bluish grey tinge, but weathering buff. The strata dip to the west at this point about 10°. The layers which are wrought for building are from eight to thirteen inches in thickness. There are numerous fossils in these beds, among which *Lithostrotion hexagonum*, *Favosites polymorpha*, with several species of *Spirifer*, *Orthis*, and *Atrypa* are quite common.

On the Iowa river, in Johnson county, the rocks are well exposed in the neighborhood of Iowa city, where there are numerous quarries, which have been opened to supply the town with lime and building materials. The layers are of very various lithological character. In a quarry opened about a mile above the city, on the east side of the river, nearly opposite the mill, there is an exposure of about forty feet of a thinbedded bluish limestone, which weathers of a dirty yellow. The layers dip about 5° in a direction S. 80° E. This rock is not durable enough to make a good building-stone when it is to be exposed to the weather : it will answer very well for underpinning. Nearer the town, on both sides of the river, the rock along the base of the bluffs is a dark-colored argillaceous limestone, which is crowded with fossils, especially corals, among which the genera *Favosites*, *Lithostrotion*, *Stromatopora* are the most frequent.

Higher up, the rock becomes more compact and less distinctly stratified : it is almost a pure carbonate of lime, containing hardly more than one percent of other substances.

It forms a durable building-stone, although not splitting or dressing handsomely. When polished, the large coralline masses which it contains, especially the *Lithostrotion*, are very beautiful; and pieces have been worked up into small ornaments, such as paper-weights, and are well known under the name of "Iowa marble". Unfortunately, the layers are not sufficiently free from flaws to be manufactured into objects of any considerable size. The same rocks may be observed at various points up the Iowa for a distance of ten or twelve miles from Iowa city. Within the limits of Johnson and Iowa counties we have not been able to find any other outcrop of the Hamilton rocks, than those on the Iowa river along this part of its course. Beyond T. 81, R. 7, there are no rocks seen in place, except a few patches of sandstone, until we reach Tama county. Not a single exposure of rock was discovered on any of the smaller streams to the south of the Iowa, although diligent search was made along the vallies of Old Man's creek and the north fork of the English river. Through Iowa county, low bluffs border the river at a distance of from half a mile to a mile from the stream ; but they are made up of finely-comminuted materials, without even so much as a loose slab or fragment of rock to indicate the character of the underlying strata. Although it would appear from the general direction of the lines of outcrop in this region, so far as they can be ascertained, that rocks of Hamilton age predominate over the large surface in Iowa and Benton counties, over which no exposures of the strata are visible ; still, there is good reason to believe that there may be considerable patches of carboniferous strata existing beneath the superficial covering of detritus. These may be either the remains of a deposit once spread continuously over a large extent of surface, or, more probably, limited deposits in pre-existing depressions of the Hamilton strata. Near Iowa city, on the left bank of the river, is one of these limited patches of rock belonging to the Coal measures, which appears to have been a deposit over a very small space, perhaps in a trough-shaped depression or cavity of the limestone. The annexed figure will give an idea of its relations.

FIG. 38 — Section of coal shales and sandstone in depression of Hamilton rocks at Iowa city.

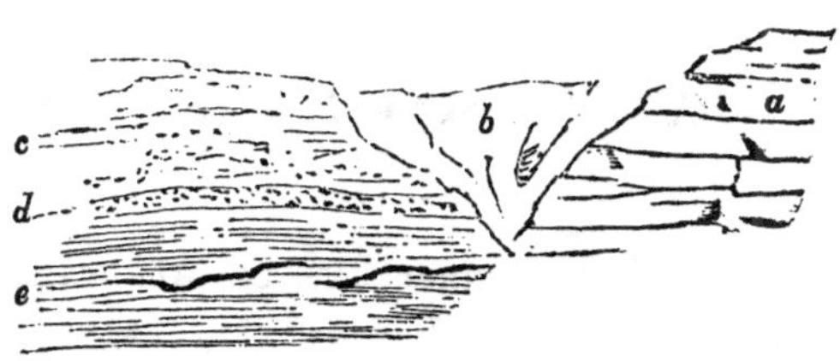

In this figure, *a* represents the limestone of the Hamilton group : *b* is a space filled with detritus, in which no rocks are visible : *c* is a mass of detritus lying upon *d*, which represents a thin bed of sandstone, from one to two feet in thickness, much broken up, and filled with coal plants. This is underlaid by *e*, a bituminous shale with numerous thin layers of coal scattered through it. The horizontal extension of the beds which belong to the Coal measures is very limited, and from their position it would appear that they must have originally occupied a pre-existing depression in the limestone.

There are also considerable patches of sandstone, which appear to belong to the Coal measures on the Iowa, near the line between Iowa and Johnson counties, forming low bluffs, but not accompanied, as far as has yet been ascertained, by any coal or Coal-measure fossils, by which it might be possibly assigned to this place in the series. That these patches are isolated, and not continuous with the strata of the same age farther west, on the borders of Poweshiek and Jasper counties, the nearest point where the Coal measures are positively known to exist, cannot be positively affirmed, but is rendered probable by the occurrence of the Carboniferous limestone farther up the Iowa, in Tama county. At all events, there is little encouragement for explorations for coal in the region in question; as even if small deposits of it should be met with, they are hardly likely to be of sufficient extent or of a good enough quality to be profitably worked.

TAMA, MARSHALL, HARDIN, JASPER AND POWESHEIK COUNTIES.

THE district occupied by these five counties closely resembles in physical character that of the group of counties lying to the east, which has been noticed in the preceding pages. The surface of the country is almost all gently-rolling prairie traversed by numerous streams, skirted with timber, and dotted with occasional groves. The exposures of the rocky strata are extremely few and imperfect, as the high ground between the principal rivers is deeply covered with the superficial detritus, and in the valleys the bluffs are low, and rarely show any rock at all. In Tama, Marshall and Hardin counties, no exposures of the rocks were observed except in the immediate neighborhood of the Iowa river. In Poweshiek, we were unable to discover a single outcrop, except along the Skunk and its branches, in the extreme southwestern corner of the county. In Jasper, there are better opportunities for making out the geology, as there are tolerable exposures on both the North and South Skunk, and some of their branches.

The same remarks in reference to agricultural capacity will apply to these counties, which were made in regard to the counties lying on the east. The soil is highly fertile, and the amount of worthless land is exceedingly small; indeed there is hardly an acre which cannot be brought under cultivation. The greatest drawback to settlement is the scarcity of wood and building materials. The deficiency of wood for fuel is in a measure compensated by existence of coal which has been opened and mined at several points in Jasper, Marshall and Hardin counties. The settlements have thus far been chiefly limited to the vicinity of the rivers; the divides, or high rolling prairies between the streams, are as yet but very sparsely populated.

All the geological formations which have been ascertained to exist within the limits of the counties under consideration, belong to the Carboniferous series; the Carboniferous limestones underlying the coal being developed along the borders of Marshall and Tama counties, and probably extending also through Poweshiek; while the Coal measures are known to exist along the Iowa in Hardin county, through the centre and western border of Marshall, and over the whole extent of Jasper county. It is very probable that the Hamilton group exists in the northeastern portion of Tama county, but no exposures of the rocks were met with in traversing that region.

The Carboniferous limestone is found cropping out at various points between Toledo and Marietta, on the Iowa and its tributaries. The following section is exposed at a quarry belonging to Carl Breniker, on Timber creek, a short distance above the bridge on the road from Marietta to Indiantown.

	1. Thinbedded, sandy limestone . .	3 feet.
	2. Thinbedded oolitic limestone . .	4 feet.
	3. Heavybedded, but somewhat irregular limestone; color grey with a bluish tinge	6 feet.
Level of the creek,	4. Thinbedded, oolitic layers, . . .	8 – 10 feet.

This quarry is worked chiefly for burning into lime. Near Indiantown, or Butlerville, the rock is exposed in numerous localities. About one-half mile northwest of the town, a thinbedded brittle limestone with a reddish tinge is seen cropping out along the summits of the low ridges. These layers occupy a thickness of a few feet, and are succeeded, in a descending order, by thin layers of white crystalline limestone filled with fragments of crinoidal columns. These layers contain intercalated masses of chert; and some of the beds are oolitic in structure, the whole assemblage closely resembling the outcrop of the Burlington member of the Carboniferous limestone, as seen at that place.

At a quarry near the town, where building stone is procured, there is an exposure of about twenty feet of a dark mottled grey magnesian limestone, which is entirely destitute of fossils. Some of the beds are hard and crystalline, with a bluish tinge, but weathering of a brownish hue. The layers are thin at the top of the quarry; but lower down, the rock is heavybedded. In some loose masses of oolitic limestone lying upon the surface in this vicinity, there were found several specimens of *Spirifer* ——? and an *Avicula* resembling *A. marionensis*, SHUMARD. No other exposures of the carboniferous limestones were noticed in Tama county along the course of the Iowa river, whose valley is bordered by bluffs of considerable height, but consisting of sand and detrital materials.

In Poweshiek county, a rock, supposed from its lithological charactèr and position to belong to the upper beds of the Carboniferous limestone, was found to crop out in the valley of the North Skunk, at Van Winkle's quarry near Walker's mill. This rock is used at Montezuma for underpinning; the larger dressed stones required for sills and caps are brought from farther south.

The series of the Coal measures probably covers nearly all of Jasper as weil as of Hardin county, and a considerable portion of Marshall is occupied by the same rocks. The exposures, however, are very unsatisfactory, and no good section of the series could be obtained. After leaving the isolated patches of sandstone on the Iowa river, near the borders of Johnson and Iowa counties, no more is seen of the Coal measures in following up the river, until we pass Marietta in Marshall county. In T. 85, R. 19, S. 16, black slate was dug up by Mr. LANCASTER BELL. On the northwest quarter of Section 34, in the same township, coal has been mined to a very limited extent on land belonging to GEORGE PATTON. On examining the excavation, in 1857, it was found to have become filled up, and no clue could be obtained as to the thickness of the bed or the character of the accompanying strata : the fragments lying upon the surface indicated a fair quality of coal.

In the vicinity of Eldora, in Hardin county, there are several localities where coal has been mined in some quantity, and where it is still procured for consumption in the vicinity and furnished to the adjoining counties on the east and southeast. The rock most conspicuously exposed in the valley of the Iowa in this vicinity is a sandstone, sometimes almost coarse enough to be termed a conglomerate, which rises to a vertical height of from fifty to seventy-five feet. These bluffs line the river on both sides from Eldora as far up as Steamboat rock; beyond which point they were not traced, for want of time. The principal excavations for coal are at the bend of the river between Townships 87 and 88.

On the northwest quarter of the northwest quarter of Section 5 in Township 87, Range 19, a bed of coal has been worked on land owned by Dr. FULLER. The principal opening is elevated a few feet above the river, and the rocks at this point present the following section :

Ferruginous sandstone, about	50 feet.
Black slate	5½ feet.
Coal	3½ – 4 feet.
Black shale	7 feet, exposed, but not cut through.

The beds dip from the river, or to the south, from ten to fifteen degrees : this rate of dip would soon bring the coal beneath the water level of the river, if it is found to be continuous. It is possible, however, that the rate of dip may decrease in penetrating beneath the bluff; or the whole mass of rock,as exposed here, may possibly have slidden out of place, and thus have had its position deranged. The appearances in the vicinity are somewhat puzzling; as there seems to be little or no regularity in the position of the coal, or of the attendant beds of rock. The coal seam of Dr. FULLER is underlaid by a dark ash-grey, soft shaly mass, without apparent stratification, of which the thickness is not known. A little farther up the stream, a dark-colored limestone, which is a nearly pure carbonate of lime colored by about a half of one per cent of organic matter, makes its appearance in a position which would indicate it to be the lowest rock of the region. It contains a few fossils; among others, a *Productus* and a new species of *Phillipsia.*

The bed of coal, which has been penetrated to a distance of a few yards, shows numerous slips passing through it from top to bottom, at distances of a few feet. The quality is fair, considering its position near the edge of the basin: it is considerably mixed with iron pyrites, but this is a fault from which none of the coals of this region are free.

About one-fourth of a mile farther down the stream, on the same side of the river, a bed of dark bituminous shale was observed at an elevation of about forty feet above the water. It is included within the sandstone, which is seen overlying it to a height of thirty or forty feet, and also beneath it as far down towards the river as the rocks are exposed. The shale is much contorted, and contains numerous crystals of gypsum, some of which are several inches long. At this point the dip of the strata is to the east, and still away from the river.

At Moran's opening, a few rods farther down the river and on the northeast quarter of the northwest quarter of Section 5, the section which is exposed is the annexed :

Sandstone, heavybedded, vertical cliff	50 feet.
Black bituminous shale	5 feet 4 in.
Coal	4 feet.
Ash-colored shale, thickness undetermined.	

The dip at this point is from five to seven degrees, in a direction a little north of east. The quality of the coal is about the same as that at Dr. Fuller's opening; and there would seem little reason to doubt that it was the same bed, were the coal not totally wanting in the section exhibited in the last described locality, which is not more than four or five rods above Moran's opening.

The same seam, apparently, has been opened on the opposite side of the river from Moran's, where it is three and a half feet thick, and it is overlaid by two feet of black shale. A little farther down the river on that side, the slate disappears entirely, and the coal has sandstone above and below it. The dip here is nearly horizontal : hence it would appear that there has been considerable disturbance of the strata in this vicinity, which has especially affected their inclination on the south side of the river, and which also renders it difficult to say what will be the depth and position of the coal seam at a distance from the river, where it would be necessary to look for it, by sinking a shaft, in case the water became too troublesome at the localities where it is now worked. No borings have yet been made for this purpose; but wells have been sunk to a considerable depth on the prairie, a little east of Eldora, and about one and a quarter mile from the river. One of these wells was 105 feet deep, of which sixteen feet was superficial detritus, and the remainder sandstone, without indications of coal. In this connection it may be mentioned, that the sandstone bluffs are not continuous above the coal openings along the river banks : on the contrary, they are intercepted for a distance of one or two miles, the rock not being exposed in that distance. Excavations which have been made for coal in that space show that there is a considerable thickness of shales accumulated at those points; but the sandstone seems to be entirely wanting. This would indicate a disturbance of the strata, the exact nature of which it is difficult to make out where the exposures are so limited.

Some of the beds of fire clay which are connected with the coal in this region are of excellent quality for the manufacture of pottery and fire bricks, and have already been made use of for that purpose. The limestones connected with the coal are not suitable for hydraulic cement, being almost pure carbonate of lime.

The only building stone furnished along this portion of the region occupied by the Coal measures is the sandstone, which is neither a very durable or handsome material for that purpose. Some of the beds are not liable to crumble on exposure to the air; but the color of the rock is too sombre and unequally distributed to produce a pleasant effect on the eye.

In Jasper county, the rocks of the Coal measures are seen cropping out along the banks of Rock creek, a branch of the North Skunk. The exposures here exhibit from ten to twenty feet of a soft, rather coarse-grained sandstone, which extends along the stream at intervals for two or three miles. No appearance of coal-shales or coal was observed anywhere in this part of the county; nor has any yet been discovered east of the town of Newton, so far as we were able to ascertain. Loose fragments of coal are occasionally found in the soil, and have led to some attempts to find valuable beds by boring. The same sandstone crops out in low ledges along the North Skunk, below its junction with Rock creek. Some of the layers are thin, highly ferruginous, and durable in their qualities as a building material.

Coal has been obtained at several points in the western part of Jasper county. At a locality about two miles west of Newton, a bed has been opened; but it was not worked at the time of our visit. The coal is of good quality, but the seam is quite thin. On Skunk river, about eight miles from Newton, considerable coal has been mined, at a locality known as Slaughter's coal-bank. A gently curving ridge extends along on the southwest side of the river for a distance of two or three miles, which rises to the height of, perhaps, a hundred feet above the river. This ridge is well-wooded and covered with soil, so that the rocks are but little exposed upon it, but it appears to form an outlier of the Coal measures. The bed of coal, where opened, is about four feet thick, and is overlaid by bituminous shale, whose thickness was not determined, for want of a good exposure. The dip of the bed is about 3°, from the river, or south 10° east. The quality of the coal obtained here is not very good, as the amount of sulphuret of iron and sulphate of lime present in the joints is quite considerable. This seems to be a characteristic feature of the coal beds on the edge of the basin, and in the limited and detached deposits which flank the main accumulations. The convenience with which coal can be obtained at Slaughter's bank, owing to the situation of the bed in relation to the river, and the fact that no workable seams have been found to the east of this in this region, makes this deposit one of importance to the adjacent country; and a considerable quantity of the coal already finds its way to the neighboring towns. There are other localities in the southern part of the county where coal is said to have been found, but none where it has been worked to any considerable extent.

MUSCATINE COUNTY.

This county is bounded on the southeast by the Mississippi river, which, at the city of Muscatine, makes a sudden bend to the south; its course from Davenport to this place being nearly west. The Cedar river flows through the county, a little west of its centre, in a direction nearly parallel with that of the Mississippi, and the Wapsinonox is its principal tributary. The route of the Mississippi and Missouri railroad runs along the northern edge of the county, and a branch from Muscatine intersects it from north to south; so that few districts in the State have greater facilities of internal communication.

The surface of the county is very uniform in its character; the streams have not cut through the prairie deposits, and, except on the Mississippi river, we have not observed any rock in place. The soil is highly fertile, and the subsoil a deep yellowish clayey loam, in the finest possible state of subdivision. The timber in this county is mostly confined to the immediate vicinity of the Mississippi and Cedar rivers and their branches. The most abundant trees are white and black oak, hickory, blackwalnut, linden and elm. The region bordering on the Cedar is rather low, and the soil somewhat sandy,: on the Wapsinonox it is more fertile, and the timber is of vigorous growth.

There are no boulders on the surface, and but few indications of transported drift, the superficial detritus appearing to have come almost entirely from the decomposition of the underlying rocks.

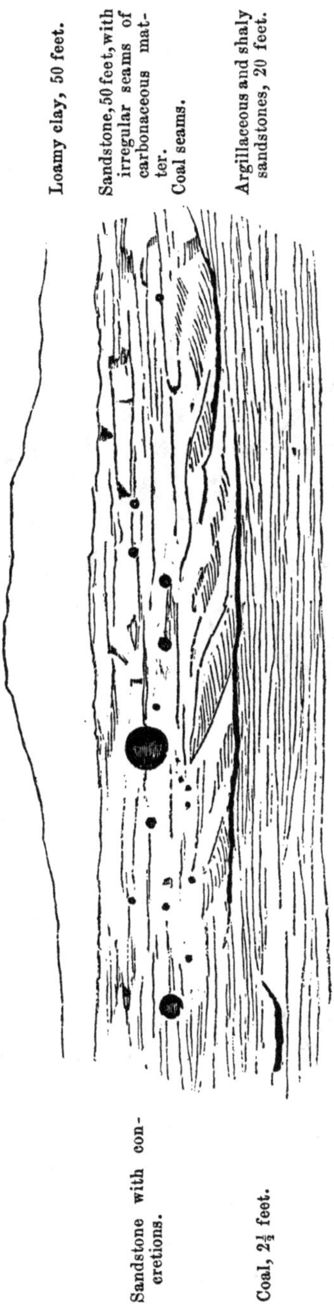

Loamy clay, 50 feet.
Sandstone, 50 feet, with irregular seams of carbonaceous matter.
Coal seams.
Argillaceous and shaly sandstones, 20 feet.
Sandstone with concretions.
Coal, $2\frac{1}{2}$ feet.

This county is chiefly underlaid by limestone of the Hamilton group, which crops out in the adjacent counties, north and west, but is not seen within the limits of this, on account of the heavy superficial deposits. There is a narrow belt of the Carboniferous series along the banks of the Mississippi, which appears to be an outlier of the Rock island coal-field (See geological map). This is finely exhibited in a section made for railroad purposes just below the steamboat landing at Muscatine, which is represented in the annexed cut (fig. 33). The superficial deposit of loamy clay is exposed to the thickness of about fifty feet. It is extremely destitute of foreign boulders, and appears to be made up almost exclusively of detritus formed from the d[illegible]position of the rocks which are in the immediate vicinity, which may be seen in numerous localities, gradually crumbling under the influence of various causes. Beneath this deposit a thickness of about fifty feet of a somewhat argillaceous sandstone may be observed. This sandstone is pretty regularly stratified in its upper portion; but lower down, it is much disturbed, as if it had been deposited under the influence of varying currents. It contains a great number of spherical concretions, which vary in size from a few inches to eight feet in diameter. Some of them are remarkably symmetrical, as shown by the annexed cut (fig. 39.), which represents

Fig. 39.

one of the most regularly-formed ones which we have observed. These concretions are distinctly stratified, and the lines of stratification pass from the adjacent rock through them without interruption. The material of which they are composed is much harder than that of the adjacent sandstone, contains more calcareous matter and more sulphuret of iron : indeed, in the smaller ones, a nodule of this substance may not unfrequently be found in the centre. The fossil stems which occur in the sandstone are seen to extend directly into, and, sometimes, through the concretions; which, as well as the other facts mentioned above, shows conclusively that they have been formed by segregating agencies, such as are often observed to have been operating in the rocky strata, but which have here caused the aggregation of larger and more symmetrically-formed masses than we have elsewhere observed.

The sandstone is filled with impressions of stems and leaves of fossil plants of the Coal measures, some of which are of considerable size. One was observed (a *Lepidodendron*, species ?), which was traced for twenty feet in length. It was eighteen inches in diameter in one direction, and nine in the other; being, like most of the stems found here, considerably flattened by the pressure of the superincumbent material*.

Beneath this sandstone is a bed of coal which is not regularly continuous, but is broken up into small independent basins at its eastern extremity, as shown in the figure. Farther west it becomes more regular, attaining a thickness of two and a half to three feet : with the highly bituminous shale which is taken down with it, it reaches a thickness of four feet. Its quality is very poor, as it contains an unusually large proportion of iron pyrites mixed with it.

The coal is underlaid by bluish argillaceous and shaly beds, of which about twenty feet are exposed in the cut; and, so far as known, this formation extends down to the level of the river.

The outliers of coal which are to be observed a short distance back from the river, at various points between New-Buffalo and Muscatine, have been already noticed in the preceding pages, in the description of the river section (See pages 120 to 126). The extent back into the interior of the Coal measures must be in some degree a matter of conjecture, as it is only in the vicinity of the river that the rocks are exposed.

* The plants collected from the coal series of the State will be noticed more particularly and described in a future Report.

SCOTT, CEDAR, CLINTON AND JONES COUNTIES.

These four counties have been placed together, owing to their general similarity of physical and geological character, and because they have been but very slightly explored, owing to want of time and the difficulty of marking out the formations which are concealed under a heavy body of sandy detritus and prairie soil.

This group of counties is watered chiefly by the Wapsipinicon and its branches; while the Mississippi forms the eastern boundary of Clinton and Scott counties, gradually bending to the west from the head of the rapids, so as to have at Rock island a due westerly course. The Cedar river also runs through the southwest corner of Cedar county. The surface of Scott county is nearly all rolling prairie : the soil is in some places rather sandy, but usually very good. The timber is confined to the vicinity of the Mississippi and Wapsipinicon, with the exception of a few small groves: the white oak, hickory and black walnut are the most common trees. The localities where rock has been observed within the limits of Scott county are but few in number, with the exception of those in the immediate vicinity of the Mississippi, which have been noticed in a preceding chapter of this Report (See pages 121 to 125). The thickness of the superficial deposits, by which the rocks are so effectually concealed, is very variable : in the vallies it appears to be quite considerable; but it is probable that on the high prairies it is not as great, although we have not observed any locality where it has been cut through in digging for water, which is usually found near the surface. In the city of Davenport, the bluffs rise gradually to an elevation of 120 to 130 feet above the river, of which the upper sixty or seventy feet are made up of a succession of irregularly-stratified layers of yellow clayey loam and bluish sand and clay, with a few small pebbles scattered through the mass, and occasional thin layers of limestone gravel. In the clayey portion there are occasional patches of coarse gravel, the whole presenting the appearance of having been deposited under the influence of somewhat turbulent currents. After rising on to the general level of the prairie we meet with no boulders, the superficial materials being everywhere fine and homogeneous.

In Clinton county, with the exception of the vicinity of the Mississippi, the rocks are almost entirely covered by the superficial deposits, until we approach the northern limit of the county, where there are numerous ledges of the Niagara limestone along the small streams. The soil of the central portion of the county is rather sandy, and in the northern tier of townships it is somewhat broken and rather inferior in quality. There are occasional groups of boulders scattered over the surface.

In Cedar county, the northern tier of townships is nearly all prairie. In the vicinity of the Cedar and its branches there is some excellent timber, especially on Rock creek, and in the space between that stream and the Cedar. The white and black oak are the predominating trees. There are a few boulders scattered over the surface. The soil varies in character, being usually of good quality, but sometimes rather sandy.

In Jones county the timber fringes the banks of the Cedar, and is abundant in the broken region in the vicinity of the Makoqueta river, in the northeast corner of the county. On this stream and its tributaries the white and black oak, linden and hickory are the most conspicuous trees. The soil is rather sandy, and in some localities decidedly poor.

The lowest geological formation observed in this group of counties is the Niagara limestone, the upper beds of which crop out on the north side of Clinton and Jones counties, giving rise to a broken and rather rocky region. Occasional fragments of iron ore are found on the surface, which have originated in this rock; it contains, however, no mineral deposit of any importance. Along the Wapsipinicon, the rocks which show themselves at various points are supposed to belong to the series intermediate between the Niagara limestone and the Hamilton group; but the exposures are so infrequent, the number of fossils so small, and the amount of time which has been bestowed on this region so short, that it is impossible as yet to trace with accuracy the limits or relations of the strata. The outcrops of rock in Jones county between the Makoqueta and Wapsipinicon, along the line of the road from Cascade to Anemosa, exhibit a thin-bedded yellowish magnesian limestone with nodules of chert, and destitute of fossils, but resembling lithologically the upper beds of the Niagara limestone. These strata weather irregularly, and stand out from the soil in low ragged ledges, as represented in the annexed figure. After arriving within six or eight miles of Anemosa, on the road from Cascade, the rocks are entirely concealed by the prairie soil. Boulders are scattered over the surface in this vicinity somewhat abundantly.

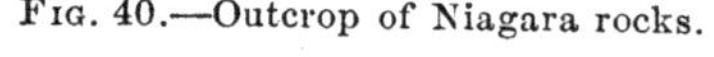
Fig. 40.—Outcrop of Niagara rocks.

Anemosa is situated on the Wapsipinicon, about a mile below the mouth of Buffalo creek. About three-fourths of a mile north of the confluence of these streams, a quarry has been opened, and material obtained for building a mill. The rock obtained here is a porous light straw-colored magnesian limestone, in layers which vary from four to five inches in thickness. The stone is soft and dresses well, answering a good purpose as a building material. No fossils were observed in it. Near the mouth of the creek, the rock is exposed in irregularly bedded layers of a grey or dove-colored limestone quite tough and compact in its texture. There are a few fragments of indistinct fossils, mostly corals, among which *Cyathophyllideæ* and *Stromatopora* were recognized, with an imperfect *Spirifer*.

On the banks of the Wapsipinicon, a short distance below the town, the rocks are exposed in bluffs about 100 feet in height. They are made up of a yellowish porous and somewhat crystalline magnesian limestone, in thick but irregularly stratified layers. Numerous traces of fossils were observed at this locality, but few of them distinctly preserved. The most common are corals, namely, *Cyathophyllideæ*, *Favosites*, *Stromatopora*, and also an abundance of fragments of the stems of crinoids. There are some good regularly-bedded layers in this vicinity, of a drab color, which are wrought into grave-stones; but the locality was not visited. It would appear that we have in these semi-crystalline porous magnesian limestones, and thinbedded drab-colored beds, the representations of the Leclaire limestone and the Onondaga-salt group as described in the section on the Mississippi river, in the preceding pages (See pages 73 to 80). A thorough and detailed examination of the valley of the Wapsipinicon, will not fail to throw much additional light on the range and extent of these groups.

Another locality where the Leclaire limestone was noticed is Walnut grove, two or three miles south of the Wapsipinicon, on the road from Dewitt to Davenport. The rocks are well exposed in the small creeks emptying into the river in this vicinity. At one locality, about a mile east of Walnut grove, there is an exposure of about thirty feet perpendicular of a magnesian limestone, of a yellowish grey color, which is filled with small cavities, which are casts of a species of brachiopod, in which the spiral apparatus of the animal is imperfectly preserved, as noticed under the head of Leclaire limestone in the preceding pages (See page 73). This outcrop continues all the way down the Wapsipinicon to the Mississippi. This is the farthest locality to the northwest, in which the Leclaire limestone has been distinctly recognized with these peculiar characters.

JACKSON COUNTY.

The Mississippi river bounds this county on the east; and the Makoqueta traverses it from west to east, with numerous branches, which head in Dubuque county and have a general southeasterly course. The surface of Jackson county is more broken and irregular than that of any other in this section of the State. The Makoqueta and its branches are skirted with timber, and the whole district between the north and south forks of that river is covered by one of the heaviest bodies of timber in Iowa. The white oak predominates here; but there are several varieties of this genus, together with hickory, black walnut, linden and sugar maple, the latter in greater abundance than is usual in this State. The soil is not, in general, of the finest quality. In the western tier of townships, the surface, where not covered by timber, is rather sandy : the same is true of portions of the township, farther east, along the course of the Makoqueta. The southern edge of the county is mostly high, rolling and somewhat broken prairie. The Tête des Morts valley in the northeastern corner of the county is one of the most picturesque and attractive in this region. On the edge of, or near, the stream there are cliffs of the Galena limestone, rising in some places fifty feet perpendicularly. Above this rock, we come upon a gently undulating region, having a rich soil, which extends back on each side of the creek, gradually rising, until it meets the bluffs, at a distance which diminishes as we ascend the stream. This undulating and fertile belt is underlaid by the soft and easily decomposed shales of the Hudson-river group, which are capped by the harder beds of the Niagara limestone, containing great numbers of silicious nodules, or flints, and forming a thickly-wooded crest around the valley, which is intersected by numerous ravines, the alternations in the character of the surface and vegetation giving a charming variety to the scene.

Nearly the whole of the county is underlaid by the Niagara limestone, which is everywhere exposed on the Makoqueta and its branches, often forming cliffs from fifty to a hundred feet in elevation. No other rock than this is seen in the interior of the county; but, on its eastern and northeastern edge, the Mississippi and its tributaries have cut down through the underlying Hudson-river shales into the Galena limestone, and exposed from fifty to a hundred feet in thickness of this latter rock. Along the east side of the Mississippi, from the northern line of the county nearly to Bellevue, the Galena limestone rises in cliffs of from fifty to one hundred feet in height near the river's edge; which are succeeded by an undulating and gently-ascending plateau of half a mile to a mile in width, formed by the Hudson-river group, which appears to have a thickness of from seventy to eighty feet, but is rarely exposed. This rock gradually sinks as we proceed down the river, and its lower edge nearly comes to a level with the water at Bellevue. The dip of the strata seems to be quite rapid in this region, as is shown by the position of the Hudson-river shales, which are met, in ascending the bluff at Dubuque, at an elevation of from 235 to 250 feet; while, at Bellevue, they have sunk to the water's edge, although the direction of the river in this part of its course is at a considerable angle with the line of greatest dip of the strata in this region. From Bellevue to Sabula, near which place the Hudson-river group finally disappears beneath the river, the dip is considerably less than it has been shown to be above the first-mentioned place.

The Niagara limestone, as developed in this district, is a

light greyish-yellow dolomite, which is generally somewhat crystalline in its texture. Its upper portion is more porous and softer than the lower, so that it is much less conspicuous than the harder strata below. In the southern part of the county these upper beds are seen occasionally, and especially in loose masses, which are characterized by the presence of numerous casts of the heads and stems of crinoids, of which the genus *Caryocrinus* is the most abundantly represented. These upper beds are not represented in any good section, owing to the facility with which the strata become disaggregated. The middle beds are, however, well exhibited in very numerous localities. The following section was measured about two miles east of Makoqueta, at Goodenow's quarry, from which building materials for the use of the town are largely quarried.

Loam and clay	8 feet.
Chert and red ferruginous clay	2 feet.
Thinbedded dolomite with flint, non-fossiliferous, the layers slightly argillaceous	8 feet.
Compact dolomite, distinctly bedded	8 inches.
Light buff-colored compact dolomite . . . . . . (This and the overlying layer are the only valuable building stone of the quarry).	1 foot.
Mass of dolomitic limestone, indistinctly bedded and not fully exposed, containing a few corals, of which *Syringopora* is the most conspicuous	90 feet.

In the above section, the eight-inch and one-foot layer, near the top of the quarry, are evenly-bedded and of the right texture for building materials : the lower ninety feet is made up of a rock too massive and unevenly bedded to be of much value.

At Tubbs's mill, near the town, there is an exposure of about thirty feet, where the following section was obtained:

Buff-colored dolomite, irregularly bedded and filled with casts of *Pentamerus* . . . . -	8 feet.
Heavybedded, greyish-yellow dolomite, in layers from eighteen inches to two feet in thickness	10 feet.
Thinnerbedded and somewhat ferruginous layers, with a few corals . :	12 feet.

The heavy beds in the centre of the section are separated from each other by cherty layers : they have been extensively quarried, and furnish a pretty good building stone.

Brush creek, which heads in the northern part of the county, and runs south through the centre of it, is bordered by bluffs from fifty to a hundred feet in height, which rise almost vertically from the river-bottom. The rock is usually a buff-colored dolomite, with numerous flinty nodules scattered through it, which impair its value as a building-stone. The only fossils which occur in any considerable abundance are corals, among which *Halysites catenulatus*, *Favosites* and *Stromatopora* are the most common. The same remark will apply to the outcrops on the North fork of the Makoqueta and Lytle's creek, a branch of the same.

The occurrence of iron ore in numerous localities in Jackson county will be noticed in the chapter devoted to economical geology; and in the same connection the diggings for lead ore, both in the Niagara limestone at various places and in the Galena or true lead-bearing rock, in the Tête des Morts valley, will be described.

DUBUQUE COUNTY.

The Little Makoqueta and its numerous branches water the northern and central portions of this county, while the larger stream of the same name, and its tributaries, run through the southern, southeastern and western townships. The Mississippi forms the eastern boundary of the county, and the Dubuque & Pacific railroad passes through the central portion of it, while other railroads are in contemplation, by which every part of the county will be rendered easily accessible. There is a considerable amount of water-power on both the Little and Big Makoqueta and their branches.

The nature of the surface and soil varies considerably in the different portions of the county. In the northeastern townships the streams have cut deep vallies, exposing the rocks in steep bluffs ; the surface is, therefore, quite broken, and a large part of it well timbered, mostly with oak of good quality. The soil of these townships is rather sandy, except in the river bottoms, where it is of the most fertile description. Dubuque township (T. 80, R. 2, E.) is mostly high rolling prairie, with very little timber except on the bluffs which line the Mississippi and mark the line of outcrop of the Niagara limestone. The township immediately west of this (T. 89, R. 1, E.) is very much broken and intersected with deep ravines ; it is almost entirely covered with timber of vigorous growth and a great variety of species. Farther west, in the same tier of townships, the country becomes more elevated and less broken, the proportion of timbered land to prairie constantly increasing. In the southern half of the county the same gradual passage from a broken timbered region, to the high rolling prairie, takes place in going from the east to the west. The central and western townships are almost entirely prairie, except in the extreme southwestern corner of the county, where the Makoqueta river and its tributaries have cut deep into the rocks. The elevation of the high prairie land in the centre of the county along the line of the Dubuque & Pacific railroad has been given in a preceding chapter (See page 3).

The geological formations which are exposed in this county include the various groups from the Trenton or Blue limestone up to the Niagara limestone; the exposures of the rocks, especially in the eastern part of the county, being numerous and satisfactory.

Beginning with the lowest group, the Trenton, and proceeding upwards in the series, the most important exposures will be noticed.

Trenton limestone. This rock first makes its appearance in ascending the Mississippi, in the neighborhood of Dubuque; and is exposed to a sufficient extent to be quarried, at Eagle point, about two miles above the city. Here the layers are from six to twelve inches in thickness, consisting of a tolerably compact bluish gray limestone, which contains *Ceraurus pleurexanthemus, Isotelus gigas, Orthis testudinaria, Strophomena alternata, Leptæna sericea* and other fossils commonly found in this geological position throughout this region. There is, at this point, a thickness of from twenty to thirty feet of this rock above low-water mark. On the opposite side of the river, at Dunleith, quarries are opened all along the bank, at about high-water mark, for a distance of a mile or two above the town. The rocks are similar in character to those of Eagle point; but certain layers near low-water mark are much more fossiliferous, and furnish the best specimens illustrating the character of organic life at this period, which have been procured in this region. These layers are of a light gray color, and thinbedded, with argillaceous partings, which become light yellow on exposure to the air, and are made up of a mass of brachiopods, crustaceans and bryozoa, weathering out with quite perfect forms, although composed of carbonate of lime, and apparently quite homogeneous in character with the surrounding rocks. The fact that this rock splits in layers of a suitable size for building purposes, and that it dresses well, being quite free from chert, renders it a desirable building stone, and it is much used for that purpose at Dubuque. The undulation of the strata are such in this region that the whole thickness of the Trenton limestone is brought up, in ascending the river, near the mouth of the Platte, the upper sandstone being exposed at that point. The strata decline to the north again rapidly, so as to bring the sandstone below the water at Cassville. The Trenton beds have not been noticed in Dubuque county, except on the Mississippi river.

Galena limestone. This rock is of great importance in this county, as the source of the lead-ore which has been so extensively mined in the vicinity of Dubuque. Bluffs of this rock border the Mississippi along its whole course on the east boundary of this county, and it is finely exposed on the Little Makoqueta and its branches, as also on the smaller streams emptying directly into the Mississippi. At Buenavista, the whole height of the bluffs which border the river is of the Galena limestone; but at a distance of between two and three miles from the river, the precipitous cliffs of the Niagara limestone may be seen, and can be followed in a southeasterly direction, passing about seven miles west of Dubuque, and gradually approaching the river again, and finally reaching it a little south of the Tête des Morts valley in Jackson county. The space thus enclosed between the Niagara limestone and the river, forming a belt some eight or ten miles wide in its widest part, is chiefly occupied by the Galena limestone, which may also be traced for some distance up all the vallies of the streams running down from the Niagara plateau.

The lithological character of the Galena limestone, as seen

in this county, where it is as well developed as in any part of the Northwest, is everywhere nearly the same. It is an almost pure dolomite, containing from three to eight percent of silicious substances intermixed with the double carbonate of lime and magnesia, and tinged of a light greyish color by a little carbonate of iron, where it has not been exposed, but which soon changes to a light buff by the oxidation of the iron, when acted on by air and moisture. A thickness of a little over 250 feet of this formation is exposed at Dubuque, and that seems to be about its maximum development.

One of the most characteristic features of the Galena limestone is its peculiar mode of weathering. It seems to decompose very unequally, and thus gives rise to a great variety of interesting forms, which give to the landscape, where this rock predominates, a singularly picturesque character. The summits of the bluffs bordering all the streams in the eastern and northeastern parts of the county are crowned with almost perpendicular ledges of this rock, which in many places have a castellated appearance, like the half ruined wall of some ancient fortified city. Occasionally isolated masses of rocks rise abruptly from the vallies, resembling lofty watch-towers. Some of the most curious of these outcrops may be seen on the Little Makoqueta, in the northeast corner of T. 89, R. 1 E. The annexed woodcut represents an isolated group of rocks of this formation, which is near the railroad, three and a half miles from Dubuque.

FIG. 41.— View of Outcrop of Galena limestone in the Catfish valley, near Dubuque.

The upper portion of this limestone is more regularly bedded than the lower, and hence the quarries near Dubuque are mostly at an elevation of about two hundred feet above the river. At this level the layers are from six to eight inches in thickness, and comparatively free from cherty nodules, which abound in the heavy-bedded portion below. As a building-stone, this rock answers quite well, having an agreeable tint; but it does not dress smoothly, or weather uniformly enough to be used for the best work. The custom-house at Galena, a city surrounded by bluffs of the *Galena*, is built of rock from the Carboniferous limestone group, brought from a point on the river two hundred miles distant. The lithological character and chemical composition of the Galena limestone, as well as of all the other rocks, will be noticed more at length in a special chapter devoted to that subject. The full description of the mode of occurrence of the various metallic ores which are found in this limestone, especially of lead and zinc, will be found farther on, in the chapter on economical geology.

Hudson-river group. For a notice of the occurrence of this group in Dubuque county, see page 64 of a preceding chapter, in which a detailed section of the strata belonging to this geological position, as exhibited on the Little Makoqueta, is given. In the chapter devoted to the chemical composition of the rocks, some farther remarks will be found on the lithological character of these rocks. In this connection, a few additional notes on the range and extent of the formation in Dubuque county will be added.

The shaly and easily decomposing nature of the rocks of which the Hudson-river group is made up, renders natural sections very uncommon; and although evidences of its existence has been obtained at many points, yet it has usually been by means of artificial excavations. In the Dubuque & Pacific railroad cut, a little west of the town of Julien, the blue shales have been intersected for a considerable distance, and the whole thickness of the group exposed; but the rock is so soft and crumbly and the sides had been so much washed down, that no satisfactory section could be observed. Within the limits of the city of Dubuque, on Julien avenue, at an elevation of two hundred and thirty-five feet above the river, the blue shales have been intersected in digging a well, and a fine specimen of *Isotelus gigas* obtained. In all the shafts which have been sunk for lead, on the highest ground between the streams in the vicinity of Dubuque, a greater or less thickness of this rock has been cut through. As the shales which are thrown out in the excavations are soon covered up at the mouth of the shaft by the underlying limestone, there is usually no opportunity to see the character of the section, except when one is on the spot at the time the digging is commenced. This accounts for the fact that the extension of the Hudson-river group over so much of the lead region was only so recently recognized. On Sections 15 and 16, in Dubuque township, the rock thrown out in the diggings consists mostly of a light grey but highly bituminous shale, with a few graptolitic impressions and occasional layers filled with Orthoceratites. On a small stream flowing north through Sections 18, 7 and 6, and a branch of the same in Sections 17 and 8, there are natural exposures of a few feet in thickness of a light-colored, coarse-grained, impure magnesian limestone, in which the Orthoceratites are crowded together in greater numbers, and in a more perfect state of preservation than at any other locality examined by us. The bed of the stream is filled with fragments of fossiliferous rock, containing great numbers of *Murchisonia* resembling *M. gracilis*, *Pleurotomaria*, *Lingula*, *Tellinomya*, and fragments of Orthoceratites. The best natural sections of the Hudson-river group, however, as before noticed, are on the Little Makoqueta river between Sims's mill and Channingsville, and in the small streams coming into it from the northwest (See section on page 66). No doubt, careful exploration will reveal other good exposures on the Middle fork of the Makoqueta and its branches. As we proceed towards the north from the Middle fork of the Catfish, where this group occupies the highest portions of the region over a width of six or seven miles, we find more and more of it removed by denudation ; and on the northern edge of the county, it forms only a very narrow strip along the base of the bluffs of the Niagara limestone.

Niagara limestone. This formation occupies all the elevated prairie region of Dubuque county, comprising about three-fourths of its surface. The line of outcrop is well marked, and may be traced in a range of precipitous bluffs, having a very irregular outline, and with occasional outliers, in a direction parallel with Turkey river, and at a distance of from one to two miles from it, diagonally across the country, gradually curving in towards the Mississippi to the south of the city of Dubuque, and approaching it within a distance of half a mile near the Tête des Morts valley. The numerous small streams which descend from the elevated plateau of the Niagara, have cut deeply down into the rocks, so that the lower formations may be followed up the vallies far above the point where the Niagara occupies the general level of the country. For this reason, and also partly on account of the irregular denudation, the range of bluffs indicating the outcrop of the Niagara is very irregular, with numerous projecting spurs, which extend out sometimes in long narrow flat-topped ridges with almost vertical sides, giving a peculiar and picturesque character to the landscape. The elevation of these ridges is usually from five hundred to six hundred feet above the Mississippi, and from one hundred and fifty to two hundred feet above the rolling and gently declining belt, occupied by the Hudson-river shales, at their base. The outlying masses capped by the Niagara limestone, which are so conspicuous in the lead-region, and which are known as *mounds*, have already been alluded to (pages 12 and 13).

The annexed section will give an idea of the relations of the different members of the series in the vicinity of the Mississippi river, and will indicate the amount of denudation to which this whole region has been subjected. The longitudinal extension of the section is about twelve miles; and the height of the Niagara limestone, as still seen in the outlier known as Sinsinnewa mound, is nearly six hundred feet above the river. That the strata were once continuous over this space, can hardly be doubted; and when it is considered that we have outliers of the same character, and about the same elevation, at various distances, for forty miles to the northeast of Sinsinnewa, some idea of the long continued action of denuding forces over this region may be obtained. In the case of the Blue mounds, the preservation of the strata seems to have been due to the great hardness of the Niagara limestone at this point, since the upper portion of the higher mound is found to have been entirely converted into a silicious mass.

Fig. 42.

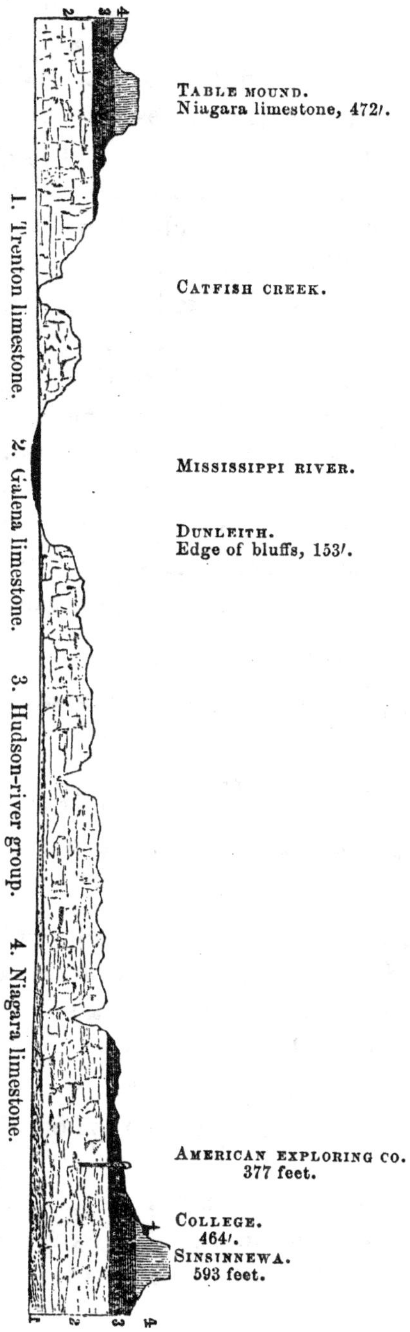

1. Trenton limestone. 2. Galena limestone. 3. Hudson-river group. 4. Niagara limestone.

Table mound. Niagara limestone, 472f.

Catfish creek.

Mississippi river.

Dunleith. Edge of bluffs, 153f.

American exploring co. 377 feet.

College. 464f.

Sinsinnewa. 593 feet.

The Niagara limestone, throughout this region, presents nearly the same lithological character. It is a nearly pure dolomite, not differing materially in chemical composition from the Galena limestone, but being usually a little less crystalline in its texture and more distinctly stratified than that rock. It contains, also, numerous intercalated bands or irregular layers of chert, which are especially abundant in the middle portion of the series, and which, as the strata become disaggregated by exposure, accumulate on the surface, especially on the elevations from which the soil has been washed down into the vallies, and which, on this account, are frequently designated as "flint-ridges". This rock, when not too cherty, forms a valuable building material and is quarried in numerous places for that purpose. The following section at a quarry on the Delhi road, about eight miles west of Dubuque, near the summit of the ridge, will give an idea of the succession of the beds in this portion of the Niagara.

Thinbedded flinty layers	4 feet.
Heavy layers alternating with cherty bands two or three inches thick	5 feet.
Fine white and compact dolomite in beds from 6 to 14 inches thick, with a few thin layers of chert	5 feet.
Irregularly stratified and somewhat concretionary beds, with shaly partings : thickness not known.	

Rocks very similar in character to these are quarried on Waddles's mound near Galena, and used for building in preference to the Galena limestone, which is less regularly bedded and weathers more unequally than the Niagara.

The exposures of the Niagara limestone in the southwestern portion of the county, on the north fork of the Makoqueta and its branches, are very numerous. There is not unfrequently a thickness of one hundred and fifty to one hundred and eighty feet exhibited in the river bluffs of that region. On the edges of the bluffs the soil is usually thin, and filled with angular fragments of chert; but on receding a short distance from the streams, the rocks are found to be covered with a heavy covering of finely comminuted materials, forming a rolling and highly fertile country.

The lower beds of the Niagara are not very fossiliferous, but the upper ones are everywhere characterized by the presence of corals, which, having been silicified, resist the influence of the weather and accumulate on the ridges in considerable quantity. Among the corals, *Halysites catenulatus* is the most conspicuous; but *Favosites, Lyellia, Stromatopora, Syringopora, Heliolites* and other genera are each represented by one or more species. *Pentamerus oblongus* is also accumulated in some localities in great numbers.

DELAWARE AND BUCHANAN COUNTIES.

THESE two counties were traversed at different times by members of the geological corps, but were not explored with any minuteness. The region is mostly rolling prairie, and the exposures of the rocks are not satisfactory, although not unfrequent on the principal streams.

The Makoqueta runs diagonally through the centre of Delaware county, and has numerous small branches flowing into it from each side, in a direction nearly at right angles to its course. The streams are fringed with timber, and there are occasional groves; but the larger part of the county is a rich and fertile rolling prairie.

The only rock seen in place in Delaware county is the Niagara limestone, which crops out on all the streams in the northeastern townships, with the same lithological characters, and containing the same fossils which have been noticed as belonging to this formation in the adjoining county to the east. The bluffs, however, are much less elevated than they are in Dubuque or Clayton counties, as the streams are smaller and have not cut their beds down so deeply. The most western exposure of rock observed in Delaware county was at Coffin's grove, where the Niagara was seen in low cliffs, containing the usual corals which everywhere in this regiòn mark the presence of this rock. Beyond this point to the westward, no rocks are exposed, either on the road to Independence, or for some distance on either side of it, until we reach the Wapsipinicon river. The outcrop of the Leclaire limestone, or of other groups intermediate between the Niagara and the Hamilton group, was sought for in vain in the district near the borders of Delaware and Buchanan counties.

No other rocks were observed in Buchanan county than those belonging to the Hamilton group, which make their appearance on the Wapsipinicon at Independence, and are seen along the river as far down as the south boundary of the county. There is a vertical thickness of about one hundred feet exposed at Independence in the ledges which border the river and the quarries which are near the town, a short distance to the east. The upper beds are made up of a somewhat argillaceous carbonate of lime, which is not crystalline, and breaks with an irregular fracture : they are highly fossiliferous, containing an abundance of *Spirifer* and *Atrypa* and a few corals. The strata near the level of the river have a brecciated character, and are less fossiliferous than those exposed at the quarry.

These rocks are burned for lime, and are valuable for that purpose, but they are too irregularly bedded to be of much value as a building material.

CLAYTON COUNTY.

THIS county is bounded on the east by the Mississippi river and is watered by the Turkey river and its numerous branches, as well as by several smaller streams which are directly tributary to the Mississippi. The Turkey runs diagonally through the county from northwest to southeast; its principal branch is the Volga, and both these streams have numerous smaller affluents, of which the Little Turkey, Cedar, Pony, Dry Mill, Bear, Elk and Cox creeks are the most important. The county is well watered, and furnished with abundant water-power. The surface of Clayton county is quite broken, and the larger part of it is covered by heavy timber. Turkey river runs between high and precipitous bluffs, and is bordered along its entire conrse with an abundant supply of oak, sugar maple, blackwalnut, ash and linden. There is an irregular belt of rolling prairie extending through the county from southeast to northwest along the divide between the streams flowing directly into the Mississippi and those which are tributary to the Turkey, and also a few small tracts between the Volga and the Turkey which are not covered with timber. The soil is, generally, excellent, especially in the river bottoms. In the southeast corner of the county it is rather clayey, and the sub-soil throughout this part of the State is usually quite argillaceous. On the whole, Clayton county stands among the first in the State, taking into consideration soil, abundance of timber, water-power and general situation.

The whole series of rocks, from the Niagara limestone downwards to the Lower Magnesian, is exposed within the limits of Clayton county; and at numerous points, especially on the Mississippi and the Turkey, good sections may be obtained.

Beginning with the southern extremity of the county and proceeding northward, which takes us from higher rocks to those which are lower in the geological series, we pass successively over the Niagara, the Hudson-river, the Galena and the Trenton limestones, which latter rock occupies the greater part of the surface in the northern tier of townships, while the streams have cut down, in that region, to a considerable depth in the Lower Magnesian. South of Buenavista, Millville and Newstand, the outcrop of the Niagara limestone is marked by an irregular precipitous line of bluffs which have an elevation of from five hundred to six hundred feet above the river. This line of outcrop is at a distance of three or four miles from the Mississippi and Turkey rivers, and is a distinctly marked feature of the country through the whole extent of the county. The Volga river intersects the Niagara a short distance above Elkport, and the high bluffs of this rock are continued along nearly parallel with the course of the Turkey, and at a distance of from one to two miles from that stream. The elevation of the outcropping edges of this rock was estimated at four hundred feet above the valley. The bluffs, however, gradually decline in height from the southeast to the northwest. On the Volga, near Volga city, they rise to an elevation of about seven hundred feet above the valley, which is here about two miles in width. The varied grouping of the bluffs, combined with the richness of the valley, give a highly picturesque character to the scenery of this part of the county. In its lithological character, the Niagara limestone of this region is very little different from that of the region farther south. It has a light buff-grey color, weathering with a decided yellow tinge, and is rather heavy-bedded, although not very distinctly stratified. At a point about three miles south of Elkader, a number of fossils were collected from this rock, among which *Favosites niagarensis* was the most conspicuous. In the bluffs south of Elgin, at a distance of about two and a half miles from that place, and an estimated elevation above the Turkey of three hundred and fifty feet, numerous corals were found, including *Halysites catenulatus*, *Heliolites* ——*?*, and *Syringopora* n.sp. The region occupied by the Niagara limestone in the southwestern corner of the county is quite elevated, and much of it is very broken. It is from one-fourth to one-third prairie, and the soil is frequently rather sandy and filled with fragments of chert.

The Hudson-river group undoubtedly extends through the county, as it has been recognized in the adjoining one on the west, although quite different in character from the same group in the vicinity of the Mississippi. A few small patches still remain, and are occasionally exposed by artificial excavations between the Mississippi and Turkey rivers. In the neighborhood of Garnavillo, the shales of this group have been intersected in several places in digging wells. The presence of these shales, which form by their ready decomposition a deep argillaceous soil, gives a peculiar character of fertility and beauty to this region.

The Galena limestone crops out on the Mississippi river, forming the whole mass of the bluffs at the southern edge of the county, but thinning out gradually to the north as the successive lower groups make their appearance above the water. It finally disappears on the river altogether in the neighborhood of Clayton, the Trenton limestone there being the highest rock exposed in the bluffs. In the interior of the county we find the Galena occupying the valley of the Turkey river, extending to the south for two or three miles, as far as the line of bluffs indicating the outcrop of the Niagara, and northward over nearly the whole extent of the county, excepting a narrow belt along the Mississippi and some of its smaller tributaries in the northeast corner of the county. The region occupied by it is chiefly prairie, with a good soil. The rocks are exposed in the vallies of all the small streams, furnishing convenient material for building.

The relations of the Galena limestone to the Trenton are well exhibited in the section exposed on Turkey river at Elkader, where a thickness of about 170 feet may be examined. At the level of the river at the bridge, there is a thickness of ten or twelve feet of thin grey layers, weathering yellow in irregular bands and patches, and containing an abundance of *Leptæna sericea, Schizocrinus nodosus, Orthis testudinaria* and other characteristic Trenton fossils, and numerous *Receptaculites*. Above this are found a succession of greyish, somewhat crystalline, limestones which are quarried to some extent for building-stones. These beds are not fossiliferous so far as observed, although not exposed in their whole thickness at any one point. At an elevation of one hundred and twenty to one hundred and thirty feet, the rock is thickbedded and crystalline, and resembles in character the Galena limestone, as usually seen in the lead region. This is succeeded by about thirty feet of a compact grey limestone, tinged with blue in some places, which is extensively quarried for building, and seems to be a pretty good rock for this purpose. The layers are from six to eight inches thick, and are separated from each other by shaly partings, which contain a few fossils, among which are *Leptæna sericea, L. planumbona, Orthis* n.sp., *O. testudinaria, O. subæquata, Lingula quadrata* and numerous very minute joints of crinoidal columns. Thus the intermingling of Trenton and Galena fossils, as well as the repetition of peculiar lithological characters, is very marked at this locality. Near the north line of the county, a short distance north of Monona, on Suttle's creek, the Galena limestone is exposed in cliffs thirty or forty feet high. The layers at this point are quite heavy, varying from two to four feet in thickness : the rock is irregular in texture, and of a light buff color. No fossils were observed except a few stems of crinoids and fragments of *Orthocerata*. This rock is quarried for use in the town of Monona, and for burning into lime. In this direction, this was the most northerly locality at which the Galena limestone was observed. Numerous diggings for lead in this rock have been carried on in this county, especially in the neighborhood of Buenavista and Gutenberg. These will be particularly noticed in the chapter devoted to the economical geology.

The Trenton limestone covers but a small extent of surface in Clayton county. It is well exposed, however, on the Mississippi, from Gutenberg northward as far as the county line, and, in occasional patches, for a distance of a few miles back from the river. At Gutenberg the Trenton limestone may be observed resting on the upper sandstone, which disappears below the level of the river near this place. The lower beds, of which about forty feet are exposed, at the south end of the bluff near the mouth of Mineral creek, three miles below Gutenberg, are heavy-bedded, and are made up of a series of layers of a bluish-grey, argillaceous limestone, weathering of a buff color. These layers are extensively quarried for building purposes and for lime, and furnish a good material for these uses. These thicker layers are succeeded by a few feet of thinbedded, brittle, light-grey limestone, filled with the usual fossils of the Trenton. Above these beds, the Galena limestone may be observed, capping the bluff, with a thickness of over one hundred feet. About two miles north of Gutenberg there is a good section of the rocks exposed along the line of the road leading westward from the town. In a distance of about a mile we attain an elevation of four hundred feet above the river; of this, three hundred and fifty-six feet is a very abrupt rise, and the rocks are exposed at frequent intervals for this distance. The remaining forty-four feet is a gradual ascent, due chiefly to the superficial detritus and soil. Of the three hundred and fifty-six feet, the lower fifty-seven are a soft white sandstone which is overlaid by thin shaly blue limestone, succeeded by thicker bedded bluish-grey fossiliferous layers, the whole thickness referable to the Trenton being a little over one hundred feet. Above this there is about two hundred feet of the Galena, with the usual characters of that rock. Throughout this region the thicker and more compact layers of the Trenton form the best material for building and for lime, which can be obtained.

The rocks beneath the Trenton are not developed in this county except on the Mississippi and in its immediate vicinity, and they have already been sufficiently noticed in a preceding chapter (See page 56).

FAYETTE COUNTY.

The position of this county is next west of the one just noticed. The main branch of Turkey river runs through its northeastern corner; and the south fork, with numerous small branches, comes in from the western side. The Volga rises in the centre of the county, and drains the larger portion of its southern two-thirds. The southwestern corner is imperfectly watered by small affluents of the Wapsipinicon. The region bordering on the Turkey is very broken, and is well timbered. The southwestern portion is high prairie land, and as yet almost entirely uninhabited, the settlements in the county being thus far chiefly confined to the north side of a diagonal drawn across it from the northwest corner to the southeast.

The Niagara limestone occupies about five-sixths of the surface of Fayette. It is well exhibited in various sections in the vicinity of West-Union, on Otter creek, and on Turkey river, at Auburn and above that point. On Otter creek, at Wiley's quarries, a thickness of one hundred and thirty-five feet is exposed, resting on dark blue shales which appear to belong to the Hudson-river group. The lower layers are somewhat soft and irregularly stratified, resembling the Niagara as seen in the immediate vicinity of the Mississippi. Above these is a very hard and almost white limestone, differing considerably from any rock seen in this geological position in the more southern portion of Iowa, but closely resembling a rock of the same age on the northern shore of Lake Michigan. This white mass, which is at least one hundred feet in thickness, is capped by a dark buff limestone, which is rather argillaceous, and contains numerous minute crystals of calc. spar scattered through it. It forms layers of about seven inches in thickness; and as it splits and dresses pretty well, it furnishes a tolerable building-stone. Above this dark limestone, there is a considerable thickness of a hard grey limestone, with seams of calc. spar running through it, which is too brittle to dress well, but is quarried near West-Union for underpinning.

Proceeding from West-Union northwestwardly, we descend into the valley of Turkey river. Here the Niagara limestone is exposed, and appears to have a thickness of something over two hundred and fifty feet. At Auburn, the lowest rock seen is a dark buff-colored, arenaceous, magnesian limestone, which crops out just on a level with the river. Rising above this, we observe a very hard dolomite, which is compact in its texture and weathers very white : the upper portion is of a light-grey color, and very compact and brittle. Nowhere in this region was there any trace of organic life observed in these rocks. Two and one-half miles south of Elgin, however, and at an estimated elevation of three hundred and fifty feet above the Turkey, a number of corals were collected, among which *Syringopora multicaulis*, *Halysites catenulatus*, and *Heliolites spinipora* were recognized. The same fossils were collected by Mr. HUNGERFORD about nine miles south of Elgin, on the head-waters of the Volga.

The only point where the Hudson-river group was noticed in this county was on Otter creek, about two and a half miles southeast of West-Union. A blue shale or clay makes its appearance at the bottom of the valley, although no good exposure was found. A small fragment was found, in which *Leptæna sericea* and *Orthis occidentalis* were observed.

The Galena limestone appears in the valley of the Turkey, through its whole length in this county. It is not, however, the lowest rock observed there, as the Trenton may be seen underlying it at various points, from near the mouth of the Volga, up at least as far as Fort Atkinson. At Elgin, the bluffs on the north side of the river, at an elevation of three hundred feet, and a distance of two miles from the stream, exhibit all the characters of the Galena limestone, but contain no fossils, as far as could be ascertained, from which their identity with this formation could be positively asserted. In the notice of the geology of Winnesheik county, some additional remarks will be made on the position of the rocks in the Turkey valley, and especially with reference to the probable existence of a fault along the course of this river.

The Trenton limestone was noticed at various points in the valley of the Turkey, underlying the Galena, and being the lowest rock exposed in this county, so far as was observed. At Elgin, near the mouth of Otter creek, and for some distance down the Turkey, below the confluence of the two streams, the Trenton limestone is seen at the level of the river, in ledges from six to ten feet in height. The rock is a thinbedded, almost shaly, limestone, portions of which are quite argillaceous, containing from eight to ten percent of clayey matter. Some of the layers are crowded with the remains of trilobites, almost all of them belonging to the species of *Asaphus* (*Isotelus*) described by Dr. D. D. Owen, from this locality, under the name of *A. iowensis*, a species closely resembling, if not identical with, *A. gigas*. Some slabs were obtained, on which the remains of perhaps a hundred individuals might be distinguished; but for some reason, only the tails were preserved, and not a single specimen of the entire animal was obtained. A few impressions of graptolites were noticed at this locality, this being the only place in this region where they were found so low down in the geological series.

The southwestern portion of the county has been but little explored, as it is still unsettled : it is mostly rolling prairie, not very well watered, and showing but few outcrops of rocks. It is supposed from its position, and from what is known of the geology of the adjacent counties, to be underlaid by rocks of Hamilton age, the space occupied by the Niagara limestone narrowing rapidly towards the northwest.

Near the western edge of the county, on Crane creek, at a point eleven and a half miles below Jacksonville, Mr. HUNGERFORD observed a section of beds which appear to belong to the Hamilton group : the section is as follows :

5. Thin shaly beds, same as No. 4	1 ft. 6 in.
4. Irregularly stratified beds, of a somewhat argillaceous magnesian limestone	6 feet.
3. Light yellowish-grey hard and brittle limestone . . .	1 ft. 1 in.
2. Fossiliferous band, same character as No. 1	6 inches.
1. Light-grey limestone ; hard but not brittle	2 ft. 2 in.
To level of Crane creek, rock not exposed	2 ft. 6 in.

No. 4 is a peculiar looking buff-grey magnesian limestone, which contains about seven per cent of insoluble matter, mostly clay. It is shaded with concentric bands of a dark buff color. When first taken from the quarry, it may be easily cut with a knife, but it grows harder on exposure. Bed No. 2 contains a small *Orthis* resembling *O. elegantula*, and an imperfect *Atrypa* like *A. reticularis*. No. 1 also contains *Atrypa reticularis*, of which well characterized specimens were obtained in loose fragments, which were supposed to be from this bed.

HOWARD, MITCHELL, CHICKASAW, AND FLOYD COUNTIES.

The reconnoissance of the district comprised in these four counties was made by Prof. Hungerford; and the following brief notice of their geology is derived from his notes, and from the examination of specimens collected by him.

This region is drained by the head-waters of the Turkey, Wapsipinicon and Cedar rivers. The Turkey heads in the centre of Howard county, and the Upper Iowa pursues a winding course through the northern tier of townships, running with a generally eastern direction. The south fork of the Turkey, or Crane creek as it is generally called, is a clear rapid stream, furnishing good water-power, which has been improved at several points. It flows through the centre of Howard, and the northeastern corner of Chickasaw county, pursuing a very direct southeasterly course. The central portion of Chickasaw, and the borders of Howard and Mitcheli are imperfectly drained by the head-waters of the Wapsipinicon, which flow through a level and rather marshy region; the streams, however, through this low country, are quite heavily skirted with timber. The larger portion of Mitchell and Floyd, as also of Worth and Cerro-Gordo counties, is drained by the Cedar and its branches, of which Lime and Shellrock creeks are the most important. These are all beautiful and rapid streams, skirted with timber and furnishing good water-power at numerous points. There are also many rock exposures in the banks of these streams, although no high bluffs occur, the ledges of rock not usually exceeding ten or twenty feet in height. The region between the vallies of the streams is mostly gently rolling prairie, destitute of timber, which is almost exclusively confined to the edges of the streams: the soil is usually highly fertile. The settlements are chiefly in the neighborhood of the rivers, where timber, water-power, and building-materials are abundant, and where the flourishing condition of most of the towns, which have only been very recently settled, attests the presence of an industrious population, possessed of unusual advantages of position and soil.

The larger portion of this extensive region, which embraces over 3000 square miles, if we include in it Worth and Cerro-Gordo counties, appears to be chiefly underlaid by rocks of the Hamilton group; which, although differing considerably in lithological characters at various exposures, are still characterized by the same fossils, which have been collected in this group at numerous points farther south. The details of some of the sections measured by Prof. HUNGERFORD are as follows:

In passing from Jacksonville to Bradford, in Chickasaw county, a distance of eighteen miles, across a region drained by the three forks of the Wapsipinicon, not a single exposure of rock was found. The whole district is one vast expanse of low level prairie, excepting the fringes of wood land along the courses of the streams.

Near the east bank of the Cedar, one and a half miles below Bradford, the annexed section was measured at the quarry of the brothers Layton:

Dark-gray thick shaly limestone	7 feet.
Buff-grey crystalline limestone with calcareous spar cavities,	5 inches.
Light-grey, fine-grained limestone	9 inches.
Hard, dark-grey shaly limestone	8 inches.
Hard, dark-grey limestone	7 inches.
Unexposed	2 feet.
Light, buff-grey limestone	1 ft. 8 in.

The limestones exposed at this quarry are of medium purity, and mostly quite hard: they are entirely destitute of fossils, so far as observed.

In passing up the Cedar river to St. Charles, on the west bank, the road lies over a rolling prairie. In the ridges limestones occur, as is shown by the presence of occasional fragments lying on the surface, or perhaps here and there an imperfect exposure. The beds, as observed, are mostly shaly, and singularly devoid of fossils. An actual river section seems necessary to the determination of their relations to each other.

On the Cedar, at St. Charles, there is a small opening in thin beds of hard, buff-colored limestone. Under these beds occurs a thick-bedded, light-grey limestone, shading off into buff-grey : it contains numerous concretions. Both the upper and lower beds contain a few fossils, all of which are in a very imperfect condition, so that only one, an *Atrypa reticularis*, could be made out. There were a few fragments of corals obtained here, which are too poorly preserved to be distinctly recognized.

The next section was taken at a quarry three-fourths of a mile above St. Charles, on the west side of the river. The beds are of very hard limestone, which is mostly fine-grained and rather brittle : they vary in thickness from four inches to one foot; and the different layers resemble each other so much that they could hardly be distinguished in hard specimens, especially as they are all equally unfossiliferous. The whole section exposed is only nine feet above the level of the dam at St. Charles, of which two at the base are concealed by detritus.

The court-house at St. Charles is built of this rock, which is a good material for building, although too brittle to dress evenly and handsomely. The quarry is conveniently situated for use, as the back-water from the dam sets up as far as that, and allows the blocks to be rafted down to the town. The beds exposed at this point are probably a little higher in the series than those of the section at St. Charles; but, as there is considerable irregularity in the dip at this point, this could not be determined with certainty. At the quarry above the dam the dip was observed to be 10°, in a direction S. 25° W.

On Lime creek, one mile above Rockford, the annexed section was measured :

Soil, &c	5 feet.
Decomposed limestone detritus with numerous fossils . . .	25 feet.
Blue clay (foot of precipitous bluff, one-eighth of a mile from Lime creek)	20 feet.
A gently inclining surface, mostly unexposed, with buff and white striped shaly limestone at the base	43 ft. 10 in.
Unexposed	2 feet.
Dark colored, hard limestone	2 feet.
White, pure limestone with shaly structure	5 ft. 6 in.
Hard, buff calcarcous sandstone, with *Spirifer*	2 ft. 8 in.
Soft ash-colored calcareous sandstone	1 ft. 3 in.
Arenaceous clay shales	2 ft. 6 in.
Beds not exposed down to level of Lime creek	3 feet.
Entire elevation	112 ft. 9 in.

The beds represented in this section as made up of decomposing limestone detritus, underlaid by a heavy deposit of clay, form the abrupt termination of one of the highest ridges in this region, which runs up from the southeast to within a short distance of Lime creek.

The upper bed of the section contains an abundance of fossils, which are washed out by the rain from the decomposing rock. Among these were observed, *Atrypa rugosa* or *spinosa*, *A. reticularis*, *Orthis* one or two new species, *Spirifer* n. sp., *Strophomena*, and a few Hamilton corals (See chapter on Palæontology).

On Shellrock creek, at Rockford, the exposures of the rocks are very limited. There is a light greyish buff-colored stratum, which is a somewhat argillaceous dolomite, but rather soft and worthless for building purposes, succeeded by a bed of a slightly darker color, but of essentially the same character. These beds are probably lower in the geological series than those indicated in the preceding section.

At Shellrock falls, in Cerro-Gordo county, about thirteen miles above Rockford, the absence of fossils in the beds exposed renders it difficult to assign them any certain place, although, from their position, they may be supposed to belong to the upper part of the Hamilton or the Chemung group. They consist of thinbedded hard and rather crystalline magnesian limestones, varying in color from light-grey to almost black. The exposure of the rocks at this locality is good, but the most careful search failed to reveal the presence of any fossils. The lithological character of the rocks at Shellrock creek and falls is peculiar, and nothing exactly like it has been observed in other parts of the State. They are all highly magnesian but not pure dolomites, as they contain rather more lime than belongs to the composition of the double carbonate of lime and magnesia. The specimens from Shellrock creek have a considerable resemblance to those from Cedar falls, which are referred to the Chemung by Mr. WORTHEN, with some doubt as to their real position, since they are quite unfossiliferous. The beds at Shellrock falls are very magnesian limestones, or dolomites with a little excess of lime, and are remarkably free from silicious and argillaceous substances. One specimen analysed from this locality, contained less than two percent of impurities mixed with the carbonate of lime and magnesia. These beds are too irregular in their texture for good building-stone, some of them being hard and brittle, and others soft and perishable. They are valuable, however, for lime, and some of them will probably furnish good hydraulic cement.

In Mitchell county, about one and a half miles above Newburg, on the Cedar, there is a tolerable exposure of the rocks where the following section was observed :

Crystalline limestone, sandy at the bottom, but growing more calcareous towards the top	2 feet.
Dark-grey thinbedded limestone	8 inches.
Dark-grey hard and brittle limestones in heavy layers, varying from 8 inches to 4 feet in thickness.	13 ft. 4 in.
Rock not exposed, down to level of dam at Newbury . . .	2 ft. 6 in.

Another section was measured at Newburg, the base of which is on the same level with the preceding one; but as there is little agreement in their details, it appears that the dip of the strata has probably carried the beds of the upper one below those of the lower.

The section at Newburg is as follows:

Beds of detritus with *Spirifer*, of irregular thickness.	
13. Hard brittle light greyish-yellow magnesian limestone .	4 feet.
12. Unexposed	4 feet.
11. Hard light-grey somewhat crystalline beds, with concretionary bands of darker color	8 feet.
10. Soft sandy beds with clay	2 ft. 8 in.
9. Hard light-grey silicious limestone	1 ft. 3 in.
8. Hard limestone like No. 9, decomposing into a sandy rock,	10 inches.
7, 6, 5, 4, 3, 2, 1. Beds of hard buff-grey limestone varying from 4 to 14 inches in thickness, and in various stages of decomposition	4 ft. 4 in.
Unexposed, to level of river at Newburg	6 feet.

In this section, No. 11 and No. 13 contain *Spirifer* closely resembling *S. mucronatus*: no other fossils were noticed.

Prof. Hungerford remarks in regard to the lithological resemblances of the rocks of these two sections, that there is a very great similarity between some of the beds of the Newburg section and those noticed on the borders of Winnesheik and Chickasaw counties, near the road from Fort Atkinson to Jacksonville, in descending the high ridge towards the Little Turkey. In this vicinity, near a lime-kiln, loose masses of limestone were observed, marked by concretionary lines, and having that peculiar softness and fineness of grain which was noticed above as belonging to bed No. 11 of the Newburg section. The same rock is seen in No. 4 of the section eleven and a half miles below Jacksonville on Crane creek.

WINNESHEIK COUNTY.

This county lies next west of Alamakee, and directly south of the Minnesota line. The Upper Iowa river runs through its northern portion, pursuing a southeast course from the northwest corner of the county, as far as Decorah, and then bending to the northeast, and keeping that direction to the eastern line of the county. The Turkey river and numerous small branches of it drain the southwestern part. The northern part of the county is much broken, while the southern is smoother and has more prairie. The valley of Turkey river, in the portion of its course which is within this county, is a beautiful farming region, having a wide bottom, bordered with low bluffs, succeeded by rolling prairie. There is an abundance of timber and water almost everywhere within the limits of the county.

The rocks which are exposed in Winnesheik county are the same as in Alamakee, namely from the Lower Sandstone as far up in the series as the lower beds of the Galena; although as we advance in a northwesterly direction the distinction between the Trenton and Galena is no longer as marked, either by lithological or palæontological characters, as it was farther to the southeast.

The Lower Sandstone occupies but a very limited space, in the bed of Bear creek and its branches, in the extreme northeastern corner of the county.

The Lower Magnesian is seen on Canoe creek, one of the branches of the Upper Iowa, as well as overlying the sandstone in Bear creek. It covers a small extent of surface in the region between these two streams. As seen on Canoe creek, six miles north of Decorah, it is a hard crystalline rock of a light-grey color, having a peculiar vitreous lustre, due to its finely crystalline granular structure. There is a section of about thirty or forty feet exposed at this point, and the same rock occurs at intervals for some distance up the stream. The Upper Sandstone caps the bluffs in this region at an elevation of about one hundred and forty feet above the stream.

The central portion of the county is chiefly occupied by the Trenton limestone, which gradually passes into the Galena as we proceed towards the southwest. At Decorah, on the Upper Iowa and in its immediate vicinity, the Trenton is finely displayed; this rock forming the whole thickness of the ridges and bluffs which border the river at this place. Near the town the rock is thinbedded and almost shaly : it is crowded with fossils, which, however, have not weathered out so as to form good specimes. There is a thickness of one hundred and thirty to one hundred and forty feet displayed in the bluffs a little southwest of the town, where the rock is a pure limestone of a light-grey color, weathering a dirty blue, and crowded with fossils. Of the *Receptaculites*, two species occur here abundantly in the upper beds, at an elevation of from one hundred to one hundred and thirty feet above the river. One of these species is the usual one of the Galena limestone ; the other is apparently identical with the fossil described by Dr. OWEN as *Selenoides iowensis*. Besides this, casts of *Murchisonia bellicincta* and *Maclurea magna* are not unfrequent at this locality ; also *Pleurotomaria lenticularis* and *Leptæna sericea*. About three miles north of the town, near a small creek which empties into the Upper Iowa at Decorah, there are good exposures of the Trenton, where the beds are crowded with fossils, although they do not weather out distinctly enough to be of much value as specimens. *Leptæna sericea*, and a small *Atrypa* resembling *A. modesta*, are the most common fossils at this locality. At Calmar, ten miles southwest of Decorah, the rocks occupying the surface are evidently the lower beds of the Galena. About three-fourths of a mile from the town there is a quarry exposing a series of thinbedded, buff-colored, somewhat arenaceous limestones. The upper beds at this point are shaly and exceedingly cherty, while the lower ones are thicker, and, when not weathered, of the usual bluish color of the beds of the Trenton in this region.

At Fort Atkinson and up the valley of the Turkey, the relations of the Trenton with the Galena may be satisfactorily observed. The annexed section was measured by Mr. HUNGERFORD one mile above the fort, at a quarry belonging to Mr. Charles Clark.

Light buff-grey shaly limestone	10 feet.
Buff and light-grey limestone	4 ft. 9 inches.
Heavy-bedded blue limestone	7 feet.
Not exposed ; to level of river	20 feet.

The plateau on which the fort stands is elevated eighty-four feet above the river, and the rock is exposed along its east side, where it has been quarried for building and for lime. The Galena limestone was traced by Prof. HUNGERFORD for a distance of four or five miles up Turkey river from Fort Atkinson. It possesses here all the characteristic features of this rock as exhibited in the lead region : its color is the same, and it weathers in the same irregular, ragged manner. The characteristic fossils of the Galena limestone, especially the *Receptaculites*, were also observed in this region. As far as known, no lead has been found in this county. At Ossian, the rocks exposed are similar in character to those noticed above as occurring at Calmar. In fact, the elevated region between the Turkey and Upper Iowa is undoubtedly occupied by the upper beds of the Trenton and the lower ones of the Galena limestone.

Proceeding southwestwardly from Fort Atkinson, we find, in the extreme southwest corner of the county, an elevated ridge, running parallel with the course of the Little Turkey, in which no rock is exposed; but which, from its position and relation to the rocks known to exist in the neighboring counties, is undoubtedly the outcrop of the Niagara limestone. In descending this ridge towards the west, Mr. HUNGERFORD observed loose masses of thinbedded, white, crystalline-granular limestone, very free from silicious matter, which appear to belong to the Niagara limestone, although exhibiting a different lithological character from that displayed by this group farther to the southeast.

The outcrop of the Niagara limestone, which is so conspicuous a feature in the topography of Dubuque county, continues to be equally well marked through Clayton. It follows the line of Turkey river, keeping at a distance of from two to five miles from it, and forming a line of precipitous bluffs elevated from five hundred to six hundred feet by estimation, above the level of the valley. No indication of the existence of the Niagara beds on the north side of the river has been detected, the highest rock exposed being the Hudson-river shales, in the vicinity of Garnavillo. Passing from Clayton into Fayette county, the Niagara bluffs gradually lose their distinct character, the line of outcrop receding somewhat from the river and becoming more irregular. At Elgin, the Trenton beds rise a few feet above the level of the water, and the lithological character of the rock in the bluffs, at an elevation of three hundred feet, on the north side of the river, would indicate that it belonged to the Galena limestone, in which case this rock would have a thickness at least equal to that which it has in Dubuque county. The bluffs on the south side of the river, which are known from their fossils to be of the Niagara age, are apparently not much higher than those on the north, which would indicate the existence of a fault which has thrown the Niagara down on one side or raised the Galena on the other to an extent of two or three hundred feet. The same conclusion may be drawn from the sections of the rocks cropping out in the valley higher up. At Elgin we have the Trenton limestone exposed, which is continuous in the bed of the stream from Elkader up to that point. Only five or six miles up Otter creek, which comes into the Turkey at Elgin, we find the Hudson-river shales at the level of the stream, near the summit at the base of the bluff at Wiley's quarry. The fall of the creek in this distance was not measured, but it can hardly exceed fifty feet; but there is a thickness of the Galena limestone equal to two hundred or two hundred and fifty feet, which should have occupied this space, unless there had been a break in the strata to nearly that amount. Again, still farther up, in Winnesheik county, we pass from beds of undoubted Galena limestone at Fort Atkinson on to those which appear to belong to the Niagara, in descending the river a few miles to the Old Mission, and without any perceptible rise to indicate the existence of the intermediate Hudson-river group, as would be the case were there no interruption of the regular stratification of the rocks in this region. The rocks seen in the bed of the south fork of the Turkey seem also to belong to the Niagara, where there is a thickness of over two hundred and fifty feet exposed. Beyond that point, towards the northwest, the Hamilton group seems to widen rapidly at the expense of the Niagara, which latter formation is reduced within very narrow limits in the northwest corner of Fayette county. This fact would indicate a depression of this region to the southwest of the Turkey, at least in this part of its course, previous to the deposition of the strata of Hamilton age. Owing to the fact that the rocks are very little exposed in Howard county, no definite information was obtained as to the outcrop of the Niagara in that direction.

ALAMAKEE COUNTY.

THIS county occupies the extreme northeastern corner of the State ; it is bounded by Winnesheik on the west and Clayton county on the south. The Mississippi river forms its eastern boundary. The Upper Iowa and its tributaries water the northern portion of the county, and Paint creek and Yellow river flow through the two southern tier of townships and empty into the Mississippi. The surface of Alamakee county is considerably broken, and the rivers have cut their channels deeply into the rocks, especially the Upper Iowa, which flows through a narrow, winding valley, which might almost be called a gorge, bordered by bluffs which have an elevation of from three hundred to four hundred feet above the stream. This county is well timbered, on the whole, although portions of it, especially on the elevated ridges, are covered with a rather scrubby growth. The soil is usually good, especially in the vallies of the streams : on the elevated ridges it is rather less desirable.

The rocks exposed in this county include all of the series from the Potsdam sandstone up to the lower beds of the Galena limestone, which latter just make their appearance on the surface along its southern edge. At the mouth of the Upper Iowa, the Potsdam sandstone is well exposed, and thence may be traced for a considerable distance up the stream, occupying the bottom of the valley. It dips to the south and disappears beneath the surface in the neighborhood of M'Gregor ; but as the limit between the upper beds of the Potsdam and the lowest of the Lower Magnesian cannot be exactly drawn, owing to the gradual passage of one formation into the other and the numerous alternations of sandstone and limestone along the lines of junction, no exact estimate can be made of the dip in this region ; it is probably not far from ten feet per mile. The sandstone is usually almost a pure silicious sand, of which the grains are rounded and of uniform size, and held together with no more than the minutest trace of calcareous or ferruginous matter. Sometimes the oxide of iron is in sufficient quantity to give the rock a dark brown color; but even then it is but trifling in amount compared with the silicious material, hardly ever exceeding two or three per cent, and usually much less than that.

The Lower Magnesian limestone caps the bluffs on the Mississippi river from the north line of the State as far down as Yellow river, and it is well exposed in the bluffs of the Upper Iowa and its tributaries. The annexed section on Bear creek near New-Galena, thirteen miles due west of the Mississippi, shows the character and relations of this rock to the over and underlying sandstones.

Soft friable red sandstone	12 feet.
White crystalline dolomite, partly concealed, but showing itself at various points	168 feet.
Beds of passage from dolomite to sandstone	30 feet.
White sandstone, to level of Bear creek	83 feet.

The base of the section is occupied by eighty-three feet of a soft white sandstone : this is succeeded by about thirty feet of beds of passage, or sandstone gradually passing into a thinbedded dolomite. A thickness of one hundred and sixty-eight feet of the Lower Magnesian limestone overlies this sandstone, of which the lower one hundred and fourteen feet are concealed by a grassy slope : the upper fifty-four feet are exposed in a vertical cliff of white hard dolomite, irregularly stratified and somewhat concretionary in its structure. Of the Upper sandstone, only twelve feet are here exhibited : it is a friable rock of a red color.

In the immediate vicinity of New-Galena, the bluffs rise to the height of three hundred and twenty to three hundred and thirty feet above the valley of Bear creek. The sandstone at their base is concealed by detritus, but the Lower Magnesian is well exposed on the face of the bluffs. The Upper sandstone as developed in this vicinity, occupying the highest ground, is not a granular rock, but a cherty or flinty mass, differing somewhat in its character at this point from that which it usually exhibits.

In the valley of Mineral creek, extending directly south from New-Galena for a few miles, the same section of the rocks is displayed as on Bear creek, except that the Lower Magnesian is still better exposed, and exhibits a decided concretionary and brecciated structure through a considerable thickness. Mining operations have been carried on here; for account of which, see chapter on Economical Geology, farther on.

The Yellow river, in the southern tier of townships, cuts into the Lower Magnesian, but not through it. At Volney, this rock is seen rising in cliffs from the bottom of the valley to the height of thirty or forty feet. The Upper sandstone may be seen cropping out, on the south side of the river, above the Lower Magnesian. On rising from the valley of the river and proceeding north, we pass successively the Upper sandstone and the Trenton, with its usual fossiliferous bluish-grey layers, and find a few thin outliers of the Galena limestone. On the highest points, these, however, soon disappear, and the Trenton occupies the elevated surface of the country, through the centre of the county, over a space of some ten or twelve miles in width. This rock is usually concealed by the superficial formations, but occasionally crops out in the vallies. About four miles south of Wakon, a well was observed on the prairie, sunk eighty-one feet in depth, chiefly in the Trenton limestone : the rock is fine-grained, and of a light bluish-grey color. An analysis showed that it consists almost exclusively of carbonate of lime, with hardly more than one per cent of other substances intermixed with it. There are occasional thin layers of sandstone near the base of the rock at this locality. The same rock appears in the bed of the creek, one of the head-waters of Paint creek, two miles before reaching Wakon. It is here quarried for lime and as a building-stone, for both of which uses the Trenton limestone in this region is well adapted.

A few remarks on the geology of the counties lying to the northeast of Skunk river, whose general features have been briefly noticed in the preceding pages, may here be appended, in order to bring out more closely the leading facts which the geological reconnoissance has developed.

An inspection of the geological map will show that the general trend of the formations over the greater part of the district in question, which comprises an area of from 15000 to 20000 square miles, is almost exactly northwest and southeast, or in the same same direction with the course of the streams, which are very nearly parallel with each other in this region. Thus, if we start from the Des Moines river, and proceed northeastwardly, we shall cross, successively, a great number of the principal tributaries of the Mississippi, and, at the same time, shall descend in the geological series from the Coal measures to lower and lower beds, until at the northeastern corner of the State, we shall reach the lowest member of the fossiliferous series. If, on the other hand, we were to start from the Mississippi river and go northwestwardly, we should hardly cross any but the smaller branches of the streams, and we might remain upon the same geological formation until we reached the limit of the State in that direction. This northwest and southeast trend of the groups is, however, not perfectly unbroken; the most important exception to its irregularity being the gradual bending of the formations more to the north as they approach the north line of the State, as will be noticed by looking at the map. This fact has an important practical bearing, as it results in bringing the Coal measures considerably nearer to the Mississippi, in the northern section of the State, than they would be if the strata were continued with the same trend from one end of the State to the other. Although no direct observations have been made on the north boundary of the State, far enough west to strike the coal-bearing strata, it appears hardly to be doubted that they must reach it near the head-waters of the Des Moines river, and that they occupy a more or less extensive tract in the territory of Minnesota. Whether the coal-beds are sufficiently developed in that region to be of importance, remains yet to be seen; and this point will be one of the first for examination during the future prosecution of the survey, as the importance of coal to this district will eventually be very great.

The gradual decrease in the space covered by some of the groups, and the increase of others as we proceed westwardly, is another interesting feature, as indicating an unequal denudation or deposition, at different geological periods. Thus the Niagara limestone, which occupies a belt thirty or forty miles in width to the southwest of Dubuque, has become contracted, on the borders of Winnesheik and Chickasaw counties, into a narrow space of three or four, while the beds of the Hamilton age appear to extend in that region over a district nearly a hundred miles wide from east to west.

The accumulation of superficial detritus in the State of Iowa is so extensive, over a larger part of its surface, that the nature of the underlying rocky strata can only be made out in the beds of the principal streams, and the lines of junction of the different members of the series being almost always along the elevated districts between the water-courses, the limits of the groups drawn upon the map must be considered as, at best, only approximations. The outcrop of the

Niagara limestone, however, owing to its peculiar lithological relations to the shales of the Hudson-river group below it, form a very marked feature of the topography of the region, and might be designated with great accuracy on a good topographical map, if any such existed.

The Hudson-river group is so liable to crumble away and become covered with vegetation, that it is only very rarely that a natural section of it can be found. When well exposed by artificial excavations, as near Dubuque, a good idea of its relations to the adjacent strata may be obtained : farther to the northwest, however, but little evidence of its existence was procured ; although there is good reason to believe that it continues its course up to, and beyond, the State line.

The eastern limits of the coal-bearing strata of Iowa, and the exact amount of space occupied by the Carboniferous limestones, in the central counties of the State, are points which still remain unsettled, and which are likely to continue so for some time, although the importance of as precise a limitation of the outcrop of the Coal measures as possible will be readily acknowledged. The accumulations of soil and drift over the whole of the region between the Cedar and the Des Moines are so great, that a distance of fifty miles may frequently be gone over without the sight of a single outcrop of rock. It is not unlikely that artificial excavations, such as wells or borings for coal, will throw some light on the geology of those counties, where natural exposures of rock are almost unknown. The lines indicating the eastern boundary of the coal was extended by Dr. Owen over a considerable area in Keokuk, Iowa, Powesheik, Tama and Marshall counties, which on our map is assigned to the Carboniferous limestone and other groups lower than the Coal measures, chiefly, as near as can be made out, to embrace the patches of sandstone lying on the Iowa river near the borders of Johnson and Iowa counties, there being no outcrop of rock visible for a distance of fifty miles to the west.

On the map accompanying this report, the line of the Coal measures has been placed considerably farther west, as being more in harmony with the general trend of the formations through the State. Still, the facts already collected in the progress of the survey show that numerous isolated patches of coal exist beyond the borders of the main basin of the Coal measures, resting not only on the Carboniferous limestone, but on strata of Hamilton, and even of Silurian age. A very considerable proportion of the space between the Iowa and Skunk rivers may be in reality covered by these outliers of coal, some of which will in all probability be hereafter discovered, and perhaps worked. It must, however, be borne in mind that these small patches, in this position, usually contain beds which are thinner and of poorer quality than those which belong to the main basin; so that explorations over this doubtful district must be conducted with caution, as the coal, even if discovered, may not be sufficiently good to pay for working, especially if any considerable amount of capital is to be invested in sinking shafts or making preliminary explorations. The quality of the coal in the State, so far as has as yet been ascertained, improves decidedly towards the southwest, or in the direction of the centre of the basin.

The surface geology, or the study of the nature and distribution of the loose materials or superficial detritus, commonly called drift and alluvium, over the surface, forms one of the most important subjects for investigation falling within the scope of the geological survey of any region, and especially in Iowa, where these transported materials are developed to such a thickness and spread so universally over the country. This subject, in its relations to agriculture, will form an important topic for consideration in a future report, when a larger part of the surface of the State has been examined, and the numerous facts already and hereafter to be obtained have been collated.

CHAPTER VII.

CHEMISTRY AND ECONOMICAL GEOLOGY.

General Remarks on the Study of the Chemical Composition and Lithological Character of Rocks, in connection with their palæontology—Chemical Composition of the Principal Rocks of Iowa, with Notices of their range, extent, peculiarities of lithological character, and the mineral substances accidentally present in them — Potsdam or Lower Sandstone— Lower Magnesian Limestone— Upper Sandstone— Trenton Limestone—Galena Limestone—Hudson-River group—Niagara Limestone—Groups intermediate between the Niagara and Hamilton — Hamilton group— Chemung group— Carboniferous Limestones — Coal Measures — General Considerations — Economical Applications of the limestones : Lime; Hydraulic Cement—Non-metallic Minerals of economical value — Coal, its distribution in the Eastern Half of the State; Chemical Composition : General Remarks on mode of working— Fire-clay—Gypsum—Metallic Ores in the various groups— Iron in Coal measures; in Niagara limestone; in Lower groups — Lead Ore; in the Niagara; in the Galena limestone — General Remarks on the mode of occurrence of ores in the unaltered sedimentary rocks — Notice of extent of Lead deposits in the Northwest — Particular Description of Workings in Iowa—Theory of Deposition of Lead—Statistics of Production of the Iowa Mines—Zinc Ores; their mode of occurrence : prospects of successful working.

THE vast basin of the Northwest, with its magnificent expanse of unaltered sedimentary rocks, offers a fine field for the study of the conditions which have determined the deposition of stratified masses, and their variations in chemical composition and mechanical aggregation. The intimate relations between these conditions and the physical character of the surface over which they prevailed, and the all-important influence which they must have exerted on the development of that organic life, whose remains often constitute so large a portion of the rocks themselves, give to this subject a peculiar interest.

The questions, what was the origin of the immense mass of material forming these widely-spread and uniformly constituted beds of rock, with their abrupt and simultaneous transitions of lithological character over so extensive a space; by what forces and under what conditions they were brought into their present situation; and what were the relations of their conditions to the structure of the various races of organized beings which inhabited the region, while the different groups of strata were successively accumulating: these questions are among the most important which can be investigated by the geologist, and, also, it must be confessed, among those which can be least satisfactorily answered.

Among the reasons which have retarded the progress of this branch of geological study, are to be mentioned, first, the want of accurate observations on the range of species, with reference to the change in the lithological character of the rocks in which they are imbedded; and, secondly and most especially, an insufficient knowledge of the conditions and distribution of life beneath the waters of the ocean, and how far such distribution is affected by the changes of temperature, pressure, presence of foreign substances accidentally intermingled, etc. The researches of EDWARD FORBES have, it is true, thrown much light on this branch of the subject; but there is no field more inviting, even now, than this; and zoologists have it in their power to advance geological science wonderfully, by making these subjects more especially the objects of their investigations.

In studying the chemical composition of the more important varieties of rocks existing in Iowa, while reference has been constantly had to the economical bearing of the information thus obtained, we have also endeavored to throw some light on the theoretically interesting subjects suggested in the preceding paragraphs, and to answer, even if only partially and imperfectly, the question, What were the changes of physical condition which have determined the corresponding changes of mechanical aggregation and chemical composition in the unaltered sedimentary strata of the vast region lying to the south of the great lakes and in the valley of the Mississippi ?

In speaking of the sedimentary rocks of the great basin of the Northwest as "unaltered", it is proper to make a reservation. It is not intended to imply, by the use of this term, that the strata in question still exhibit precisely the same conditions of structure and chemical composition which they possessed at the epoch of their deposition. It is, on the contrary, highly probable, and in some cases certain, that considerable changes have taken place in this respect; but the agencies by which these changes have been procured have not been of such a nature, or so general in their action, as to have entirely obliterated the original character of the strata, and brought them into the condition of "metamorphic rocks", as that term is generally understood by geologists. More especially are all traces of metamorphism by igneous agencies entirely wanting, at least so far as the actual presence of masses of eruptive or igneous origin, any where in the region in question, is concerned, at any period later than that of the deposition of the earliest sedimentary strata. On the northern borders of the basin there was, during a certain length of time after the first appearance of organic life in the region, a vigorous display of igneous phenomena, by which the character of the detrital deposits were greatly influenced; but this action gradually became less marked, and finally ceased altogether before the close of the Lower Silurian period; nor was its influence felt at any time over more than a small portion of the northwestern basin. We have, therefore, in this region a better opportunity than is, perhaps, offered in any part of the country, of studying the the whole series of palæozoic rocks, where it has been least subjected to such disturbances as might lead to any misapprehensions in regard to the order of succession of its fossil remains, and where the connection of lithological with palæontological characters is least obscured by changes which the rocks have undergone subsequently to their deposition.

For the purposes of the present chapter, the rocks of the region in question will be taken up consecutively, in chronological order, beginning with the lowest, or first deposited, group, and ascending in the geological series. After thus noticing the chemical composition and lithological peculiarities of each set of beds, as displayed in the valley of the Upper Mississippi, and especially within the limits of Iowa, some general remarks will be added as to the relations of one group to another, and the probable difference of physical conditions during their deposition.

The basin on which all the palæozoic rocks of the Northwest have been accumulated is the azoic series, whose characters may be studied conveniently on the northern border of the basin of the Great Lakes in Canada, and on the south shore of Lake Superior, where it is developed on a grand scale. It is made up of slates, quartz-rock, and occasional belts of saccharoidal limestone with numerous intercalated masses of trappean rock, the whole in a highly crystalline state, and, so far as is yet known, absolutely destitute of every trace of organic life, and presenting in its stratigraphical position the evidence of having originated during a period of disturbance and powerful igneous action. The line which is drawn between the azoic series and the palæozoic, in this region, is a strongly marked one, and indicates the most striking difference in the physical conditions prevailing at the time of the deposition of the rocks which make up the two sets of strata.

POTSDAM, OR INFERIOR SANDSTONE.

The extent of country covered by this rock is very considerable, especially within the limits of Wisconsin, where it occupies a broad belt, extending entirely around the azoic, and spreading out to the south and west of that central nucleus over a space of from fifty to sixty miles in width. In Iowa, the region covered by it is limited to a small part of the northeastern corner of the State. The entire thicknsss of this subdivision of the series is quite variable, and cannot be exactly stated, as the passage of the sandstone into the overlying limestone (the Lower Magnesian, or Calciferous of the N. Y. geologists) is effected by numerous repetitions and alternations of the two rocks, giving rise to a series of beds along the line of junction, which from their chemical composition might as well be reckoned to one rock as the other. We have no evidence of a thickness, at any point away from the influence of the igneous rocks, exceeding four hundred feet, and probably the mean thickness of the purely silicious strata does not vary much from two hundred and fifty feet. This is about the thickness which it has in Canada and in the State of New-York.

In its normal condition, this sandstone is an almost chemically pure silicious mass, containing only one or two-tenths of a per cent of other substances besides silica, oxide of iron usually predominating among the accidental ingredients. The silica is almost invariably in the form of nearly spherical grains, of the size of a large pin's head, sometimes showing crystalline facets, but not well developed ones. These grains seem to be held together with the minutest possible quantity of a calcareous ferruginous cement. When this is wanting, the mass is friable, and crumbles so readily under the fingers, that it is with difficulty that specimens can be preserved. Sometimes the sandstone has a concretionary structure, which is not visible except upon the weathered surfaces, which then assume botryoidal forms : this, however, is not a common occurrence. The sandstone is frequently tinged by oxide of iron, which gives it a dark color and cements it into a firm mass, even when present in minute quantity. When the ferruginous matter is abundant, it collects in nodules and stalactitic masses, apparently the result of infiltration after the deposition of the strata in which it occurs.

Among the most important characteristics of the Lower sandstone, may be noticed its very great freedom from argillaceous substances : shaly bands and intercalations of clayey matter are almost unknown throughout the rock, and up to the summit of the overlying limestone. There are occasional thin layers of greenish, soft material, which might at first sight be supposed to be quite argillaceous; but chemical analysis shows that they are, on the contrary, almost purely calcareo-magnesian : they seem to be the result of trituration of the calcareous layers. In this connection it may be mentioned, that there is no purely calcareous matter in the series until we reach the middle beds of the Blue or Trenton limestone; all the limestones of the lowest groups, whether they form thin bands in the sandstone, or the great mass of the Lower Magnesian, being true dolomites, and containing, in every instance in which they have been chemically examined, almost exactly one atom of carbonate of lime to one of carbonate of magnesia. It may also be remarked, that with the exception of the thin pulverulent layers before noticed, the dolomitic strata are uniformly quite crystalline in their structure. Towards the base of the Lower Magnesian, the occurrence of bands having an oolitic structure is not uncommon. These bands consist of spherical particles of soft calcareous matter, having evidently a concretionary structure, and surrounded by an amorphous or finely crystalline mass of silicious material; as if the calcareous matter had separated itself, or segregated out, in the midst of a silicious magma.

One of the most interesting facts in relation to the Lower sandstone is the entire, or almost entire, absence of conglomerate bands, or layers of sandstone containing pebbles or rolled masses of either quartz or any other material. In the vicinity of the trappean ranges of Lake Superior, such conglomerate bands form an important portion of the Lower sandstone series; but, as we recede from the trap, they soon disappear, and throughout the whole region occupied by this rock we have never yet observed a distinctly marked bed of heterogeneous water-worn materials. Another marked feature of the sandstone, in its normal state, is the comparative rarity of the lines of oblique deposition, lamination, or cross-stratifiction, which indicate the existence of shifting currents and shoal water at the time of the deposition of the beds thus marked. The influence of the igneous rocks in giving rise to these movements of the medium in which the sandstone was depositing, seems to be indicated by the much greater frequency of these indications of disturbance in their vicinity.

In general, the sandstone is extremely deficient in organic remains : none have been found within the limits of the State of Iowa, so far as we know; but there are localities, in Wisconsin and Minnesota, where, within a limited space, the beds of rock are crowded with the remains of a former existence. These localities are all on, or near, the borders of the sandstone towards the north, or in close juxtaposition with the underlying azoic rocks. The strata which contain the *Lingula* in such abundance, on the St.Croix river, consist of a ferruginous sandstone, mixed with a considerable amount of calcareous and magnesian carbonates. The manner in which the fossils are crowded together at this point indicates the prevalence over a very limited area, and, perhaps, during a comparatively short proportion of the whole time of deposition of the sandstone, of conditions highly favorable to the development of organic life.

The accidental minerals accompanying the sandstone are very few in number, and none are of any economical importance. Oxide of iron, or hematite, is occasionally present in small nodules, or minutely diffused through the mass, tinging it of various shades of yellow and brown, according to the quantity. There are no geodes of quartz crystals, or crystallized calcareous spar. Traces of carbonate of copper, staining the sandstone, have been occasionally noticed, but nowhere in the undisturbed district in quantity sufficient to be worthy of notice. The mineralizing effect of the trappean ranges on this rock, as exhibited in the Lake Superior region, extends but to a short distance, especially on the south side of the axis of elevation. In that district, the metalliferous veins pass through the trappean beds into those of conglomerate and sandstone, and are sometimes developed for a considerable length in the sedimentary rocks; but the profitable workings have, thus far, been entirely confined to the trap, no mine having been found remunerative in the sandstone.

The agricultural character impressed by the sandstone on the region which it covers, would be one of great sterility, were not the accumulations of northern drift over so large a part of the region occupied by this rock so considerable as to mask the character of the underlying strata. Still, the sandy character of the soil shows itself in the extent of the pine region of Wisconsin. In Iowa the surface covered by this rock is so small that its influence on the soil is hardly perceptible, although a portion of the silicious matter of the drift spread over the State undoubtedly had its origin in the denudation of beds of the Lower sandstone.

LOWER MAGNESIAN LIMESTONE,

(or " Calciferous Sandstone" of the New-York Reports.)

The great dolomitic mass which overlies the Lower Magnesian in the valley of the Mississippi, is known throughout that region as the "Lower Magnesian limestone". The term "Calciferous sandstone", which has been given to the rock succeeding the Potsdam sandstone of the N. Y. geologists, however applicable to this formation, as it is developed farther east, cannot properly be used to designate the parallel group at the west, since the rock is remarkable as being, throughout nearly its whole thickness, an almost chemically pure dolomite.

The extent of this rock on the surface is by no means as great as that of the sandstone which underlies it. It forms a narrow belt, in Wisconsin, surrounding the sandstone, and gradually becoming a more conspicuous member of the series as it sweeps round to the west, and forms the bluffs which overhang the Mississippi from Prairie du Chien, far up the St. Croix. The undulations of the strata bring the Lower Magnesian to the surface in many vallies in the Wisconsin lead region, where the Galena or the Blue limestones occupy the elevated prairie. It is exposed on the Platte, Grant, Peccatonica and Sugar rivers, through a very considerable part of the course of those streams. Within the limits of Iowa, the Lower Magnesian is most conspicuous along the Upper Iowa river : it also crops out in the vallies of Paint creek and Yellow river, but the amount of surface covered by it is quite small.

The thickness of the Lower Magnesian, as near as can be determined, is about the same as that of the Lower sandstone. At Prairie du Chien there are over two hundred and twenty feet of exposed ; but the lowest beds are not observed. On a branch of the Upper Iowa, near New-Galena, there is a thickness of one hundred and ninety-eight feet of pure dolomite, and thirty feet of beds of passage into the Lower sandstone exposed. On the Upper Iowa, there seems to be in places a thickness of over two hundred and fifty feet which must be considered as belonging to the Lower Magnesian.

The variations of lithological character in the Lower Magnesian, in point of texture and color, are very considerable; but the chemical composition of the mass varies but little from that of a pure dolomite, with a slight admixture of silicious sand, and a little carbonate of iron : it usually contains also traces of oxide of iron, and sometimes of manganese, and a minute quantity of chloride of sodium, and, more rarely, a still smaller amount of sulphate of lime.

The brecciated and concretionary character of the Lower Magnesian is the principal feature which distinguishes this dolomitic mass from those of the Galena and Niagara, which are higher up in the series. This peculiar condition, however, is not universal; but is, rather, confined to certain localities which seem to have been the scenes of more or less disturbance while deposition was taking place.

The chemical composition of this rock will be seen from the annexed analyses of some of the most characteristic varieties.

Specimen marked "Oolitic sandstone", M'Gregor's landing.

This is a very light-buff rock, made up of a somewhat crystalline dolomitic mass, filled with minute spheroidal cavities, many of which are empty, while others are occupied by silicious matter, which sometimes entirely fills the cavity, and, at others, forms a thin shell around its walls. The mass of the rock is composed of about equal quantities of dolomite and silicious sand, as is shown by the annexed analysis :

Silicious sand, with trace of iron	54.30
Carbonates of lime and magnesia, with traces of iron	45.70
	100.00

This is one of the beds of passage which mark the transition from the almost purely silicious strata at the base of the fossiliferous series of the Northwest, to the very pure dolomites of the Lower Magnesian limestone proper.

Specimen collected at Prairie du Chien, from quarries at base of bluffs.

The specimen of which the analysis follows, was taken from the quarry which has been quite extensively opened, for the use of the town of Prairie du Chien, at the base of the bluffs about a mile and a half from the river. This is a semi-crystalline rock, with a faint greenish tinge, and having thin bands and lines of a darker color traversing it horizontally. It lies in regular beds of a convenient thickness for building, and is a good material for that purpose. The analysis gave, the material having been dried at a temperature a little above 212° F.,

Insoluble in acid	14.26
Carbonate of iron and trace oxide of iron	.67
Carbonate of lime	46.98
Carbonate of magnesia	37.55
Trace of chlorine, sulphuric acid, soda, potash and loss	.54
	100.00

The insoluble portion consists of silicious sand, slightly tinged by iron, but containing hardly a trace of alumina. It is not unlikely that this rock would make a good hydraulic cement.

Lower Magnesian limestone, Pike's Hill, M'Gregor.

The specimen analysed was a crystalline rock with an irregular fracture, and weathering with irregular cavities : it is of a light-flesh color. It is almost a pure dolomite, containing hardly more than a trace of foreign matter, as the annexed analysis shows :

Silicious substance	0.96
Carbonate of iron and manganese	.54
Carbonate of lime	54.03
Carbonate of magnesia and traces of chlorine and soda	44.47
	100.00

The specimen was tested for sulphuric acid, but was found to contain none. It contains a minute trace of chloride of sodium and a small proportion of manganese ; but in addition to the double carbonate of lime and magnesia, there is all-together only about one and a half per cent of other substances. The rock is valuable for lime ; but, to judge from the specimen analyzed, too hard and irregular in its fracture and mode of weathering to be conveniently used as a building-stone, although a durable material.

Lower Magnesian limestone, New-Galena.

This is a light-yellow rock, quite crystalline in its structure, but not very compact, being made up of an aggregation of minute crystals of dolomite, and presenting the external appearance of a quite arenaceous limestone, although, in reality, almost a pure dolomite. Its chemical composition is as follows :

	I.	II.
Insoluble (silicious sand)	3.58	2.75
Carbonate of iron	.83	1.78
Carbonate of lime		52.47
Carbonate of magnesia		42.13
Traces of soda, potash, and chlorine and loss,		.87
		100.00

The lower portion of the Lower Magnesian is often rather thinbedded ; but there is no regularity in this respect, as, in some localities, the very lowest strata are thick and regularly-bedded, and better adopted for building-stone than any other portion of the formation. Still these heavy-bedded layers usually alternate with thinner and almost shaly ones ; although, even in the shaliest strata, the amount of argillaceous matter present is very minute. In the central portion of the mass of Lower Magnesian the presence of nodules and layers of flint may be noticed as rather characteristic, while the rock itself is hard, crystalline and very irregularly-bedded, the original lines of stratification being almost entirely obliterated. This character is intimately connected with another peculiarity which manifests itself in the Lower Magnesian limestone, and especially in its upper beds. This is the concretionary and, occasionally, brecciated structure of the rock, which, taken in connection with the obliteration of the planes of stratification and the crystalline structure of the associated beds, indicates that considerable chemical changes, probably accompanied by more or less mechanical disturbance, took place about the time of their deposition. The concretionary structure of the upper beds of the Lower Magnesian is particularly well manifested at several localities where lead ore has been mined from this formation; a fact which leads us to infer a close connection between the chemical agencies to which were due the formation of the metalliferous deposits, and the rearrangement of the strata with which they are associated.

The accidental minerals which occur in the Lower Magnesian limestone are few in number, and of little economical value. Sulphuret of lead, or galena, is the most important; and this ore has been found in such quantities in some localities as to lead many persons to suppose that this rock might one day become of as much importance, as a source of lead, as the Galena, or proper lead-bearing, limestone has been. With this opinion we are unable to coincide; but the matter will be discussed farther on in this chapter, in connection with the description of the lead region of the Northwest. The occurrence of copper pyrites, or sulphuret of iron and copper, in the Lower Magnesian, in small irregular "pockets" or cavities, has been occasionally noticed, within the borders of Wisconsin. There is no reason to suppose, however, that this formation is destined to become productive in any of the metalliferous ores.

The non-metalliferous minerals of the Lower Magnesian are of no importance whatever. The layers and nodules of chert in this formation occasionally contain geodes lined with small quartz crystals; but the whole rock, from the bottom to the top, although itself usually highly crystalline in its texture, is remarkably destitute of crystallized minerals.

There are numerous small irregular caves in the Lower Magnesian, which are sometimes lined with stalactitic deposits as in the lead-bearing rock.

The indications of the existence of organic life, during the deposition of the Lower Magnesian limestone, are but few. In Iowa, indeed, we have observed nothing of the kind; but, within the limits of Wisconsin, we have noticed beds of rock in this position whose weathered surfaces were covered with the indistinct silicified remains of *Orthoceratites*. It is an interesting fact, in connection with these appearances, that on breaking the rock and exposing a fresh fracture, it was hardly possible to detect in the interior the slightest appearance of those organic forms which were so distinctly and abundantly revealed on the weathered exterior. Other beds in the same neighborhood (near Wauwatosa), are filled with small cavities, which are the casts of fragments of the stems of crinoids, about one-sixteenth of an inch in diameter. The very small number of fossils hitherto found in the Lower Magnesian warrants the conclusion, that during the period of its deposition, the physical conditions were not suited to the development of organic life. Occasionally, as in the case of the underlying sandstone, there may have been a circumscribed locality where animals flourished; but the great mass of the formation appears to have been accumulated as a chemical precipitate, and not to have been eliminated from the surrounding ocean by organic forces, as we know to have been the case with most of the more recent calcareous strata.

UPPER, OR ST. PETERS' SANDSTONE.

The characteristics of the Upper Sandstone are in most respects those of the Lower; and what has been said of the one is applicable to the other, without much modification. Being, however, very much thinner, its range and extent on the surface, throughout the Northwest, is proportionally less: in Iowa, however, it occupies a more extensive region than both the formations below it. The principal exposures of this rock are on the streams running into the Wisconsin river from the south, and, in Iowa, on the Upper Iowa river and its tributaries. The undulations of the strata within the Wisconsin lead-district bring the Upper sandstone to view in the vallies of several of the streams for a considerable part of their course. Thus, it is well exposed on Grant and Big Platte rivers, as also on the Peccatonica, and, to a limited extent, along Sugar river. To what distance towards the northeast, along the east side of the outcrop of the Lower Magnesian, in the direction of the Upper Peninsula of Michigan, this formation may be traced, has not yet been ascertained. It appears to gradually thin out between Sugar river and Green Bay, as it has never been discovered in the Northorn Peninsula of Michigan. It certainly disappears before reaching the Menomonee river, at which point there is a good section of the lower rocks exposed, but no traces of any sandstone between the Lower Magnesian and Trenton were observed.

The thickness of the Upper sandstone within the limits of the lead region, and in the northeastern corner of Iowa, is remarkably persistent, as are also its lithological characters. At numerous points in the bluffs along the Mississippi, the entire thickness of this rock, and its relations to the over and underlying strata may be well observed. It is usually an almost pure silicious mass, made up of minute grains, which are somewhat rounded, but not as if worn by attrition, and remarkably uniform in size, as well as free from any admixture of foreign ingredients. In general, the grains are not held together by any cement, and consequently the rock is very friable, especially after the exterior crust is removed, as the sandstone often seems to have the property of hardening on the surface exposed to the weather, probably from the infiltration of water holding calcareous matter in solution derived from the adjacent limestones. This peculiarity renders the sandstone, both of this and the lower series, much more durable than it would otherwise be, and more so than the overlying strata of the Blue limestone. Sometimes the sandstone loses its granular structure and assumes the form of a compact silicious rock, almost as vitreous as the quartzose members of the azoic series; but this is a rare occurrence, and appears to be limited to small areas, although in those localities apparently affecting the formation through its whole thickness. We have never noticed any appearance of pebbles or foreign detrital matter in the Upper sandstone, or any instances of cross stratification: neither does this rock ever appear to contain any intercalated beds of dolomite or limestone. The persistence of the mass in thickness is as remarkable as its homogeneity in lithological character. From La Salle on the Illinois river, where it makes its appearance in a low axis of elevation, underlying the Coal measures unconformably, to St. Paul in Minnesota, a distance of over four hundred miles, the sandstone hardly varies at any point more than ten feet from its normal thickness of about eighty feet. These facts indicate a remarkable uniformity in the physical condition prevailing at the time of the deposition of this comparatively thin mass.

This sandstone is almost wholy destitute of any accidental minerals. In a very few localities it contains nodules of brown oxide of iron, which is not unfrequently diffused through the rock itself in minute traces, giving it a light-yellowish tinge. The lead deposits of the overlying Galena and Trenton limestones never penetrate the sandstone; and although we have heard it asserted by miners that the lead-bearing crevices do sometimes extend into this rock for a short distance, we have never had an opportunity of proving this from our own observations, and have never known an instance of any successful working for lead being carried below the limestone.

The occurrence of fossils of any description in this sandstone has never been noticed by any observer, so far as we have been able to ascertain.

With the Upper sandstone, that peculiar condition of things which gave rise to a deposit of pure silicious matter seems to have come to a close. We find no occurrence of sandstones similar to these in the overlying groups ; the silicious shales of the Hudson-river and Chemung groups being evidently the result of detrital accumulations, and bearing all the evidences of having a purely mechanical origin, in their texture and chemical composition. So, too, the sandstones and fine conglomerates, which occur still higher up in the series, in the Coal measures, are very different in their character from the lower sandstones, and exhibit much more distinct evidence of being made up of the detritus of quartzose rocks.

The origin of these immense accumulations of silicious matter in so pure a form, and with such peculiarities of lithological character, is a matter of great theoretical interest. It has been generally assumed, without much examination of the subject, that all such sandstones were originally formed by mechanical agencies, the material being supposed to have gradually accumulated from the grinding down of previously existing quartzose rocks. The facts collected above, however, seem rather to point to chemical than mechanical causes, as having been the chief agents in the deposition of the sandstones. If these silicious strata, developed over so extensive a surface, and with such a thickness as they are, were the result of the trituration of the azoic rocks which everywhere underlie them, and it is difficult to conceive of any other source from which the material could have been obtained, unless we adopt the chemical theory, we can hardly understand how such an amount of quartzose sand could have been accumulated, without its containing, at the same time, a considerable quantity of detritus which could be recognized as having come from the destruction of the schistose, feldspathic and trappean rocks which make up the larger portion of the azoic series, wherever it has been examined. The uniform size of the grains of which the sandstone is composed, and the tendency to the development of crystalline facets in them, are additional facts which suggest the idea of chemical precipitation rather than of mechanical accumulation.

The space which can be given to purely theoretical subjects in a Report like this, will not admit of a full discussion of this question : it is sufficient, at this time, to have directed attention to some of the difficulties in the way of accepting the views usually entertained in regard to the origin of these sandstones.

TRENTON, OR BLUE LIMESTONE OF THE WESTERN GEOLOGISTS.

The Blue limestone is worthy of especial notice as being, throughout the Northwest, the first group of strata which indicates anything approaching to an abundant distribution of living beings during its deposition. From Eastern Canada to the region of the Upper Mississippi, a distance of fully fifteen hundred miles, this limestone has been traced continuously, and it is everywhere characterized by a surprising similarity of organic forms and a hardly less remarkable persistence of lithological character. In the groups below this well-marked horizon there is a surprising paucity of organic forms, especially as compared with the thickness of strata which have been accumulated, and the necessary great length of time which must have elapsed since the first known appearance of life on the globe. The strata of Trenton age, however, are crowded with a great number and variety of forms of animal life, which are often in the most perfect state of preservation, and can, therefore, be studied and compared with facility.

The area occupied by the Trenton limestone, in the Mississippi valley, is very considerable. It may be found cropping out in the bluffs of almost all the streams in Wisconsin south of the river of the same name; and in the northern portion of the mineral region it covers most of the elevated region between the streams. It is spread out, in Iowa, over the larger portion of the region lying to the northeast of a line drawn from M'Gregor in a northwesterly direction. Its course through Minnesota has not yet been traced; but it reappears at the Falls of St. Anthony, with nearly the same characters which it has three hundred miles farther south.

The term "Blue limestone", as used in the Mississippi valley, includes all the strata from the top of the Upper sandstone to the base of the Galena limestone. The name indicates the peculiar light bluish drab-color of the large portion of the beds, a tint which contrasts with the light-buff or yellowish color of the groups above and below. In Dr. OWEN'S Report on the geology of the mineral region, published in 1844, the lower portion of the series of beds between the Upper sandstone and the Galena is separated from the rest, and designated as the "Buff limestone". This seems to be a very proper subdivision, at least as the rocks are developed in the lead-region; since the beds immediately overlying the sandstone are, in most respects, quite different from those a little higher up in the series. There is, indeed, considerable variation of lithological character in the different beds of the Trenton in the Northwest; but in Iowa and Wisconsin, the only subdivision which can be recognized over a large area, is that indicated above, namely, the separation of the lower beds under the term "Buff limestone", from the upper or "Blue limestone" proper.

The thickness of the lower division, or Buff beds, is quite constant where it has been examined by us: at Gutenberg it is fifteen feet; at Prairie du Chien, eighteen; and on Grant river in Wisconsin, it is twenty feet. The whole thickness of the Blue limestone cannot be so accurately stated, as there is a gradual passage, in most sections, from the beds of this group into those of the next succeeding. As near as can be made out, the beds which should be considered as belonging to the Blue limestone proper have in the lead-region a thickness of from seventy to eighty feet, which, with the twenty feet of the Buff beds, makes the entire series from the Upper sandstone to the Galena from ninety to one hundred feet.

The chemical composition of the Buff limestone will be seen from the following analyses of that rock, the specimens having been selected, as representing fairly that part of the series as it exists in the Mississippi valley.

Specimen from layers next above the Upper sandstone, at Clayton.

This is a light yellowish-grey or slightly ash-colored rock : its texture is finely subcrystalline, with occasional admixture of more earthy portions. It exhibits numerous small cavities, which are seen, with the aid of a microscope, to be lined with minute crystals of brown spar.

The analysis gave :

Insoluble in acids	18.36
Carbonate of iron and a little oxide of iron	1.69
Carbonate of lime	44.90
Carbonate of magnesia	34.23
Loss, which includes carbonate of soda, a trace of chloride of sodium and of sulphate of soda	.82
	100.00

The insoluble portion consisted of silica, mixed with a little clayey matter. The soluble part has nearly the composition of dolomite, as 44.9 per cent of carbonate of lime requires 37.7 of carbonate of magnesia to form the double carbonate.

Specimen from Grant river, Wisconsin.

The specimen of which the analysis follows was taken from the bluffs on Grant river, near the crossing of the road from Platteville to Prairie du Chien, and at an elevation of one hundred and fifty-three feet above the valley, in a position a few feet above the Upper sandstone.

It is a light-yellowish brown rock, mottled with shales of buff : its texture is somewhat earthy in part, with some granular crystalline portions, the layers not being very homogeneous in structure or in composition.

The analysis gave the following results :

Insoluble in acid	22.86	
Carbonate of iron	4.56	
Carbonate of lime	42.97	
Carbonate of magnesia	29.49	(by loss).
Alumina, in soluble portion	.12	
	100.00	

The insoluble portion was analysed by itself, and found to contain 63.7 per cent of silica : the remainder consisted of alumina 14.7, oxide of iron 3.5, and a little magnesia with the alkalies, potash predominating. The composition of this residuum will be seen, therefore, to be nearly that of orthoclase (common feldspar), in which a portion of the alumina is replaced by oxide of iron. (Orthoclase contains silica 64.8, alumina 18.4, potash 16.8.)

Specimen from Clayton, Iowa, marked " Base of the Trenton".

This is a light buff-colored rock, resembling in texture and color the beds of the Lower Magnesian. It is more crystalline and homogeneous than the specimens from the same geological position of which the analyses are given in the preceding pages. The chemical analysis showed it to be considerably more free from insoluble matters than the other samples of the Buff limestone.

The following are the results :

Insoluble in acids	7.07	
Carbonate of iron, with a little oxide of iron	4.95	
Carbonate of lime	52.55	
Carbonate of magnesia, and traces of chloride of sodium and carbonate of soda	35.43	(by loss).
	100.00	

This specimen is almost the only magnesian limestone analyzed from rocks of Silurian age, which was not found to contain magnesia and lime in very nearly the proportion required to form dolomite. The amount of carbonate of lime given above, 52.55 per cent, would require 44.13 of carbonate of magnesia for that purpose. Thus it appears that the lime is a little in excess, even reckoning the iron as replacing a portion of the magnesia.

The limestones at the base of the Trenton appear, from their chemical composition, to be better qualified to make good hydraulic cements than any others found in the State of Iowa, as far as has yet been ascertained.

The Buff limestone seems to be entirely destitute of fossils; at least, none have been noticed by us in that position. In some localities in Wisconsin, markings resembling fucoids have been observed; but whether they are the result of organic structure, or merely concretionary arrangement of the slightly argillaceous layers, we have not examined sufficiently to decide.

After the deposition of the Upper sandstone, there seems to have been a sudden return of the conditions under which the Lower Magnesian had been accumulated, the transition from one rock to the other being everywhere an abrupt and strongly marked one. To the chemical precipitate of the carbonates of lime and magnesia, was added, however, at this period, a considerable proportion of finely-divided sediment or mud, evidently the result of mechanical agencies, and brought into the basin in which deposition was going on from a considerable distance. The composition of this sediment indicates that it may have originated from the trituration of feldspathic rocks, such as everywhere underlie the fossiliferous strata of this region. The conditions of the ocean during the deposition of these beds became gradually better adapted to the growth of organized beings; and we find the strata rapidly becoming more purely calcareous and at the same time more and more crowded with the remains of animal life. During the latter portion of the Trenton period, the deposition of detrital material was repeatedly intermitted for long periods of time; and the accumulation of the nearly pure carbonate of lime of which the strata were formed, may be due chiefly, if not entirely, to the agencies of organic life eliminating the calcareous matter from the surrounding ocean.

Rising in the series above the Buff beds of the Trenton, we come to a series of thinbedded and highly fossiliferous layers of limestone, alternating irregularly with more compact and thicker beds of equally pure carbonate of lime, but which are much less crowded with organic remains. There does not seem to be any very considerable persistence in these changes of character over a wide area. There are, however, few good sections exposing at one view the whole of the series, the easily decomposing shaly beds usually concealing with detritus a portion of the more resisting ones. The lower layers, however, appear on the whole to be more evenly and thicker-bedded, and to contain fewer fossils. Some of the layers have a peculiar compact structure, and break with a conchoidal fracture : these are known among the miners as the "glass-rock". Their color varies from light to dark-grey, and they consist of an almost chemically pure carbonate of lime; the fossils which they contain being chiefly confined to the shaly partings between the layers. The upper portion of the series is made up of more shaly and thinner beds, most of which are crowded with fossils. There are also numerous thin layers, which are quite argillaceous, and decompose to blue and yellow clays, leaving the fossils in a perfect state of preservation.

The following analyses will give an idea of the composition of the Trenton limestone, as it exists in the lead-region and in the northeastern corner of Iowa.

Specimen from a quarry four miles south of Wakon, Alamakee county.

This is a very light drab-colored rock, not materially changing its color or appearance by weathering. It breaks with a smooth fracture into rectangular fragments. Its texture is finely-crystalline, and it is very compact and homogeneous, with the exception of minute specks of crystallized calcareous spar and bitumen, which are sparsely scattered through it. It is in all respects a good building-stone, splitting out in good shape, dressing easily and keeping its color well. This is not from one of the very fossiliferous layers of the Blue limestone; but it contains a few fossils, and is colored by a trace of organic matter.

The analysis showed the following composition :

Insoluble (silicate of alumina)	4.07
Carbonate of iron	.62
Carbonate of lime	94.08
Carbonate of magnesia, alkalies, chlorine, sulphuric acid and loss	1.23
	100.00

The specimen analyzed above represents in character and composition the lower portion of the Blue limestone, as developed throughout the northeastern corner of the State. It is quarried in numerous places, and affords the best material both for building-stone and for lime, being an almost pure carbonate of lime. It sometimes fades slightly on exposure, by the gradual disappearance of the organic matter which it contains; and is not unfrequently colored of a light-buff on the exterior, by the oxidation of the iron which it contains in the form of carbonate of the protoxide.

Specimen from a quarry on Limestone creek, near Platteville, Wisconsin.

This rock has a dark brownish drab-color, gradually shading off on some of the layers into a light-drab. It has a very smooth fracture, breaking readily into large cuboidal blocks. Its texture is fine-grained and imperfectly crystalline, and it has an oily lustre. It is colored by a trace of organic matter, which gradually fades out on exposure to the sun and air. This is an excellent building-stone, and furnishes the best of lime. Like the preceding specimen, it is nearly a pure carbonate of lime, containing hardly three per cent of other substances.

The composition is as follows :

Silicate of alumina	0.75
Carbonate of iron	.26
Carbonate of lime	97.25
Carbonate of magnesia	1.13
Carbonate of soda	.27
Chlorine, sulphuric acid, and loss	.34
	100.00

This specimen approaches nearly in character to the so-called "glass-rock" of the miners, which is also a pure carbonate of lime, but rather more compact and brittle, and therefore not so well adapted for a building-stone, as it does not break or dress smoothly, and is usually quite thinbedded.

The section at the quarry from which the above specimen was taken gave the following series of beds :

Thinbedded layers, highly fossiliferous	8 feet.
Thinbedded layers, without fossils	2 ft. 3 in.
Not exposed	4 ft. 9 in.
Shale and clay in alternate layers	2 ft. 5 in.
Hard light-grey fossiliferous limestone (containing numerous trilobites)	1 ft. 7 in.
Thin bands of clay	9 inches.
Hard dark-grey and somewhat brittle limestone in layers from 6 inches to 1 foot in thickness	4 ft. 3 in.

Specimen from Elgin, at junction of Otter creek and Turkey river.

The beds exposed at this point are somewhat shaly, and more argillaceous than most of the fossiliferous strata of the Trenton. The rock is a rather dark yellowish-grey, and not crystalline : it is too easily decomposed to be of much value as a building-stone.

The analysis of this specimen gave :

Insoluble in acid (clay)	8.37
Soluble alumina, and trace oxide of iron	.33
Carbonate of lime	90.58
Carbonate of magnesia	.50
Carbonate of soda, and trace of chloride of sodium	.20
	99.98

Some of the beds in this position, in Wisconsin, have been found to furnish a good hydraulic cement ; but in Iowa, the Buff beds at the base of the Trenton seem better adapted for that purpose, the Blue limestone above not containing a sufficient quantity of silicious and argillaceous substances, except in very thin layers.

The passage from the Trenton into the Galena limestone above is not an abrupt one : on the contrary, there are in many localities, several alternations of calcareo-magnesian and purely calcareous layers between the two formations, indicating that the change of conditions, which resulted in the deposition of the highly crystalline magnesian rock which overlies the Trenton, was not effected at once and without occasional partial returns to the former state of things. The beds of the Trenton intercalated in the Galena resemble those of the last named rock in being comparatively destitute of fossils.

GALENA LIMESTONE.

The Galena limestone closely resembles in lithological character, as well as in chemical composition, the Lower Magnesian, from which it is separated by the Blue or Trenton limestone. It is, however, more uniform in its texture, and does not exhibit the brecciated and concretionary structure which the Lower Magnesian frequently takes on.

The Galena limestone is a member of the series which, although of importance in the Mississippi valley, both from its thickness and mineral contents, has not been distinctly recognized in its eastern extension beyond the borders of the State of Wisconsin. It gradually thins out, as we proceed northwards through that State, on the east side of the axis of elevation which passes through Rock, Jefferson and Dodge counties. This rock is most fully and characteristically developed on the Mississippi river, in the neighborhood of Galena and Dubuque, and occupies a large portion of the elevated prairie region in Wisconsin, south of the river of that name and east as far as Rock river; although, throughout the whole of this part of the State, the large streams have cut down to lower formations. In Iowa, the Galena limestone has been traced as far to the northwest as Fort Atkinson, where it has all its usual characters, although apparently somewhat thinner than on the Mississippi. The greatest thickness of this rock which has been measured, is in the vicinity of Dubuque, where it equals about two hundred and fifty feet. This appears to be the point of its maximum development, from which it gradually thins out in all directions.

The term "Upper Magnesian" has been frequently applied to this division of the geological series, but including, at the same time, the Niagara limestone, the former being distinguished as the "Lead-bearing beds", the latter as the "Coralline and Pentamerus beds", of the Upper Magnesian limestone. In this nomenclature the existence of the Hudson-river group, which lies between these two divisions, was overlooked; the two magnesian limestones, which differ entirely in the nature of their included fossils, although strikingly alike in lithological characters, being in point of fact separated from each other by from sixty to eighty feet of shales, which, in their turn, are characterized by a peculiar set of animal remains. Besides, the Niagara itself is not the highest magnesian rock of the region, the Leclaire limestone and portions of the Carboniferous series being also nearly pure dolomites.

The Galena limestone, as usually developed, is a rather thick-bedded, light-greyish or light yellowish-grey dolomite, distinctly crystalline in its texture and usually rather coarse-grained, although occasionally so finely granular as to be almost compact. The coarse-grained portions not unfrequently contain small cavities, which are lined with minute crystals of brown spar.

This limestone is remarkably uniform in its lithological character, from the bottom to the top of the group of strata. It contains but little insoluble matter, usually not more than two or three per cent; a little carbonate of iron, which partially decomposes on exposure, giving to the rock the light-yellow or buff tinge which it generally has when weathered.

The following analyses will give an idea of its chemical composition.

Specimen from Garnavillo, Clayton county.

This is a massive limestone, of a very light yellowish-brown color, like all the rocks of this formation, where it has been exposed to the weather even for a short time. It is quite crystalline in its texture, and has occasional irregular-shaped cavities, or portions liable to form cavities by decomposition; which portions, on examination with the magnifying-glass, are seen to be made up of, or lined with, minute crystals of brown spar, or dolomite. There are a few imperfect traces of fossils in the rock, usually cavities once occupied by stems of crinoids.

The results of the analysis were as follows :

Insoluble in acids	4.43
Carbonate of iron	.93
Alumina and oxide of iron	traces
Carbonate of lime	52.01
Carbonate of magnesia	42.25
Carbonate of soda and potash	.38
Chloride of sodium and sulphate of lime,	traces
	100.00

The insoluble portion is mostly silica, but slightly colored by oxide of iron. There is hardly a trace of alumina in the rock : neither was the presence of sulphuric or phosphoric acids detected.

An additional determination of the alkalies was made by burning a fragment, in order to decompose the combination of the alkalies, and then exhausting the ignited mass by water. In the solution the lime was removed by saturation with carbonic acid, evaporating to dryness, adding a little water and filtering off the carbonate of lime. 50 grammes of the rock treated in this way gave .0724 of alkaline carbonates, or 0.14 per cent, which contained .03089 of potash, or .04531 of carbonate of potash, and .02709 of carbonate of soda; or, in per centage, 0.0906 per cent of carbonate of potash and 0.0542 of carbonate of soda.

Analysis of a specimen collected near Burton's furnace, Dubuque county.

This specimen has the usual characters of the Galena limestone : it differs from the preceding one, however, in having a somewhat greyer tinge of color, and in being a little more compact and tougher. It weathers a dirty-yellow, and the occasional minute specks of iron pyrites which it contains become evident as the rock is exposed to the weather.

The analyses of two specimens gave :

	I.	II.
Insoluble in acid	10.69	12.08
Carbonate of iron	.84	1.42
Oxides of iron and manganese	trace	trace
Carbonate of lime		48.81
Carbonate of magnesia		37.49
Carbonate of soda		.17
Chloride of sodium		trace
Loss		.58
		100.00

No sulphuric acid, phosphoric acid or potash was detected in this limestone : neither were there, in this or the preceding specimen, any traces of a metal precipitable by sulphuretted hydrogen in the acid solution. A number of specimens of this rock have been tested in this way for lead, without any indication of the presence of this metal having been obtained.

Specimen from Dubuque, collected at an elevation of one hundred and fifty feet above the river.

This rock is hardly to be distinguished from the preceding one, except by a slightly deeper tinge of yellow in its color. The minute crystals which line the irregular cavities are of a decided yellow tinge.

The composition of this rock, as indicated by the analysis, was as follows :

Insoluble in acid	2.46	
Carbonate of iron and manganese	1.35	
Alumina in soluble portion	none	
Oxide of iron and manganese	trace	
Carbonate of lime	52.00	
Carbonate of magnesia	43.93	by loss.
Carbonate of soda	0.26	
Chlorides of sodium and potassium	traces	
	100.00	

This rock is largely quarried for building purposes about the city of Dubuque, although not dressing smoothly, and weathering somewhat irregularly, owing to the numerous crystalline cavities it contains. Caps and sills are usually made from the Blue limestone, from the opposite side of the river, or else iron is used for this purpose.

The character of this rock is somewhat different as de-developed in different localities; usually, the upper portion is more argillaceous and somewhat more regularly and thinly bedded, so that it is preferable as a building material. In the vicinity of Dubuque, the principal quarries are in the upper fifty feet of the rock where the layers are usually from seven to eight inches in thickness, and regular in their bedding. At the very summit of the formation the rock is frequently quite shaly and argillaceous, indicating a passage into the overlying shales of the Hudson-river group. The middle portion of the series is more crystalline, heavier-bedded, and marked by an abundance of silicious nodules or flints, which are frequently arranged in regular layers, although sometimes scattered indiscriminately through the rock. The lower portion of the Galena limestone is the most variable in its lithological character. It is sometimes sufficiently regular in its bedding to be of value as a building-stone; but more frequently it is intersected by seams and floors of crystallized calcareous spar, or even by masses of silicious matter.

The Galena limestone is of great importance economically, not only as a valuable building-stone, but as the depository of the lead ore, which has been so extensively worked in this region. Sulphurets of lead, zinc and iron, are almost the only metalliferous ores which occur, although these metals are occasionally found in their oxidized combinations, the results of the decomposition of the sulphurets. The particulars of the mode of occurrence of these ores will be given at length farther on in this chapter.

Among the few simple non-metalliferous minerals found in the Galena limestone, silica is by far the most abundantly distributed, in the form of irregular nodules or flat sheets of varying thickness, which are especially abundant in the middle portion of the series, and in connection with the lead-openings near the base. It is remarkable that the silicious matter is very rarely found crystallized : in a large collection of the minerals accompanying the lead ores in this geological position, we have not discovered a single crystal of quartz. Carbonate of lime occurs at numerous localities, in connection with the mineral openings ; and, in the lower part of the series, in flat crystallized sheets, the individual crystals often being of very large size, and usually in the form of the scalene-triangular dodecahedron : these crystals occur up to six inches in length. Sulphate of baryta is of not unfrequent occurrence in the Galena limestone, both as an accompaniment of the lead ore and otherwise. At Scale's mound, in Illinois, it occurs in fine crystallizations, associated with crystallized pyrites and brown spar, forming geodes in the upper beds of the Galena.

The Galena limestone, as a whole, is by no means a highly fossiliferous rock, and, in this respect, it offers a striking contrast to the underlying Blue limestone. The lower portion, especially, is almost entirely destitute of organic remains. In the argillaceous and shaly partings of the beds, near the top of the series, there are, in many localities, somewhat numerous casts of shells. The remarkable and conspicuous coral, generally known at the West as the *Coscinipora*, or "Sun-flower coral", but which is considered by Mr. Hall as belonging to the genus *Receptaculites*, is found through nearly all the strata of the Galena limestone, and in the lead-region proper is quite characteristic of this rock, as it has never been found in the beds of the Trenton limestone within the mineral district : farther to the northwest, however, in the valley of the Turkey and Upper Iowa rivers, it has been observed at several localities, abundantly scattered through the shaly beds of the Blue. Almost equally conspicuous with the *Receptaculites*, as a characteristic fossil of the Galena limestone, is the *Lingula quadrata*, which is quite frequently noticed in the upper beds of this group. Besides these, the most common fossils are a few gasteropods, among which several species of *Murchisonia* are most frequently met with. *Pleurotomaria* is another genus of not unfrequent occurrence. Of bivalve shells, imperfect casts of the genera *Edmondia* and *Ambonychia* are occasionally observed.

With the exception of the *Lingula*, all the organic remains of the Galena limestone are in the form of casts, no vestige of the original shells remaining, except when it consisted of *phosphate* of lime instead of *carbonate*, as is the case with this genus. Hence it appears, that the chemical changes which this rock has undergone since its deposition have been of a nature to remove the carbonate of lime, but to leave the phosphate untouched.

HUDSON-RIVER GROUP.

Next above the Galena limestone, in the Upper Mississippi valley, we find a series of beds which differ entirely in lithological character from any which have preceded them. Up to the close of the period during which the various groups, from the Potsdam sandstone to the Galena limestone, were deposited, rocks of a purely detrital origin, that is to say, such as were formed by the wearing down of pre-existing strata, seem to have been almost entirely wanting. A little argillaceous sediment occasionally found its way into the basin in which the deposition of silicious or calcareo-magnesian strata was going on, under the action of chemical, and sometimes of organic forces; but the quantity of detrital matter thus introduced previous to the epoch of the Hudson-river group was very small. While the shales of this period were accumulating in the Mississippi valley, the material from which they were formed seems to have been a fine mud, made up of the detritus of argillaceous and silico-argillaceous rocks, with but a trifling amount of calcareous matter; while limited portions of the series are crowded to repletion with the remains of organic forms, which seem to have flourished in countless multitudes, and which have been preserved in the greatest perfection.

The variations in physical condition under which different portions of the Hudson-river group were deposited are made evident by tracing the rocks of this geological age along the line of their outcrop, between New-York and Iowa, and noticing the different characters which they exhibit at different points in a distance of more than twelve hundred miles.

In Eastern New-York, the series is made up almost exclusively of detrital materials, the larger portion of which is finely comminuted, while in some districts coarser grits and sandstones predominate. The thickness of this group, including the Utica slate, Hudson-river shales, and the Grey sandstone, seems not to be very accurately known. In the eastern part of the State it is very considerable, exceeding a thousand feet; but there is a rapid diminution towards the west, and where the series appears to have been accumulated more nearly in its normal condition, in the upper part of the Mohawk valley, it is probably not over four hundred feet.

Following the course of the group still farther west, we find it bending north in the direction of the northeast corner of Lake Ontario, thence crossing Canada to Lake Huron, where excellent exposures are to be observed along the south shore of Georgian Bay and on the Grand Manitoulin and Drummond's islands. In this region there has been a great accession of calcareous matter; and there is a thickness of nearly five hundred feet of somewhat argillaceous limestones, belonging to this series, exposed near Cabot's Head. This thickness rapidly diminishes in a westerly direction; but the predominating material of the group is calcareous, until we reach the borders of Wisconsin, where silicious shales begin to predominate again, and the limestones are reduced in the neighborhood of the Mississippi to a few very thin bands, collectively hardly equal to five feet in thickness. The entire thickness of the group, as it exists in the Upper Mississippi valley, is probably about seventy-five or eighty feet, and in some localities may be as much as one hundred; but it is very difficult to find a natural section exposing more than a few feet of it, so easily do the beds decompose and form grassy slopes. The best natural section we have seen is on the Little Makoqueta, where about twenty-five feet is exposed; and in the most satisfactory artificial one, at Scale's mound, about forty-two feet were measured, of which all but four feet were silicious and argillaceous shales.

Throughout the whole region in which the Hudson-river group occurs, it appears to be more or less charged with carbon; but some portions of the series, in certain districts, contain so large an amount of this substance, that its occurrence becomes a question of economical importance.

From some experiments made, at our request, by Dr. C. F. Chandler, it appears that the black, highly glazed and apparently very carbonaceous shales from the Hudson-river valley contain from one-half to one per cent of fixed carbon, but no volatile bituminous matters. The Utica slate, on the other hand, is rich in carbonaceous substances, chiefly in the form of fixed carbon : some specimens lost one-sixth of their weight when burned in oxygen. In Canada, according to Mr. Logan's Reports, the Utica slates are highly bituminous; so much so, that they are considered as likely to become of economical value as a source of oil and bitumen.

In the Mississippi valley, the amount of carbonaceous matter in the Hudson-river shales has been found to form one-tenth to one-fifth of the weight of the material examined; and the quantity of volatile substances is so great, that all the specimens examined have taken fire and burned with a brilliant flame when heated in the crucible.

The following examinations will show the large amount of combustible matter present in these shales. Farther examinations will be made to acquire a more exact idea of the nature of the combinations in which the carbon occurs, and especially to determine the economical value of the rock, and whether it can be profitably used as a material from which to obtain oil or illuminating gas.

Specimen marked "One mile east of Savannah (Ill.), from a well ten feet below the surface".

This is a dark chocolate-colored shale, which weathers white on exposure. Heated in the closed crucible, it gives off a considerable amount of gas, which takes fire and burns with a clear bright flame.

The analytic determination gave :

Moisture	.75		
Volatile combustible matter	14.12	total combustible substances	20.96
Fixed carbon	6.84		
Incombustible residuum	78.29		
	100.00		

The residuum consists mainly of silica, the substance being a silicious shale highly impregnated with bitumen. It contains no trace of organic remains, either of animals or plants.

The rock was pulverized and digested in chlorohydric acid, which took up only a small portion, without producing any effervescence. The solution contained 0.75 per cent of lime and 3.22 of oxide of iron, with traces of magnesia and the alkalies.

Specimen from Hawley's mill, Little Makoqueta river, near Channingsville.

This is a rather dark yellowish-brown shale, which contains a few fragments of *Lingula* and numerous minute black points, which appear to be organic matter, scattered through the mass.

Its composition was found to be as follows :

Moisture	1.20		
Volatile combustible substance	8.16	total combustible substances	11.01
Fixed combustible substance	2.85		
Silicious incombustible residuum	87.79		
	100.00		

Specimen from near Dubuque, taken from a shaft near Levins's diggings.

A light yellowish-brown rock, fading to light ash-color, with a tinge of blue, on being exposed for some to the air. The rock is somewhat shaly in structure, but the layers are rather thick, and between them are numerous fossils, chiefly very minute *Lingulæ*. Both this and the preceding specimen turned jet-black when heated in the closed crucible, and gave off considerable gas, which burned with a bright clear flame.

The rock contains :

Moisture	.54		
Volatile combustible substance	8.26	total combustible substances	16.29
Fixed combustible substance	8.03		
Silicious incombustible residuum	83.17		
	100.00		

The presence of carbon in the shales of the Hudson-river group, over so extensive a region, and in such large quantity, is not only a matter of very considerable economical importance, as indicating a source from which, in those parts of the country where the true Carboniferous rocks, or Coal measures, are wanting, a supply of material for lighting and, perhaps, heating purposes, may hereafter be obtained; but it is also of great interest in a theoretical point of view, as bearing on the question of the origin of the carbon of the Coal measures themselves. The Hudson-river shales, with the closely allied Utica slates, seem to have been deposited under conditions somewhat resembling those under which the true coal-bearing rocks were accumulated. The presence of so large a proportion of carbon in the Northwest becomes still more striking from the circumstance, that neither do the rocks below, nor those above, up as high in the series as the Coal measures, contain more than the merest trace of carbonaceous matters. From the base of the Potsdam to the top of the Galena, the whole amount of carbon present in the series would not, if collected into one layer, make a deposit of more than an inch or two in thickness; but if the bituminous portion of the Hudson-river group at Savannah, Illinois, had all been deposited by itself in one stratum, instead of having been diffused through eighty feet of shale, that stratum would have equalled at least twenty feet, and perhaps twenty-five in thickness.

The question arises, whence did this large amount of bituminous matter derive its origin? If identical in this respect with the carboniferous layers of the true Coal measures, why do we find so few traces of the existence of vegetation during the period of the deposition of the Hudson-river shales? Admitting, as most geologists do, that the carbon of the Coal-measures were derived from the growth and decay of that vegetation whose remains are so abundantly scattered through the rocks which are associated with the coal, and which are often seen to make up so large a proportion of the coal itself, why should we not find some indications of similar conditions having prevailed during the accumulation of so large an amount of carbon, as has been shown above to be present in the Hudson-river series, over so wide a region? There are layers in which animal remains are accumulated in great numbers; but no trace of vegetable life has yet been observed in this group, anywhere in the Northwest: in New-York a few obscure fucoids have been found in some portions of the series; but the most highly bituminous strata seem to present but little evidence to justify the conclusion that the carbon which they contain was due to vegetation alone. It is to be hoped that future researches into the nature of the carbonaceous matter of the Hudson-river group may throw some light on the interesting question whether it was of organic or inorganic origin; and, if derived from organized bodies, whether these were of animal or vegetable character.

NIAGARA LIMESTONE.

The Niagara limestone is the third great mass of dolomite, which throughout the valley of the Upper Mississippi lies next above the Hudson-river shales, and which, from its thickness and persistency of lithological and palæontological characters over a vast extent of surface, forms one of the most important members of the geological series. It is the rock which, prior to the recognition of the Hudson-river shales in the northwestern mineral region, was known under the designation of the "Coralline and Pentamerus beds of the Upper Magnesian limestone".

This limestone occupies a very considerable extent of surface in the State of Iowa, as will be seen by reference to the geological map accompanying this Report. It has been traced from the centre of New-York, where it is first recognized as a distinct formation, across the river at Niagara falls, from which locality it receives its name, and where it is well developed and admirably exhibited in the gorge of the falls. It is also seen in fine sections on the islands which lie to the south of Georgian bay, as well as along the north shore of Lake Huron, and in the vicinity of the mouth of the St. Mary's river. It crops out on the north shore of Lake Michigan and on the east side of Green bay, where it forms bold bluffs in which its characters may be conveniently studied. Bending to the south, it forms the western side of Lake Michigan, passes through the north of Illinois and crosses the Mississippi into Iowa, pursuing its course in a northwesterly direction to the Minnesota line, beyond which it has not yet been traced.

In its lithological character, the Niagara limestone, as developed in the Mississippi valley, is quite homogeneous, the variations of structure which it presents being much less marked than those which the same formation exhibits farther east. In its normal condition it is a light yellowish-grey rock, varying in shade from a warm and decidedly yellow tinge to a cooler brown. Its structure is somewhat less crystalline, and more compact than that of either of the magnesian rocks below it, and its stratification is more distinctly marked. Still, in hand specimens, it would often be difficult to distinguish the Niagara from the Galena limestone. The former does not, however, weather as unequally as the latter, so that it does not present such fantastic and picturesque forms, where exposed to the weather in elevated cliffs. Silicious matter is abundantly present in the Niagara, especially in its middle and lower portion, in the form of nodules of flint arranged in irregular layers. This tendency to silicification exhibits itself, throughout the formation, in the fact that all the corals which occur in it so abundantly have been converted into silica. In the Blue mounds, in Wisconsin, the whole thickness of the Niagara which is exposed has been converted into flint; and, thus hardened, it has been able to resist the denuding influences which have swept off the rocks in the adjacent region, down as low as the upper surface of the Galena limestone.

The entire thickness of the formation in Iowa cannot be accurately given, as there is no section in which the whole of the Niagara is exposed in its relations to the over and underlying rocks. As developed in Western New-York, the Niagara shales and limestone together have a thickness of about two hundred and sixty feet. There seems to be a gradual thickening of this member of the series towards the west, as in the sections measured by the different geological corps along the north shores of Lakes Huron and Michigan, a development of the Niagara and Clinton groups, which throughout the West cannot be separated from each other, equal to from three hundred and fifty to five hundred and sixty feet has been shown to exist. In Iowa, the greatest thickness observed in any one section is about two hundred and fifty feet, and probably three hundred and fifty may be taken as the maximum development of this limestone. The observations made lower down on the Mississippi river appear to indicate a rapid thinning out in that direction.

The Niagara limestone, in its chemical composition, hardly differs at all from the Galena, being essentially a nearly pure dolomite, with a small quantity of insoluble matters, which rarely exceeds two or three per cent of the whole. There is usually, however, a trifling excess of carbonate of lime over what would be required to form a compound consisting of one atom of each of the carbonates of lime and magnesia. The insoluble portion consists chiefly of silica, or silicious sand, without much alumina.

The annexed analyses will serve to illustrate the chemical composition of the Niagara limestone :

Specimen from Hickory grove, Jackson county, from the upper beds of the Niagara.

The color of this rock is a decided yellow or straw-color, deeper than has been observed in any other rock in this region. It is somewhat crystalline; but the crystalline character is masked by the numerous minute cavities it contains, which give it the appearance of a soft porous rock. These cavities are seen, on examination with the magnifying glass, to have been once occupied by organic bodies, mostly the stems and plates of minute crinoids.

The analyses gave :

	I.	II.		
Insoluble in acid	.90	.96		
Protoxide of iron, and a little perox.	.35	.45	=	.72 carb. iron
Lime	30.98	30.67	=	54.76 carb. lime
Magnesia	21.05	20.69	=	43.46 carb. mag.
Soda, and trace potash	(.18)	.18		
Chlorine and sulphuric acid	traces	traces		
Carbonic acid	46.54	46.54		
Loss		.51		
	100.00	100.00		

46.4263 grammes of this limestone were burnt in the crucible, and exhausted with water. In the solution there was 0.0149 gramme of the carbonates of the alkalies, in which soda greatly predominated in quantity.

This is nearly a pure dolomite, there being but a very trifling excess of lime over that required to form the double carbonate. The rock is valuable for lime, but is too porous to be used with advantage as a building-stone.

Specimen from Wiley's quarry, one mile southeast of West-Union, Fayette county.

This is a dark yellowish-grey limestone, with a few very minute cavities scattered through it, which are in some instances filled with bituminous matter. On examination the rock is found to be made up of a compact, crystalline, dolomitic mass, through which are disseminated numerous imperfectly developed crystals of calc. spar, which give it a peculiar vitreous lustre when held in such a position that the light is reflected from the faces of the crystals to the eye.

This rock forms a good and durable building-stone for common purposes, and is used in the town of West-Union.

The analysis gave as follows :

Insoluble in acid	4.16
Alumina and a little oxide of iron	1.01
Carbonate of lime	66.01
Carbonate of magnesia	28.52
Carbonate of soda	.25
Chlorine	trace
Loss	.05
	100.00

There was no potash present, and only a faint trace of sulphuric acid. In this case, the amount of carbonate of lime present is considerably greater than would have been required to form a pure dolomite with the magnesia which the specimen contains. The insoluble portion consists of a little argillaceous matter mixed with fine silicious sand.

Specimen from Goodenow's quarry, near Makoqueta, Jackson county.

This is a light buff-colored rock, more compact than the specimen from Walnut grove, although containing minute cavities, which were once occupied by stems of crinoids. It has a few nodules of silicious matter scattered through it; but is, on the whole, a good building-stone, and is quarried for that purpose extensively and used in the town of Makoqueta.

The analyses gave :

	I.	II.
Insoluble in acid	4.35	3.88
Alumina and peroxide of iron		.63
Carbonate of iron		trace
Carbonate of lime		52.18
Carbonate of magnesia	42.65	42.64
Carbonate of soda, and trace of potash		.35
Loss, and traces of chlorine and sulphuric acid		.32
		100.00

The above analyses will be sufficient to exhibit the chemical composition of the Niagara limestone in the Mississippi valley, and will demonstrate how nearly it approaches in character to a pure dolomite, and how nearly allied it is to the two great masses of the same material which lie beneath it.

Remarkable as is the resemblance in lithological character between the various dolomitic beds of the Silurian series in the Northwest, the fossils which they contain are entirely different. The Niagara limestone, as developed in that region, is peculiarly a coralline rock, as this class of fossils is usually found in it in much greater abundance than any others. There are localities, however, where great masses of the *Pentamerus oblongus* are crowded together into a limited space; as is also the case along the north shore of Lake Michigan, where this rock has already assumed nearly the same character, both lithological and palæontological, which it maintains as far west as it has yet been traced. Hand specimens of the Niagara limestone, from the region of Big Bay des Noquets, could with difficulty be distinguished from others collected at various points in Iowa.

The brachiopods of the Niagara in the western region are almost exclusively preserved as casts; the original shell being generally entirely removed, although occasionally partially retained, and, in such cases, converted into silex. In some localities, the cavity left by the shell is often lined with small crystals of dolomite. The corals, which have frequently been preserved in a tolerably perfect condition, are always converted into silex; and being consequently but little liable to destruction, they collect in considerable quantities in some localities where the rock itself has been decomposed. This would give the formation the appearance of being a highly fossiliferous one; whereas, in truth, the actual number of individual specimens present in this limestone is everywhere small in comparison with the mass of the rock, except in the case of the occasional Pentamerus beds. The silicified corals are frequently covered on the exterior with a fine network of concentrically-circular markings or grooves, evidently due to a peculiar concretionary arrangement of the silicious particles, which probably pervades the whole mass, and has been made apparent on the surface by weathering.

The accidental minerals of the Niagara limestone, in the Mississippi valley, are exceedingly few, and in no locality are they of any economical importance. The localities of brown hematite in Jackson and Clinton counties are numerous; but the ore has never been found in regular beds, or in sufficient quantity to be worked for iron. It seems from its peculiar position, and from the fact that it is often found in crystals which are pseudomorphs of those of iron pyrites, to have been derived from the decomposition of this substance. Sulphuret of lead is reported to have been found in many places in the Niagara limestone, but has never been worked to a profit in that rock: indeed, it appears most probable that the larger portion of the reported localities have their origin in some speculative attempt to sell land, on the strength of its presumed mineral value. The lithological character of the Niagara being so similar to that of the real lead-bearing rock, it is not surprising that it should often have been regarded as identical with it, and mineral treasures presumed to exist in it.

When the Niagara limestone is regularly bedded and not filled with cherty masses, it becomes an excellent building stone, as it usually proves durable and unchangeable in color when exposed to the weather. The thick and unevenly stratified layers, as well as the more brittle ones, have much less value for architectural purposes.

GROUPS INTERMEDIATE BETWEEN THE NIAGARA AND HAMILTON.

The Leclaire limestone appears to resemble the Niagara pretty closely in chemical composition, although differing from it somewhat in its external characters. A partial analysis of a specimen from near Leclaire were made, at our request, by Dr. C. F. Chandler, with the following results :

Insoluble silicates, or sand	0.42
Oxide of iron and alumina	0.53
Carbonate of lime	57.54
Carbonate of magnesia (by loss)	41.51
	100.00

The specimen analysed was a light grey crystalline rock, filled with small cavities, which were once occupied by a species of brachiopod, the remains of whose spiral apparatus may still be observed in numerous instances. These cavities are seen, on examination with the magnifying glass, to be lined with small crystals of pearl-spar or dolomite. The very small amount of insoluble matter present in this rock is remarkable.

This limestone is too porous to be of any value as a building-stone : it will make good lime. What may be the conditions of structure and composition with which the Leclaire limestone appears in other localities is not known : this peculiar rock has only been noticed on the Mississippi, and a few miles back in the interior, near Walnut grove.

Two specimens from the vicinity of Leclaire were analysed, which are supposed to belong to the Onondaga-salt group.

Specimen from Quarry creek.

This specimen, which was marked "Quarry creek—middle of the quarry" (see section on page 79), was found to be a soft and somewhat friable rock, without any decided crystalline structure, although nearly a pure dolomite. It has a greyish-yellow color, with delicate bands of a dark ferruginous stain crossing it in a direction parallel with the lines of stratification.

The analysis gave :

Insoluble in acids, mostly sand	3.77
Carbonate of iron and a little oxide of iron	2.23
Carbonate of lime	53.76
Carbonate of magnesia	39.05
Carbonate of soda, chlorides of sodium and potassium, sulphate of lime and loss	1.19
	100.00

This specimen does not differ much in composition from the average of the Niagara beds, except that it contains a little more iron; but it is softer and less crystalline than that rock, as it is usually seen. It would appear, as far as can be judged from the examination of a hand specimen, that this is rather too soft a material, and too much exposed to become stained by the oxidation of the iron it contains, to be recommended as a building-stone.

Specimen marked "Leclaire, Upper beds."

This rock is of a rather dark brownish-yellow color. It is soft and rather friable, having very little crystalline structure. There are occasional minute black specks scattered through it, which appear to consist of bituminous matter.

The analysis gave as follows :

Silica and insoluble silicates	6.70	
Peroxide of iron, and a little protoxide	.80	
Lime	29.06	= 51.89 carb. lime.
Magnesia	19.32	= 40.49 carb. mag.
Soda	.11	
Sulphuric acid and chlorine	minute traces	
Carbonic acid	43.55	
Loss	.46	
	100.00	

For particulars as to the thickness and range of the beds referred to the geological position of the Onondaga-salt group, see page 76, of a preceding chapter. It does not appear that any of the economically valuable products peculiar to this group in New-York have been discovered in this region. The existence of strata of this age had not been previously recognised at any point west of Mackinac and its immediate vicinity, where the Onondaga-salt group occurs in isolated patches of considerable thickness, but of limited extent, and characterized by the presence of gypsum, although not in sufficient quantity to be of much economical value. The peculiar character of the surface in Iowa will render the farther tracing into the interior of a group, of which only a few thin fragments are left, a matter of considerable difficulty.

HAMILTON GROUP.

The rocks which may be referred to this geological position cover a very considerable extent of surface within the State of Iowa, expanding in a northwesterly direction, so as to occupy, near the Minnesota line, a space over a hundred miles in width from east to west. The series of strata described in the New-York Reports under the name of the "Upper Helderberg group" has not been distinctly made out in the interior of the State of Iowa; and whether this group does occur, to the west of the Mississippi, remains yet to be decided, the limited exposures rendering the tracing out of any beds, which are not marked by an abundance of fossils, a very difficult task, after leaving the river. The complete connection of the Upper Silurian and Devonian strata, as developed in the West, with the groups of the same age, recognized by the New-York geologists, requires much more extended and careful observations of these rocks in the States of Ohio, Michigan and Indiana than has as yet been made; the subdivision of the wholesale grouping adopted in the first, necessarily rapid, reconnaisance of an extended region, being always a matter demanding much careful investigation on the part of the geologist.

In the State of New-York, the predominating materials of the Hamilton group are silicious and argillaceous : the series being made up of slates, shales and sandstones, in which the amount of calcareous matter present appears to be usually quite small. A black and probably quite carbonaceous slate seems to be characteristic of this period throughout a large portion of the West : in Canada, indeed, the shales of this age are highly bituminous, yielding, in some localties, large quantities of naptha, on distillation. Beyond the Mississippi, however, the rocks referred to the age of the Hamilton are almost exclusively calcareous, or calcareo-magnesian : the carboniferous shales appear to be wholly wanting in that region. Near the eastern line of Iowa the purely calcareous beds predominate, but they contain occasional bands in which argillaceous matter is abundant, and these are usually crowded with fossils. Farther to the northwest, near the northern boundary of the State, we find the rocks of Hamilton age, quite varying in their lithological characters, but always containing more or less carbonate of magnesia, not in sufficient quantity, however, to form dolomite. The quantity of argillaceous and silicious matter present in these magnesian limestones is quite variable, but never very large.

In regard to the thickness of this group as developed in

Iowa, we find it impossible to offer anything more than conjectures. Generally, the exposures of the rock are such as only to display a few feet in thickness, while its junction with the over or underlying groups is rarely to be seen. The greatest thickness exposed in a single section, referable to the Hamilton group, is about 100 feet. There seems to be considerable irregularity in the dip of the rocks of this region, especially after rising above the Silurian series; so that any calculations of the thickness of the group in question, based on the width of the area occupied by it, would have little value.

The annexed analyses will show the chemical composition of some of the most important varieties of this rock, as exhibited in the Mississippi valley.

Limestone from a quarry one mile above Rock island, Illinois.

This specimen was selected for analysis as representing the character of a large portion of the beds of the Hamilton group in this region. It is a fine-grained, compact and homogeneous rock, hardly exhibiting any trace of crystalline structure, until examined by the magnifying glass. It has a somewhat conchoidal fracture, and is somewhat soft, but appears to grow harder after being taken from the quarry : its color is a light bluish-grey. It is one of the purest limestones which has been found in the whole western country, as will be seen from the following analysis :

Insoluble in acid	.42
Carbonate of iron	.36
Carbonate of lime	98.77
Loss, alkalies, etc	.45
	100.00

This rock is largely quarried for lime, and furnishes the best possible material for that purpose.

Limestone from Independence, Buchanan county, Barker's quarry, lower beds.

This is a dull, earthy-looking rock, with a close texture and homogeneous structure. It is of a light yellowish-grey color, and is stained in fine waving lines with oxide of iron. It is quarried for building-stone and for lime, for either of which purposes it is well adapted.

It contains :

Insoluble in acid	10.02
Carbonate of iron	.98
Carbonate of lime	87.95
Alkalies, magnesia, etc	1.05
	100.00

Magnesian limestone, Shellrock creek, Rockford.

The rocks from this neighborhood are quite destitute of fossils, and are referred with some hesitation to the upper part of the Hamilton, or, possibly, the Chemung group. The specimen of which the analysis follows, is a light buff-grey rock and not crystalline, but rather earthy in its texture.

The analysis gave :

Insoluble in acid, clay	6.56
Peroxide of iron and a little alumina	1.01
Carbonate of lime	55.09
Carbonate of magnesia (by loss)	37.34
	100.00

Another specimen from the same locality was found, on examination, to be a soft argillaceous magnesian limestone, closely resembling the preceding one in composition, but containing a trifle larger percentage of argillaceous insoluble substance, namely, 8.3 per cent.

Magnesian limestone from Limekiln at Newburg, Mitchell county.

This specimen was taken from a quarry near Newburg, on Cedar river, and probably belongs to bed No.10, of the section at that place, given on page 311 of the preceding chapter. It is a dull earthy looking limestone, of a light-yellow color, with concretionary bands of a darker shade of a brownish-yellow : it has an imperfect laminated structure. This rock, when first quarried, is quite soft, so that it may be easily cut with a knife ; but it soon hardens on exposure. There are occasional blotches of calc. spar scattered through it.

The analysis gave :

Insoluble clayey substance	2.52
Carbonate of iron, with traces of oxide of iron and alumina	.48
Carbonate of lime	81.06
Carbonate of magnesia	15.72
Carbonates of soda and potash, with traces of the chlorides	.19
Trace of sulphuric acid and loss	.03
	100.00

A rock very similar to the one of which the analysis is given above was observed by Prof. HUNGERFORD in the section at Crane creek (No. 4 of section on page 305). A specimen from this locality, however, was found to contain more argillaceous matter and iron. A partial analysis was made of the Crane creek specimen, which gave :

Insoluble, mostly clay	10.07
Alumina, in soluble portion	2.40

The remainder consisted of the carbonates of lime and magnesia, the former in somewhat greater quantity than the latter.

Dark-brown Magnesian limestone from Shellrock falls.

This is a dark-brown rock, somewhat crystalline and rather close in its texture. It has an irregular fracture, and is interspersed with occasional blotches or irregular nodules of calcareous spar. It is too tough and not sufficiently homogeneous to make a good building-stone.

According to the analysis, it contains :

Insoluble in acid	4.58
Alumina and trace of iron	0.77
Carbonate of lime	57.06
Carbonate of magnesia	37.31
Carbonate of soda	.23
Chloride of sodium and loss	.05
	100.00

Sparry Magnesian limestone from Shellrock falls.

This specimen is a light-grey, hard, crystalline, sparry limestone, differing somewhat in texture and appearance from any other collected on the survey, but most resembling some of the rocks belonging to the Carboniferous limestone series.

The analysis gave :

Insoluble in acids	.80
Alumina and trace oxide of iron	1.10
Carbonate of lime	64.50
Carbonate of magnesia, including a little carbonate of soda and loss	33.60
	100.00

The Hamilton group does not contain, in the State of Iowa, any metalliferous ores of importance, nor are there any accidental crystallized minerals found in it.

The number and variety of the organic remains which characterize the rocks of this age are very great, although there are some districts, towards the north boundary of the State, where there is a considerable thickness of the strata referred to this group, without any traces of fossils. The similarity of lithological character between the Trenton and Hamilton rocks, in the Northwest, is worthy of being noticed as connected with the remarkable number of organic remains found in the two groups. They are the first accumulation of nearly pure carbonate of lime which took place in the earlier geological period; and it is reasonable to infer that the large part of the material of which the fossiliferous beds consist was eliminated from the surrounding water by the animals whose remains are entombed in the rocks. When carbonate of magnesia begins to be present in considerable quantity, we find the number of the individuals and species much less than it was where the rocks were almost purely calcareous.

We notice, as we ascend in the geological series, a greater variety of lithological character in the rocks of each successive group; which, taken in connection with the more irregular accumulation of the sediments in the district under consideration, as evinced by the unequal thickness of the various groups and their subdivisions, exhibited in sections taken at different points, indicates that the great uniformity of condition which prevailed over the region during the earliest period was gradually broken up, and modified by the action of local causes.

CHEMUNG GROUP.

The rocks which are referred to this position, in the State of Iowa, cover but a very limited surface, and they have been as yet but little investigated in reference to their connection with the strata of the same age at the East. In the State of New-York, the Chemung group is made up of a highly fossiliferous series of shales and thinbedded sandstones, with occasional calcareous layers resulting from the aggregation of organic remains.

In Iowa the group is chiefly represented by certain silicious shales, which vary much in lithological characters at different points in close proximity to each other. There is a thickness of somewhat over a hundred feet of beds, which are referred to the Chemung group, exposed at Burlington, and this appears to be its maximum development in this region. The strata at that place are chiefly silicious shales, irregularly bedded, and readily breaking up on exposure to the weather : they are, consequently, of no value whatever, either for lime or as a building material. Towards the north line of the State, the rocks of this age appear to become more calcareous. This would agree with the composition of the rocks of the Chemung group in Missouri, where the series referred to that position by the State Geologist is composed chiefly of one set of calcareous and another of calcareo-magnesian limestones, with a variable thickness of impure shale and sandstone between them.

Specimen from Lower beds at Burlington.

This is an earthy easily-decomposing rock, of various shades of bluish-grey. It is rather thinbedded, and not very distinctly stratified, having in many places a concretionary structure. From its appearance, it was supposed that it might possibly be valuable as a hydraulic cement : but it appears to be, in reality, a very silicious rock, containing only a small per-centage of carbonate of lime.

The analysis gave :

Insoluble in acid	92.69
Carbonate of lime	3.24
Carbonate of magnesia	2.57
Carbonate of iron	1.16
Chlorides of sodium and potassium	.08
Loss	.26
	100.00

The insoluble portion consisted chiefly of silicious matter, as appears from the following analysis of it by fusion with carbonate of soda :

Silica	87.46
Oxide of iron	2.75
Alumina	5.94
Lime	none
Magnesia	.43
Alkalies (by loss)	3.42
	100.00

The quantity of calcareous matter in different layers, and in different portions of the same layer of this rock, is quite variable.

Limestone from Cedar falls.

A very light grey rock, weathering dark brown, and occasionally stained in the interior with spots occasioned by the decomposition of iron pyrites. It has a somewhat conchoidal fracture, with a compact structure and finely crystalline texture. It is too hard to dress easily, and stains on exposure, which faults take from its value as a building-stone. It is almost a pure limestone, as will be seen from the analysis :

Insoluble in acid	2.10
Carbonate of lime	97.48
Carbonate of magnesia	trace
Carbonate of iron	.16
Alkalies, not determined, and loss	.26
	100.00

The limestone, of which the analysis is given above, is referred by Mr. WORTHEN, with some doubt, to the Chemung group : it is entirely destitute of fossils, and the exposure is but limited, so that its place in the series must remain uncertain for the present. The quality of the rock is such as to make it valuable for lime; and judging from the specimens collected, those portions which are not injured by sulphuret of iron will make a good material for building.

CARBONIFEROUS LIMESTONES.

The series of rocks constituting the Carboniferous limestones of the Mississippi valley have been, as yet, but imperfectly studied in relation to lithological characters and chemical composition, and any general remarks on these subjects will be deferred until a future report. It may, however, be mentioned that, as we rise in the series, we are constantly meeting with the evidences of the action of local causes; the members of each successive group varying more and more in lithological character and thickness, as developed at points not very remote from each other, and no longer maintaining that uniformity of texture and composition over large areas, which is so noticeable in the lower groups. On the whole, the predominance of the detrital beds, and especially of those formed from the accumulation of organic remains, becomes more and more marked. Magnesian limestones gradually disappear, and, in the Carboniferous series appear to be only met with in a few thin layers, between purely calcareous masses.

The Burlington limestone is a white sparry limestone, frequently highly crystalline in its texture. It contains numerous intercalated irregular masses of chert, and is characterized by a profusion of organic remains, especially of crinoids, which sometimes make up nearly the whole mass of the rock. No analyses have yet been made of specimens from this subdivision of the Carboniferous limestone group. It furnishes, however, a tolerable building-stone, and is much sought for that purpose, especially in Des Moines county.

The Keokuk limestone is an important member of the series in an economical point of view, as it furnishes a large amount of good building material. At its base, it is made up in series of thin bands of cherty matter, alternating with grey sub-crystalline limestone, and is rarely of any value : this portion of the rock is about forty feet thick in the south-eastern corner of the State, but it rapidly thins out towards the north. The beds above the cherty layers consist chiefly of bluish grey sub-crystalline limestone, which is rather apt to be injured as a building material, by the presence of seams and nodules of chert. Some of the layers appear to be highly magnesian, but the thickness and extent of these beds is not exactly known, although probably not exceeding a few feet.

An analysis of a specimen from the Asylum quarry at Mount-Pleasant, will exhibit the chemical composition of the magnesian layers in this portion of the series.

Limestone from the Asylum quarry, Mount-Pleasant.

This rock is of a dark yellowish-brown color. It has rather an earthy texture, although neither very homogeneous or compact in its structure. It contains blotches and seams of calcareous spar, and occasional stains of copper as well as of oxide of iron. Although resembling in appearance a rather argillaceous rock, it is, as appears from the following analysis, a quite pure dolomite :

	I.	II.	III.
Insoluble in acids	2.81	2.18	2.16
Alumina and oxide of iron	2.02	1.06	
Carbonate of lime	57.00	57.15	
Carbonate of magnesia		39.24	
Carbonate of soda and trace of potash		.31	
Chlorine (no sulphuric acid)			.04
		99.94	

This very magnesian limestone resembles greatly, in composition and external characters, the dolomitic members of the Silurian series. Like those, it weathers irregularly, and thus does not furnish a handsome building-stone, although its composition indicates it to be a durable material.

Specimen marked " Sipes's best layer", Mount-Pleasant.

The color of this rock, taken as a whole, is a light-buff ; but it is not homogeneous in its structure, being made up of numerous small irregular crystalline plates of calcareous spar, which are nearly transparent and colorless, scattered through a somewhat silicious mass of a buff color.

The analysis gave as follows :

Silica and insoluble silicate of iron	9.23	
Protoxide of iron, and a little peroxide	.27	
Manganese	trace	
Lime	50.01	= 89.30 carb. lime.
Magnesia	.54	
Soda and potash	.21	
Chlorine	trace	
Carbonic acid	38.80	
Loss	.94	
	100.00	

This specimen contained no sulphuric acid, and only a trace of chlorine. The appearance of this rock indicates that it would be an excellent material for building, as it dresses well under the hammer, and has a pleasing shade of color, which does not appear to change materially on exposure.

Specimen from M'Mahon's quarry, Mount-Pleasant.

This is a light bluish-grey rock when first quarried, but it soon weathers of a dirty yellow. It is made up in great part of small crystals of calcareous spar, disseminated through, or surrounded by, a soft and almost pulverulent substance. It contains numerous fragments of fossils scattered through it, especially of bryozoöid forms.

The analysis gave :

Insoluble in acid	10.69
Alumina, oxide of iron and trace of manganese	.75
Carbonate of lime	79.36
Carbonate of magnesia	7.90
Loss, soda, potash, chlorine, sulphuric acid	1.30
	100.00

The preceding analyses of the limestones belonging to the Keokuk series show that they are usually pretty pure carbonate of lime. Some of the layers contain, however, minute particles of sulphuret of iron scattered through the mass; and, in this case, they soon stain on exposure to the weather. Some of the rocks quarried at Mount-Pleasant and used in building the Asylum for the Insane, have been found, on actual trial, not to endure as well as would have been expected from an inspection of them when first quarried. When the material is so distinctly stratified as is the case in this region, it not unfrequently happens that the blocks have not sufficient coherence between the laminæ to admit of their being set up on edge in the building. They should be laid in the walls in the same position which they occupied in the quarry; that is, with the planes of deposition horizontal. There seems to be a want of coherence between the particles, which causes the blocks to split in the direction of the stratification, even when no perceptible parting of the layers can be observed, and when the whole rock seems to have a crystalline structure.

Specimen marked "Hartnett's quarry, southwest of Mount-Pleasant".

This is a light-grey limestone, of a decidedly crystalline texture, and quite compact and homogeneous in its structure. It breaks with a tolerably smooth fracture, and dresses handsomely ; but is much injured for building purposess by the occasional occurrence of sulphuret of iron, which is found in minute crystallizations in the joints of the rock. This limestone weathers a dirty yellow, which is rather extraordinary, considering that it only contains a quarter of one per cent of carbonate of iron.

The analysis gave the following results :

Silica and insoluble silicates	2.05	
Peroxide of iron	.29	
Oxide of manganese	trace	
Lime	54.23	= 96.84 carb. lime.
Magnesia	.52	
Soda and trace potash	.26	
Chlorine, sulphuric and phosphoric acids,	traces	
Carbonic acid	42.82	
	100.17	

The above limestone represents the composition of the St. Louis or Concretionary subdivision of the Carboniferous series : it is a very pure calcareous rock, and is well adapted for burning into lime. Those portions which are sufficiently heavy-bedded, and free from sulphuret of iron, answer well for architectural purposes.

The tendency to the formation of geodes, lined with crystals of various minerals, is peculiarly characteristic of the Carboniferous limestones, although not limited to that part of the series. The beautiful crystallizations of pyrites, barytes and pearl-spar which occur in geodes in the Galena limestone at Scales's mound, have already been noticed : in this particular rock, instances of this mode of occurrence of crystallized minerals seem to be quite rare and confined to localities of limited area. In the carboniferous series, however, the geodiferous bed which lies next above the Keokuk limestone is remarkable for its persistency of character and thickness over a considerable area, as well as for the size of the cavities and the beauty of the crystals with which they are more or less completely filled. Quartz, crystallized or in form of chalcedony, is the most common mineral substance occurring in this way; but some of the geodes are lined with fine crystallizations of calc. spar, or, less frequently, of dolomite, with which are occasionally associated blende (sulphuret of zinc) and pyrites. This geode bed is from twenty-five to forty-five feet in thickness, and is made up chiefly of an impure argillaceous and sometimes shaly limestone : the cavities in which the crystals occur are from two or three inches up to fifteen in diameter. The comparative abundance of sulphuret of zinc, and the almost entire absence of galena in rocks of this age, is worthy of notice. Geodes are occasionally found in all the members of the Carboniferous limestone series, but they are far more common in the position noticed above, between the Keokuk and Warsaw limestones.

COAL MEASURES.

The predominance of detrital rocks, including clays, shales and sandstones, over those of chemical origin, is the characteristic feature of the Coal-measure strata. It is in this formation that we first meet, in the Mississippi valley regions, with coarse quartzose sandstones, bearing in their physical characters marks of having been formed by the abrasion and grinding up of silicious rocks.

The most prominent member of the Coal-measure group in the eastern part of Iowa is a ferruginous sandstone, composed of rounded grains of quartz which vary in size and shape, although usually minute and nearly spherical. These grains are held together by a cement of oxide of iron, mixed with a little lime, giving the rock a dark brown color. This is the character of the sandstone along the eastern outcrop of the coal, in Jasper, Powesheik, Hardin and Marshall counties. At Muscatine, the sandstone is destitute of ferruginous matter, having a light bluish-grey tint, with minute specks of black coaly matter. It is very fine-grained and homogeneous, and thinly laminated. The position of the sandstone in regard to the beds of coal, at least on the eastern outcrop of the basin, is not a uniform one. In general, the larger portion of this rock appears to underlie the principal coal-beds; but in some localities, especially in Hardin county, there is a thickness of from seventy-five to one hundred feet above the coal-bed opened at several localities in that region. Throughout the whole of that portion of the State, the exposures are too imperfect to afford a clear idea of the order of succession of the rocks of this epoch. As we go farther south and west, we find the amount of calcareous matter in the coal series gradually increasing, although shales and sandstones everywhere predominate. Some of the beds of limestone associated with the Coal-measures are white and crystalline; the crystalline structure having obliterated all traces of the fossils these beds once contained, and which become apparent on the weathered surface of the rocks, sometimes showing the whole mass to be made up of fragments of shells, crinoids, etc. The larger part of the limestones in this geological position, are, on the other hand, dark-colored and earthy, containing more or less bituminous matter, but consisting, with the exception of from two to ten per cent of insoluble argillaceous matter, almost entirely of carbonate of lime. No limestones containing more than one or two per cent of magnesia have been noticed in the Coal measures.

The silicious shaly beds of the Coal measures sometimes contain calcareous concretionary masses, which at Muscatine are often of great size and remarkable regularity (see page 276).

The annexed analyses will serve to indicate the composition of some of the limestones associated with the coal.

Specimen from Eldora, Hardin county.

This specimen was taken, from the immediate vicinity of Dr. Fuller's coal-bank, where it seems to have a position underlying the coal. It is a dark-colored, almost black, fine-grained earthy limestone, and destitute of any trace of crystalline structure. Like most of the limestones of this period, it contains a little bituminous matter : it contains only a small amount of magnesia.

The results of the analysis are as follows :

Bituminous substances	1.09
Earthy substances, insoluble in acid	8.04
Carbonate of iron and manganese	3.00
Alumina, dissolved by acid	.35
Carbonate of lime, and trace sulphate	85.74
Carbonate of magnesia	1.00
Chloride of sodium, carbonate of soda, and loss	.78
	100.00

This limestone appears, from its external character, to be likely to possess hydraulic properties : its chemical composition, however, when compared with that of other limestones, suitable for this purpose, does not indicate it to be of much value except for burning into lime : for this purpose it is well adapted. The rock is of no use as a building-stone, owing to its softness and to the fact that it breaks too irregularly to be easily quarried; besides, the exposure is too limited to allow of any considerable quantity of material being obtained.

Specimen marked "Hydraulic limestone, Business corner, Van Buren county."

This limestone is a dark bluish-grey rock, very fine-grained, and having but little trace of a crystalline structure. The dark color is owing to the presence of a little bituminous matter which is uniformly diffused through it.

The analysis gave the following results :

Carbon	.56	
Insoluble (clay)	3.57	
Protoxide of iron	.56	
Lime	52.16	= 93.14 carb. of lime.
Magnesia	.91	
Soda and trace potash	.21	
Sulphuric acid	.51	
Chlorine	trace	
Carbonic acid and loss	41.52	
	100.00	

This specimen is nearly a pure carbonate of lime, as shown by the analysis : it is, therefore, not adapted for use as a hydraulic limestone, although valuable for common lime. It contains a larger amount of sulphuric acid than any other limestone examined from this region.

The analyses which have been given above, will serve to convey an idea of the chemical composition of the calcareous and calcareo-magnesian rocks of Eastern Iowa. Farther examinations will be made of the limestones, shales and sandstones of the upper members of the series, the investigation of which in the central and western portion of the State will be the object of the future prosecution of the Survey. A few remarks may here be appended in regard to the methods pursued, and the general results which have been obtained.

The substance used for analysis was always dried at a temperature a little over that of boiling water, by which, in all the crystalline rocks, at least, all the water was removed. The shaly and argillaceous limestones contain, however, a little water combined with silicate of alumina, in such a condition, that a heat greater than 212° F. is required for its expulsion. These specimens show a small loss, which sometimes, in the very argillaceous limestones, amounts to three or four per cent.

The residuum left after digestion with chlorohydric acid of moderate strength, was occasionally analyzed by itself, as a silicate, by fusion with carbonate of soda, or examined with the microscope. A careful analysis of the insoluble portion, in every case, with especial reference to the amount of alkalies present in the rock, would be desirable. It will be noticed, on inspection of the analyses of about forty different limestones given above, how small an amount of insoluble matter is present in the large majority of the limestones of the Mississippi valley : indeed, several of them are almost pure carbonate of lime, or carbonate of lime and magnesia, containing no more impurities than the finest crystallized marbles. In the lower dolomites, the insoluble portion consists mainly of silicious sand, apparently derived from the destruction of the underlying sandstones. In the more calcareous and shaly beds of the Trenton and Hamilton, the insoluble portion consists chiefly of a mixture of clay and sand.

The limestones analyzed all contain at least a trace of iron, and but rarely more than one per cent. In the rocks which have not been weathered, the iron is usually present in the form of a carbonate : when the rock has been exposed, more or less of the iron is found to be oxidized, the substance having acquired a yellow tinge of color. As the amount of iron present is so small, it has usually been reckoned as a carbonate, except in those cases where the reaction and color of the specimen showed distinctly that the larger portion of it had been converted into the peroxide. The amount of alumina dissolved by the acid and precipitated by ammonia, has usually been found to be quite small.

In some instances the carbonic acid has been directly determined ; but, in most cases, the lime and magnesia have been reckoned as carbonates, without making a separate analysis for that purpose.

Most of the limestones analysed have been carefully tested for the alkalies. Potash has almost always been found to be present, although usually only in minute quantity. Soda has always been detected, and generally in amount sufficient for determination.

The uniformity in the quantity of this alkali given by the analyses, it being almost always between one and two tenths of a per cent, would lead to the idea that this supposed amount might be, in reality, the expression of some constant impurity in the reagents employed, or of some error in the methods adopted. As, however, the same results have been obtained, when different modes of analysis, and the most carefully prepared reagents, have been employed, there can be little doubt that the results are substantially correct. From some experiments which have been made, it would appear that the potash contained in the limestones exists principally in the clay, or insoluble portion of the rock; and that this combination was acted on by being ignited so as to become partly soluble in water, while the soda remains in a state in which it is not capable of being dissolved without the aid of an acid. The quantity of chlorine which exists in the limestones is very minute, never, in the case of any specimen examined, exceeding three or four hundredths of one per cent: it is evident, therefore, that the larger portion of the soda must be in combination with carbonic acid; and, if so, as it is not in a soluble condition, it is probably also combined with silica, forming a complex silicate, perhaps analogous in composition to Cancrinite, a silicate of alumina + carbonate of soda and lime. That a portion of the lime is present in the form of a silicate is also made probable by the fact, that in a large number of analyses the amount of carbonic acid has always been found to fall a little below what would be required to saturate all the bases, supposing them all to exist as carbonates. Besides, a portion of the silica in the insoluble residuum is almost always found to be capable of being taken up by carbonate of soda, indicating that it is not all in the form of sand, but, rather, of silica set free from chemical combination.

Sulphuric acid has almost always been found to be present in minute traces in the limestones examined : in some of the dark-colored calcareous rocks, associated with the Coal measures, its quantity is sufficient to make it worth while to determine it quantitatively : in one case it amounted to one-half of one per cent of the substance. It is undoubtedly present in the form of sulphate of lime.

Phosphoric acid probably exists in many of the limestones, but its quantity is so minute that it is very difficult to detect its presence and positively identify it. The usual test for minute quantities of this acid, by means of molybdate of ammonia, seems not to be a reliable one; and it is proposed to reject the results which have been obtained by its aid, and to repeat the investigation under different circumstances, the results to be given in a future Report.

ECONOMICAL APPLICATION OF THE LIMESTONES AND OTHER ROCKS.

Building-stone. In the preceding pages of this Report, frequent notices have been given of the value of the rocks described as building materials; and in the chapters devoted to the county geology, a sufficient amount of detail on this subject has already been incorporated. A few general remarks will here be added on the choice of stone for architectural purposes, with reference to the condition of things in Iowa.

As there are no igneous or metamorphic rocks within the limits of the State, so far as we have yet observed, except in the form of boulders, which, of course, will give but a limited supply of material, although very useful in some localities for a time, the builder will be obliged to confine himself exclusively to the stratified rocks, either sandstones or limestones.

Sandstone, or freestone as it is generally termed by builders, occurs in every variety of form, from the softest material, yielding as readily between the fingers as sugar, to the hardest quartzose rock, which is almost absolutely indestructible by exposure. The medium hardness is, of course, the most desirable, as the material used must be capable of being worked with tools, as well as of enduring after it has been brought into shape. The beautiful freestone, so much used in the Atlantic cities, a sandstone colored and held together by a ferruginous cement, is extensively wrought at several localities, especially in Connecticut and New-Jersey. It belongs to a geological position higher in the series than that of any sandstone yet noticed in Iowa.

The Potsdam sandstone, as usually developed in the Northwest, is too friable to be a good building-stone, the silicious grains being held together by the merest trace of a ferruginous cement. In the vicinity of the trappean ranges, however, and in certain limited localities, at a distance from any igneous rocks, there are beds of this material which are sufficiently durable to be employed to advantage in building. Some of the beds of passage from the Potsdam to the Lower Magnesian limestone appear to be well adapted for architectural purposes, as they are made up of a mixture of sandstone and limestone, which seems to possess a high degree of strength and durability, and which also splits and dresses with facility. The Upper sandstone is hardly ever coherent enough to be made use of for any purpose, where a durable material is required.

The dolomites, which cover so large a portion of Northeastern Iowa, are capable of furnishing a great variety of building-stone, some of which is of an excellent character, both in point of strength, color and durability. There is a considerable diversity in the external appearance of these rocks, however, even in cases where the analysis indicates no great difference of chemical composition. In the Lower Magnesian, the principal defects are, that the rock is too heavybedded, or not regularly stratified, so as to split into layers of convenient size, or else that its texture is not sufficiently homogeneous. Layers may usually be found in which these defects are not apparent. In the Galena limestone, the unequal weathering of the rock is a very great drawback to its value, and it does not split and dress with the facility requisite to form a first-class material for architectural purposes. The Niagara limestone is, usually, more compact, and has less of the peculiar tendency to disintegration which seems to characterize the Galena, and which is apparently due to its peculiar crystalline structure. One defect is common to portions of all the dolomitic masses in the Mississippi valley : this is the presence of silicious nodules, or layers of chert, which materially impair the value of the rock in which they occur. Still, the pure crystalline dolomites are classed by competent authorities among the most durable materials used for architectural purposes; and the sections and exposures of the three great dolomitic masses of the Northwest are so numerous within the limits of Northeastern Iowa, that a good stone may almost always be obtained without the necessity of going to any considerable distance.

The pure limestones of the Trenton, the Hamilton and the Carboniferous limestone groups furnish a great variety of building-stones, of very different character and value in different parts of the State. The Trenton limestone is much wrought along the upper portion of the Mississippi, within the limits of Iowa, as it is easily accessible and furnishes a rock which, on the whole, splits better and dresses more evenly than the average of the dolomitic strata above and below. There is a very great difference between the different beds of limestone of the Carboniferous series : some of them are worthless, whilst others furnish an excellent material. The most reliable guide to a knowledge of their actual value for building, is to examine the outcrop of the rock, where it has long been exposed to the weather, and observe what effect this has had upon the texture and color of the different strata : if they appear discolored and softened, or irregularly worn away on their projecting edges, it may safely be inferred that the same appearances will be exhibited, although not perhaps in so great a degree, by the freshly-quarried blocks after they have been for a time exposed to the action of the elements. If nodules of pyrites, or sulphuret of iron, are noticed, it may be taken for granted that they will decompose and discolor the rock in which they occur. As far as possible, the blocks should be laid in their natural position, and not set up on their edges, as they are much more liable to crack in the direction of the planes of stratification than across them.

There is hardly anything so much felt throughout the West, as the absence of good materials for road-coverings. None of the sandstones or limestones are suitable for this purpose, since only the trappean, hornblende or quartz rocks have the requisite hardness and toughness. The cherty masses associated with the different limestones and dolomites are, indeed, a most excellent material for roads; but there are few localities where they can be obtained in quantity, without a good deal of expense. Railroads, iron pavements, and, to some extent, plank roads, must be relied on to facilitate traffic. The prairie roads are excellent in dry weather, when not too much cut up by heavy vehicles, and much may be done for their improvement by a suitable and thorough system of drainage.

Hydraulic lime. The importance of good hydraulic lime to engineers and architects, for use in a great variety of constructions, is so evident, that all will admit the necessity of a thorough investigation into the qualities of the different limestones occurring in the State, with special reference to their value for this purpose. This object has been had in view, in making the chemical analyses, which have been recorded in the preceding pages; and after collecting and examining the principal varieties of rocks from other parts of the State not yet visited, it is proposed to make a series of practical trials, with a view of ascertaining in that way, more definitely than can be learned from analysis alone, which among all the limestones possessing hydraulic properties in different degrees, are the most to be recommended. The difference in the composition of the rocks used for water-lime in various parts of the world is very great, and there is a corresponding difference, no doubt, in the material manufactured from them; and numerous and elaborate researches have been made by able chemists, with the view of determining the character of the reactions which take place in the process of preparing and using hydraulic cements. From these investigations it appears that a limestone, containing a certain amount of silica only, is capable of making a lime possessing hydraulic properties; the setting of the lime being caused by the hydratation of the silicate of lime, which is produced by burning the mixture of carbonate of lime and silica. The rock of the Theil (Ardèche), in France, is a hydraulic limestone of this character : it consists of almost exclusively of carbonate of lime and silica, having the following composition, according to RIVOT :

Lime	46.3
Oxide of iron	0.7
Silica, quartzose sand and clay	15.0
Carbonic acid and water	37.6

The lime prepared from it contains only 1.8 per cent of alumina to 18.2 of silica and 1.71 of quartzose sand; and yet it furnishes a most excellent water-lime, and one which has been found especially valuable in marine constructions.

In most of the limestones furnishing water-lime on being calcined, however, clay or silicate of alumina takes the place of pure silica; and it appears, from the results of numerous analyses, that mixtures of carbonate of lime with clay, in various proportions, constitute by far the larger proportion of the hydraulic limestones used in Europe. Argillaceous limestones containing less than 10 per cent of clay have hardly any hydraulic properties; and the value of the material for this purpose increases with the quantity of the clay, until the latter reaches 30 or 40 per cent.

None of the *non-magnesian* limestones of Iowa, which have yet been examined, have been found to contain a sufficient amount of silica and alumina to justify the expectation that they will yield good hydraulic lime. It is not improbable, however, that beds of limited extent will be found in the Trenton limestone, or in the Carboniferous series, which may hereafter be made available for this purpose.

The *magnesian* limestones, however, appear to be capable of furnishing a good hydraulic lime, even when a considerably less quantity of silica and alumina is present in them than is required to give hydraulic properties to a purely calcareous rock. The effect of the presence of magnesia in altering the character of a limestone, and imparting to it hydraulic properties, has not been sufficiently studied in Europe; since almost all the limestones used for cements contain only a small per-centage of magnesia, and not enough to produce any sensible effect on the reactions of the lime. From the experiments of VICAT, however, it would appear that the carbonates of magnesia and lime alone, without the addition of some clay, will yield only a feeble hydraulic lime. The only dolomite used for hydraulic lime in Europe, so far as we have been able to ascertain, is at Robache, near Saint-Dié in France. This material gives a lime which is eminently hydraulic, and is used for the public works, under the direction of the Government, in the region of the Vosges. As this dolomite agrees nearly in composition with many of those of the Upper Mississippi valley, a transcript of the analysis will be given.

It contains :

Lime	29.38	= 51.46 carb. lime.
Magnesia	21.55	= 45.27 carb. magnesia.
Carbonic acid	45.80	
Clay	3.25	
	99.98	

The Magnesian limestones and dolomites have long been used in Virginia for hydraulic purposes; and attention was called to the fact that the magnesia imparts the property of hardening, under water, to limestones which contain but a small proportion of silica and alumina, by W. B. ROGERS, in 1838, who has given in his report for that year a number of analyses of hydraulic limestones, some of which agree closely in composition with the dolomite rocks of Iowa, and lead to the supposition that these will be equally available for this purpose.

The annexed analyses, from the report above cited, will show the resemblance between the hydraulic magnesian limestones of Virginia and those of Iowa:

	I.	II.	III.	IV.
Carbonate of lime	51.84	46.20	52.04	57.16
Carbonate of magnesia	37.40	34.16	17.12	23.80
Silica	8.36	12.68	19.36	8.52
Alumina and oxide of iron	1.48	4.00	8.60	9.12
Water	.56	.60	1.60	1.40

No. I is from the eastern side of Price's mountain, given as "highly hydraulic": No.II, from near Big Lick, Roanoke county, also "highly hydraulic": No. III, from the Coal measures, "very hydraulic": No. IV, "very hydraulic", from the same geological position.

The best hydraulic cements used in the State of New-York are highly magnesian, although they contain a little larger proportion of the insoluble silicates than is found in most of the Iowa dolomites. The materials from which the Chittenango and Manlius cements are made, both of which are considered of good quality, agree pretty nearly in composition with some of the Iowa rocks. According to L. C. BECK's analyses they contain:

	CHITTENANGO.	MANLIUS.
Lime	29.00 (= 51.78 carb. lime).	25.24 (= 45.07 carb. lime).
Magnesia	17.30 (= 36.34 carb. mag.).	18.80 (= 39.44 carb. mag.).
Carbonic acid	40.95	39.80
Silica & alumina,	11.00	13.50
Peroxide of iron,	1.10	1.25
Water and loss	.65	1.41
	100.00	100.00

The subject of the influence of magnesia in the composition of hydraulic limes, and how far it can replace the argillaceous element, without injury to the result, is one which has not yet been sufficiently studied, and it is proposed to make this a special subject of investigation during the progress of the Survey; so that, in connection with the additional analyses and practical experiments, as much light as possible may be thrown on this branch of the economic geology of Iowa.

Lime. The materials for burning into lime are to be found in every part of the State of Iowa, where there are any rocks exposed, without the necessity of going to any considerable distance. The kilns are usually located with reference to abundance and convenience of fuel, rather than of rock. The Trenton, Hamilton and Carboniferous limestone groups all contain considerable masses of nearly pure carbonate of lime, which of course afford the best of lime. The Magnesian limestones are also largely burned for lime, less sand being required for making mortar with this kind of limestone than with the purely calcareous.

NON-METALLIC MINERALS OF ECONOMICAL VALUE.

COAL.

The investigations of the geological corps in Iowa have been, up to the present time, confined almost exclusively to the region lying to the north and east of the Des Moines river, and the explorations to the south of that stream have been limited to its immediate vicinity. As the great body of the coal region of the State is believed to lie to the south-west of the Des Moines, it would be premature, at the present stage of progress of the Survey, to attempt to enter into a general account of the coal-bearing strata of Iowa. The localities which have thus far been examined are chiefly along the edge of the basin, and in detached patches of limited extent, where the beds of coal are thinner, and of poorer quality than they will be found to be farther in towards the centre of the basin, as we are justified in asserting from the results of the explorations which have already been made. To attempt to estimate the number of square miles occupied by workable coal-beds, or to give an approximation to their average thickness, would be entirely premature at the present time. There is an extensive district in the portion of the State which has already been explored, over which the superficial deposits are so deeply spread, that but little more can be said of it, than that it is, in all probability, in part occupied by limited patches of rocks belonging to the Coal-measures; while the question whether there are workable beds of coal associated with these outliers can be only decided by borings and other expensive explorations, which it was not within the province of the Geological Survey to have carried on.

An examination of the preceding pages, especially of Mr. WORTHEN'S Report on the Des Moines valley, and of the chapters devoted to the county geology, will serve to give an idea of the nature of the deposits of coal along the eastern edge of the basin. It will be seen that there is no regularity in the number or thickness of the beds at localities which are comparatively near each other, the whole arrangement of the materials of the coal and the associated rocks indicating great irregularity in their mode of deposition and of the surface on which their accumulation took place. There appear to be in most of the localities, where the rocks are best exposed, two beds of coal; and where best developed, the heaviest may sometimes reach five feet in thickness. On the north side of the Des Moines, the beds rarely exhibit that amount of good workable coal, but such have been already noticed on the south side. At one locality, near Hillsborough, in Henry county, two beds of four and three feet in thickness, are so near each other that they may be profitably worked as one, since they are only separated by about ten inches of shale. A little west of Ottumwa, there is a thickness of five feet of good coal exposed, and probably a second seam which has not yet been found.

The explorations which have been made in search of coal in Iowa have been but limited, and it has been nowhere wrought, except where cropping out naturally in exposures convenient of access, and for local consumption. The demand has, as yet, been small, owing to the recent settlement of the interior of the State, and to the fact that the beds on the west side of the river, in Illinois, are more conveniently situated for supplying the valley : as the interior counties become filled up with inhabitants, the use of this kind of fuel will rapidly increase; and the time will soon come, when coal-mining will become an important branch of business, and one in which all will be more or less directly interested. Up to the present time, however, this kind of work has not been prosecuted with any regularity or systematized organization of labor by skilled workmen, so that the price of the coal has been much greater than it will be hereafter, when the mines come to be worked on a more extensive scale and in a more business-like manner.

The coals of Iowa are all of the bituminous class. They are fat, adhesive and close-burning, the coke melting down into a solid mass, and, therefore, requiring frequent stirring to effect a complete combustion. There is no essential difference between the average of Iowa coals and of those of Illinois : they contain from thirty-five to forty per cent of volatile bituminous matter, and from forty-five to fifty of fixed carbon. The amount of ash varies from one to twenty per cent; but, in the better class of coals, it does not usually much exceed five per cent.

A considerable number of analyses have been made, in order to acquire a correct idea of the constitution of the coals in Eastern Iowa, and specimens will hereafter be examined, as they are collected from other portions of the State during the progress of the Survey. No ultimate analyses, or determinations of the amount of oxygen, hydrogen, nitrogen and carbon, have been made, this matter being left for future investigation. In a practical point of view, the most important question in regard to the condition of the western coals is one that could not well be answered by chemical analysis, but, rather, by a mechanical operation performed on larger quantities of the material than it was always in our power to collect, even had it been desirable. The question to which reference is here made, is in regard to the quantity of sulphuret of iron, or pyrites, mechanically mixed with the coal, the amount being frequently so considerable as to materially impair its value. Besides the sulphuret of iron, there is often more or less gypsum, and, occasionally, carbonate of lime, present in the coal, the gypsum and pyrites being frequently associated together and forming thin plates filling the joints of the coal. Near the outcrop of the beds where the coal has been exposed to the weather, the sulphuret of iron is found to have become decomposed, and a large portion of it removed as a soluble sulphate, while the remainder of the iron, in the form of a hydrated peroxide, discolors the coal and the adjacent rock. The presence of these substances renders the coal unpleasant to burn in open grates, and injurious in its effects on the metals in contact with which it is ignited. Besides this, those coals which contain pyrites and gypsum cannot be transported to any distance, without losing much of their value by slacking, or crumbling into small fragments. The quantity of these deleterious substances, disseminated through the coal, is so variable in different portions of the same bed, and even in samples taken from the immediate vicinity of each other, that no inference could be drawn from the analytical examination which would be of much value, unless an average was taken of several hundred pounds of the material, carefully sampled, and even then a more reliable opinion could be obtained from an inspection of the coal lying in quantity at the mine.

The method of analysis adopted, was as follows : All coals contain a little hygrometric water, or moisture mechanically disseminated through their mass, which must be taken into account in estimating their value. This water is entirely driven off at a temperature of 212° F.; and the quantity present was determined by drying a small sample of the coal, coarsely pulverized in the air-bath at a temperature a little above that of boiling water, until no farther loss of weight took place.

The amount of water in the different specimens analyzed is very different, but appears to be dependent, in a great degree, upon the length of time which has elapsed since the coal was taken from the bed, and the conditions under which it has been kept. That this is the case, will be evident from the following experiments. A sample of coal from Rock-Island, taken from the bed, in September 1856, and analyzed in November, was found to contain 7.96 per cent of water; but, after having remained another year in a dry and warm room exposed to the air, it was ascertained to have parted with over half its hygrometric moisture, losing at that time only 3.44 per cent by exposure to a temperature of 212–220° F. Another sample of coal from Webster county (northeast quarter of Sec. 18, T. 88, R. 28), gave the following results : The specimen analyzed, after having remained about two months exposed to a summer temperature in a dry room, gave 14.95 per cent of water : the same, after remaining a further period of six months under the same conditions of dryness, contained only 6.6 per cent of moisture. Another sample of coal, from the Big Muddy river in Illinois, which was collected in 1852 and had remained in a dry place for five years, lost 5.37 per cent of water on being dried at 212°. The slowness with which these coals part with the moisture which they contain, and which appears to be only mechanically mingled with the carbonaceous matter, is indeed surprising. The amount of water in the different coals examined varies from three to fifteen per cent : the specimens which came from the smaller detached basins, or the edge of the basin, evidently contain considerably more water than those which were obtained farther to the southwest. This is, undoubtedly, owing to the greater solidity of the coal, when it occurs in heavy beds and has been pressed down by a heavier weight of superincumbent rock.

A remarkable fact, in connection with the determination of the water present in the specimens of coal, has been noticed. In numerous instances, after the sample, in the form of a coarse powder, had been dried for several hours in the air-bath, at a temperature a little above that of boiling water, during which time it had gradually lost weight until all the water seemed to have been expelled, on continuing the operation for some time longer, a slight increase of weight would become perceptible, and the coal would continue to grow heavier, until a gain of several tenths of a per cent of the original weight had been made. This appears to be owing to the slow oxidation of the sulphur which all these coals contain in a very finely-divided state, disseminated in invisible particles through the mass, and, perhaps, partly in combination with iron.

After thus determining the amount of water, the quantity of matter volatilized from the coal by ignition in a closed crucible was ascertained, and then the amount of fixed carbon by burning the coal with access of air. As the result of these operations, we have the proportion of gaseous or volatile matter and that of the coke or fixed residuum, and, finally, that of the ash, or the inorganic and incombustible portion of the coal.

The quantity of sulphur was determined, on samples of the coal picked clean from all the pyrites visible to the eye, by digesting the substance with chlorate of potash and chlorohydric acid until complete oxidation had taken place. The solution was then evaporated down to expel the excess of acid, and the sulphuric acid precipitated by a salt of baryta.

The following analyses will exhibit the general composition of the coals of Iowa basin, and a few samples of coals used in Iowa from the adjacent State of Illinois have also been examined for comparison.

Specimen collected at Havill's coal-bank, near New-Buffalo.

This is an impure cannel coal, holding a position in point of chemical composition about midway between a pure cannel coal and a highly bituminous shale. It has a finely laminated structure, a rather dull lustre, and a tendency to a conchoidal fracture. It is traversed by numerous joints, or thin cracks, which are filled with sulphuret of iron.

The analyses gave :

Water	2.87	Total volatile matter	39.26
Volatile bituminous matter	36.39		
Fixed carbon	40.82	Coke	60.72
Ash	19.90		
	99.98		99.98

The amount of sulphur present, in a form not perceptible to the eye, was found to be 0.19 per cent, that being the smallest percentage of sulphur observed in any specimen analyzed. The ash was pulverulent, and of a light reddish grey color.

Composition, calculated on the coal dried at 212°:

Volatile	37.47
Fixed carbon	42.03
Ashes	20.48
	99.98

This coal would be a good material for the manufacture of gas; but it appears to occur in too thin a stratum to be capable of being worked with profit (See section of Havill's coal-bed, page 124).

Specimen marked "Lower coal : 28-inch seam, near New-Buffalo, Iowa."

This is a coal of a rather irregular fracture, having tolerably well-marked lines of bedding. The fractured surface in the direction of these lines is rough and uneven, being made up of portions having a pitch-black color and brilliant lustre, and other portions with a dull surface and lighter shade of color. It is intersected by numerous thin seams of sulphate of lime, which are perpendicular to the lamination of the coal, and divide it into small blocks of irregular shape and size.

The analysis gave, on the substance dried at the ordinary temperature :

Water	3.13	Total volatile	41.90
Other volatile substances	38.77		
Fixed carbon	49.08	Coke	58.10
Ash	9.02		
	100.00		100.00

Reduced to substance dried at 212° F. :

Volatile combustible matter	40.02
Fixed carbon	50.67
Ash	9.31
	100.00

The color of the ash was light red : it was quite pulverulent and infusible. The coke is hard and brilliant, and thoroughly fused.

A separate determination of the amount of sulphur present in the picked portion of this coal, gave 1.57 per cent.

For a description of the bed from which the above sample was taken, see page 124. The thickness of the bed does not appear to be sufficient to encourage working, although the quality of the coal, to judge from the specimen, is fair.

Specimen from Rock island, Illinois.

This coal is nearly connected in geographical position with those which have been previously noticed. The specimen analyzed was from the bed of Messrs. Thomas & Co., and is extensively mined for the supply of the river towns, from Davenport as far up as Dubuque. It has a rather regular fracture, with well-marked lines of bedding. The fractured surfaces, parallel with the thin lines, are coated with a dull fibrous material, which has a perceptible vegetable structure, and resembles charcoal in appearance, and is usually called *mineral charcoal*. It soils the fingers readily when handled, while the fractured surfaces at right angles to the bedding are quite clean. The specimen analyzed is intersected by numerous minute seams, or thin plates, of gypsum; while portions of the coal from the same locality contain sulphuret of iron, although less in quantity than in most of the coals of this region. When heated it swells up a very little, and leaves a porous coke, which retains the form of the original coal.

The analysis gave, on a specimen which had remained in a dry room for one or two months :

Hygrometric moisture	7.96	Total volatile	45.73
Volatile combustible matter	37.77		
Fixed carbon	53.15	Coke	54.27
Ash	1.12		
	100.00		100.00

Or, calculated on the coal dried at 212° F. :

Volatile combustible substances	41.03
Fixed carbon	57.75
Ash	1.22
	100.00

The amount of ash is smaller than in any coal which has yet been analyzed from this region. Its color is light reddish gray, and it is light and infusible.

The quantity of sulphur present in the clean picked coal was 0.72 per cent.

Specimen from the Lower coal seam at La Salle, Illinois.

As the La Salle coals are extensively used in Northeastern Iowa, analyses were made of the samples collected at that place, one from the lower and the other from the upper bed. The specimen from the lower bed which was analyzed is a tolerably firm coal, breaking with a rather smooth fracture, and exhibiting alternate bands of more and less compact glossy substance. It contains some gypsum in thin plates scattered through it. When heated over the spirit lamp, it softens and swells up a very little and burns, leaving a very porous coke.

The analysis gave the following results :

Water	5.62	Total volatile	42.59
Volatile combustible matter	36.97		
Fixed carbon	51.15	Coke	57.41
Ash	6.26		
	100.00		100.00

Composition calculated on the substance dried at 212° :

Volatile combustible matter	39.17
Fixed combustible	54.19
Ash	6.64
	100.00

The ash is pulverulent, and of a deep chocolate-brown color. The coke has a metallic lustre and is thoroughly fused, without having swollen up to any considerable extent.

A separate trial gave as the amount of sulphur present in the coal, in the picked portions, 1.18 per cent.

The mean of five analyses of specimens from the lower bed of the La Salle coal basin, by Mr. PRATTEN, of the Illinois Geological Survey, gives the following results* :

Moisture	6.2
Volatile	39.2
Fixed carbon	45.7
Ash	8.9
	100.00

Specimen from the Upper Coal-seam at La Salle, from the shaft of the La Salle Coal Mining Company.

This coal, in hand specimens, closely resembles that from the upper bed, and the analysis does not indicate any material difference. The lower bed is generally preferred, as being a little more free from pyrites, and bearing transportation better. When heated over the spirit-lamp, this coal swells up a little, and bakes together into a spongy coke with a metallic lustre on the surface.

The analysis gave :

Moisture	7.67	Total volatile matter	42.19
Volatile and combustible	34.52		
Fixed carbon	46.53	Coke	57.81
Ash	11.28		
	100.00		100.00

Composition of the coal dried at 212° - 220° :

Volatile combustible matter	37.39
Fixed combustible matter	50.40
Ash	12.21
	100.00

The ash is light and infusible, and of a reddish-grey color. A separate determination gave as the amount of sulphur, 0.63 per cent.

The La Salle coals, together with those from the vicinity of Rock island, are supplied in large quantities to the towns bordering on the Mississippi river, north and south from the last named place.

* Report on La Salle Coal Mining Company's property, by the State Geologist. La Salle, 1856.

Specimen from Cox's coal bank, two miles north of Hillsborough, Van Buren county : Upper portion of seam.

A pretty compact and tolerable firm coal, with indications of fine lines of bedding : fracture, parallel with these lines, somewhat conchoidal ; color pitch-black, and lustre quite brilliant, with the exception of occasional patches of fibrous material ; intersected by plates of sulphate of lime, which are parallel with each other, and hardly exceed writing-paper in thickness : tarnished with pavonine tints.

The analysis gave :

Moisture	7.92	Total volatile	49.66
Volatile combustible	41.74		
Fixed carbon	46.76	Coke	50.34
Ash	3.58		
	100.00		100.00

Composition of the coal reduced to the dry substance :

Volatile combustible substances	45.33
Fixed carbon	50.78
Ash	3.89
	100.00

The amount of sulphur present in the specimen analyzed was only 0.29 per cent. The ash is white and light.

This coal contains quite a small amount of ash, as compared with other samples from this region ; and is, altogether, one of the best varieties which has been met with in Iowa.

Specimen from Dr. Crail's bank, two miles north of Hillsborough, Van Buren county.

This specimen closely resembles the last described one from the same locality. It has, however, more fibrous substance, or mineral charcoal, between the layers ; but is almost entirely free from foreign substances, such as pyrites and sulphate of lime. When heated over the lamp, the fragments swell up and fuse together into a porous coke.

The analysis gave :

Moisture	5.30	Total volatile	43.28
Volatile and combustible	37.98		
Fixed carbon	54.35	Coke	56.72
Ash	2.37		
	100.00		100.00

The composition of the coal, as fully dried at the temperature of 212°, is :

Volatile and combustible substances	40.11
Fixed carbon	57.39
Ash	2.50
	100.00

The amount of sulphur in this coal is 0.55 per cent. The ash is flocculent and white.

This specimen and the preceding one are among the best which have, thus far, been obtained in the State. The amount of ash which they contain is small, and the quantity of sulphur less than is usual in western coals.

Specimen from Slaughter's coal bank, two miles above Farmington, Van Buren county.

This coal is quite compact and breaks with an irregular fracture, somewhat conchoidal, in a direction parallel with the lines of bedding, which are very numerous and close together, but almost obliterated. The lustre is not very brilliant. It contains a little pyrites and sulphate of lime, in occasional irregular plates and blotches. The coal, on being heated, fuses readily to a porous coke.

The analysis gave as follows :

Moisture	8.62	Total volatile	46.70
Volatile combustible substances,	38.08		
Fixed carbon	47.42	Coke	53.30
Ash	5.88		
	100.00		100.00

As calculated on the coal free from moisture, the composition will be :

Volatile and combustible substances	41.67
Fixed carbon	51.90
Ash	6.43

The ash is reddish-white in color. A special determination of the sulphur in the clean picked coal gave 1.02 per cent.

This coal, to judge from the specimen analyzed, is of fair quality, and will bear transportation rather better than the average of Iowa coals.

Specimen from south side Des Moines river, one-half mile from Farmington, Van Buren county.

This specimen is a tolerably compact coal, with indistinct and irregular lines of bedding. Its fracture parallel with the bedding is irregular, being partly conchoidal and exhibiting patches of mineral charcoal, alternating with pitch-black brilliant and highly bituminous portions. It contains some sulphuret of iron irregularly scattered through the mass, in thin layers parallel with the bedding and in small nodules. When heated, it swells up and fuses to a porous mass.

The results of the analysis were as follows :

Moisture	4.62	Total volatile	41.89
Volatile combustible matter	37.27		
Fixed combustible matter	51.10	Coke	58.11
Ash	7.01		
	100.00		100.00

The composition, as reduced to the coal when entirely free from moisture, will be :

Volatile combustible	39,07
Fixed carbon	53.58
Ash	7.35
	100.00

The ash is bulky and of a light reddish color. For a notice of the locality where the coal was obtained, see page 155. There appears to be a thickness of four and a half feet of coal, separated into two seams by sixteen inches of slate.

Specimen from Manhard's coal bank, two miles southwest of Iowaville, Van Buren county.

This coal is, as far as can be judged from the sample taken for analysis, of rather inferior quality, being much mixed with sulphuret of iron, which has decomposed and incrusted it with a white efflorescence. It is thinly laminated, and breaks with an irregular fracture, which is somewhat conchoidal on the surfaces parallel with the bedding, and exhibits portions of jet-black color and brilliant lustre in which no structure is visible, intermixed with small patches of fibrous material.

The analysis gave :

Moisture	7.76	Total volatile	47.99
Volatile combustible matter	40.23		
Fixed carbon	48.11	Coke	52.01
Ash	3.90		
	100.00		100.00

Or, reduced to the dry coal :

Volatile combustible	43.62
Fixed carbon	52.15
Ash	4.23
	100.00

The ash is small in bulk and of a dark color, indicating the presence of considerable iron in the sample. The amount of sulphur present in portions of the coal, which have been picked, was 1.69 per cent.

From Mr. WORTHEN's description, on page 161, this sample appears to have been taken from a bed of coal of irregular thickness, varying from three to five feet, which has been opened at several points within the distance of a mile.

*Specimen from **Business-corners, Van Buren** county.*

This coal is finely laminated, and tolerably compact. Between the layers there are thin portions of fibrous substance or mineral charcoal, so that it cannot be handled without crocking the fingers. In the specimen analyzed there is no pyrites or gypsum present in visible particles, but the joints perpendicular to the bedding are stained with iron rust.

The analysis gave :

Moisture	5.42	Total volatile	44.81
Volatile combustible substance	39.39		
Fixed carbon	47.80	Coke	55.19
Ash	7.39		
	100.00		100.00

Which, reduced to the dry substance, gives :

Volatile combustible matter	41.65
Fixed	50.54
Ash	7.81
	100.00

The ash is light-colored and pulverulent. A determination of the sulphur present gave 0.49 per cent.

This appears to be a fair quality of coal, containing but a moderate amount of sulphur. It is not, however, as well calculated to bear transportation as some of the Iowa coals, nor is it as cleanly to handle.

For a notice of the locality from which this specimen was obtained, see page 225.

Specimen from Colburn's bank, opposite Fort Dodge, Webster county.

This coal is made up of alternate layers of more or less dense material. The most compact pitch-black and brilliantly lustrous layers break with a conchoidal fracture : between them there is some fibrous substance, which contains iron pyrites finely disseminated through it. There is a little gypsum in fine reticulations scattered through the mass.

The following are the results of the analysis :

Moisture	13.02	Total volatile	50.56
Volatile combustible matter	37.54		
Fixed carbon	43.06	Coke	49.44
Ash	6.38		
	100.00		100.00

Reduced to the perfectly dry material, the composition will be as follows :

Volatile combustible matter	43.16
Fixed carbon	49.50
Ash	7.34
	100.00

The ash is light-reddish in color. The sulphur was not determined.

The quality of this coal, to judge from the sample analyzed, is tolerably fair. The quantity of water it contains is uncommonly large.

The bed from which this specimen was obtained, as noticed by Mr. WORTHEN on page 178, is about 2½ feet in thickness.

Specimen from the northeast quarter of Section 18, *T.* 88, *R.* 28, *Webster county.*

The specimen from this locality is of a very fair quality, being tolerably compact, finely, but indistinctly, laminated, and quite homogeneous in its texture. It breaks into cubical fragments ; the partings between the layers exhibiting traces of fibrous structure. There are but few traces of sulphuret of iron or gypsum in the specimen.

The following are the results of the analysis :

Moisture	14.95	Total volatile	49.93
Volatile combustible substance,	34.98		
Fixed carbon	42.89	Coke	50.07
Ash	7.18		
	100.00		100.00

Or, reduced to the substance as dried at 212° :

Volatile combustible substances	41.13
Fixed carbon	50.43
Ash	8.44
	100.00

The ash is light and pulverulent, and of a reddish color. A determination of the sulphur gave 0.81 per cent.

The bed from which this specimen was taken is given by Mr. WORTHEN, on page 174, as being from 4½ to 5 feet in thickness. The specimen, of which the analysis is given above, is probably better than the average of the bed from which it was taken, as this is noticed as containing rather more than an average amount of sulphuret of iron.

Specimen from the southeast quarter of Section 13, *T.* 88, *R.* 28.

This specimen is of quite inferior quality, and not at all suited for transportation to any distance. It is very distinctly bedded, and liable to fall to pieces by breaking parallel to the lamination, in consequence of the oxidation of the sulphuret of iron, which occupies innumerable small fissures, both parallel with, and at right-angles to, the bedding. A considerable portion of this specimen is made up of the soft fibrous mineral charcoal.

The analysis gave :

Moisture	9.46	Total volatile	43.15
Volatile combustible matter,	33.69		
Fixed carbon	39.66	Coke	56.85
Ash	17.19		
	100.00		100.00

Or, as calculated on the dry substance :

Volatile and combustible	37.21
Fixed carbon	43.80
Ash	18.99
	100.00

The ash was of a dark color and quite ferruginous. The amount of sulphur was determined on a sample of the specimen pulverized, without picking out the particles of visible pyrites ; which, in this case, was impossible, owing to the intimate mixture of the pyrites with the coal. As thus estimated, the quantity of sulphur was found to be 2.52 per cent, equivalent to 4.37 of sulphuret of iron. It is evident from the above analysis, that if the specimen analyzed was a fair specimen of the coal from this locality, it is not fit for use, if anything better can be obtained. (See page 174.)

Specimen from Dr. Fuller's bank, near Eldora, Hardin county.

The specimen analyzed was taken from the lower part of the bed, and represents its least sulphurous portion ; but there is a considerable amount of pyrites irregularly disseminated through it. Like much of the coal of this region, it contains so much of the soft fibrous charcoal-like substance, that it cannot be handled with convenience. When heated in the crucible, it swells up a very little and splits into thin plates, but does not fuse.

The following are the results of the analysis :

Moisture	12.45	Total volatile	48.18
Volatile combustible substance,	35.73		
Fixed carbon	43.64	Coke	51.82
Ash	8.18		
	100.00		100.00

As calculated on the dry substance :

Volatile combustible substances	40.81
Fixed carbon	49.85
Ash	9.34
	100.00

The ash is a mixture of white and light-red portions : the sulphur was not specially determined.

For a notice of the locality, thickness of the bed and other particulars in regard to its occurrence, see pages 269 – 271.

Specimen from Slaughter's bank, near Newton, Jasper county.

The quality of the coal at this locality varies considerably in different portions of the bed : most of it is very sulphurous, containing a great deal of pyrites and gypsum deposited in all the minute seams and cracks, giving some of the specimens, when freshly broken, the appearance of having been gilded. The fractured surfaces, parallel with the planes of deposition, are covered with fibrous, soft, charcoal-like substance. Fragments heated over the spirit-lamp fuse to a porous but coherent mass, having a spongy texture and a brilliant metallic lustre on the exterior.

The analysis gave the following results :

Moisture	8.33	Total volatile	50.05
Volatile combustible matter,	41.72		
Fixed carbon	44.51	Coke	49.95
Ash	5.44		
	100.00		100.00

The composition reduced to the entirely dry substance, is as follows :

Volatile combustible substances	45.51
Fixed carbon	48.56
Ash	5.93
	100.00

The ash is of a light-reddish color.

In this and the preceeding specimen the quantity of sulphuret of iron was not only large, but was so irregularly distributed throughout the mass, that no opinion could be formed of the value of the coal from the analysis of a single specimen. To determine its amount satisfactorily, a portion taken so as to represent the average composition of the coal would be required ; for this purpose, a large quantity of the material should have been pulverized and properly sampled. As near as could be estimated by the eye, the amount of sulphuret of iron present in this coal, was not, on the average, less than three or four per cent.

From the analyses which have been given in the preceding pages, an opinion can be formed as to the quality of the coal on the eastern borders of the coal-field of Iowa. As before remarked, it would not be proper to infer, from the character of the beds occurring in this part of the basin, that thicker and heavier deposits may not be found in a southwest direction, towards the centre of the basin. The extreme tenuity of the formation, as we approach its limits on the north and northwest, would give ground for expecting thinner beds and a poorer quality of coal, than would be found where the strata belonging to this period are developed on a more extensive scale. According to the reports of the Geological Survey of Missouri, the thickness of the Coal measures, in the northern part of that State, exceeds 700 feet; and in Central Illinois there seems to be an equal, if not greater, development of the series. On the Des Moines, however, the actual amount of strata belonging to this position, observed in any one section, is evidently considerably less than this, no exposure having been yet measured which would give much over a hundred feet; and how much the entire thickness of the coal-series exceeds this, in that region, is still a matter of uncertainty, although it is not probable that it goes over a hundred and fifty feet, in its maximum development.

One effect of the thinness of the series will be, that few underground workings, or expensive shafts and machinery for raising water, will be required. The coal will be wrought in numerous localities, by small parties, to satisfy the demand of the vicinity, and not on a large scale, by companies, for export to distant regions.

Fire-clay. This substance is the usnal associate of coal,

being, almost everywhere, the floor on which that substance has been deposited, and, in the quadruple association of coal, iron-ore, limestone for flux and fire-clay, in the Coal measures, completing the series of materials required for the rapid and cheap production of iron.

There are numerous localities in Iowa, where a clay suitable for making fire-bricks, pottery, and other useful articles of the kind, has been noticed : they are all in strata belonging to the Coal measures. It is not known that the manufacture of fire-brick has been attempted; but there are several places in the State, where pottery of the coarser kind is turned out in considerable quantities. For reference to the locality of various beds of fire-clay already discovered, see pages 197, 207, 218, 230, 257 and 272.

Material for common bricks. The manufacture of common bricks is one of the most important branches of that industry to which the resources of the State are made available, with the exception of coal-mining : there is no business depending on the use of material furnished by the inorganic kingdom which will continue to employ so large an amount of capital and labor, as this does. In those regions of the State where outcrops of rock are distant, the chief dependence of the inhabitants for building materials will be brick; and as the scarcity of good building material is chiefly in the district occupied by the Coal measures, the want will be more easily supplied, since fuel for burning the brick will be found close at hand, in those places where the rocks are not durable enough for use, as it is frequently the case in this portion of the series. The material for brick-making is found everywhere in this State, in the superficial formations, which are spread so thickly over the surface. The mixture of clay and sand, which constitutes the larger portion of the prairie deposits, is usually well adapted for this purpose, although sometimes too calcareous to burn into a strong compact brick. By judicious selection of material, however, good material for this manufacture may be obtained in almost every district of the State, without going to any considerable distance.

Gypsum. The presence of gypsum in large quantities in the interior of the State seems to be a well-ascertained fact, and there can be no doubt that Iowa will be able to supply the neighboring States with an abundance of this valuable material. The localities where gypsum has been found, are in the vicinity of Fort Dodge : for a notice of them, see Mr. WORTHEN'S Report in a preceding chapter, pages 175 to 178. There is every reason to suppose that farther explorations will reveal the existence of other deposits ; but those which are already known are capable of furnishing an almost inexhaustible supply.

METALLIC ORES ASSOCIATED WITH THE VARIOUS GROUPS.

IRON.

Iron-ore in the Coal measures. The presence of iron ore in connection with the coal-bearing strata, throughout the Mississippi valley, seems to be rather an exceptional occurrence than a general condition of things, as it may be said to be in many other parts of the world. In England, especially, the iron ores associated with the coal are of the greatest importance, and furnish the larger portion of the material from which this metal is obtained. In this country, Pennsylvania, Maryland, Virginia and Ohio seem to be the most favored States in regard to the abundance of iron ore in the Coal measures. The more Western States, Illinois, Michigan, Missouri and Iowa, are much less bountifully supplied with ore in this geological position ; although there are immense deposits in some portions of the Mississippi valley, in rocks belonging to various members of the geological series below the coal. Thus, on Lake Superior and in Missouri, the accumulation of the best and purest ores in the azoic series are truly astonishing in quantity; and in Wisconsin, Illinois and Missouri, there are very important deposits in the palæozoic series, in various positions from the Lower Helderberg limestone downwards as far as the Clinton group. It is possible that future investigations in the Coal series of the Western States may reveal deposits of iron ore in that position; but, taking into consideration the character of the coal, and other circumstances, it is hardly possible that, even if such were discovered, they would become of much importance for a long time to come.

However, as the geological surveys are still in progress in several of the States bordering on the Upper Mississippi, in which a large amount of surface is covered by the coal-bearing strata, and which have been as yet but imperfectly explored, it would be premature to speak positively on this matter.

The extreme tenuity of the Coal measures in that part of Iowa which has already been examined, would, of itself, lead to the idea that heavy deposits of iron ore would not be likely to be found in that geological position. There are some localities, however, where the presence of iron has been noticed: the only one which has fallen under the notice of the geological corps, is that at Crawford's mill on Skunk river, described by Mr. WORTHEN on page 213 of this Report. The bed is stated to be from two and a half to three feet thick; but as nothing is known in regard to its superficial extension, it would be impossible to pronounce positively on its value. The ore is a hydrous peroxide of iron, containing considerable insoluble argillaceous matter, but no carbonic acid. A partial analysis gave:

Water	17.69
Insoluble silicates	24.52
Sulphuret of iron	trace
Peroxide of iron	58.27
Alumina, lime, magnesia and phosphoric acid	traces
	100.48

58.27 of peroxide of iron = 40.79 of metallic iron.

The slight excess in the analysis indicates that a little of the iron was present as the protoxide.

The amount of earthy matter in this ore is too great to allow of its being considered a good ore, although it might possibly be used to advantage, if its association were such that it could be mixed with other ores. The fact that it is a hydrous peroxide, and not an earthy carbonate, would indicate that it was not likely to form a very persistent mass; but, on the other hand, that it would probably be found to be a mass of limited extent, which had originated from the decomposition of pyrites.

Iron-ore in the Niagara limestone. The deposits of ore in connection with the strata of the Clinton group in New-York and Wisconsin are of considerable importance; and the Clinton and Niagara groups being merged together west of the Mississippi, and, so far as we yet know, not to be separated from each other, it was natural to suppose that the extensive deposits of iron ore, which have been reported as occurring in the Niagara limestone of Iowa, might prove to be of considerable importance. The results of all the explorations we have made in the region in which iron has been noticed in this connection are, that there is little probability of workable beds of ore being discovered in any of the groups below the Coal measures. The Lower Helderberg rocks occupy so small a space, and are so diminished in thickness from what they are in New-York and to the southwest, that there is but little chance of finding anything of importance associated with that group; while the character and position of the ore found in the Niagara beds in Iowa is such as to indicate that it will not be found in extensive and persistent beds, but only in irregular and disconnected patches, and not of sufficient extent to be capable of being worked with profit.

The reported localities of iron-ore in Iowa are situated chiefly in Jackson county, near the Makoqueta river and on the branches running into it from the north side, especially Brush, Farmer's and Lytle's creeks; and this district has been pretty thoroughly examined during the progress of the Survey, but no discoveries of any importance have been made. There are, it is true, numerous fragments and small masses of brown hematite ore lying upon the surface in some portions of that region; and these have, naturally enough, among those not acquainted with the mode of occurrence of the metalliferous ores, been presumed to indicate the existence of heavy beds of the same material in the rocks below. We have, however, never been able to discover a continuous stratum of ore, having anything like the dimensions necessary to justify the erection of furnaces for smelting iron. The ore seems to have originated, in some instances, in the decomposition of nodules of iron pyrites distributed irregularly through the rock; in other cases, it has been deposited in the fissures and cavities of the limestone by springs charged with ferruginous matter, itself probably also the result of the decomposition of the sulphuret. That this last-named ore has been the source from which much of the peroxide was derived, is proved by the fact that the masses of the hematite ore are not unfrequently found, when broken, to contain undecomposed sulphuret of iron in the interior; besides, they sometimes occur in crystallizations, which are pseudomorphs of this mineral, showing conclusively that, in such instances at least, they were derived from its decomposition. In general, the fragments of iron ore lie scattered singly over the surface, and this is not an uncommon occurrence over the whole region underlaid by the Niagara limestone; but there are some limited districts, where the quantity of fragments, which have been liberated by the decomposition of the rock, is considerable. Usually, these loose masses are quite small, the size of a man's fist being the most common. Occasionally, the ore may be observed in the rock, although this is not frequently the case. When thus seen, the evidence of its local origin and of its necessarily limited range, is conclusive. The most interesting locality of this kind which was noticed was on land belonging to Mr. Bowman, 2½ miles southeast of the town of Makoqueta. Here is an elevated bluff of Niagara limestone, at whose base lie large masses of hematite ore, some of which are from four to six feet in length and made up of an aggregation of stalactitic columns. On tracing these masses to their origin, at the summit of the cliff, a tunnel-like cavity was discovered, lined with iron ore, as represented in the annexed wood-cut, figure 43, in which the part shaded with oblique lines indicates the ore, which had in some places a thickness of several inches. It was evident, that in this locality the ore had been deposited from a ferruginous spring percolating through a gradually tapering cavity, which had become exposed to view by the wearing away of the rock, while portions of the ore had become broken out and slid down the face of the bluff. We need hardly add, after this description, that the locality is not one at which the erection of a furnace could be advised, although perhaps a few tons of ore might be got out of the cliff, or picked up in loose pieces around it. Several other localities were examined, in which iron ore was supposed to be present in inexhaustible quantity; but, as not one was discovered in

FIG. 43.— Section of iron ore deposit near Makoqueta.

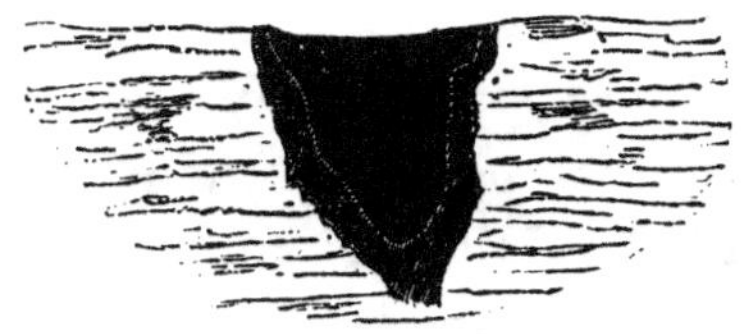

which a regular and continuous stratum of ore could be traced, a recapitulation of the places examined will not be necessary.

It is not at all likely that, for a long time to come, deposits, situated as these are with reference to fuel and a market, could be worked to a profit, even if the conditions were favorable in respect to quantity and quality of ore.

On the whole, it is surprising how little ferruginous matter is disseminated through the rocks of the palæozoic series in this part of the valley of the Mississippi. A reference to the analyses of the limestones given in the preceding pages of this chapter will show, that iron, in its various forms of combination, rarely constitutes more than from one-half to one per cent of the mass of the strata; a quantity surprisingly small, as compared with the amount of the metal present in the azoic series, which constitutes the floor on which the fossiliferous rocks of this region were deposited. Periods of disturbance of the strata, and the presence of the intrusive rocks, seem to have acted powerfully on the dissemination of ferruginous matter.

LEAD.

The great lead deposits of the Mississippi valley may be classed, according to their geographical position, under two heads: the Upper Mississippi and the Missouri mines; at the West, they are commonly distinguished as the Upper and Lower mines. The first of these divisions embraces the lead-region lying in the southwestern portion of Wisconsin, and including a small portion of each of the adjacent States of Illinois and Iowa: the second comprehends the mines in the State of Missouri, which lie chiefly to the south of the river of that name. These lead-producing districts possess many features in common, both in regard to the geological position and the mode of occurrence of the ore; but the

Upper mines have always been, and will probably continue to be, much the most important.

It is with that portion of the Upper Mississippi mining region which lies within the limits of Iowa, that we have to do in this Report; but, as a correct idea of the character of the lead-deposits could hardly have been acquired, had the examination been confined to that narrow space, it will be necessary, for the purposes of comparison, to take into consideration and develope in as brief a manner as possible, the principal features of the occurrence of the lead ores, as deduced from repeated examinations of different portions of the lead-region within the boundaries of each of the three States in which it is included. It is only after a comparison of the phenomena exhibited by the deposits of metalliferous ores in many different regions, that general opinions can be formed with any reliability as to the value of particular localities; and even then, after the most careful investigation of vein-phenomena in all their forms, the difficulty of the subject becomes apparent in the impossibility of deciding some of the most important questions in regard to them. Those who have not been made familiar with the appearances presented by metalliferous deposits, in many different geological positions, and under a great variety of circumstances, are very likely to be led to form erroneous opinions in judging of matters in which there is so little seeming regularity, and in regard to which the almost invariable tendency of the human mind seems to be to exaggerate.

The existence of lead deposits in the Northwest was undoubtedly well known to the aboriginal inhabitants; but whether they were worked and the ore smelted into metallic lead, previous to the time of the whites, is a question of some doubt. It is stated that, although galena has been repeatedly found in the mounds, no metallic lead has ever been discovered among the relics of the former occupants of the soil. It would seem, however, highly probable that the race which had skill and perseverance enough to mine the native copper of Lake Superior, in numerous localities, and, in some places, to a depth of fifty feet, in a rock much more difficult to work than the limestone accompanying the lead ore, would also have understood the simple process of smelting the lead from its pure and easily-reducible ore.

The first discovery of lead by the white race in this region dates back as far as 1700, when LE SUEUR made his famous voyage up the Mississippi, as far as the St. Peters; up which stream, near the mouth of the Mukahto or Blue river, he supposed that he had discovered a mountain of copper ore. Although this supposed discovery was a great mistake, yet there is reason to believe that he did find lead ore at different points along the Mississippi. About twenty years after this, mining was actually commenced in the Missouri lead-region; although it was not until 1798 that it became a regular business, and was carried on with any system. It was nearly a century after LE SUEUR's discoveries, before any attempt was made to open the lead mines of the Upper Mississippi. In 1788, however, JULIEN DUBUQUE, an Indian trader of French extraction, who had previously settled on the site of the flourishing city which is now called by his name, obtained a grant from the Councils of the Sacs and Foxes, which was afterwards confirmed by Carondelet, at that time Governor of Louisiana, of a large tract of land situated on the western bank of the river, including the rich mineral lands of that vicinity. Here he remained, engaged in mining and trading with the Indians, until his death, which took place in 1810.

It was not, however, until about the year 1822 that mining was regularly commenced in the Upper Mississippi valley. In that year, a number of individuals settled in the vicinity of Galena, and engaged in the business of digging for lead; and so rapidly did the excitement, consequent on the discovery of such rich deposits, spread, that by the year

1827, mines had been opened and worked over nearly the whole extent of the lead-region on the east side of the river. Up to the year 1830, the Indians had held possession of the west bank of the river, and had not permitted any encroachments of the miners on to their domain, which had not yet been ceded to the United States : in that year, however, in consequence of the hostility of the Sioux, the Foxes abandoned the vicinity of the river, and thus that region was opened to the whites, who immediately crossed over and commenced exploring and mining. They were soon driven away by the United States troops, as the land had not yet been purchased of the Indians. A small military force was stationed here, and under this protection the Indians returned and began to work at the localities abandoned by the whites, but probably under their direction, and chiefly for the benefit of the traders stationed on the other side of the river. After the close of the Blackhawk war, in 1832, which resulted in the ceding to the United States of a large tract of land, including the eastern portion of Iowa, a considerable number of miners crossed over and resumed operations on that side. They were again driven off by the Government troops, as the treaty had not yet been ratified by the Senate. Finally, in 1833, permission was given to take possession of the much-coveted region. Attempts were made by the government to collect rent for the mineral lands, which, by the act of Congress of March 3d, 1807, had been reserved from sale. The system of leasing the reserved mineral tracts was kept up for a few years, with great expense and trouble to the government, and finally abandoned in 1847, when lands supposed to contain valuable ores, and previously reserved on that account, were thrown open for entry and purchase.

Previous to this abandonment of the system of leasing, a geological survey of the lead-region had been authorized by Congress in 1839, for the purpose of ascertaining the extent of the productive lead formation, with a view to the preparation of a place for the sale of the lands reserved as mineral. The conduct of the Survey was intrusted to Dr. D. D. OWEN, by whom, with the aid of a hundred and thirty-nine assistants, it was accomplished in the autumn of the same year, and printed without the maps and illustrations in 1840, and afterwards reprinted with these, in 1844. During the prosecution of the State Geological Survey of Wisconsin, the lead-region has been made the subject of two Reports, which were published by the late Dr. PERCIVAL, the State Geologist, and which are chiefly devoted to the discussion of the subject of the occurrence of the lead ores, and the stratigraphical geology of the region in which they occur.

The productive lead-region of the Upper Mississippi occupies the larger portion of the territory south of the Wisconsin river, between the east branch of the Peccatonica on the east, and the Mississippi on the west, and extends south into Illinois as far as Apple river. The Mississippi runs near the western edge of the mineral district; but there is a considerable area of productive territory on the west side of that river; the limit beyond which no ore has been worked on that side being the outcrop of the Niagara, as seen in the Geological Map accompanying this Report.

Nearly the whole of the area thus bounded, and which is peculiarly the lead-producing region of the Northwest, is underlaid by the Galena limestone, of whose lithological character and distribution on the surface, within the limits of Iowa, enough has been said in the preceding pages of this Report. Although this limestone occupies most of the elevated prairie region of the lead district, the larger streams are found almost universally to have cut down to lower groups; while undulations of the sandstones bring up these, so that they occupy sometimes a considerable extent of surface, where, if the dip were uniformly regular throughout the region, we should expect to find the Galena limestone occurring. The whole thickness of the series, from the top of the Lower sandstone to the bottom of the Galena, is only from four hundred to four hundred and twenty-five feet, so that slight undulations of the strata, in a region irregularly denuded and furrowed deeply by the river-channels, will naturally give rise to considerable irregularity in the distribution of the groups upon the surface. The general southern dip of the strata, by which we are carried to lower rocks as we proceed northward, causes the Galena limestone to thin out gradually in that direction, and to be more and more restricted to the most elevated part of the region; so that, by the time that we have reached the water-shed between the streams flowing into the Wisconsin, and those running south into the Mississippi and its tributary Rock river, we find the Blue limestone occupying more space on the surface than the Galena; and we have to descend the vallies to the north but a short distance, before we come upon the Upper sandstone.

The occurrence of lead ore in the region under consideration, is limited to the groups between the Hudson-river shales and the Lower sandstones; and it appears that no profitable workings have ever been carried on for any length of time, except in that part of the series which lies between the Upper sandstone and the Hudson-river group; while much the larger portion of the lead hitherto obtained has been raised from the Galena limestone proper. Within the limits of Iowa and Illinois the diggings are exclusively confined to this position, and, in Wisconsin, there are no productive workings in any other rock, except on the northern and eastern borders of the district. The distribution of the lead ore seems, in reference to its position in the geological series, to have been influenced by the geographical position and the development of different members of the series. Thus, where the Galena limestone has its maximum thickness, it will be found that the lead-deposits are limited to the central and lower portions of this rock, and by far the most abundant in the central, never penetrating the Blue limestone. For instance, in the region between the Mississippi and Fever rivers and its immediate vicinity, which has always been the most productive part of the lead-region, in proportion to its superficial extent, and where the Galena limestone is developed to its full thickness of two hundred to two hundred and fifty feet, we know of no lead-bearing crevices extending down as low as the Blue limestone; and we have become satisfied that, in the great majority of cases, at least, the deposits have diminished in productiveness rapidly, after passing below a limit perhaps fifty feet above the base of the Galena. Neither have we ever known of profitable mining in the Upper portion of this rock : the first fifty feet seem to be almost as barren of ore as the Niagara limestone itself. If, however, we go from the district specified above, we find the thickness of the Galena limestone diminished, partly by denudation and partly by the original thinning out in that direction; and at the same time we notice the fact, that the lead deposits are found in lower and lower positions in reference to the geological horizon, until, at last, we reach the bottom of the Blue limestone. Here, however, the Upper sandstone entirely cuts off the ore, there never having been a single instance, so far as we can ascertain, of a crevice having been worked in that rock. Below this sandstone, in the Lower magnesian limestone, the rock becomes metalliferous again, but in a highly diminished degree ; and it is not possible to include this formation in the productive lead-bearing series, as will be more fully set forth, farther on in this chapter.

The sulphuret of lead, or galena, is almost the only ore of that metal which is found in the Upper Mississippi mines; the oxidized combinations being exceedingly rare, and not of the slightest importance in an economical point of view. The carbonate of lead has been observed at the Blue-mound diggings, in reniform and stalactitic masses of considerable size : it is also said to have been found, in connection with the sulphate, at Mineral Point ; but, so far as we know, no traces of arseniates, phosphates or any other of the numerous oxidized combinations of lead have ever been observed in this region. Within the limits of Iowa, we have never noticed any other form of ore than the sulphuret, with occasionally a thin incrustation of the carbonate over it.

The chemical composition of the pure sulphuret of lead is :

Lead	86.6
Sulphur	13.4
	100.00

The galena of the western mines contains only the most minute trace of silver, a metal which is almost invariably found associated with lead, and frequently in sufficient quantity to be separated with profit. This is usually the case, however, only in the ore obtained from the crystalline and metamorphic rocks : the unaltered sedimentary strata furnish a much less argentiferous ore. The quantity of silver in the galena of the Upper Mississippi mines is by far too small to be worth separating; the smallest amount which can be profitably separated, under the most favorable circumstances, being from six to eight ounces per ton of lead, while the western lead ores rarely contain more than a fraction of an ounce to the ton.

The crystalline forms in which the galena presents itself in the western mines, is almost exclusively the cube. Occasionally the angles of the cube are replaced by the planes of the octahedron ; but the simple cubic form is infinitely more common than any other. The crystals are usually rough and irregular, as if somewhat corroded on their faces, and grouped together into a variety of irregular forms. Occasionally, single crystals are of very great size : one presented to the State Collection by A. ESTEY, Esq. of Galena, measured about seven inches along one of its edges, and weighed over sixty pounds.

Different names are given by the miners to the different forms of the galena, according to the form and size of the crystals and their arrangement into groups. The terms "dice-mineral", "cog-mineral", "sheet-mineral", "chunk-mineral", etc. explain themselves, the ore of lead being universally designated by them as "mineral".

The freedom of the galena from intermixture with other metalliferous ores throughout the Upper mines, and, more especially, in Iowa, is remarkable. Sulphuret of zinc is almost the only one which occurs in any quantity intimately associated with the galena, and the large majority of the diggings do not show even a trace of this. Hence, the great softness and purity of the metallic lead of this region, and the high price which it bears in comparison with most of the imported metal.

Having, in the preceding pages, given a brief sketch of the geographical and geological position of the lead-region of the Upper Mississippi, and noticed the mineralogical associations of the ores, we come next to examine their *mode of occurrence;* by which term is meant, the relations of the metalliferous deposits to the rocks in which they are enclosed, as to their form, extent and origin; on the careful study and complete understanding of which conditions depends our knowledge of the value of all mining property; as, the more thorough our acquaintance with the peculiarities of any class of ore-deposits, the less will be the risk in opening and working them. And before proceeding to describe the mode of occurrence of the lead ores of the region in question, it will be advisable, in as brief a manner as possible, to give a general idea of the most important varieties of form in which the metalliferous ores occur, as well as to define some of the terms used in speaking of them.

The forms assumed by the deposits of the economically valuable ores are various and complex, and the limits between them are not always capable of being drawn with such sharpness as to admit of their being satisfactorily classified. For convenience of description, however, it has been found best to arrange all the metalliferous deposits under two heads : the *stratified* and the *unstratified*. The first of these classes comprehends such masses of ores as are included within rocks of sedimentary origin, and which are in every way identical in their epoch and mode of formation with the strata in which they occur : this class of deposits may be illustrated by reference to the beds of iron ore in the Coal measures, which were deposited in the regular order of succession of the members of that series, one bed differing from another only in the chemical composition of the material of which they are made up.

The unstratified deposits, on the other hand, which class includes most of the forms of occurrence in which the metals other than iron and manganese are found, present a series of phenomena of a complex character, the real nature of which cannot always be easily made out. In the most general way, they may be divided into *irregular* and *regular*. The irregular, unstratified deposits include : igeneous eruptive masses of ore, as for instance, the iron mountains of Lake Superior and Missouri; stockwerk deposits, or bodies of rock impregnated over an irregular space with metalliferous particles ; contact-deposits, or accumulations of ore between the planes of contact of two different kinds of rock-masses. From this last class, we pass by gradual steps to that of the regular unstratified deposits, or mineral veins, the term by which this division may most properly be designated. A mineral vein may be defined as an aggregation of mineral matter, of indefinite length and depth and comparatively small thickness, differing in character from, and posterior in formation to, the rocks in which it is enclosed. Veins may be divided into three classes, *segregated*, *gash* and *true veins*. Segregated veins, which are peculiar to the altered crystalline stratified or metamorphic rocks, are usually parallel with the stratification and of limited depth. Gash veins may cross the strata at any angle; but are limited to one particular group of strata, and are peculiar to the unaltered sedimentary rocks. True veins are aggregations of mineral matter, accompanied by metalliferous ores, within a crevice or fissure which had its origin in some deep-seated cause, and which may be presumed to extend for an indefinite distance downwards.

True veins are almost universally admitted by geologists to have originated in "faults", or dislocations caused by great dynamical agencies connected with extensive movements of the earth's crust, and for this reason they are believed to extend indefinitely downwards; an assumption which is supported by facts, since no well-defined vein has ever been found entirely terminating in depth, at any point which has yet been reached by mining industry. Gash-veins, on the other hand, are supposed to have originated in fissures produced by shrinkage, or some other cause confined in its action to a certain set of beds, and not extending into strata of a different character from that in which they originated. The principal distinction between true and gash veins, is, that the former may be worked to an indefinite depth; while the latter, however rich they may be for a certain distance, are sure to give out, or be cut off, on passing into another set of beds of a character unsuited to their development; so that no one vein can be made the seat of permanent mining operations, requiring a large amount of costly machinery, as is the case with true veins, some of which extend for miles in length, and have been worked downwards for centuries, without a permanent diminution of their metalliferous contents. Among the most striking characteristics of true veins, besides their persistence in depth, are : 1st, The presence of a peculiar gangue or vein-stone, which consists most frequently of quartz, calc. spar or heavy spar, forming the bulk of the vein, through which the metalliferous portions of the ore are disseminated; 2d, A peculiar symmetrical arrangement of the contents of the vein, especially of the gangue, which is called the *comby structure* of the lode, lode being synonymous with vein : this consists in a disposition of the different mineral substances of which the vein is composed, in parallel layers on each of the walls, with their crystalline faces turned inwards towards the centre of the lode; so that, if the vein were divided longitudinally into two portions, each of these halves would correspond with the other in the nature and arrangement of the material of which it was composed: 3d, Well-defined walls, or sides of the vein, which are often grooved and polished as if motion, accompanied by immense pressure, had taken place along these surfaces, and which are usually separated from the mineral substances forming the vein-stone, by thin bands of clayey matter, called *selvages*, the clay itself being known as *flucan*.

True veins are usually observed to traverse the rocks without being influenced by their stratification, sometimes coinciding in direction with the strike of the enclosing beds, but more usually cutting them at a greater or less angle. On passing from one set of strata into another of a different nature, they often undergo changes in the character of the vein-stone and the accompanying ore, but the fissure remains, even if quite barren of ore; persistence in depth being the most marked feature of this class of deposits.

Having thus noticed the most important characteristics of the different classes of mineral deposits, we shall be able to proceed more intelligibly to a discussion of the varieties of forms under which the very remarkable deposits of lead ore in the Upper Mississippi valley present themselves. These deposits approach most nearly in character to what have been designated above as *gash-veins ;* but they are, in some respects, peculiar in character, no mining-region exactly resembling this in the mode of occurrence of its ores ever having been observed by us in any part of the world, unless it be in the Missouri mines, in which the conditions of the Upper mines are closely imitated, although on a somewhat more limited scale.

To go into the details of the arrangement of the lead-bearing crevices or veins, and to give all the minute particulars of the mode of occurrence of the ore in the great variety of localities which have been examined in the lead-region, will be impossible in this place, as a full treatment of the subject would require far more space than can be allotted to it in this Report. It must suffice, at the present time, to set forth the general results which have been obtained in a number of examinations of portions of the lead-region made since 1852, and, illustrating the subject by reference, particularly, to localities within the limits of Iowa, to make a practical description of these principles to a discussion of the probable future of the lead-mining interests of the Northwest, and the best course to be followed in order to their most economical and satisfactory development.

The first thing which impresses the mining-engineer, who visits the Upper Mississippi region, having an acquaintance with the important mining districts in other parts of the world, is the fact, that the mines here have only been wrought to a very limited depth and then abandoned; so that, throughout the whole lead-region, where he will see one excavation where persons are still at work, he will notice a hundred others, where nothing is doing, and most of which appear to have been abandoned forever. Again, he will observe, that, instead of an extensive and costly *plant* (as the machinery and fixtures of a mine are called) and a large body of miners, there will be usually no more than two persons engaged on any one vein or crevice, and that their machinery will be limited to a windlass and a bucket. Moreover, he will visit many diggings where no ore is raising, before he comes upon one which is producing lead; and this will, perhaps, astonish him by the extraordinary amount of ore which is presented to view within the excavations, and the facility with which it can be mined and brought to the surface. Some persons who have been accustomed to deep mining in Europe, have visited the Northwest and returned full of contempt for the system adopted, as if the shallowness of the mines were the fault of the miners, and not the necessary result of the mode of occurrence of the ore itself. To maintain that the deposits of ore in this region are continuous in depth, is to attempt to convict all the miners who have ever worked here of imbecility. Did the directors of the Cliff or Minnesota mines propose to suspend operations, when they had reached the point where costly machinery was needed to drain their works? There are, undoubtedly, some instances in which valuable bodies of ore have been left going down, on account of water; but it was because the general experience of the region has fully impressed the miners with the belief, that, in the large majority of cases, the outlay required for the costly machinery by which deep mines are kept free from water will not be reimbursed, as the distance to which the crevices can be followed and ore found in them is always limited, and does not generally extend far below the point at which the water becomes too abundant to be kept under by simple machinery. We have mentioned before, that no crevice has ever been traced into the Upper sandstone, at least for more than a very short distance, or found in the slightest degree productive in that rock. The extreme depth to which a mine might be wrought, under the most favorable circumstances, if we suppose the crevice to extend from the top of the Galena to the bottom of the Trenton limestone, would be about three hundred and twenty-five feet in that part of the district where the first named rock has its full development. In point of fact, however, the actual extent of metalliferous ground is much less than this; since where the crevices are developed in the upper and middle portion of the Galena, they do not extend down as far as the Trenton, the deepest workings never having penetrated more than two hundred feet below the surface, and the actual mining ground, in the very large majority of instances, being comprised within fifty feet of vertical height.

The lead-deposits of the Northwest do not, therefore, present the most important feature of true veins, namely, persistency in depth; neither do they, on the other hand, exhibit the character and disposition of vein-stone, or of wall-rock which have been noticed above as belonging to that class of deposits.

On attempting to classify the mineral deposits of the Northwest, according to their predominating forms, we find that they may be conveniently arranged under three heads: Surface deposits; Vertical crevices, and Flat sheets. The surface deposits are not peculiar to this region, or to any particular class of ores : they depend for their existence on the destruction of previously formed accumulations of ore, by the denudation or gradual decomposition of the rocks in which they were contained, and the consequent liberation of the metalliferous portions, which may remain irregularly scattered through the superficial detritus near the place of their origin, or be carried by currents of water or other causes to a distance from their native bed. In the forms of the vertical crevice and the flat-sheet deposit, and their combinations with each other, we have the modes of occurrence of the lead ore which are peculiar to this region, and which will be explained as briefly as possible.

SURFACE DEPOSITS. The masses of ore which have been liberated by the decomposition of the rock near the surface, lie imbedded in the clayey loam which forms the bulk of the prairie soil, and are called by the miners "float-mineral". The amount of lead obtained from this kind of diggings is small; but the occurrence of float-mineral is of importance to the miner, as being his chief guide to the discovery of the ore in the crevices. The fragments have not usually been transported far from their original position; and the discovery of loose pieces in the soil is an almost certain indication of the proximity of a deposit of more or less value in the adjacent rock, and it is the only one which can be relied on by the "prospecter". (Searching for ore, or *shoding*, as it is termed by the Cornish miners, is called in the lead region *prospecting*.)

In prospecting, the crevices are usually discovered at their outcrop in the vallies, where the denudation of the surface has exposed a considerable thickness of rock in the sides of the bluffs. When thus found and traced as far as is necessary to ascertain the direction of the lode, shafts are sunk along its presumed course, through the superficial detritus into the rock, until the crevice is struck; or, if not hit upon exactly in the shaft, drifts are extended each way until it is discovered. When the rock is not well exposed in the river sections, the difficulty of ascertaining the position of the crevices is vastly increased; and there are extensive tracts in the mineral districts where no lead has been discovered, simply because the rock is so deeply covered with soil and detritus, that explorations cannot be carried on without too great an expenditure of money.

VERTICAL CREVICES. The term *crevice*, as generally applied, in the lead-region, is nearly synonymous with vein or lode as used in other mining districts. It designates the vein-like fissures, or gash-veins as they may be termed, in which the ore is found occurring, and especially those portions of them where the walls are near each other, and the fissure has not widened out into what is called an *opening*. A more general term still, for the accumulation of ore along a certain series of crevices and openings, is that of *range*, and with this the word *lead* is nearly synonymous. To "strike a lead" is to come upon, or discover, a productive mineral deposit. The term "lead" may be a corruption of *lode*, by which miners usually designate a vein producing ore; or it may be a contraction of *leader*, a Cornish term for a branch of ore falling into the main lode, and thus *leading* the miner to its discovery. On account of the inconvenient similarity in spelling between the metal *lead* and the ore-bearing *lead*, the use of the latter should be dropped, and lode or range substituted for it.

The mineral-bearing crevices may be described individually, or in reference to their form, dimensions, the position of the ore in them, and other such conditions as appertain to each taken by itself: they may also be considered collectively, in their relations to each other, their grouping and general surface arrangement, as well as the limitations of their peculiar forms to the different subdivisions of the geological series.

The simplest form in which lead ore is found occurring, in the region under consideration, is the vertical sheet, or upright crevice filled with galena, where the whole remains in the same condition in which it was when the ore was first deposited in the fissure, the rock not having undergone decomposition, so as to allow the mineral to be washed out of its place. The thickness of these sheets varies from that of a knife blade up to several inches: in very rare cases, a solid sheet of ore may extend for some distance, having a thickness of a foot or more; but bodies of ore of this magnitude are usually connected with "openings", as will be explained farther on, or they have a nearly horizontal position, and belong to the class of "flat-sheet deposits". The vertical sheet is usually from one to three inches in thickness, and is pretty regular in its form, the walls maintaining their parallelism for some distance and then gradually closing up, the ore thinning out and disappearing. In these crevices there are rarely any of the usual accompaniments of a vein, such as a gangue or vein-stone, and never smoothed and striated walls : there is sometimes a little clay, or ferruginous matter between the ore and rock ; but, more generally, the one is directly adherent to the other without any separating substance. When the crevice is barren of ore, it is usually filled with clay, or, more rarely, with brown oxide of iron. Sometimes when the ore gives out, calcareous spar takes its place, especially in the lower part of the Galena limestone ; but neither does this mineral, or any other vein-stone, ever appear in the vertical crevices with the comby structure characteristic of the true vein.

Vertical sheets of the kind just described are rarely of great extent in any direction ; but a number of them are sometimes grouped together, so that they may be profitably mined in one excavation. Single sheets are said to have been followed down uninterruptedly for nearly one hundred feet, but no such instances have ever fallen under our observation. On the whole, but a small portion of the ore raised occurs in the vertical sheet form : in much the larger number of instances, the vertical crevice is connected with what is called an *opening*, and this may be considered as the characteristic mode of occurrence of the lead ore in the middle and upper portions of the Galena limestone, the flat sheet being almost exclusively limited to the lower part of that rock and the upper portion of the Trenton.

The *opening* is the expansion of the crevice in a single stratum or a set of strata, in which the conditions were more favorable to the accumulation of ore, and, on passing into which, the previously nearly closed fissure widens out suddenly and becomes productive. This change from a mere seam to a wide opening is the more marked, because, in the metalliferous stratum, the rock adjacent to the crevice has usually undergone decomposition, and been partially or entirely removed, leaving a cavity of irregular dimensions, which sometimes expands out into what may, with propriety, be called a cave. To this peculiarity the term *opening* owes its derivation.

In different localities, the forms and dimensions of the openings vary considerably. Their vertical height is not usually less than four, or more than fifteen feet; and the same opening may vary between these limits, in different parts of the course. The opening is equally liable to expansion and contractions in width; and, while from four to ten feet may be considered as being the usual dimensions, there are localities where the rock retains its metalliferous character, and is more or less marked with the peculiarities of the opening, for a width of forty feet. The number of openings, or productive strata, which may in any one locality be found occurring, one below the other, is variable in different districts of the mining region. In the majority of cases, there is only one; and, although there may be as many as five, one is usually much more productive than the others.

The transition from the unproductive into the metalliferous stratum is usually a sudden one, so that the rock above the opening is firm and solid, and covers it like a cap, and is for this reason called, by the miners, the *cap-rock*. Not unfrequently, however, the expansion takes place more gradually, and often, in the same crevice, unequally, so that the opening will in one place be capped over by a flat stratum, in which nothing more than a mere seam is discernible; while, in other places, the cavity will extend far up into the cap-rock, gradually diminishing in width as it is followed upwards. When the opening presents itself with irregular forms, and with a solid cap above, it is called a square-opening : when it becomes irregularly elliptical in form and expands to a great size, it comes under the denomination of a cave-opening. Some openings exhibit irregularly-formed conical cavities passing up into the cap-rock, which are called chimneys, and which are often lined with a stalactitic deposition of carbonate of lime. The annexed wood-cut, figure 44, will serve to convey an idea of these singular forms, which have, apparently, been worn out by the percolation of water. This particular instance of the occurrence of chimneys was observed at Schaffner's diggings, near Dubuque, where a cave-like crevice, filled with clay, but barren of mineral, was opened for some five hundred feet in length. The opening itself was from six to eight feet in height, and about the same in width; but numerous chimneys were observed extending up into the cap-rock, sometimes to a distance of twenty-five or thirty feet : many of these were beautifully rounded, and tapered upwards to a fine point, being lined with incrustations of calc. spar, and, in some cases, with this mineral in layers alternating with clay.

FIG. 44.—Opening with chimneys, near Dubuque.

The manner in which the ore is disposed in the openings is very simple. More generally, the opening is only partly filled, and the materials which occupy it are of such a nature as to show that they have been derived from the decomposition of the rock which once occupied the opening, and through which galena was disseminated in various forms, such as nodules, strings, bunches and flat-sheets. Often, the arrangement of the material in the opening is such that it may be observed to have undergone decomposition without having been removed from its place; as the stratification may be traced distinctly across the decomposed mass, from one side of the crevice into the other. Again, in other cases, the whole, or the larger part of the contents of the opening, have been washed out by currents of water; leaving an irregular cavity, at the bottom of which a mass of detritus is accumulated, and which will be found filled with fragments of ore, if the opening was a rich one. Sometimes, after the contents of the opening had been removed, it has become filled up again with clay, which has slowly filtered into it from above, through crevices communicating with the surface. This clay has, in numerous instances, been found to contain the remains of a former generation of animals, once the inhabitants of this region, among which the peccary, mastodon, wolf and buffalo have been observed; the two former species in so many localities, as to lead to the inference that they were once abundantly distributed through the valley of the Upper Mississippi.

In some instances, the opening seems to have been formed previous to the introduction of mineral matter into it; although, more usually, it appears to have depended for its existence on the change which took place in the character of the rock, at the time of the deposition of the ore. This change, however, was not always necessarily connected with the presence of lead ore; as there are cavities resembling, in most respects, the mineral-openings, and yet entirely barren of mineral. Such cavities have also been formed, and ore has been afterwards introduced into them, either depositing itself on their walls, and lining them like a shell, or filtering in from above and forming a crystallized mass, hanging down into the vacant space below: instances of these forms will be described, in noticing particularly some of the more interesting mines near Dubuque, farther on in this chapter.

FLAT SHEETS. The deposits in the form of horizontal sheets, or in flat openings, are mostly limited to the lower part of the Galena limestone, and the upper and middle portion of the Trenton : where horizontal layers of ore occur in the upper portion of the Galena, it is chiefly as subordinate to the vertical crevices; the latter sending off branches or lateral offshoots, of moderate dimensions compared with the principal vertical mass. This arrangement of a vertical crevice, with flat sheets subordinate to it, is intimately connected with the form of the openings themselves; since it is by the decomposition of the rock surrounding the deposits of lead, that the dimensions of the cavities have been determined.

The deposits in flat sheets are quite various in form; but, in the greater number of instances, they are imbedded in, or interstratified with, the solid rock, the strata with which the ore is associated not having undergone decomposition, so as to give rise to a cavity. Much more frequently than in the vertical crevices, the galena is found associated with other metalliferous ores, especially with blende and pyrites; while the presence of such mineral substances as are of common occurrence in other mining regions, as veinstones, is almost exclusively confined to the flat-sheet deposits. The mineral most frequently found in this connection is calcareous spar, or *tiff*, as it is usually called by the miners; and heavy spar is not uncommon, but crystallized quartz is almost unknown. In some instances the larger portion of the metalliferous layer is made up of the sulphurets of zinc and iron, the galena appearing to be quite subordinate in importance to these substances. The different ores and minerals associated together in the flat-sheet deposits not unfrequently assume something of the arrangement which they would be likely to have in regular veins : for instance, at Mineral Point, a deposit of blende and pyrites about eighteen inches thick was noticed, in the centre of which were large cavities lined with crystallized galena. More frequently, the galena occupies the lower side of the metalliferous layer, the other ores lying above it in alternating layers, as shown in the annexed wood-cut (Fig. 45), which represents a section of a portion of the mineral deposit at the "Marsden lode" near Galena; the thickness of which, at the point represented, was about twelve inches. In this case there was a shallow cavity beneath the ore, partially filled up with detritus and fragments of ore; but usually, throughout the mine, the ore was solidly imbedded in the rock. In the flat openings, the galena may also occur without any trace of gangue associated with it; the pure ore being attached to the solid rock in a thin sheet, or in irregular bunches of crystals. The annexed figure (Fig. 46) represents an opening of this description observed at Shullsburg, in which the galena, represented by oblique

FIG. 45.—Section of Marsden lode.

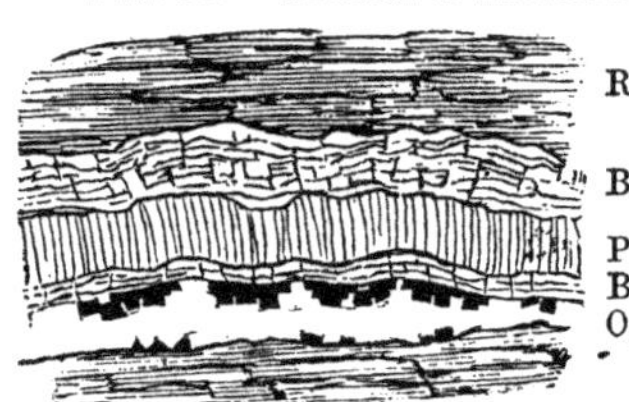

FIG. 46.—Flat opening at Shullsburg.

lines of shading, may be seen to be adherent to the cap rock, the bottom of the opening being covered with decomposed rock and fragments of ore which have fallen from above. In other instances, at the same locality, the opening had an almost spherical form, heavy bunches and plates of ore lining its interior like the crystals of an immense geode.

The general shape of these flat sheet-deposits is very irregular; but in many instances they are rudely circular in their outline, the deposit gradually thinning out in all directions from the centre. At the "Marsden lode", for instance, the metalliferous mass has something like the form represented in the annexed section (Fig. 47); the sheets of ore descending, by steps, from the interior towards the limits of the mass in each direction, and the diameter of the whole being about one hundred feet. On the summit of the dome-shaped mass, galena was the predominating ore; but the quantity of blende and pyrites appears to increase considerably as the mass descends.

Fig. 47.— Section of Marsden lode.

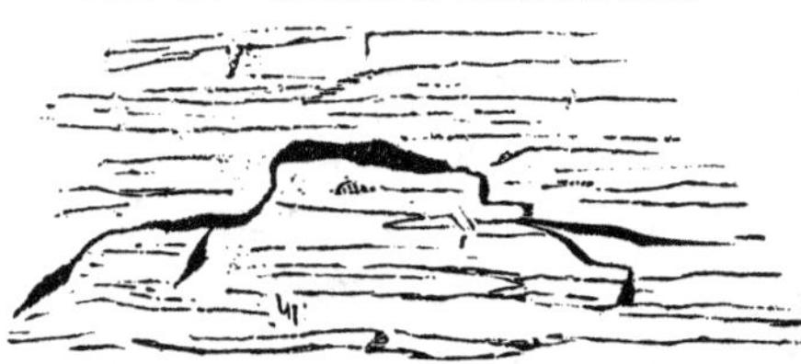

The most remarkable instance of this form of deposit observed by us, and probably one of the largest accumulations of ore ever met with in this region, was at "Mills's lode", near Hazle Green, which, when examined in 1857, presented the following appearances. A mass of ore was exhibited in the workings, of a saddle shape from east to west; the flat part above being twenty feet across, and varying from two to three and a half feet in thickness of solid galena, which was separated from the rock by thin selvages of a decomposed ferruginous substance : in each direction, as observed in the east and west cross section, this mass falls off at a steep angle, varying from 30° to 45°; and it had been worked on one side to the depth of twenty, and on the other, fifteen feet, the ore slightly diminishing in thickness in its descent, but still exceeding one foot on each side. In a north and south direction, the mass had been removed for a length of a hundred and twenty-five feet, the last forty feet rising gradually towards the surface. Thus it will be seen that a face of nearly one hundred square feet of solid ore was exposed in one section of the workings, presenting a truly interesting spectacle ;— one of the great prizes which are occasionally drawn in the lead-mining lottery. About twelve hundred thousand lbs. of galena had been taken out from this place previous to May 1857, and there could be no doubt that several millions more remained to be removed, at an almost nominal expense, the deposit being near the surface and entirely free from water.

We have thus briefly sketched some of the most important forms of occurrence of ore in the lead region; but to give the minute details of all the variations which have been observed would be quite impossible, for want of room. We must therefore be contented with a somewhat particular description of the principal workings which have been accessible in the vicinity of Dubuque, within the last four or five years, and which we have had an opportunity of examining.

The surface occupied by the Galena limestone on the Iowa side of the Mississippi, is but small in extent compared with its area in Wisconsin; and the profitable workings have been chiefly carried on in the immediate vicinity of Dubuque, a large part of the district occupied by the lead-bearing rock in Iowa not having as yet been found to contain any productive crevices.

Beginning at the southeast and proceeding northwestwardly, we first notice the diggings in the valley of the Tête des Morts, along which stream the Galena limestone is exposed in low cliffs for some distance. So far as we could ascertain, these diggings have never been very productive; and as they are now entirely abandoned, we have no definite information concerning them.

The mines in the vicinity of Dubuque come next in order. These occur over most of the space extending from Catfish creek, in a northwesterly direction, as far as the middle fork of the Little Makoqueta, occupying a belt from three to four miles wide to the west of the Mississippi. The Hudson-river shales cover the elevated surface over a considerable portion of this area; but as the streams have cut down into the Galena limestone, the crevices are first discovered by their outcrop in the vallies, and then worked, frequently, by shafts sunk through a considerable thickness of detritus and shale before reaching the lead-bearing rock (Compare the geological map and the diagram of the lead-bearing crevices in the vicinity of Dubuque, accompanying this Report).

The mines in the vicinity of Dubuque are among the most interesting and remarkable of the whole lead-region. Extending over an area, on the surface, of hardly more than twelve to fifteen square miles, there is probably no district of equal extent in the Mississippi valley, which has produced so large an amount of ore. The crevices are more extensive, both vertically and longitudinally, than in any we have observed in Wisconsin; and their whole arrangement and grouping exhibits a degree of regularity which is rarely exhibited by this class of mineral deposits, and which most closely assimilates them, in this respect, to true veins.

The characteristic form of occurrence in the Dubuque district is the vertical crevice with openings, which frequently expand into large caves several hundred feet in length, and from which, not unfrequently, several millions of pounds of mineral have been taken.

A somewhat particular description of the mines which have been accessible during the past four or five years, in the vicinity of Dubuque, will serve to illustrate the character of the deposits on the west side of the Mississippi. In general, during the time since our personal acquaintance with this portion of the lead-region commenced, there have not been, at any one time, more than one or two important localities where working was carried on, and where any considerable amount of lead was raised. In 1852, Levins's lode was yielding very large amounts : this was mostly worked out during that year and 1854. In 1853 and 1854, Stuart and Bartlett's lode was producing extensively. In 1855, there does not appear to have been any one mine at work which was yielding a large amount of ore. In 1856, Kennedy's was the most important lode worked. In 1857, Kerrick & Jones had erected a steam engine and were taking out large quantities of ore from their mine, which had been for some time lying dormant on account of the water. These are the principal mines which have been accessible to us since the commencement of the Survey, and they have together furnished a large portion of the lead which has been raised since 1852.

STEWART AND BARTLETT'S LODE. This very interesting locality was still partially open for examination in 1854 and 5, although most of the lead had been taken out. Some of the appearances observed

FIG. 48.— Section of opening at Stewart & Bartlett's mine.

Cap rock.
Opening with galena along the north wall.
Drift.
Platform.
Galena in sheets and bunches near the wall.
Rubbish.
Bottom of the opening.

here are peculiar, and throw some light on the mode of deposition of the ore, as well as on the action by which the crevices have been formed.

A space was worked out, open to day, at one end of which a good exhibition was afforded of the mode of occurrence of the ore at this locality, and of the manner in which the strata had been impregnated with it, through the limited space called the opening ; the rock remaining, in this part of the mine, nearly in its original position, not having been washed away. The wood-cut, figure 48, on preceding page, represents the general appearance of the rock at this point. The width of the opening, between the walls, is about fifteen feet, and its vertical height not far from thirty-five feet. Within this space, it will be seen, that the strata are slightly bent downwards and broken in numerous places, leaving cavities between the fractured edges of the strata in which a portion of the ore has been deposited, as represented by the patches of oblique shading. The larger part of it, however, is collected along the walls of the opening, especially on the north side, where the rock is broken up into small pieces and somewhat decomposed, forming with the ore a brecciated ferruginous mass. The decomposition of the rock had evidently not proceeded quite as far in this case as in some others, or we should have had, instead of the mass of fractured strata still in place, a cave limited by the walls of the opening on each side and filled partially with detritus, clay and " tumbling rock ", with fragments of galena scattered through it.

The workings at this locality have been on two different levels, in an irregular crevice, or two crevices connected together by flat openings. The excavations on the upper level follow an irregular crevice for several hundred feet, which had been entirely worked out before being examined by us, and which is said to have produced but little mineral. The lower drift is forty-two feet below the level of the upper, and was extended a little over two hundred and seventy feet to the west of the shaft, and a considerable distance in the other direction, but how far, was not ascertained, as it had become filled up in that direction; probably over eight hundred feet. This lower drift runs in a crevice of varying width and height, sometimes widening out to twelve or fifteen feet, in other places closing within a few inches, and chiefly filled with clay and decomposed rock with fragments of ore. At the extremity of this drift the crevice comes to an abrupt termination, in a cavity such as would have been produced by the sinking down of a portion of the rock shaped something like a flat-bottomed boat, as represented in the annexed wood-cut, figure 49, in which the part left white indicates the vacant space, the flat upper part of which is fourteen feet wide and two and a

FIG. 49.—Section at west end of Stewart and Bartlett's lode.

half feet high, while the crevice runs off on each side at a steep angle, to an unknown depth. At the upper right-hand corner, the crevice is seen continued upwards in the cap rock : this probably connects with the crevice worked in the upper drift as noticed before, and which was somewhat to the north of the lower one. The section is an interesting one, as showing how the formation of the crevice, in this portion of it at least, was due to a mechanical cause originating within and confined to a limited space in the rock.

We were informed that four millions of pounds of mineral had been taken from these excavations, which, when visited by us last year, seemed to have been entirely abandoned, and were rapidly filling up again with clay and sand.

LEVINS'S CAVE. For a description of this very interesting locality, as it appeared when first discovered, we are indebted to C. WHITTLESEY, who visited it immediately after its discovery by Mr. LEVINS, and before it had been at all disturbed. This was in October 1850 : it was first visited by one of us two years later, after about two million pounds of ore had been removed from it. The locality, as at first seen by Mr. WHITTLESEY, presented a narrow cave or crevice entering from the side of a hill, and capable of admitting, although in some places with great difficulty, the passage of a man : the crevice had a nearly east and west direction in general, with many small deflections from a straight course. We annex Mr. WHITTLESEY'S description of his visit to the locality in question. After speaking of the difficulty of squeezing between the walls of the narrow and winding crevice, he goes on as follows : "We had not gone far in this uncomfortable manner, when a handsome cave appeared before us, illuminated by the lights in front. It was a square room, with a mud floor and a rock ceiling, along the middle of which was a seam or vertical crevice, containing galena. This crevice was about two feet broad, the sides covered with mineral six to eight inches thick, leaving a space between the inner faces of the mineral up which we could see several feet. There was about this crevice an entirely new feature, so far as I know. The solid mineral projected from this crevice downward, a foot to a foot and a half in a 'sheet', as they call it, eight to ten inches thick, and twenty-five to thirty feet long, spreading fan-like as it descended. (The annexed wood-cut, figure 50, will convey an idea of this peculiar and interesting feature : it represents a section across the cave at the point where the depending sheet of ore was observed, as described above.) A part of the way there were three sheets, two thick and heavy ones, with coarse irregular surfaces, composed of aggregated cubes from two inches to ten inches on a side, and one thin or light sheet, the whole covered with oxide (carbonate ?) of lead, and having, in consequence, a pure white color. This depending mass was wholly clear, except where it was attached to the rock above and projected downwards in space, the most rich and beauti-

FIG. 50.—Section in Levins's cave.

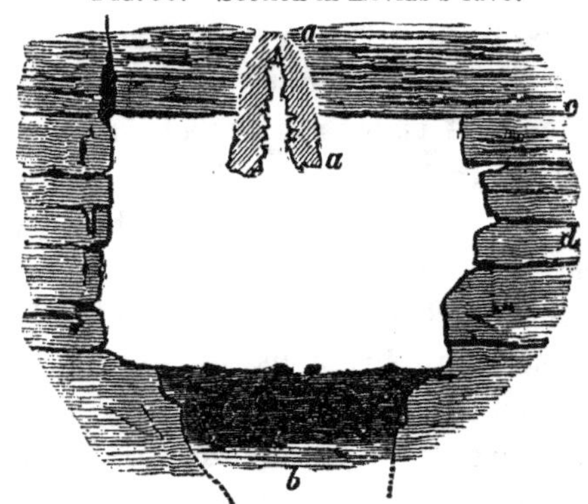

a. Depending mass of galena.
b. Detritus and clay with galena.
c. Cap rock.
d. Galena limestone.

ful object I ever saw of a mineral kind. About two hundred feet more of twisting and squirming brought us to the leaden temple, where lay the fortune of our bold explorer. It is a cave, or pocket, some hundred and thirty feet long, twenty feet high in the dome or cavern part, and twenty to thirty feet wide, the sides and roof arched in an irregular manner. Probably it extends in this oval shape to a depth equal to the clear space above. The whole appears to have been ceiled with lead; and although its size is not as great as that of many (?) other mineral caves, the amount of galena in view at any one time is said to exceed that of any 'pocket' yet opened. Much of the lead lining the roof and sides had fallen down in immense blocks, some of them very recently. This mineral incrustation was, in places, two feet thick, and one of the fallen masses was estimated to weigh twenty-three thousand pounds. In the mud and clay that formed the bottom, or floor, of this spacious room, they said that mineral would be found buried, or enclosed, in large lumps to the bottom, probably fifteen feet deeper."

Such was the appearance of things at this most interesting locality, certainly one of the most remarkable ever discovered, in 1850. In October 1852, about two million pounds of ore, worth, at the then current price of lead, about fifty thousand dollars, had been removed; and there was still left in the mines about one and a half millions of ore, which was taken out in 1853 and 1854. A shaft had been sunk from the surface to strike the rich cave spoken of above, the top of which was reached at the depth of about ninety feet, and the bottom of the excavation was about forty-five deeper. The length to which the crevice had been traced was about twelve hundred feet; and the cave-like expansion extended for nearly three hundred feet, widening out in some places to twenty-five feet. The galena at this time could be seen, in some places, occupying a fissure extending upwards into the cap-rock: it also formed flat sheets running into the sides of the opening, in some places, with a thickness of three or four inches of solid ore; but by far the larger portion lay in loose masses in the bottom of the elliptical cave-like opening, mixed with clay, sand and loose masses of partially disintegrated limestone, called "tumbling rock". Besides the shell-like deposit of ore which lined the walls of this cave, as described by Mr. WHITTLESEY, there seem to have been horizontal layers which once extended through the opening : these had been broken up, and the rock surrounding them removed by the action of currents of water, of which the evidence could be seen in every part of the crevice, especially in the water-worn and grooved lower surface of the cap-rock, and in the rounded edges and angles of the projecting strata of the sides of the opening.

Kerrick and Jones's lode. This is one of the most important and interesting deposits of lead which has been worked in recent years. The crevice is remarkable for its length and regularity as well as for its productiveness, it having already yielded over a million and a half of ore. It has almost exactly an east and west direction, the magnetic bearing between the shafts, proceeding in a westerly direction, being from No. 1 to No. 2, S. 85° W. ; No. 2 to No. 3, S. 83° W. ; No. 3 to No. 4, S. 83½° W. (the magnetic variation is about 8° E.). It has been opened for a length of nearly fifteen hundred feet, having a width of from six to eight feet, except where divided into two portions by the "key-rock", when it widens out to twelve or fifteen.

At the time this locality was visited by us, in October 1857, the end of the drift going west was distant about three hundred feet from the engine-shaft, and the crevice presented the appearance represented by the annexed section (Fig. 51), its width at this point being about six and its height eight feet. The opening was filled with soft clay; the ore occupying a fissure extending upwards in the top of the drift, and having a width of nineteen inches (represented at *a* in the figure), all of which was solid galena, with the exception of a narrow irregular space in the centre, the ore having crystallized on both sides of the fissure, but not filling it up entirely. Twenty feet before reaching this point, a solid sheet of mineral had been struck, which extended from the floor to the top of the crevice. Between this point and the shaft the crevice appears to have a quite variable height, the excavation having a height of forty or fifty feet,

Fig. 51.— Section at Kerrick and Jones's lode.

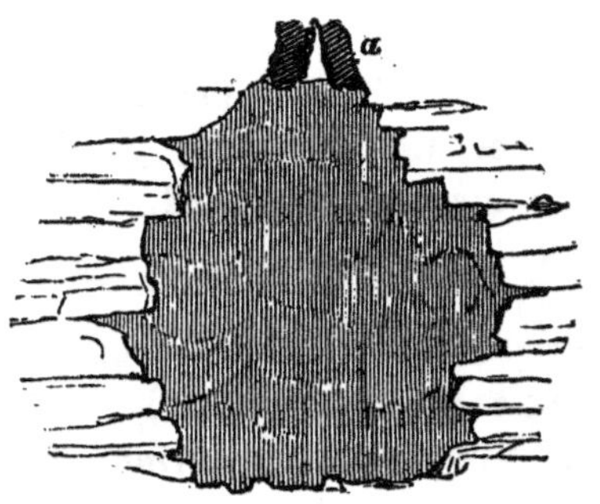

the crevice having extended upwards in the cap-rock and carried ore for a considerable distance. A section of the crevice at another point is represented in the annexed wood cut (Fig. 52), which shows the position of the so-called "key-rock", an irregular mass of limestone remaining undecomposed along the centre of the crevice, which divides into two parts, as is frequently the case in the wide vertical openings : this disposition resembles the splitting of veins, so as to include large masses of rock, called by the Cornish miners "horses", and which are common in other mining regions.

FIG. 52.— Section at Kerrick and Jones's lode.

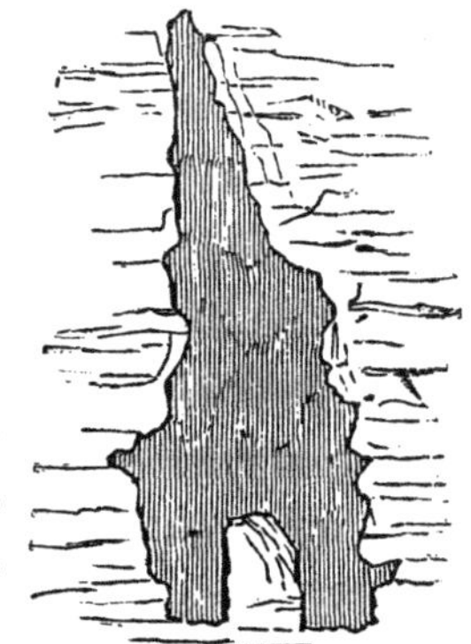

The workings on the crevice have been several times suspended and resumed, on account of the abundance of water, the shaft having reached a depth of a hundred and ten feet. After several abortive attempts to introduce new-fangled and ill-contrived machinery for pumping, a steam engine was erected in 1857, which operated a suitable pump with 21-inch lifts, raising seven hundred gallons per minute, and with the aid of which it was intended to sink the shaft twelve feet deeper.

This was the only locality, at this time, where steam power was in use on this side of the river for draining a mine. Another engine was erecting at Riley's lode, a few rods south of this, and which had been worked for some years, over an extent of several hundred feet longitudinally and to a depth of a hundred and thirty-seven feet, and much mineral raised; two millions, it is said. The crevice, which was not accessible, was found to be almost exactly parallel with that of Kerrick & Jones, its mean direction being N. 86° E., S. 86° W., magnetic.

KENNEDY'S LODE. This mine was producing largely in October, 1856. At that time the drift had been extended in the crevice to a distance of three hundred and thirty feet from the shaft, which was one hundred feet deep. The opening was about thirty-five feet in height, and the crevice extended upward in the cap-rock, sometimes to a distance of fifteen feet or more. The galena was said by the miners to have formed, for some distance, a solid sheet three and a half feet thick : in some places the rock was undecomposed ; in others, the crevice was filled with tumbling rock mixed with galena. Over a million of pounds of ore had been taken from this rich deposit in the six months preceding our visit.

LANGWORTHY LODE. This was one of the most extensive and best developed crevices ever discovered in the lead-region. It has been opened and worked in different places along a line nearly three-quarters of a mile in length ; and is said by E. H. LANGWORTHY, Esq., to have produced about ten millions of pounds of ore. The crevice was irregular, sometimes expanding, for a distance of one or two hundred feet, to a width of from fifteen to twenty feet, and then contracting within narrow limits. There are said to have been usually three openings, of which the upper was the most productive, the entire thickness of the productive ground being about forty feet. This interesting lode was one of the first discovered and worked in the district, and has not been accessible in later years. We are informed that a large portion of the ore obtained from it was taken out within a length of three hundred feet.

M'KINZIE'S LODE. The mine worked by Mr. M'KINZIE for several years, but which is not now accessible, is said to have been carried to a greater depth than any other in the lead-region, having nearly reached the bottom of the Galena limestone; the deepest workings having been extended two hundred and ninety feet below the surface, as was stated to us by Mr. M'KINZIE. In the fourth opening, at the depth of two hundred and eighty feet, a mass of ore was discovered, " shaped like a counter ", which weighed seventy-five thousand pounds : this is the only instance, so far as we have been able to ascertain, where any ore has been obtained in this vicinity, so low down in the rock. The opening was about three or four feet wide and six feet in height. MANGOLD'S workings, near M'Kinzie's, had reached, in the spring of 1857, a depth of a hundred and seventy-three feet; but had not been found productive in the third or lower opening : the upper one was twenty-six feet in height, and from this most of the lead had been taken.

Among other celebrated crevices which have been worked in former years, and which have been noted for their productiveness, are the following :

Booth & Carter's : Cave-opening, forty feet deep, produced 3,500,000 lbs.

Kilbourn : Shallow; no cap-rock, produced 4,000,000.

North Langworthy : Produce, 3,000,000.

Ames : Two crevices; mineral to the surface and to the depth of sixty or seventy feet, produce estimated at 2,000,000.

Madden : Amount of ore raised, 2,000,000.

M'Nair : Three or four parallel crevices, with very heavy masses of ore in two crevices; amount of ore raised, 2,000,000.

Dubuque cave : Worked by Julien Dubuque; supposed to have produced 2,000,000 of mineral.

Many other crevices might be mentioned; but the information in regard to them is so indefinite, that, for the present at least, it is not deemed best to attempt to give a complete catalogue, as may perhaps be done hereafter. The difficulty of procuring exact accounts of long abandoned workings is so great, that no complete history of the old mines in the vicinity of Dubuque will ever be put on record, as so many of the old miners are dead or have removed from the country, leaving no account of their work behind them.

The diagram of the lead-bearing crevices in the vicinity of Dubuque which accompanies this Report, will serve as the first attempt to bring together such information as could be procured in regard to the position of the productive lodes which have been worked in former years, as well as those which are still accessible. For much of the information upon it, we are indebted to Messrs. RICHARD BONSON and R. OSEE ANDERSON; as also to H. VON WERTHERN, Esq., of the Surveyor General's office, who has kindly aided in the collection of materials.

Although there is indeed a surprising regularity in the direction of the crevices in this district, their parallelism being much more marked than in other portions of the lead region, the diagram must not be taken as representing them with absolute accuracy in this respect. Where the workings have been for some time abandoned, they are, in most cases, entirely or nearly obliterated; and the recollection only remains that they had the general direction of the ranges of the district, which is nearly east and west, in many instances not varying more than a degree or two from that course. It is much to be regretted that a careful record has not been preserved, by those residing at Dubuque and interested in the mines, of the position and course of all the lodes which have been opened, and, especially, of the depth to which they were worked : the information which would be supplied by a map based on accurate data, and with correct topography, might hereafter be of the greatest importance, not only scientifically, but in its practical bearing on the interests of the mining region.

Before proceeding, however, to general considerations on the mode of occurrence of the lead ore in Iowa, it will be proper to notice what has been done in the way of mining in other districts farther to the northwest, in the direction of the outcrop of the lead-bearing rock.

The diggings on the Little Makoqueta river, near Durango, were formerly very productive, having given employment to more than one hundred and fifty men at one time : they are now almost entirely abandoned, and in 1856, when this district was last visited by us, only a few persons were engaged in washing over the old rubbish. There is a very remarkable range or series of crevices, running N. 80° W., S. 80° E. for a distance of between one and two miles along the middle fork of the Little Makoqueta : in this range, the indications of heavy workings may be seen on almost all the points of the bluffs coming down to the river on the south side. On the southwest quarter of Sec. 31, T. 90, R. 2 E. at Ewing's diggings, the crevice is said to have been thirty feet wide, and to have produced large quantities of lead. This locality will be noticed farther on, under the head of zinc.

There have been, in former times, some diggings in the neighborhood of Sherald's mound : those on Sherald's creek, about a mile west of the mound, are said to have been tolerably productive. Beyond this, to the northwest, we know of no mining of any importance, until we reach the neighborhood of Buena-vista. Here, in the ravine extending back from the river in a nearly southwest direction, are several excavations which were not working, when examined by us in 1857. One crevice was noticed, extending to a distance of two hundred and fifty or three hundred feet, in a direction N. 83° to 85° E., forming a square opening from which considerable mineral had been taken.

Lead is said to have been raised in some quantity, on Bluebelt creek, which runs into Turkey river, from the south, near its confluence with the Mississippi, on the northeast quarter of Section 13; also on the north side of the Turkey, on Sections 10 and 11, T. 91, R. 2. At the locality on Section 13, the crevice has been worked at intervals along a line twelve hundred feet long, to a depth of from twenty to thirty feet. The crevice is wide and regular; but the mineral does not hold in it to any considerable depth.

The next diggings of importance, and the farthest in this direction yet discovered and proved to be of any importance, within the limits of Iowa, are those in the vicinity of Gutenberg. The Galena limestone is well exposed in this region, having a thickness of nearly two hundred feet, and is very much cut up by ravines, so as to afford the best possible opportunities for exploration. The localities which have been worked are near Miner's creek and its branches, on the northeast quarter of the southeast quarter, and the north half of Section 12, T. 92, R. 3 west, and on the north half of the southwest quarter, and the southwest quarter of the northwest quarter of Section 7, T. 92, R. 2 west. The workings in this vicinity are all in the flint-bed, just at the base of the Galena limestone, and from one hundred and twenty to one hundred and forty feet above the Mississippi. The mineral lies within a space from two and a half to three and a half feet in vertical height, very irregularly disseminated in the rock, from which it has to be got out by blasting. Some of the excavations were said to be three hundred feet wide, and to extend for a length of eighteen hundred feet, the roof being supported on pillars. There are no crevices extending upwards into the rock, and no "float-mineral" has been found at a higher level than the flint opening. The presence of crystallized calcareous spar, in the dog-tooth form and in very large crystals, is to be noticed as characteristic of the openings in this position. At Glenhaven, on the opposite side of the river from Gutenberg, where the workings are in a position exactly similar to that which they have at the diggings just noticed, there is a sheet of calcareous spar thirty inches in thickness, below which the galena lies, disseminated through a stratum of rock eighteen or twenty inches thick. Some of the crystals of this mineral were six inches in length. Barytes is also found in the Gutenberg diggings, and, sometimes, in handsome crystals. These mines have produced several million pounds of ore, it is said; but, at present, they are not much worked.

Although the Galena limestone extends to the northwest from this point for some distance, with but slightly diminished thickness, and occupying a much greater space on the surface than it does near Dubuque, we know of no crevices having been worked in it anywhere beyond Gutenberg. The position of the diggings at this place, in the lowest beds of the Galena, seems to indicate, as may be inferred from the condition of things in Wisconsin, that we are on the borders of the productive lead-region in this direction. Still, we know of no decisive reason why ore should not be found up the valley of the Turkey, either in the lower beds of the Galena or in the Trenton limestone; but the probability of the discovery of heavy deposits is, of course, diminished by the fact that, up to this time, little or nothing of importance has been found.

There are, however, some localities in the northeastern

corner of the State, where galena has been mined to some extent in the Lower Magnesian limestone, and which may here be noticed. The most important deposits of lead in this rock, and, indeed, the only ones which have been observed, within the limits of Iowa, are situated in the valley of Mineral creek, a stream flowing north, through a valley lined with precipitous bluffs, into the Upper Iowa river, and about three miles south of a small settlement called New-Galena : the diggings are on the southwest quarter of Section 13, T. 99, R. 6 west. In this vicinity, the Upper sandstone is well exposed on the top of the bluff, and a shaft has been sunk in it to a considerable depth. Along the face of the bluff, in which a thickness of one hundred and twenty to one hundred and fifty feet of the Lower Magnesian limestone is exposed, a number of drifts have been extended into the rock, a little below its junction with the sandstone, and considerable galena has been taken out. The limestone at this point is brecciated in its structure, appearing as if it had been partially broken up after its deposition, and then recemented : portions of the rock have also a concretionary structure, and its whole appearance is that of a material which has been subjected to both mechanical and chemical disturbances. The ore appears to be associated with irregular strings and bunches of calcareous spar, ramifying through the rock, but nowhere assuming a regular form, like that of a vein, or appearing to occupy a well developed fissure. Sometimes a little decomposition of the rock has taken place, which has given rise to a sort of opening; but none were observed which were more than a few inches wide and a few feet long. It is said that between fifty and one hundred thousand pounds of lead had been obtained from these diggings; but it seems hardly possible that the operation should have been, on the whole, a profitable one; and, taking into consideration the hardness of the limestone, and the very limited extent to which it has undergone decomposition in the vicinity of the mineral deposits, we see little to encourage farther expenditures at this point.

The question whether the Lower Magnesian limestone contains deposits of lead ore which can be worked for any length of time with profit, is one which has, of late years, been much agitated by those interested in the mining district. For some years after the lead-region was first opened, it was generally supposed that the productive deposits of lead was limited to the Galena limestone; and Dr. OWEN gave as the result of his official examination of the country, that "when a mine is sunk through the Cliff limestone to the Blue limestone beneath, the lodes of lead shrink to insignificance, and no longer return to the miner a profitable reward for his labor. Indeed, the small quantities of lead ore which have been found in the Blue limestone occur in veins not much thicker than writing paper, which have insinuated themselves into the slender seams of the stratification". Further examinations, and the results of longer experience, have shown that this statement was erroneous; as considerable deposits of ore have been worked in the Blue limestone, although by far the largest portion of the lead of the Upper mines comes from the proper lead-bearing rock. In reference to the occurrence of lead in the Lower Magnesian, we find in Dr. OWEN's Report, published in 1852, that a number of localities in this rock are given as having yielded more or less lead ore; and, on the strength of this evidence, the formation is pronounced "lead-bearing, but whether productively so or not, cannot be fully determined until the rock is scientifically mined". Some of the localities here specified are not in the Lower Magnesian limestone, but in the Galena: the others seem, up to the present time, not to have been profitably worked. In regard to the lead-deposits in the Kickapoo river, which have been much relied on by those anxious to make out the Lower Magnesian to be a good mineral-bearing rock, we have learned from intelligent miners who have worked in that vicinity, that the ore lay in flat sheets in the hard limestone, and that there were no crevices, nor any decomposed material connected with the mineral; so that the workings were uniformly abandoned after having been carried in for the short distance, beyond which atmospheric agents had ceased to operate on the rock. More recently, the occurrence of ore in this geological position, at Oleking's diggings, near Blue river, in Wisconsin, has been described by Dr. PERCIVAL, and considered by him as sufficient evidence "that the Lower Magnesian is a good mineral-bearing rock". Not having visited and examined this locality, we are not disposed to question the fact of considerable ore having been found at this place; but we are disposed to doubt the existence of mineral deposits in the Lower Magnesian, on any scale which will compare with those of the proper lead-bearing rock. Did any such exist, they would long since have been found; and a few isolated instances of lead ore obtained in this formation are not sufficient evidence of its productiveness, and much less are they to be considered as an argument in favor of the galena having originated in the igneous rocks beneath the Lower sandstone.

The most important practical questions to be asked, in regard to the occurrence of the lead in the Dubuque region, are the following :

1st. *Do the lead-bearing crevices extend indefinitely downwards, and is deep mining ever likely to prove profitable?* This question can be answered, unhesitatingly, in the negative. There is very little evidence that the crevices continue to be productive in this part of the lead-region, even as low down as the Blue limestone ; and it is certain, from the study of the whole region, that they are everywhere completely cut off by the Upper sandstone. In no instance, so far as we have been able to learn, have the lodes been found to extend more than a very short distance into the sandstone, or to be productive of galena in that rock. It is true, that in some localities, ore has been found in the limestone underlying this sandstone (the Lower Magnesian), where this rock occupies the surface; but the deposits in that geological position are very few in number, and the ore limited in quantity : we have yet to learn of a single instance in which diggings in that rock have been profitable for any length of time. But, again, even if the Lower Magnesian were a good mineral-bearing rock, there would be little encouragement to continue sinking from the Galena limestone, through the sandstone, into the underlying limestone; for there is no reason to suppose that a crevice, after being entirely interrupted in the sandstone, would be resumed in the limestone below, or that any other one would be hit upon, at a point exactly in the line of direction in the workings above. The fact that the mode of occurrence of the lead in the Lower Magnesian is so very different from what it is in the Galena limestone is an additional reason for believing that there could be no grounds for expecting continuity in the direction of the crevices in both the rocks. A miner would be no more justified in sinking through the sandstone, in the expectation of meeting a continuation of his crevice in the Lower Magnesian, than he would be in commencing a shaft anywhere at random in this rock, without regard to surface indications, and expecting to strike a valuable lode. He might possibly find one; but the chances would be more than ten thousand to one that he would not.

There are, occasionally, instances where water is reached before the principal portion of the ore has been taken out, and where more expensive machinery than the horse-whim is required to keep the mine free. In such cases, the so called "bull-pump" has been found very serviceable. This is an inclined wheel, from twenty-five to thirty feet in diameter, on which one or two oxen work, and which is geared to a suitable pump. With a machine of this kind, which costs about $1500, it is said that two hundred gallons of water per minute may be raised; while the expense of running it is but little more than the wages of the two men who alternate in keeping the oxen to their work, and does not exceed, with necessary repairs of the machinery, $800 per annum. The use of the steam engine may be occasionally advisable ; but in the large majority of instances in which steam has been employed in this region, we are assured that the enterprise has not been found profitable. We are not aware of any instance in which the attempt has actually been made, in any part of the lead-region, to sink through the Upper sandstone into the Lower magnesian, in order to follow a crevice through one rock into the other; but the idea has repeatedly been advocated by a certain class of persons interested in mining property, that in the execution of such a plan, great discoveries would be made, and the resources of the country developed. We believe, however, that a large majority of the intelligent miners would be willing to admit that any such operation would be a mere throwing away of money.

2d. *What can be done to farther develope the not yet discovered deposits of ore in the Dubuque district, and what method of exploration ought to be adopted for this purpose?* Is it not possible to combine capital and labor, in such a manner that results may be obtained which shall be of value to the mining interest, and which shall render the business less precarious and uncertain than it now is? There are undoubtedly extensive regions underlaid by the Galena limestone, especially in Wisconsin, where rich deposits of ore are concealed by the thick covering of superficial detritus, which forbids all explorations from the surface, except at great expense. What means are there of ascertaining whether these districts may not contain valuable bodies of ore; and, if so, how may they be most economically opened and worked? To this we reply, that the proper method to be adopted will, in a good degree, depend on the situation of the locality, and the known relations of those deposits of ore in the vicinity, which have already been discovered and worked. Before any safe directions can be given, the whole lead-region must have been carefully mapped, and the crevices laid down with minute attention to their position and direction. A more or less symmetrical distribution of them will be found to prevail; and from this symmetry of the known, the position of the unknown may possibly be arrived at; but, above all things, it must be borne in mind, that in a region like the one we are now engaged with, *horizontal excavations or drifts are the proper means of exploration*, and *not vertical ones or shafts*. By sinking a shaft in a region in which the ore is distributed as it is in this district, we prove nothing except the identical spot on which the shaft is placed. By drifting, on the other hand, we can, if our drift be judiciously laid out, prove an extensive region with one excavation. Not only is this true, but it is also to be remembered, that when a shaft is sunk, we have often to encounter the difficulty of water, which is an almost insurmountable one in a region where the rocks are so cut up by crevices, which allow the flow of currents in every direction; while in running up an adit-level from a suitable position, we not only prove the country, but effectually drain it at the same time. Of course, reference is here made to explorations carried on by an association of labor and capital : as long as mining continues under the present system, there will necessarily be but little change in the methods of explorations adopted.

Let us illustrate by taking into consideration the circumstances of the region immediately about Dubuque. We have here a very large number of crevices, many of which are regularly developed, extensive and highly productive : furthermore, they are concentrated within a limited space, as will be seen by reference to the diagram of the lead-bearing crevices. If now, by a careful series of levellings over the ground occupied by these crevices, and by ascertaining, as far as practicable, what position the productive openings had occupied with reference to the horizontal plane assumed as a base, it should be made apparent that the principal body of ore in the various ranges was approximately on the same level : then it would become a question of great interest whether an adit-level could not be carried in from the Mississippi, at the proper height to drain all the crevices which should be intersected, and at the same time to afford the greatest chance of making discoveries of ore; and whether such an undertaking might not prove remunerative, provided the many conflicting interests connected with such an enterprise could be harmonized. Let any one lay out an imaginary drift on the diagram, running from the Mississippi river, at its intersection with the line between Sections 25 and 36, to a short distance beyond the southeast corner of Section 22, and then turning nearly at right angles and extending the level, in a direction of about N. 55° E., for two miles, and he will be surprised to see how many of the most important lodes which have been worked in the vicinity of Dubuque would be intersected by an adit-level only about five miles in length. Still, we would not be understood as decidedly recommending a work of such a character, in this or any other part of the lead-region : such a step should only be taken after a much more thorough study of the ground than has been as yet made in any portion of the mining district. What we would insist on, is the superiority of the method of proving the country by horizontal, rather than by vertical, excavation, in a region where the body of ore is known to be within such a moderate depth from the surface.

The amount of lead produced by the mines of the Upper Mississippi has been gradually falling off, of late years, owing to the superior attractiveness of the gold fields of California, and to the fact that the larger portion of the mineral region has been pretty thoroughly explored, and the most easily discovered crevices worked out. Occasionally, a very rich lode is struck by some persevering miner; but, on the whole, the number of men engaged in this business is much less than it formerly was; and some districts, which were once thickly inhabited by the lead diggers, are now almost entirely deserted by that class, the plow having taken the place of the pick and the drill.

From the records kept at Galena by Captain BEEBE and others, it appears that the amount of lead annually produced by the Upper mines gradually increased from five thousand to ten thousand tons (of 2240 lbs.), during the years from 1829 to 1839 : after that it rose rapidly, and attained its maximum from 1845 to 1847, nearly reaching twenty-five thousand tons in those years. Since that time, the decline has been marked, the amount raised in 1853 being only thirteen thousand three hundred tons : since that year no exact record of the shipments has been kept, so far as we have been able to ascertain, the railroads beginning about that time to divert a part of the trade from the river. A large portion of the lead manufactured now goes across the country to Chicago, which formerly all found its way to the Mississippi. Of the remainder, a part is consumed in the country, and the rest goes down the river to St. Louis, where it is reshipped up the Ohio and to New-Orleans. If, therefore, we could ascertain accurately the amount of lead received at Chicago and St. Louis, we should have a near approximation to the entire amount produced. Such statistics as we have been able to procure, for the last few years, are given below :

Tons of Lead received,	1853.	1854.	1855.	1856.	1857.
At Chicago	1452	1895	4449(?)	2919	?
At St. Louis	14248	10123	9757	6076	6347
Total from Upper mines...	15700	12018	14206	8990	

The amount given as received at St. Louis in 1857 includes the receipts from the Missouri mines, which is but an insignificant quantity.

The proportion of the produce of the Upper mines which comes from Iowa we have been unable to ascertain with accuracy. From the statements of the best informed smelters, however, it appears, that the amount of ore smelted in the vicinity of Dubuque has been about six million of pounds yielding from sixty-eight to seventy per cent of lead, in the most prosperous year, and that it has not probably in any year fallen much below four millions; equal to about seventeen hundred tons of metallic lead, and worth in New-York city about a quarter of a million of dollars, at the current price of that metal for the last few years.

The figures given above indicate a considerable decrease in the production of lead in the Northwest during the last few years; but the diminution is not so great as would appear at first sight, since the amount required for home consumption at the West is rapidly increasing. Within the past year a shot-tower and white-lead works have been erected at Dubuque, which will probably consume a considerable proportion of the lead mined in this vicinity, and supply the Northwestern States with the manufactured articles heretofore drawn from the southern and eastern cities in exchange for the crude metal exported.

The amount of lead supplied to the eastern market from the western mines is quite insignificant, the actual produce of those mines being hardly more than sufficient to meet the requirements of the West for its own consumption. Only about one hundred tons of this metal arrived in New-York from the West in 1857, the Atlantic States being now almost entirely supplied from the English and Spanish mines.

ZINC.

The occurrence of ores of zinc, in connection with those of lead, has been repeatedly noticed in the preceding pages. They are, throughout the lead-region, chiefly associated with the flat-sheet deposits; and, therefore, most abundant in the lower part of the Galena limestone and the upper and middle portion of the Trenton. The districts in which zinc ores are found in the largest quantity in the flat openings, are those of Mineral point, and to the west of Shullsburg. In the Galena limestone, in the vertical crevice deposits, there are usually but few traces of other metalliferous ores associated with the galena.

The most abundant combination of zinc found associated with galena is the sulphuret, or blende, containing, when pure, sulphur 33, and zinc 67 parts in a hundred : all the blende of this region, however, contains more or less iron. These ferruginous blendes are usually called "black-jack" by the miners. The blende sometimes forms flat sheets, nearly a foot in thickness; but is almost always associated with iron pyrites, and layers of these two substances occasionally alternate with each other, as noticed above in describing the Marsden lode. When the sulphurets of zinc and lead occur together, the zinc seems almost invariably to have been the first metal deposited. Calc. spar and barytes are frequently associated with these ores, where they occur together; and when the deposits of galena are unaccompanied by zinc, they rarely have any earthy gangue connected with them.

The blende is frequently found more or less oxidized, and converted into the carbonate or silicate, or an impure mixture of both. That the sulphuret was the ore originally deposited, and that it was afterwards acted on and changed to these oxidized combinations, is proved by the fact that the layers of blende are sometimes only partially decomposed, still retaining portions of the original sulphuret in the interior.

Within the limits of Iowa, the only ore of zinc which we have noticed in any considerable quantity, was the carbonate associated with the silicate, at Ewing's diggings on the Little Makoqueta, a few miles northwest of Dubuque. Although the interior of the excavations was not accessible, it was evident from the inspection of the rubbish lying on the surface, that a considerable quantity of these ores, called by the miners " dry bone ", had been raised, in connection with the galena. Much of the ore at this locality has a cellular structure and an earthy texture, and portions of this variety are covered with stalactitic and botryoidal incrustations. The chemical examination of some of the cellular masses showed them to consist of mixtures of the hydrous silicate of zinc, or electric calamine, with the carbonate, or smithsonite, and more or less argillaceous matter. The first-mentioned of these ores contains 67.4 per cent of the oxide of zinc; the other, 64.8 of the same. Analyses of the incrustation and of the stalactitic masses proved them to consist of nearly pure carbonate of zinc, giving the following results:

Insoluble in acid, silica, chiefly	.14	
Oxide of iron and alumina	2.96	
Oxide of zinc	61.89	= 49.67 zinc.
Carbonic acid, water and loss	35.01	
	100.00	

A specimen of the stalactitic variety gave:

Insoluble silica and clay	2.56	
Oxide of iron and alumina	.66	
Oxide of zinc	61.53	= 49.38 zinc.
Carbonic acid	32.03	
Water and loss	3.22	
	100.00	

The question whether these ores occur in sufficient quantity in the lead region ever to become of value for the manufacture of metallic zinc and its oxide, now so much used for paint, is one which we are unable to answer in the affirmative. Blen le is a substance as yet but little used for this purpose, as there are difficulties in the way of its reduction which make it less available than the oxidized ores. In this country the manufacture of the oxide has been carried on for some years, the material used being the red zinc ore, or oxide, which occurs in large quantity in New-Jersey, and the silicate of zinc, which is abundant in the Saucon valley in Pennsylvania. The quality of the ore found at Ewing's diggings is good; but from the known mode of occurrence of the metalliferous ores throughout the lead-region, we are inclined to doubt whether it could be obtained in sufficient quantity to justify the erection of the expensive furnaces, etc. required for the manufacture of the oxide; that of the metal has not yet been attempted in this country. At none of the localities examined by us in Wisconsin, have we found the ore in sufficient quantity and purity to justify the erection of zinc-works at present, even were the conditions in regard to fuel and labor as favorable as they are in Pennsylvania and New-Jersey, which is not the case.

GOLD.

While these sheets are passing through the press, many statements are going the rounds of the newspapers in regard to the occurrence of gold in Iowa, according to which this metal exists in large quantities in some of the central counties of the State. It may therefore be advisable to state, that no rocks, such as, in other parts of the world, have been found to be auriferous, occur within the region mentioned, or, so far as we know, in any part of the State. If gold has been found, it must have been carried a great distance from the place where it originated, by currents of water; and it is not likely to occur, except in very fine particles in the sands of the streams. All that we know of the occurrence of gold and of the geology of Iowa, makes it highly improbable that any auriferous sands will be found containing enough of the precious metal to pay, even at a very moderate rate, for the labor of washing it out.

SECTION AT BURLINGTON.

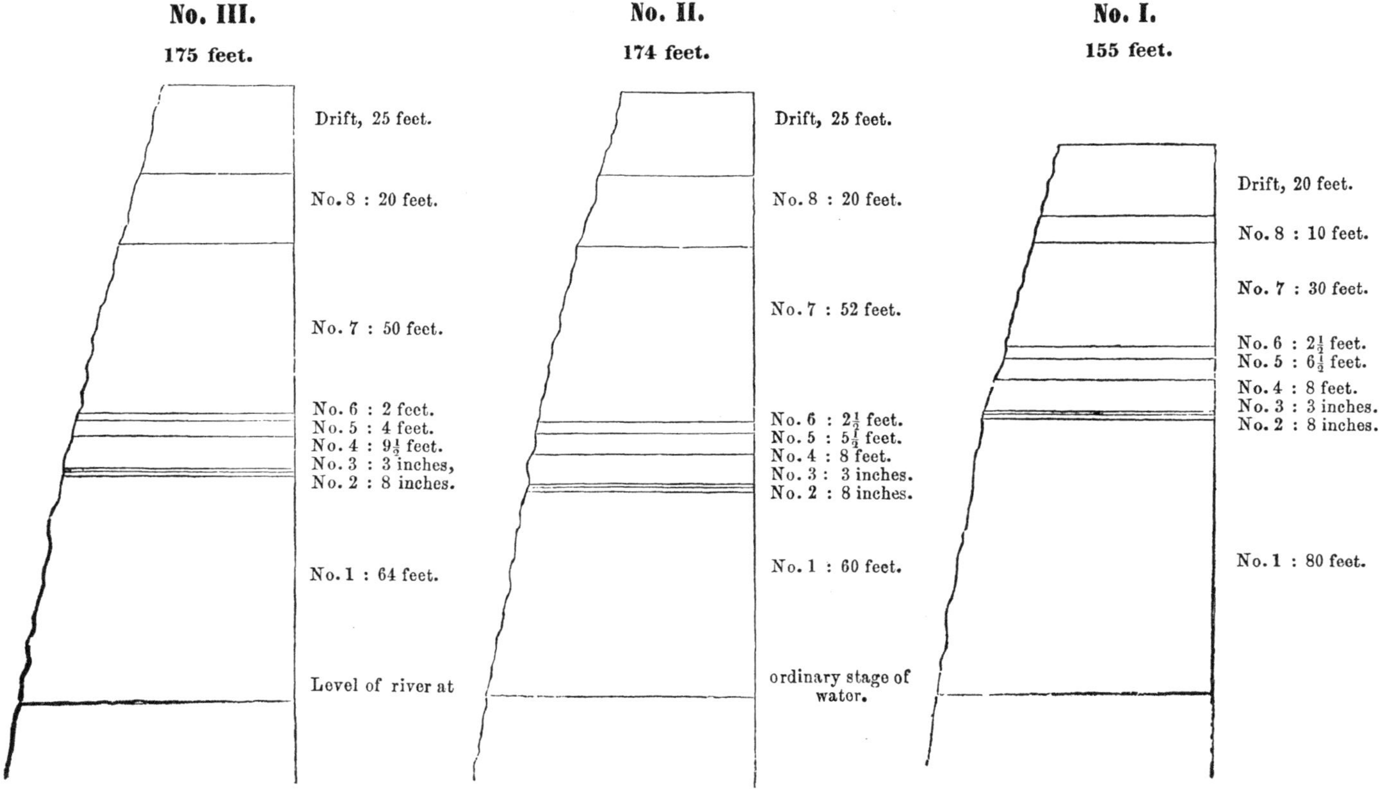

No. III.
175 feet.

Drift, 25 feet.
No. 8 : 20 feet.
No. 7 : 50 feet.
No. 6 : 2 feet.
No. 5 : 4 feet.
No. 4 : $9\frac{1}{2}$ feet.
No. 3 : 3 inches,
No. 2 : 8 inches.
No. 1 : 64 feet.
Level of river at

No. II.
174 feet.

Drift, 25 feet.
No. 8 : 20 feet.
No. 7 : 52 feet.
No. 6 : $2\frac{1}{2}$ feet.
No. 5 : $5\frac{1}{2}$ feet.
No. 4 : 8 feet.
No. 3 : 3 inches.
No. 2 : 8 inches.
No. 1 : 60 feet.
ordinary stage of water.

No. I.
155 feet.

Drift, 20 feet.
No. 8 : 10 feet.
No. 7 : 30 feet.
No. 6 : $2\frac{1}{2}$ feet.
No. 5 : $6\frac{1}{2}$ feet.
No. 4 : 8 feet.
No. 3 : 3 inches.
No. 2 : 8 inches.
No. 1 : 80 feet.

APPENDIX.

LIMESTONE OF LECLAIRE.

This limestone, which is so well marked at the Rapids above Davenport, and with the Onondaga-salt group occupies a broad belt along the river, cannot be traced far into the interior, and the coloring upon the map is terminated in accordance with our present knowledge of the extent of these rocks. This rapid disappearance of a limestone which causes such a conspicuous feature on the Mississippi river, renders a farther investigation desirable; and from the great irregularity of the beds, there is a possibility that its thickness on the river has been over-estimated. The results of farther inquiry will be given in a future Report.

NOTE ON THE SECTIONS OF STRATA EXPOSED AT BURLINGTON, IOWA.

Mr. Charles A. White, of Burlington, has furnished me with the following carefully measured sections of the strata exposed at that place, together with the accompanying memoranda. Section No. I is at the north part of the city; No. III is about one and one-third miles south of the first, and No. II is between one and three. Nos. 4, 5 and 6 of the strata are thicker at a point some three miles north of the city, and have diminished considerably below the measurements of the sections at a point two miles south of the city. About one mile south of Burlington, No. 8 is over twenty-five feet in thickness; and at a point three miles southwest, it is about forty feet thick.

"At the point where the section No. II was made, the bed No. 1 is known to extend sixty-five feet below the bed of the river, without any apparent change of composition, and at this point the boring was discontinued. This gives a greater thickness to the strata of the age of the Portage and Chemung groups than had heretofore been proved in that part of the country; and we have yet an unascertained depth below this point, which may bring the entire thickness up to the measurements made in Missouri, which are about two hundred feet. At the same time the more northerly localities of these strata have not yet shown more than half this amount of thickness.

[Iowa Survey.]

"The bed No. 1 is composed principally of a light blue indurated clay, effervescing freely with acids, somewhat arenaceous, and passing upward insensibly into a greenish-yellow fine grained sandstone: the greenish color seems to be due to the yellow sand mixing with the blue clay. Fossils are very rare in this bed, but are oftenest found in the upper part. Concretions of yellow bisulphuret of iron are frequently found in it. Sometimes the stone of the upper part of this bed is of sufficient hardness to withstand the action of the atmosphere and frost, but is too soft for building purposes. Lower down in the bed, although too hard for removal by the pickaxe, in most places it crumbles into a soft clayey substance upon exposure to the atmosphere. It sometimes presents a shaly appearance, and, throughout the bed, the lines of stratification are rather indistinct.

"No. 2 is a thin bed of limestone of a bluish-brown color, and is composed principally of very small bivalve shells, indistinctly preserved in consequence of the compactness of the stone. It sometimes thins nearly out in the vicinity, and is not inclined to disintegrate or become fragmentary. It contains corals of the Genera *Favosites* and *Syringopora*, and a few remains of crinoids.

"No. 3 is a distinct and sometimes beautifully oolitic limestone. The dividing line between this and No. 2 is often obscure. Fossils are not abundant in this bed, although so abundant in No. 2.

"No. 4 is a dark gray compact limestone, very fragmentary, even when not exposed to the atmosphere. It contains comparatively few fossils, but many of them are better preserved than those of the other Devonian beds. The oolitic structure is sometimes seen passing upwards into the bed, a foot or two from No. 3. It contains *Spirifer*, *Productus*, *Orthis*, *Chonetes* and *Rhynchonella*.

"No. 5 is a yellowish fine-grained sandstone, very closely resembling that which No. 1 passes upwards into; but is rather firmer in its texture, and the lines of stratification are more distinct. It contains casts, only, of fossils; nearly all of them quite small, but abundant. They are of the Genera *Spirifer*, *Productus*, *Orthis*, *Chonetes*, *Euomphalus* and others.

"No. 6 is a grayish-white oolitic limestone, which is quite a firm and good-looking stone when taken from the quarry, but becomes shelly and fragmentary upon exposure to the atmosphere and frost, and finally crumbles into small fragments, and is consequently wholly unfit for a building material. It seldom changes in color or texture; but at one point in the north part of the city, it loses its oolitic structure; and at this point the fossils are rather more numerous and better preserved, and the stone assumes a brown color and becomes softer. It contains corals of the Genera *Cyathophyllum* and *Syringopora;* also *Euomphalus*, *Orthoceras*, *Spirifer*, *Productus*, *Orthis*, and the large *Gyroceras* of OWEN.

"No. 7 is a reddish-brown semicrystalline limestone. From fifteen to twenty-five feet from the base it is tolerably solid, and is a very good building stone, notwithstanding the action of the frost. The stone, from some of the quarries, makes a good lime. Above this it consists of thin beds of limestone, chert, and earthy material. Fossils are not so abundant in the upper part of this bed as in the lower part, which is composed almost entirely of fossil remains. It contains crinoids in great abundance, *Spirifer*, *Productus*, *Orthis*, *Rhynchonella*, *Euomphalus*, *Syringopora*, *Cyathophyllum* and trilobites (the latter very rare).

"No. 8 is generally a white crystalline limestone, but often assumes a brown color similar to that of No. 7. It is a very good building stone, and the purer parts make a very good lime, but it contains considerable silex. The fossils imbedded in it are frequently found silicified, while the stone surrounding them is a very pure limestone; and fossils that are partly weathered out present a siliceous blossoming on the exposed surface, even when the imbedded part is quite calcareous. This bed contains crinoids in great abundance; also *Spirifer*, *Orthis*, *Terebratula*, *Capulus*, *Pecten* and *Lingula*; also corals of several genera and species."

The subdivisions of the sections given by Mr. White from Nos. 1 to 6 inclusive, constitute what I have referred to the Chemung and Portage groups, or to the Chemung group alone; and Nos. 7 and 8 constitute what I have designated the Burlington limestone (See pages 89 and 90 of this Report).

The occurrence of *Favosites* and *Syringopora* in the bed No. 2, and of *Syringopora* in bed No. 6, had not been previously noticed, so far as I know, in any strata of this age in the West, and is an interesting fact in the palæontology of the group.

Mr. White has made extensive collections of the Crinoideæ of the Burlington limestone, and finds that certain species are restricted in their vertical range to the lower or brown beds, while others are limited to the upper or white beds of the series. The species from the lower beds have, to a great extent, a different aspect and expression from those of the upper beds. Although no attempt has been made to recognise this distinction in the published species of this Report, for I had not sufficient information at the time, yet among the *Actinocrinus*, Plate 10 illustrates the prevailing character of those from the brown beds, or No. 7; while Plate 11 expresses the character of those from the white beds, or No. 8 of the sections.

NOTE.

I am informed by Mr. Worthen, since the printing of this volume, that in Southern Illinois the thinning of the sandstone between the St.Louis limestone and the Kaskaskia limestone brings the two rocks so nearly in contact, that it is probable the relative position of the fossils has not always been properly discriminated. Some of the species on Plate 25, as fig. 1 and fig. 4, may belong to the horizon of the St.Louis limestone; and I suspect also that *Pentremites symmetricus* may be of the same age. The lines of separation between the members of the Carboniferous limestone series, as indicated from examinations towards their northern limits, are not always as well marked at the south, and some confusion may exist for a time. No reasonable effort will be spared to follow out these investigations; and whatever error may be discovered, will be corrected on a future occasion.

The *Actinocrinus pentagonus*, page 577, is apparently identical with *A. concinnus* (Shumard, Geol. Rep. of Missouri, 1855, page 189, plate A, fig. 5). The specimen figured presents some modifications of structure, which are abnormal.

GEOLOGICAL SECTION ALONG THE MISSISSIPPI RIVER, FROM THE UPPER IOWA RIVER TO St. LOUIS, &c.

The geological section accompanying Part I of this volume is constructed from actual observations made along the Mississippi, and illustrates the features presented, upon the western or Iowa side of the river, from the northern limit of the State, to below the mouth of the Desmoines river. From that point to Clarkesville (Mo.), the section is constructed from observations made on both sides of the Mississippi; and from Clarkesville to the mouth of the Missouri river, the structure presented is that which is seen upon the eastern or Illinois side.

The section from Prairie du Rocher to Thebes, Illinois, is introduced for the purpose of showing the relations of the Kaskaskia limestone to the limestones below, from which it is separated by the intervening ferruginous sandstone.

INDEX TO PART I.

www.ingramcontent.com/pod-product-compliance
Lightning Source LLC
LaVergne TN
LVHW021321110826
845150LV00003B/638

* 9 7 8 1 4 2 5 5 5 7 0 7 2 *